Explaining the Brain

Explaining the Brain

Mechanisms and the Mosaic Unity of Neuroscience

Carl F. Craver

CLARENDON PRESS · OXFORD

OXFORD

UNIVERSITY PRESS

Great Clarendon Street, Oxford OX2 6DP

Oxford University Press is a department of the University of Oxford.
It furthers the University's objective of excellence in research, scholarship,
and education by publishing worldwide in

Oxford New York

Auckland Cape Town Dar es Salaam Hong Kong Karachi
Kuala Lumpur Madrid Melbourne Mexico City Nairobi
New Delhi Shanghai Taipei Toronto

With offices in

Argentina Austria Brazil Chile Czech Republic France Greece
Guatemala Hungary Italy Japan Poland Portugal Singapore
South Korea Switzerland Thailand Turkey Ukraine Vietnam

Oxford is a registered trade mark of Oxford University Press
in the UK and in certain other countries

Published in the United States
by Oxford University Press Inc., New York

British Library Cataloguing in Publication Data

Data available

Library of Congress Cataloging in Publication Data

Craver, Carl F.
  Explaining the brain : mechanisms and the mosaic unity of neuroscience / Carl F. Craver.
    p. ; cm.
  Includes bibliographical references and index.
  ISBN-13: 978-0-19-929931-7 (alk. paper)
  ISBN-10: 0-19-929931-5 (alk. paper)
  1. Neurosciences—Philosophy. 2. Brain—Philosophy. I. Title.
  [DNLM: 1. Neurosciences. 2. Philosophy. WL 100 C898e 2007]
  QP356.C73 2007
  612.8—dc22   2006103230

Typeset by Laserwords Private Limited, Chennai, India
Printed in Great Britain
on acid-free paper by
Biddles Ltd., King's Lynn, Norfolk

ISBN 978-0-19-9299317

10 9 8 7 6 5 4 3 2 1

For Pamela

Preface

There are neurophilosophers, and there are philosophers of neuroscience. Neurophilosophers use findings from neuroscience to address traditional philosophical puzzles about the mind. Philosophers of neuroscience study neuroscience to address philosophical puzzles about the nature of science. Philosophers of neuroscience are interested in neuroscience because it has distinctive goals, methods, techniques, and theoretical commitments. In this book, I propose a unified framework for the philosophy of neuroscience. Because neuroscience is like other special sciences in many respects, this framework contains lessons for the philosophy of science generally.

I develop this framework by addressing the following question: what is required of an adequate explanation in neuroscience? Debates frequently arise among neuroscientists and philosophers about whether a proposed explanation for a given phenomenon is, in fact, the correct explanation. Does Long-Term Potentiation (LTP) explain episodic memory? Do size differences in hypothalamic nuclei explain differences in sexual preference? Does the deposition of beta-amyloid plaques in the hippocampus explain memory deficits in Alzheimer's disease? Do 40 Hz oscillations in the cortex explain feature-binding in phenomenal consciousness? While the answers to these questions depend in part on specific details about these diverse phenomena, they also depend on widely accepted though largely implicit standards for determining when explanations succeed and when they fail. My goal is to make those standards explicit and, more importantly, to show that they derive from a systematic and widespread view about what explanations are, namely, that *explanations in neuroscience describe mechanisms*.

My project is both descriptive and normative. My descriptive goal is to characterize the mechanistic explanations in contemporary neuroscience and the standards by which neuroscientists evaluate them. This cannot be accomplished without attention to the details of actual neuroscience. I illustrate my descriptive claims with case studies from the recent history of neuroscience. For neuroscientists, I present enough detail to make the philosophical views concrete. For philosophers, I limit myself to the details required to demonstrate that the view corresponds to real neuroscience. This descriptive goal helps to keep the philosophical discussion targeted on issues relevant to the neuroscientists building the explanations.

The goal of searching for mechanistic explanations is now woven through the fabric of neuroscience: it is taught through examples in classrooms and textbooks; it is propagated in introductions, discussion sections, and book chapters; and it is enforced through peer review, promotion, funding, and professional honors. To understand contemporary neuroscience, one has to understand this form of explanation. A second reason to pursue this descriptive project is that questions often arise about the adequacy of widely accepted strategies of explanation in neuroscience (see, for example, Uttal 2001; Bennett and Hacker 2003). We can address the question of whether the norms of neuroscience are justified only when we have an idea of what the norms are and of how they can be defended.

The descriptive project, in other words, is the first step in a normative project: to clarify the distinction between good explanations and bad. As the body of neuroscience research continues to expand, it is worth pausing periodically to reflect on the goals of explanation and on the standards by which explanations should be evaluated. Similarly, as neurophilosophers learn more about neuroscience and seek to apply neuroscientific explanations to philosophical problems, they also need to learn to reflect critically on the standards for evaluating the explanations that they adopt. Here the philosopher of neuroscience can help. They can use the long tradition of philosophical literature about the nature of scientific explanation (see, e.g., Salmon 1989) to reveal crucial features of explanation in neuroscience specifically, and they can use neuroscience to reveal previously unrecognized features of explanation across the sciences (or at least the special sciences) generally.

The relation between the descriptive and normative projects is complex, however. One cannot simply read off the norms of explanation in neuroscience from a description of what neuroscientists actually do when they form and evaluate explanations. Neuroscientists sometimes make mistakes. They sometimes disagree about whether a proposed explanation is adequate and even about what it would take to show that it is adequate. Explanatory standards change over time, and it is possible that the standards endorsed now might some day be rejected as inadequate. What role, then, can descriptions of explanations play in the search for norms of explanation?

First, even if scientists often disagree about particular explanations, there are nonetheless clear-cut and uncontroversial examples of successful and failed explanations. Almost everyone (among scientists and philosophers) can agree that action potentials are explained by ionic fluxes, that some forms of neurotransmitter release are explained by calcium concentrations in the axon terminal, and that protein sequences are explained, in part, by DNA sequences. And almost everyone (scientists and philosophers) can agree that memory is not explained by the vibration of vital fluids through the cerebral ventricles, that the shape of a person's skull does not explain their artistic talents, and that memory loss does not explain the deposition of beta amyloid in the cortex. Philosophical analyses of explanation should deliver the correct verdicts on these clear and uncontroversial examples unless there is compelling reason to suspect that the judgments of science are wrong. It is open to deny my verdict on these standard examples and to abandon widely accepted scientific ideas about what does and does not count as an explanation, but only at the risk of stretching the term "explanation" so far that it no longer looks at all like the scientific phenomenon that we are trying to characterize in the first place. Of course, people disagree about problem cases, but disagreement need not prevent one from using the agreed-upon examples as touchstones in formalizing an adequate account of explanation. The controversial cases can then be decided according to the account that best accommodates the central and uncontroversial cases. I argue (in Chapter 2) that many of the standard accounts of explanation in the philosophy of science fail to accommodate even the central and widely held examples of successful and failed explanation in science. In contrast, my account accommodates them directly.

Second, in neuroscience, and in other sciences as well, explanations are not developed merely for the explainer's intellectual satisfaction?—the ineffable "a ha" feeling that comes with understanding something. Such emotions and feelings are terrible indicators of how well someone under-stands something (see Keil and Wilson 2000; Trout 2002). Explanations in neuroscience are frequently developed with an eye to possibilities for manipulating the brain. The widespread goal of finding mechanistic expla-nations in neuroscience is a consequence of the fact that the discovery mechanisms provides scientists with new tools to diagnose diseases, to correct bodily malfunctions, to design pharmaceutical interventions, to revise psychiatric treatments, and to engineer strains of organisms. One way to justify the norms that I discuss is by assessing the extent to which those norms produce explanations that are potentially useful for intervention and control. While this is not the only touchstone that one might use, it is nonetheless one, and it is objective. This aspect of my account is introduced through my view of causation in Chapter 3 and my view of interlevel relevance in Chapter 4.

Third, although norms of explanation should not be identified with historical regularities in scientific practice, analysis of the history of neuroscience provides a rich source of compiled hindsight about which kinds of explanatory projects work and which do not (Darden 1987). The science has collectively, if implicitly, thought about the nature of, and standards for, explanation. One goal of the book is to make these norms explicit. This involves not merely reporting what neuroscientists do, but looking at what they do for clues of the norms of explanation they endorse. Those clues can be found in exemplars of successful and unsuccessful explanation. They can be found in the kinds of arguments that neuroscientists use to argue for and against particular explanations. They can be found in the experimental practices that neuroscientists use to evaluate explanations. They can be found in scientists' historical reflections on what they were trying to do and how they failed. Occasionally they can be found in scientists' explicit statements about the goals and standards of neuroscience. There is now a large set of exemplars of successes and failures that students of neuroscience must learn: the Hodgkin and Huxley model, the neuron doctrine, Broca's localization of the language faculty, Gall's organology, McConnell's purported demonstration of cannibalistic learning in planaria, and Eccles's electrical models of synaptic transmission. The philosopher of neuroscience must learn them too because they embody the collective wisdom in neuroscience about what constitutes an acceptable explanation. Paradigmatically successful explanations reveal features of successful explanations, and paradigmatic failures of explanation reveal the norms by which bad explanations are rejected.

Finally, I intend this book to be part of the process of formulating explanatory norms for neuroscience. It is an entry to a conversation rather than its end. I present my view of these norms of explanation, I systematize them, and I show that they are justified. This opens the door to a more precise debate about what the norms of explanation in neuroscience ought to be and about the limits of mechanistic explanation. In the final analysis, even if it is false to state that all explanations must describe mechanisms, many of them do. This book can be read as an instrumental guide to discovering and evaluating mechanistic explanations.

This book is primarily for neuroscientists, philosophers of science, philosophers of mind, and students of these subjects. There are inherent difficulties in writing to address such different audiences, but this is a difficulty that any adequate philosophy of neuroscience must face. The philosophy of neuroscience lies at the intersection of the philosophy of science, neuroscience, and the philosophy of mind. It will show its worth only to the extent that it recognizes the distinctive concerns of these three fields and to the extent that it constructs the bridges required to connect them.

My neuroscience adviser once said of philosophy that he could not see how anyone could think without data. This view of philosophy is widespread among neuroscientists. I conjecture that this is in part because neuroscientists have mostly encountered philosophers of mind and metaphysicians. In many cases, these philosophers come to neuroscience with a set of concerns and a technical vocabulary that is out of touch with the way that neuroscientists think about their own work. Many metaphysical projects are fascinating, but the most interesting metaphysical disputes are often irrelevant to building explanations in neuroscience. One goal of this book is to convince neuroscientists and neurophilosophers that the philosophy of science can contribute meaningfully to how they think about the goals of their work and about the strategies for reaching those goals. A philosophy of neuroscience constructed by reference to the goals and strategies of contemporary neuroscience can create a bridge between the way that neuroscientists think about science and the way that philosophers think about causation, explanation, and levels. This point of agreement can then be the starting place for evaluating how, and if, neuroscientists and neurophilosophers can explain what they hope to explain with the tools that the explanatory framework of contemporary neuroscience affords.

I have wrestled with this book for roughly a decade. It began as my dissertation in the Department of History and Philosophy of Science at the University of Pittsburgh. The central ideas first came into view, though darkly, during a three-year stretch in the Department of Neuroscience at the University of Pittsburgh. Patrick Card, Jon Johnson, Robert Moore, Steven Small, Edward Stricker, Alan Sved, Floh Thiels, and Nathan Urban introduced me to different aspects of experimental and theoretical neuroscience. Peter Machamer, Wesley Salmon, Kenneth Schaffner, and Lindley Darden deeply influenced my approach to the philosophy of science.

I worked on aspects of this book during my two years at Florida International University, but I did not think of writing a book until I moved to Washington University in St Louis in 2001. At Washington University, I have worked with scholars in philosophy, neuroscience, and psychology. Gualtiero Piccinini and Eric Schliesser each read the entire manuscript and inspired me, chapter by chapter, to keep writing. Red Watson also read the entire book while trying to teach me to write. Other colleagues at Washington University who have impacted directly or indirectly on this book include Adele Abrahamsen, Garland Allen, Joel Anderson, Bill Bechtel, José Bermúdez, Eric Brown, Sara Bernal, Dennis Des Chene, John Doris, Stan Finger, Marilyn Friedman, Jonathan Halverson, John Heil, Marcus Raichle, Steve Peterson, Philip Robbins, Mark Rollins, Walt Schallick, Witt Schoenbein, Paul Stein, J. R. Thompson, Kurt Thoroughman, Joe Ullian, Dan Weiskopf, Wayne Wright, Alison Wylie, and Jeff Zacks. I would also like to thank the students in my Philosophy of Neuroscience seminar in Spring 2006, especially Santiago Amoya, Don Goodman, Juan Montana, and Sarah Robbins.

I owe a special debt to the Department of Philosophy at the University of Cincinnati. John Bickle taught an early draft of this book in his Philosophy of Neuroscience class, the students of which provided detailed comments. Chris Gauker, Larry Jost, Tony Landreth, Tom Polger, Bob Richardson, and Rob Skipper have provided years of conversation and feedback.

I have also had extended conversations about the topics in this book with Ken Aizawa, Anna Alexandrova, Jim Bogen, Keith Dougherty, Phil Dowe, Paul Draper, Chris Eliasmith, Carl Gillett, Stuart Glennan, Valerie Hardcastle, Eric Marcus, Robert Northcott, Stathis Psillos, Adina Roskies, Marcel Weber, Ken Waters, Rob Wilson, Jim Woodward, and Arno Wouters. Per Andersen, Carole Barnes, Tim Bliss, Bruce McNaughton, and Lynn Nadel have been especially helpful in thinking about the history of LTP. One anonymous referee provided detailed and very helpful feedback.

Work on Chapter 7 was supported in part by the National Science Foundation under grant number SBR-981792 and by a small research grant from the McDonnell Center for Higher Brain Research. Any opinions, findings, conclusions or recommendations expressed in this material are those of the author and do not necessarily reflect those of the National Science Foundation.

Kim Haddix, Phil Valko, and Youngee Choi each provided editorial assistance. Pamela Speh designed and polished the figures. Tamara Casanova, Kimberly Mount, and Mindy Danner have provided administrative assistance. Finally, I would like to thank Darlene Valot Craver for helping to care for Anna in Fall 2004, a crucial stage in the preparation of this manuscript.

Contents

Detailed Contents

List of Figures and Tables

Figures

Tables

1

Introduction: Starting with Neuroscience

Summary

Explanations in neuroscience describe mechanisms, span multiple levels, and integrate multiple fields. I articulate and defend these descriptive claims. I also describe a set of criteria of adequacy for an acceptable account of explanation in neuroscience.

1. Introduction

Neuroscience is driven by two goals. One goal—the primary focus of this book—is explanation. Neuroscientists want to know how the brain develops from infancy to adulthood, how the visual system gives rise to the perception of color, and how the vestibular system helps to keep us upright. In the popular press (but also in textbook introductions), one frequently finds claims that neuroscientists are on the verge of explaining the mysteries of consciousness, the illusion of free will, the frailty of human memory, and the nature of the self. If neuroscience succeeds in these explanatory goals, it will revise our self-conception as radically as Copernicus' decentering of the earth and Darwin's humbling vision of our origins.

The second goal of neuroscience is to control the brain and the central nervous system. Neuroscience is driven in large part by the desire to diagnose and treat diseases, to repair brain damage, to enhance brain function, and to prevent the brain's decay. This goal is evident in the many designer pharmaceuticals promising to ameliorate psychiatric and physiological symptoms, in the skill of the brain surgeon, and in the confidence of behavioral and psychiatric geneticists. If neuroscience succeeds in this second goal, it will open medical possibilities that now seem like science fiction, and it will provide human beings (for good or ill) with new and powerful forms of control over the human condition.

These two goals of neuroscience are complementary. Explaining the brain is one way to figure out how to manipulate it, and manipulating the brain is one way to discover and test explanations.

My aim in this book is to construct a model of explanation that reflects, rather than merely accommodates, the structure of explanations in neuroscience. I do not start with a philosophical view of explanation in mind and then attempt to graft it onto what I find in the discussion sections, review articles, and textbooks of neuroscience. Instead, I develop a view of explanation that does justice to the exemplars of explanation in neuroscience and to the standards by which these explanations are evaluated. Starting with neuroscience, as opposed to physics or chemistry, three main features of explanation demand attention: (i) explanations describe mechanisms; (ii) explanations span multiple levels; and (iii) explanations integrate findings from multiple fields. In this overview chapter, I show that explanations in neuroscience typically have these features. I thus prepare the ground for the normative theory to be developed in the rest of the book.

2. Explanations in Neuroscience Describe Mechanisms

Judging from the literature in contemporary neuroscience, the brain is composed of mechanisms.[1] Here are some titles:

Disinhibition of Ventrolateral Preoptic Area Sleep-active Neurons by Adenosine: A New Mechanism for Sleep Promotion (Morairty et al. 2004)
Neural Mechanisms of Cortico–Cortical Interaction in Texture Boundary Detection: A Modeling Approach (Thielscher and Neumann 2003)
Mechanisms and Regulation of Transferrin and Iron Transport in a Model Blood–Brain Barrier System (Burdo et al. 2003)

---

[1] Clifford Morgan and Eliot Stellar, whose textbook defined the field of physiological psychology through the mid-twentieth century, say that, "The primary goal of physiological psychology is to establish the physiological mechanisms of normal human and animal behavior" (1950: vii). Gordon Shepherd, whose neurobiology textbook was a late twentieth-century introduction to the field, writes that, "The main aim of neurobiology, therefore, and the main aim of this book, is to identify the principles underlying the mechanisms through which the nervous system mediates behavior" (1994: 4).

Coordinate Synaptic Mechanisms Contributing to Olfactory Cortical Adaptation (Best and Wilson 2004).
GPCR-Mediated Transactivation of RTKs in the CNS: Mechanisms and Consequences (Shah and Catt 2004).
Central Sensitization and LTP: Do Pain and Memory Share Similar Mechanisms? (Ji et al. 2003)
Na+ Channel Na$_v$1.9: In Search of a Gating Mechanism (Delmas and Coste 2003)

Neuroscientists sometimes use other terms to describe their explanatory achievements. They say that they are searching for the neural *bases,* the *realizers,* and the *substrates* of a phenomenon.[2] They say that they discover *systems* and *pathways* in the flow of information, and molecular *cascades, mediators,* and *modulators.* The term mechanism could do the same work.

But what is a mechanism? History cannot answer this question. The term mechanism has been used in too many different ways, and most of those uses no longer have any application in biology.[3] No single, coherent mechanical philosophy passed from Archimedes or Democritus (via Descartes, Huygens, and Boyle) to the present. Those who have been called mechanical philosophers differ from one another, for example, about whether mechanisms are abstract or concrete, about the activities that can legitimately appear in explanations, about the relationship between mechanism and teleology, and about whether the doctrine of mechanism, however that is to be understood, is advocated as a scientific method or as a metaphysical thesis (see, for example, Allen 2005; Craver and Darden 2005; Des Chene 2005). Few if any contemporary neuroscientists are committed to a world that contains nothing but geometrical properties (as Descartes recommends) or to the idea that everything must be explained in terms of attraction and repulsion (as du Bois Reymond requires[4]).

---

[2] Wimsatt (1976b) points out that scientists rarely use the term "reduction" in the strict philosophic sense, but use this term merely to describe the search for lower-level mechanisms.

[3] Crane's (1995) claim that the contemporary conception of a "mechanical mind" is continuous with those of the seventeenth century is true only in the very broadest sense of continuous.

[4] In a letter to a friend, du Bois Reymond (1831–96) wrote "Brücke and I pledged a solemn oath to put into power this truth: no other forces than the common physical-chemical ones are active within the organism. In those cases which cannot at the time be explained by these forces one has either to find the specific way or form of their action by means of the physical-mathematical method, or to assume new forces equal in dignity to the chemical-physical forces inherent in matter, reducible to the force of attraction and repulsion" (in Sulloway 1979: 14).

Nor is it helpful to note that mechanisms are machines, or that they are machine-like. For what is a machine? The concept can be made more precise in a variety of ways: one can restrict the class of machines to heroic simple machines (levers, pulleys, and screws), or to extended things colliding (as in Cartesian mechanism), or to things that attract and repel one another (as du Bois Reymond held). Each of these restrictions makes the concept of a mechanism too narrow to accommodate the diverse kinds of mechanism in contemporary neuroscience.[5] Second, machines often have easily identifiable parts contained within well-defined boundaries. We look into a clock and readily identify the pendulum, the counterweights, its ratchets and gears. The parts of neural mechanisms are in many cases not so visible, not so readily distinguished from their surroundings; in some cases, they are widely distributed and dynamically connected, defying any attempts to localize functions to particular parts. In that case, the machine analogy provides a misleadingly simplistic view of the mechanisms in nature. Finally, machines and mechanisms are in most cases individuated according to different criteria. Automobiles, for example, are composed of many distinct mechanisms—one for shifting gears, one for cleaning windshields, one for lighting the road, and one for signaling an empty tank. Automobiles also have a number of nonmechanical parts. The hubcaps, the mud flaps, and the fuzzy dice are features of a fine machine, but none of these is a part of any of its mechanisms. If these features are removed, the machine changes, but the mechanisms remain the same.

Rather than starting with the machine analogy, it is better to start thinking about mechanisms with the help of an example. Consider the mechanism by which a neuron releases neurotransmitters (Südhof 2000, 2004). The mechanism begins, we can say, when an action potential depolarizes the axon terminal and so opens voltage-sensitive calcium (Ca^{2+}) channels in the neuronal membrane. Intracellular Ca^{2+} concentrations rise, causing more Ca^{2+} to bind to Ca^{2+}/Calmodulin dependent kinase. The latter phosphorylates synapsin, which frees the transmitter-containing vesicle

---

[5] Compare Brandon: "But what is a mechanism? Here I cannot be precise. Sometimes old-fashioned spring-wound clocks and watches are called mechanical devices. Clearly I cannot use 'mechanism' in such a narrow sense. Mechanisms may consist of springs and gears, they may consist of computer chips and electrical pulses, they may consist of small peripheral populations and geographic isolating barriers. I cannot delimit all possible mechanisms because it is the business of science to discover the mechanisms of nature. At best I could list the sorts of mechanisms that science, or more specifically, biology has discovered" (Brandon 1985).

from the cytoskeleton. At this point, Rab3A and Rab3C target the freed vesicle to release sites in the membrane. Then v-SNARES (such as VAMP), which are incorporated into the vesicle membrane, bind to t-SNARES (such as syntaxin and SNAP-25), which are incorporated into the axon terminal membrane, thereby bringing the vesicle and the membrane next to one another. Finally, local influx of Ca^{2+} at the active zone in the terminal leads this SNARE complex, either acting alone or in concert with other proteins, to open a fusion pore that spans the membrane to the synaptic cleft. There is room for debate about aspects of this description, but this explanation nonetheless displays the general form of mechanistic explanation that is my focus.

This is a mechanism in the sense that it is a set of entities and activities organized such that they exhibit the phenomenon to be explained.[6] In this case, the phenomenon to be explained is the vesicular release of neurotransmitters. This phenomenon is multifaceted. One wants to explain, for example, why depolarization leads to neurotransmitter release, why neurotransmitter release is blocked by calcium chelators, why neurotransmitters are released in quanta, and so on. The explanation includes various entities (N-type Ca^{2+} channels, Ca^{2+} ions, active zones, a host of intracellular molecules such as Rab3A, Rab3C, VAMP/synaptobrevin, SNAP-25, and syntaxin, vesicles containing neurotransmitters, fusion pores, and neural membranes) and their various activities (opening, clamping, diffusing, docking, fusing, incorporating, phosphorylating, and priming). Entities are the components or parts in mechanisms. They have properties that allow them to engage in a variety of activities. They typically have locations, sizes, structures, and orientations. They are the kinds of things that have masses,

---

[6] I borrow extensively from a long tradition of interest in mechanistic models of explanation. Herbert Simon (1969) described this explanatory strategy as the search for nearly decomposable systems and inspired others to write about this style of explanation (Fodor 1968; Haugeland 1998; Wimsatt 1974; 1976b; Kauffman 1971; Lycan 1987). Peter Railton (1978) appeals to mechanisms in his deductive-nomological model of probabilistic causation, but he says little about what constitutes a mechanism. Wesley Salmon (1984) argues forcefully for a causal-mechanical approach to explanation, although he pays little attention to constitutive mechanisms. Robert Cummins (1975, 1983) emphasizes the importance of explanation by functional analysis in psychology. Dennett (1978) stresses the role of "reverse engineering" in building explanations. I discuss these latter two in Chapter 4. More recent discussions of mechanisms trace back to Bechtel and Richardson's (1993) account of decomposition and localization. There have been numerous attempts to say what mechanisms are (Glennan 1996; Machamer et al. 2000; Skipper 1999; Thagard 1998; Woodward 2002), and to explore how they are discovered (Bechtel 2006; Burian 1996; Craver and Darden 2001; Darden 2002, 2006; Darden and Craver 2002; Thagard 1999), but there is so far no univocal account of mechanistic *explanation* (although see Bechtel and Abrahamsen 2005; Glennan 2002; and Thagard 2003 for important steps forward).

carry charges, and transmit momentum. They also act in a variety of ways, by binding to other objects, opening and closing, and diffusing. Activities are the causal components in mechanisms. I use the term "activity" here and throughout the book merely as a filler term for productive behaviors (such as opening), causal interactions (such as attracting), omissions (as occurs in cases of inhibition), preventions (such as blocking), and so on. In saying that activities are *productive*, I mean that they are not mere correlations, that they are not mere temporal sequences, and, most fundamentally, that they can potentially be exploited for the purposes of manipulation and control (see Chapter 3). I do not require in my account that mechanisms must be composed of some restrictive set of activities; I do not require that causes act on contact, or that activities must involve transmission, or that all activities involve attraction or repulsion. There are many kinds of activity, and it is the task of science rather than philosophy to sort them out. The mechanism of neurotransmitter release includes different forms of chemical bonding, conformation changes, diffusion, attraction and repulsion. These are familiar and accepted activities that the entities in this mechanism are known to exhibit.

Finally, the entities and activities in mechanisms are organized together spatially, temporally, causally, and hierarchically such that transmitters are released when the axon terminal depolarizes.[7] The voltage-sensitive ion channels are located in the terminal, they span the membrane, and they open to expose a channel. Biochemical cascades in the cytoplasm have sequences or cycles of interactions, they are organized in series and in parallel, and their steps have different orders, rates and durations. The components in the mechanism often stand in mechanism/component relations, a species of part–whole relation. As a result the mechanism is hierarchically organized. The behavior of the mechanism as a whole requires the organization of its components (see Wimsatt 1997; Craver 2001).

So I begin with this skeletal description: mechanisms are entities and activities organized such that they exhibit the *explanandum phenomenon*. The components of this most abstract sketch of a mechanism are illustrated in Figure 1.1. At the top is the phenomenon to be explained. For economy, I often refer to the phenomenon, the property or behavior explained by

---

[7] Not all forms of organization are important in every mechanism, and different kinds of organization predominate in different forms of mechanisms.

Phenomemon

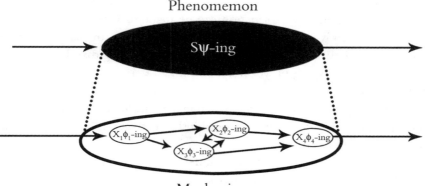

Mechanism

Figure 1.1. A phenomenon (top) and its mechanism (bottom).

the mechanism, as ψ (pronounced psi, as in psychological), and I use S (English pronunciation) to refer to the mechanism as a whole. Beneath S's ψ-ing are represented the entities (circles) and activities (arrows) that are organized together in the mechanism. For economy, I use X (English pronunciation) to describe the component entities in the mechanism and ϕ (pronounced phi, as in physiological) to refer to the component activities in the mechanism. S's ψ-ing is explained by the organization of entities $\{X_1, X_2, \ldots, X_m\}$ and activities $\{\phi_1, \phi_2, \ldots, \phi_n\}$.[8]

It is not clear why mechanistic explanations of this sort have been neglected in the philosophy of science. One reason is the long-term dominance of the covering-law (CL) model of explanation. According to that model, explanations are arguments. One explains an event by showing that it was to be expected on the basis of (that is, can be predicted from) the laws of nature plus antecedent or background conditions. The CL model states clear criteria for success in explanation: the premises of the argument must be true, some of them must be laws, and the occurrence of the phenomenon must follow from the premises according to well-defined rules of inference. Philosophers of the special sciences,

---

[8] Jon Elster has developed two senses of "mechanism" for discussions in the social sciences. According to one sense (1983), mechanisms are the working components revealed by opening black boxes. This idea is roughly the sense of "mechanism" that I have in mind. More recently, Elster (1989) describes "mechanisms" as irregular but intelligible kinds of change that ground explanation but do not allow prediction. This latter notion involves features (especially irregularity and the failure of prediction) that are not built into my view of mechanisms.

such as neuroscience, have often embarked by first asking whether the covering-law model of explanation can be made to work in that science. Debates inevitably arise as to whether there are laws of nature in these sciences and about whether ceteris paribus laws (asserting that the regularity holds unless something prevents it from holding) are truly explanatory (as opposed to trivial or vacuous). But the discussion only rarely pulls back far enough to question whether the logic of mechanistic explanation is most perspicuously described as a relationship between law statements and descriptions of phenomena.

The clearest alternative to the CL model of explanation, the causal-mechanical view espoused by Salmon (1984, 1998) among others, emphasizes that explaining a phenomenon is not a matter of showing that it was to be expected on the basis of the laws of nature (or suitable generalizations). Rather, it is a matter of showing how a phenomenon is produced by its causes. To explain neurotransmitter release, one shows that the depolarization *opens* the Ca^{2+} channels, that opening the Ca^{2+} channels *allows* Ca^{2+} to *diffuse* into the cell, that vesicles *dock* to the membrane by forming SNARE complexes, and that the *influx* of Ca^{2+} *triggers* the formation of a fusion pore. But Salmon, and most of the others who have paid attention to causal explanation, have focused exclusively on *etiological* causal explanation, that is, explanation of some event by its antecedent causes (as when a virus causes the flu). The variety of explanation that I am interested in is *constitutive* (or componential)[9] causal-mechanical explanation: the explanation of a phenomenon, such as the opening of a Ca^{2+} channel, by the organization of component entities and activities.

In Chapter 2, I argue that analyses of explanation must include reference to causal relationships if they are to distinguish good explanations from bad. The difficulties that noncausal models of explanation (such as the CL model (Hempel 1965), Philip Kitcher's (1989) unification model, and Paul Churchland's (1989) representational model) have in delivering the right verdicts on standard test cases argue collectively for a causal approach to explanation in neuroscience. Those who are already convinced of the shortcomings of the covering-law model, Kitcher's unification

---

[9] Salmon (1984) spoke of a "constitutive aspect" of causal-mechanical explanation. Metaphysicians reserve the term "constitutive" for a specific relation that has more entanglements than I intend. The word "componential" is more apt, but I will occasionally use "constitutive" in Salmon's sense (and never in any other).

model, and Churchland's representational model, or who already believe that explanation in neuroscience crucially involves describing causes, can skim this chapter. In Chapter 3, I ground the distinction between productive activities and pseudo-activities in relationships of manipulability (see Woodward 2003), thus adding a crucial normative component to the analysis of mechanisms. I develop that account in Chapter 4, and I show how it constitutes a significant improvement over, for example, Robert Cummins's account of explanation by functional analysis (1975, 1983) and William Lycan's (1987) homuncular functionalism.

3. Explanations in Neuroscience are Multilevel

Explanations in neuroscience refer to the behaviors of organisms, the processing functions of brain systems, the representational and computational properties of brain regions, the electrophysiological properties of nerve cells, and the structures and conformation changes of molecules.

Consider, as a simple and uncontroversial example, Edward Stricker's and Joseph Verbalis's sketch of the explanation for fluid homeostasis:

An increase in plasma osmolality, as occurs after one eats salty foods or after body water evaporates without being replaced, stimulates the release of vasopressin [from the pituitary], increasing the conservation of water and the excretion of solutes in urine. This is accompanied by increased thirst, with the result of making plasma osmolality more dilute through the consumption of water. (Stricker and Verbalis 1988: 261)

This explanation sketch oscillates among multiple levels to link such diverse phenomena as the behaviors of organisms (drinking), drives (thirst), the working of bodily organs (conservation of urine in the kidneys), the flux of bodily molecules (such as the pituitary's release of vasopressin), and swarms of ions (the concentration of salt in the blood). If one views neuroscience through the lens of explanation in physics and chemistry, one is tempted to organize multilevel explanations by sorting the different components into complete explanations at each level and then relating the levels to one another by deduction. But this explanation of the osmoregulatory system is more local and fragmentary than that. There is no need for a complete theory of organisms, organs, cells, molecules, and atoms to understand enough about the activities of the entities at each level to explain, in sketch, how fluid and solute levels are regulated. The explanation oscillates up and down in a hierarchy of mechanisms to focus on just the items that are relevant to different phenomena or different aspects of the same phenomenon. Food consumption, perspiration, and breathing explain the changes in plasma osmolality. Changes in plasma osmolality explain the pituitary's release of vasopressin. Vasopressin concentrations explain the kidney's filtration of the blood. In Chapters 4 and 6, I develop a notion of relevance that shows why different levels are explanatorily relevant to different phenomena and so shows why this explanatory oscillation among levels is often necessary for adequate explanations.[10]

Some neuroscientists explicitly define neuroscience as a multilevel science. Gordon Shepherd, for instance:

From these considerations we can deduce a basic premise, that an understanding of nervous function requires identifying the elementary units at different levels of organization and understanding the relations between the different levels. We can summarize this view with a more precise definition of the subject matter of contemporary neurobiology and of this book: Neurobiology is the study of nerve cells and associated cells and the ways that they are organized into functional circuits that process information and mediate behavior. (Shepherd 1994: 4–5)

Donald Perkel agrees:

Theoretical neurobiology, in parallel with its experimental counterpart and in similarity with the theoretical aspects of other sciences, operates simultaneously at a number of levels. The hierarchy of levels is governed by the organization of the nervous system itself. (Perkel 1990: 39)

The suggestion (one that I defend in Chapter 6) is not merely that the central nervous system *can be* explained at different levels, but that an adequate explanation of many phenomena in the central nervous system *must* bridge phenomena at multiple levels.[11] Judging from statements of this sort, there is no *single* neural level, or neurophysiological level, or neuroscientific level of explanation. Neuroscientific phenomena span a

---

[10] How many levels there are and which levels are relevant depends on what phenomenon is being explained and on facts about the organization of the portion of the world relevant to that phenomenon. I do not require that all explanations span multiple levels, but many do.

[11] I argue for the necessity of higher-level explanations in Chapter 6.

hierarchy of levels from the activities of molecules to the behaviors of organisms.[12]

In this respect, neuroscience is typical of other sciences *in the middle range* between elementary particles and astronomical phenomena. As Schaffner notes, such explanations are, "typically interlevel in the sense of levels of aggregation, containing component parts which are often specified in intermingled organ, cellular, and biochemical terms" (Schaffner 1993b: 321). This is an apt description of most explanations in contemporary neuroscience. This descriptive point makes a strong, albeit prima facie, case against fundamentalism.[13]

Fundamentalists demand that neuroscientific explanations bottom out in some privileged set of entities or causal relations. Some fundamentalists believe that neuroscientific explanations bottom out in the behavior of neurons. Gold and Stoljar (1999) catalogue a number of such claims. For example, Patricia Churchland and Terrance Sejnowski, who stress the importance of levels elsewhere (1992: 11–27), nonetheless claim that:

in the last analysis, the heart of the problem [of memory] is to explain the global changes in a brain's output, on the basis of orderly, *local* changes in individual cells (1992: 239; emphasis in original)

In 1972, Horace Barlow wrote that:

A picture of how the brain works, and in particular how it processes and represents sensory information, can be built up from knowledge of the interactions of individual cells. (1972: 384)

Other fundamentalists—molecularists—ground neuroscientific explanations in molecules. Consider how Samuel Barondes describes the relationship between molecules and mental illness:

---

[12] Lycan, the foremost advocate of a multilevel view of psychological explanation, objects to "two-levelism" in the philosophy of psychology: "Very generally put, my objection is that 'software'/'hardware' talk encourages the idea of a bipartite Nature, divided into two levels, roughly the physicochemical and the (supervenient) 'functional' or higher-organizational—as against reality, which is a multiple hierarchy of levels of nature, each level marked by a nexus of nomic generalization and supervenient on all those levels below it on the continuum" (in Lycan 1999: 50). Lycan's discussion is similar to the distinction be between levels of mechanisms and levels of realization that I introduce in Chapters 5 and 6.

[13] The term "fundamentalism" is meant to pick out those who think that good explanations can be formulated only at the most fundamental level, be that the physical level or some other level. Fundamentalists are often called reductionists, physicalists, and smallists (Wilson 2004), but the term fundamentalism captures the central conviction that these individuals have in common without begging any questions against them.

molecules are the chemical machinery of our brains, so that to study them is to study the actual brain components involved in feeling and remembering, instead of contemplating them at a higher level of abstraction. (1999: 46)

John Bickle (2003) agrees, insisting that higher levels are merely of heuristic value and that all real causes and explanations are ultimately to be found at the cellular and molecular levels. Most fundamentalist philosophers do not stop at neurons or molecules but descend to the most fundamental phenomena of the physical world. Wherever the bottom is, that is where the real explanations are to be found.

Ian Gold and Eliot Stoljar (1999) argue that fundamentalism (in the form of what they call the "neuron doctrine") is both widely accepted in contemporary neuroscience and philosophy *and* completely lacking in evidential support. They explain this fact by appealing to an ambiguity between the trivial neuron doctrine (that is, the doctrine that some theory of cognitive neuroscience is the best explanation for the mind and brain) and the radical neuron doctrine (that is, the doctrine that some exclusively biological theory of cognitive neuroscience is the best explanation for the mind and brain). The trivial doctrine is a wise bet, given that some theory in cognitive neuroscience will almost surely explain aspects of the mind. But the explanatory success of neuroscience provides no support for the thesis that this explanatory theory will be exclusively biological, neural, molecular, or physical. The successful explanations in neuroscience today typically span multiple levels.

Radical fundamentalism, then, is the claim that the only real explanations are to be found at some fundamental level (for example, the biological, neural, molecular, or atomic level). Gold and Stoljar are right to point out that the radical doctrine is implausible. It is not supportable by appeal to the best explanations in contemporary neuroscience, which tend to be multilevel;[14] nor is it supportable by the structure of theories and explanations elsewhere in the biological and physiological sciences. Why then is fundamentalism so common? There are many reasons, of course.

Sometimes scientists assert fundamentalism as a matter of disciplinary pride. Scientists in one field are convinced that they know more about

[14] Bickle (2003) argues that there are good explanations that are exclusively molecular. I believe that close examination of those cases reveals more significant multilevel explanation than Bickle acknowledges. Compare his discussion of LTP with mine in Chapter 7.

the world than scientists in other fields. They are convinced that their techniques are more useful for intervening to change the brain than are the techniques used by other fields, and they believe that they have identified the items that are most explanatorily relevant to the phenomenon to be explained. Debates about the relevance of different fields and levels are part of the sociology of neuroscience. To defend such disciplinary isolationism, however, one must have a principled reason for accepting one set of items as privileged over all others. In this book, I defend the *explanatory relevance* of nonfundamental items. I leave open the question of whether metaphysical arguments can be mustered to support a principled ontological fundamentalism. The most potent metaphysical arguments, as clearly formulated by Jaegwan Kim over the last quarter century, will not settle disciplinary disputes among nonfundamental disciplines. Rather, those arguments, if they work, would show that there are no nonfundamental objects or properties full stop. (There are no brains, no cells, and no receptors either). The metaphysical fundamentalist argues that nonfundamental things have no causal powers over and above fundamental things. They believe, roughly, that everything has a complete cause at the fundamental level (the principle of the causal completeness of the physical) and that nothing has more than one complete cause (the principle of non-overdetermination). If so, it follows that no nonfundamental things are causes.[15] There might be predicates that describe nonfundamental goings-on, says John Heil, but it is a classic mistake to assume that there must be some thing to which such predicates refer. The metaphysical arguments that drive philosophers to fundamentalism, in short, lead one to abandon commitment to the existence of nonfundamental properties and nonfundamental causal powers generally. Given that no neuroscientists work at the fundamental level, such arguments provide little solace to those who would wish to establish that one nonfundamental level is metaphysically privileged over another nonfundamental level. My focus is therefore on the question of whether nonfundamental phenomena are causally and explanatorily relevant, and this issue is independent of how and whether these metaphysical arguments resolve.

Fundamentalism sometimes is presented as science itself. Gerald Edelman says that the goal of neuroscience is to:

---

[15] Some defend the thesis that nonfundamental items are explanatorily, but not causally, relevant. I will defend the view that they are explanatorily relevant because they are causally relevant.

construct a scientific theory of the mind based directly on the structure and workings of the brain. By "scientific" in this context, I mean a description based on the neuronal and phenotypic organization of an individual and formulated solely in terms of physical and chemical mechanisms giving rise to that organization. (Edelman 1989: 8–9)

Francis Crick endorses a similar fundamentalist attitude:

The scientific believe that our minds—the behavior of our brains—can be explained by the interactions of nerve cells (and other cells) and the molecules associated with them. (1994: 7)

Neither Edelman nor Crick argues for this fundamentalist view of science. Few philosophers of science recognize a hard and fast criterion of demarcation between science and non-science anymore, and none that I am aware of draw the line at cells or molecules. According to most attempts at demarcation, science is distinctive by virtue of its attitudes toward nature and its policies of belief formation, not by virtue of its subject matter. Furthermore, as I noted above, many scientists endorse multilevel explanations. For example, Gordon Shepherd defines neurobiology as multilevel science: "Neurobiology is the study of nerve cells and associated cells and the ways that they are organized into circuits that process information and mediate behavior" (1994: 5). In fact, the vast majority of scientists working in contemporary science are working well above the fundamental level—or at least well above what we now think that the fundamental level is. At any rate, it will require a very strong argument to show that those who study economics, or animal behavior, or cerebral blood flow, or physiological systems of any sort have, by virtue of their chosen subject matter, ceased to do real science.

Some argue for fundamentalism on historical grounds. They believe that science exhibits a trend toward explanation in terms of ever more fundamental ontological units. Social phenomena are explained in terms of psychological phenomena, psychological phenomena in terms of neurons, neural phenomena in terms of molecules, and molecular phenomena in terms of particle physics (Oppenheim and Putnam 1958). But these claims are generally based on historical reconstructions of a few examples and not on statistical data adequate to define a trend (see, for example, Bickle 2003). Even granting that a few examples might serve as evidence for a trend in recent neuroscience, one could just as easily choose different examples, or—as I demonstrate in the closing chapter of this book—find evidence of contrary trends in the same examples. Most importantly, though, historical trends indicate nothing about whether explanations *ought* to be multilevel. Even if all neuroscientists were to embrace the techniques and explanations of molecular biology or to formulate explanations exclusively in terms of patterns of action potentials—and they do not, as the prevalence of, for example, neuroimaging studies, multiunit recording studies, and psychological experiments attests—it could turn out in retrospect that they were wrong.

Finally, some endorse fundamentalism as a reaction to a fear of the dark (cf. Haugeland 1998: 116). Some think that higher-level entities and activities are akin to ghostly entelechies (that is, vital forces), souls, or "spooky" emergent properties. But the comparison is unfair. There is no evidence that souls or entelechies exist. They cannot be detected by measuring devices, let alone with multiple methods embodying different theoretical perspectives. There are no clear criteria for determining when souls and entelechies are present or absent, and there are no clear criteria for individuating souls and entelechies (that is, clear and objective criteria according to which one could count them). We cannot intervene with predictable outcomes to change souls and entelechies, and we cannot use them to intervene in other states of affairs. For all these reasons, we are justifiably suspicious of claims that such things exist. But none of these reasonable criteria fails for higher-level items in neuroscience. Molecules, neurons, brain regions, and brain systems all clearly satisfy these standards. Fear of the dark, extended beyond its reasonable domain of application, can seem to justify fundamentalism. But nonfundamental levels in neuroscience should not spook us in this way.

In short, fundamentalism cannot be justified as definitive of science, as a finding of science, as a scientific trend, or as a unique antidote to souls. One goal in this book (Chapter 6) is to argue for the causal, and so explanatory, relevance of phenomena at multiple levels in a hierarchy of mechanisms and to show why nonfundamental explanations are required for most phenomena. This argument depends upon a view of causal and explanatory relevance (see Chapter 3) and on the assumptions that justify the use of controlled experiments to test causal and explanatory claims (see Chapter 6).

Let me be perfectly clear: my reason for being an explanatory antifunda-mentalist is not because I believe that there are gods or goblins. There are not. Nor am I an explanatory antifundamentalist because I believe that there are "emergent properties." I agree with the fundamentalist (although I will not argue for it) that talk of "emergence" or "irreducible complexity" is in many cases unintelligible. My argument for explanatory antifundamentalism is premised on nothing but well-established facts about the material world and on the assumptions underlying the use of controlled experiments to test claims about causal and explanatory relevance. In Chapter 5, I disambiguate several senses of the term "level" in order to clarify the sense in which I think that the mechanisms in neuroscience are multilevel. In Chapter 6, I present positive arguments for accepting multilevel explanations. I do not pretend to defend nonfundamental explanations against all metaphysical challenges. Instead, I content myself with presenting a positive view of levels, causal relevance, experimentation, and explanation that allows one to accept the explanatory relevance of nonfundamental phenomena.

4. Explanations in Neuroscience Integrate Multiple Fields

Neuroscience has always been an explicitly multifield discipline. The Society for Neuroscience (SfN), which came into existence with 500 members in 1970 and has over 37,000 as of 2006, is a menagerie of researchers with different explanatory goals, different concepts and vocabularies, and different techniques and methods.[16] Neuroscience includes and draws upon aspects of anatomy, behavioral psychology, biophysics, cognitive and developmental psychology, computer science, evolutionary and molecular biology, endocrinology, ethology, immunology, neurology, neurophysiology, mathematics, pharmacology, physics, physiology, and psychiatry. One explicit aim of the SfN is to integrate these fields in the common goal of understanding the central nervous system.[17] In the first edition of his *Neurobiology* text, Gordon Shepherd writes:

---

[16] These are the distinguishing features of *fields* as described by Darden and Maull (1977). One should not expect sharp boundaries for fields in sciences such as neuroscience, where interfield interaction is so diffuse and multidirectional. The boundaries of fields are also fluid and depend as much on sociological factors (e.g., who talks, publishes, and travels with whom) as they do on theoretical, technical, and explanatory differences. Despite the fuzziness of these boundaries, I use the term "field" to group researchers with overlapping interests, perspectives, techniques, and languages.

[17] See the mission statement of the SfN at <*www.sfn.org*>.

many fields of learning involve the nervous system. We may think of them as overlapping spheres of interest, and where they overlap defines the field of *neurobiology* or *neuroscience*. Some of its features may be pointed out immediately. It is a relatively *new* field, reflecting the fact that many component disciplines had not advanced far enough to intersect significantly until fairly recently. It is obviously a *multidisciplinary* field; this means that no one approach has a corner on the truth, and we need to correlate the results from several methods in order to understand any particular brain function. Finally, it is a field *without distinct boundaries*. Just as students in other fields may be drawn to the nervous system, so, when investigators start with a problem in the nervous system, they soon find themselves dealing with fundamental aspects of other fields. (Shepherd 1983: 4; emphasis in original)

More recently, Churchland and Sejnowski write:

There is now a gathering conviction among scientists that the time is right for a fruitful convergence of research from hitherto isolated fields. The research strategy developing in cognitive neuroscience is neither exclusively from the top down nor exclusively from the bottom up. Rather it is a coevolutionary strategy, typified by interaction among research domains, where research at one level provides constraints, corrections, and inspiration for research at other levels. (In Gazzaniga 2000: 14)

Neuroscientists emphasize the extent to which their best explanations integrate or unify findings from several different fields, the way that different fields constrain such explanations, and the way that techniques and vocabularies in different fields co-evolve (that is, change to accommodate one another) under the pressure of those constraints (see, for example, Nadel and O'Keefe 1974).

What does the unity of neuroscience amount to in practice? Oppenheim and Putnam argue that the unity of science consists in a chain of reductive explanations that link phenomena at the highest levels (for example, the behaviors of societies) to phenomena at the lowest levels (for example, elementary particles). Most philosophers of neuroscience have followed Oppenheim and Putnam in using reduction models to describe the multi-level structure of neuroscientific explanation (Schaffner 1967, 1993a, 1993b; Hooker 1981; P. S. Churchland 1986; Bickle 1998). Although these later models differ in details, each descends from Nagel's (1949, 1961) classical reduction model.[18] According to this model, reduction is achieved by

---

[18] Oppenheim and Putnam explicitly reject Nagel's view of reduction in favor of the Kemeny-Oppenheim model of reduction, which can be thought of as explanatory subsumption.

identifying the kind of terms in higher-level theories with those of lower-level theories and deriving the higher-level theories from the lower-level theories. On the assumption that different fields of science have their own theories, and on the assumption that their theories describe different levels, the reduction model then provides a view of the unity of neuroscience.

If Nagel had started with neuroscience as his example, however, it is very unlikely that he would have developed this model of the unity of science. Neuroscience textbooks contain few, if any, explicit derivations (I consider the best example of such—the Hodgkin and Huxley model of the action potential—in Chapter 2). More to the point, however, debates about the adequacy of an explanation almost never turn on whether it is possible to derive a description of a phenomenon at one level from its description at another. Because of this mismatch between reduction and the practice of building explanations, Schaffner defends his model merely as a "regulative ideal," an ideal end point that guides the search for explanations even if that end point is never achieved in practice. He admits that reduction is largely "peripheral" to the practices of historical and contemporary neuroscientists, who typically content themselves with partial and fragmentary descriptions of mechanisms (Schaffner 1974, 1993a). Churchland and Crick likewise claim that reduction in Nagel's sense can be achieved, if ever, only after most of the interesting science has been completed (Churchland 1986: 285). I argue in Chapter 7 that reduction is so peripheral to the practice of neuroscience that it is misleading to think of it as a regulative ideal for integrating neuroscience.[19]

As I argue in Chapter 7, the unity of neuroscience is effected when researchers collaborate to build multilevel mechanistic explanations. Different fields approach a mechanism from different perspectives using different techniques. Their findings place constraints on the mechanism. It is not the case that theories at one level are reduced to theories at another. Rather, different fields add constraints that shape the space of possible mechanisms for a phenomenon. Constraints from different fields are the tiles that fill

---

[19] Wimsatt (1976b) and Sarkar (1992) recommend that the term "reduction" be used to describe the explanation of a phenomenon by its mechanism. Peter Smith (1992) suggests that the reductive ideal can be maintained by appeal to "modest reductions." Many scientists use the term "reduction" in this way. The notion of "weak reduction" has yet to be fully explicated, and I hope that defenders of weak reduction will find my view of mechanisms congenial.

in the mechanism sketch to produce an explanatory *mosaic*. To the extent that different fields have independent perspectives and techniques, the ability of a hypothesized mechanism to satisfy their diverse constraints simultaneously counts as an impressive epistemic success. The explanation is more likely to be correct if it is consistent with multiple theoretically and causally independent techniques and perspectives. The collaborative nature of explanation building in neuroscience, in other words, provides the kind of multiple-points-of-view robustness discussed by, for example, Culp (1994, 1995), Salmon (1984), and Wimsatt (1981). I describe this view of the unity of science as a mosaic unity in which distinct fields contribute piecemeal to the construction of a complex and evidentially robust mechanistic explanation.

5. Criteria of Adequacy for an Account of Explanation

In the rest of the book, I develop my model of explanation. I hold the account to the following criteria of adequacy.

First, the account of explanation should be *descriptively adequate*. Hempel insists that his models of explanation, "constitute ideal types or theoretical idealizations and are not intended to reflect the manner in which working scientists actually formulate their explanatory accounts. Rather they are meant to provide explications, or rational reconstructions, or theoretical models, of certain modes of scientific explanation" (1962). This is similar to Schaffner's claim that his reduction model is merely a "regulative ideal." Descriptive failures are not, by themselves, decisive against a normative account of explanation. Nonetheless, as the number of descriptive inadequacies mounts, one begins to wonder whether the model actually reflects what science is like or whether it reflects a philosopher's idea of what science should be like. Such descriptive inadequacies can perhaps be accommodated by the standard models of explanation, I argue, but only at the risk of losing the elegance, simplicity, and unity that made those models so attractive in the first place. By paying close attention to these descriptive inadequacies, one can develop new rational reconstructions—models that reflect the ideals of explanation implicit in the practice of neuroscience. The account of explanation that I give is idealized and normative, but it is modeled upon the ideals of neuroscientists rather than those of philosophers and physicists.

Second, the account of explanation should *demarcate* explanation from other kinds of scientific achievement.[20] For example, an account of explanation should make sense of the difference between simulating or modeling a phenomenon and explaining it. Ptolemeic models can be used to simulate and predict planetary motion across the night sky but they do not explain it; the epicycles, deferents, and equants are merely mathematical tools in the models with no basis in the structure of the heavens. An explanation, in contrast, shows why the planets move as they do and allows one to say how they would move if conditions were different. Similarly, the account should distinguish explanation from categorization. Merely sorting neurons or glial cells into different subtypes, or carving the brain into different spatial regions (for example, frontal, occipital, parietal, temporal), while certainly useful, is not explanatory. Explanation is a distinctive scientific achievement. In the account of explanation developed in this book, I show what is so distinctive about it.

Third, the account of explanation should reveal criteria for *assessing* explanations. The account should not merely describe the form of explanation in neuroscience. It should prescribe norms of explanation as well. In what follows, I develop a view of what counts as an acceptable mechanistic explanation.

---

[20] Although the word "demarcation" is sometimes used to distinguish science from pseudoscience, I am not doing that here.

2

Explanation and Causal Relevance

Summary

I defend a causal–mechanical view of explanation in neuroscience by arguing against three other philosophical accounts of scientific explanation: Paul Churchland's representational account, Carl Hempel's covering-law (CL) model, and Philip Kitcher's unification model. Each of these models struggles to recover commonly accepted constraints on explanations, constraints that are easily satisfied by the causal–mechanical view. To illustrate this point, I consider two examples: the explanation of neurotransmitter release and the explanation of the action potential. The first example reveals several common constraints on acceptable explanations. The second example shows that even the most compelling example of covering-law explanation in neuroscience is, in fact, more accurately understood as an example of causal–mechanical explanation.

1. Introduction

All scientists are motivated in part by the pleasure of understanding. Unfortunately, the pleasure of understanding is often indistinguishable from the pleasure of misunderstanding. The sense of understanding is at best an unreliable indicator of the quality and depth of an explanation.

In this chapter, I argue that good explanations in neuroscience show how phenomena are situated within the causal structure of the world (Salmon 1984). There are other ways of thinking about explanation. One can think of explanation as a psychological process in which a representation or a prototype is applied to a phenomenon (Section 3). One can think of explanation as a logical relation by which a description of a phenomenon follows from premises describing laws of nature and antecedent conditions (Section 4). And one can think of explanation as the unification of disparate phenomena within a given argument schema (Section 5). I argue, however, that these approaches fail to articulate a core set of norms for, or constraints upon, acceptable explanations in neuroscience. I draw out these core constraints by examining the claim that neurotransmitter release is explained by an influx of Ca^{2+} into the pre-synaptic axon terminal (Section 2). One might object that other explanations in neuroscience are, in fact, most clearly reconstructed as arguments or instances of unification. The most compelling example of such is the Hodgkin and Huxley model of the action potential. In Section 6, I show that the example, properly understood, shows that complete explanations in neuroscience describe the causal structure of the world.

2. How Calcium Explains Neurotransmitter Release

To draw out some scientific commitments about explanation, consider the crucial role of Ca^{2+} in the mechanism of neurotransmitter release. This is an example of etiological explanation, in which an effect is explained by its causes. An action potential arrives at the cell's axon terminal, raising the membrane voltage sufficiently to open Ca^{2+}-specific ion channels. The resulting influx of Ca^{2+} initiates a cascade of intracellular reactions that terminates in the creation of a pore between a transmitter-containing vesicle and the membrane. The *explanandum* (the thing to be explained) is the release of one or more quanta of neurotransmitters into the synaptic cleft. The *explanans* (the thing that does the explaining) is the mechanism linking the influx of Ca^{2+} into the axon terminal. Ca^{2+} influx is only part of the explanation, of course, but for now I focus on the evidence used to justify this step of the explanation. Several norms of explanation are implicit in this evidence (see Bennett 2001 for a detailed review of the primary literature).

Bernard Katz and Ricardo Miledi did much of this experimental and theoretical work. In one experiment, they took a motor nerve and a muscle and put them in a controlled fluid bath designed to mimic the extracellular fluid environment of the synapse in vivo. They delivered current to the nerve and recorded a change in the electrical potential of the muscle. Then they varied the Ca^{2+} concentration in the bath. They found that as Ca^{2+} levels drop, neurotransmitter release diminishes and ultimately stops. In some synapses, the quantity of neurotransmitter released with an action potential varies as the fourth power of external calcium concentrations.

They then used a micropipette to deliver a puff of Ca^{2+} onto the synapse in a Ca^{2+}-free bath. The puff of extracellular Ca^{2+} alone does not cause the neuron to release neurotransmitters. Nor does the neuron release transmitters if the puff of Ca^{2+} is applied during the short time-window starting after the action potential reaches the terminal and ending when the muscle responds (or would normally respond). However, if the puff of Ca^{2+} is applied just before the action potential reaches the terminal, the neuron releases neurotransmitter. Fluorescent Ca^{2+} markers and electrophysiological evidence show that Ca^{2+} diffuses into the terminal with each action potential (Ashley and Ridgway 1968). If one blocks the influx of Ca^{2+} by raising the extracellular Mg^{2+} concentration (which blocks Ca^{2+} channels), the neuron releases no neurotransmitter. However, one can induce cells to release neurotransmitters by injecting Ca^{2+} directly into the post-synaptic terminal and by freeing caged sources of Ca^{2+} within the terminal (Miledi 1973), thus circumventing the Mg^{2+} block.

Other factors are explanatorily irrelevant. Action potentials are partly constituted by the diffusion of large quantities of sodium (Na^+) into the cell. When the action potential reaches the terminal, intracellular Na^+ concentrations rise. If one blocks the Na^+ channels at and near the terminal with tetrodotoxin (TTX), one blocks the release of neurotransmitters. This finding is consistent with the possibility that the *influx of sodium* into the terminal causes transmitter release. This finding is also consistent with the possibility that depolarization is the relevant variable, Na^+ being only one means to that end. One can decide between these possibilities by depolarizing the TTX-treated cell by some other current. Katz and Miledi (1967) demonstrated that the rise in Na^+ concentration is not, per se, explanatorily relevant to the release of neurotransmitters. Depolarization explains transmitter release. Similar experiments (using TTX together with a tetraethyl ammonium, TEA, a K^+ blocker) show that K^+ ions are not relevant for neurotransmitter release either.

This brief example contains a number of implicit norms about what does and does not count as an acceptable explanation in neuroscience. These norms of explanation have been used by defenders of the causal-mechanical account to challenge the sufficiency of alternative models of scientific explanation (Salmon 1984, 1989). A first step toward a normative account of explanation in neuroscience is to make these norms explicit.

One reliable but fallible guide to explanatory relevance is statistical relevance. One expects explanatorily relevant phenomena to *make a difference* to the *explanandum*, and statistical relevance is one way of making a difference. Explanatory factors sometimes fail to raise the probability of the *explanandum*. In some cases there are two independent possible explanations, one of which will be true if the other is false. There might, for example, have been two independent release pathways such that preventing Ca^{2+} influx would trigger the other as a failsafe. Ca^{2+} influx would, in those conditions, still be said to cause neurotransmitter release even if its behavior does not raise its probability over what it would be if the other pathway had been activated. Sometimes explanatory factors reduce the probability of the *explanandum*. Philosophers discuss examples of "making it the hard way" in which an event comes about through a sequence of improbable events that, taken together, make the event to be explained less likely than it would otherwise have been (see Salmon 1977 for a lengthy discussion).

Not all correlations are explanatory. The rise in intracellular Na^+ concentration and the subsequent efflux of K^+ during the action potential are correlated with the release of neurotransmitters, but the rise in Na^+ concentration and the drop in K^+ concentration are not explanatorily relevant to neurotransmitter release. The rise in membrane voltage explains why neurotransmitters are released (via the opening of Ca^{2+} channels). For these reasons, it seems best to say that although correlation is perhaps a reliable indicator of explanatory relationships, such simple statistical measures do not pick out the set of all and only relevant factors.

This example also illustrates the norm that in order to establish that a factor is explanatorily relevant, it is not sufficient to show that the factor regularly *precedes* the *explanandum* event. To use Aristotle's example, the rooster's crowing and the sunrise are sequential, and they are sufficiently regular that one could predict the sunrise from an occurrence of crowing, but the crowing is explanatorily irrelevant to the sunrise. No doubt, it is an important piece of evidence that Ca^{2+} influx precedes the release of neurotransmitters. If the Ca^{2+} influx occurred after the neurotransmitter release, it would not be considered part of its explanation. This idea is implicit in the logic of Katz and Miledi's experiment. Application of Ca^{2+} to the cell after the terminal depolarizes but before the post-synaptic response has no effect on the post-synaptic response. Even if there are domains of physics within which it is possible to explain present or past events by reference to future or present events, there are no such explanations in neuroscience.[1] In etiological explanations, the factors in the explanans generally precede (or at least, do not follow) *explanandum* factors.[2] Bad explanations mistake effects for causes. Bromberger's (1966) example of the shadow and the flagpole is the classic philosophical example, and one that I discuss further below. One can derive the length of a flagpole's shadow from the height of the flagpole, the elevation of the sun, and laws about the rectilinear propagation of light, and one can also derive the height of the flagpole from the length of the shadow, the elevation of the sun, and laws about the rectilinear propagation of light. The point of this example is that explanation follows the direction of causal influence: light from the sun travels past the flagpole and on to the ground. This norm is clearly enforced in the evidence for the Ca^{2+} hypothesis. The empirical fact that most explanations in neuroscience run from earlier to later is explained by the hypothesis that these explanations track causal relationships and by the fact that causal relationships in the domain of neuroscience tend (as far as is now known) to run from earlier to later.

Another norm of explanation implicit in this example is that one cannot explain one effect of a common cause by reference to another effect. Hans Reichenbach's (1956) classic example is that of the barometer and the

---

[1] I do not claim that all explanations or causes work from earlier to later. There might be certain areas of physics in which backwards causation remains a live possibility (see Dowe 2000), and it might be that bona fide backwards causes are rare (owing to the absence of initial or boundary conditions) rather than impossible (see Price 1996). The account of causal relevance I develop in Chapter 3 does not prohibit backwards causation. For my purposes, what matters is not temporal asymmetry in explanation per se, but rather the asymmetry of causal relevance that explains it.

[2] This can be difficult to tease apart in practice. The brains of patients with Alzheimer's disease regularly contain dense plaques of a substance known as β-amyloid and with pockets of withered neuronal processes known as neurofibrillary tangles. Suppose one believes that the presence of tangles is explained by the deposition of β-amyloid in the brain. One should abandon this explanatory hypothesis if one discovers that neurofibrillary tangles appear in the brain long before β-amyloid is deposited. But in a stain on a microscope slide, it is impossible to establish which factor precedes the other. This was the source of considerable debate at one time in the history of research on Alzheimer's disease.

weather. Despite the regularity obtaining between falling barometers and storms, changes in barometers do not explain storms. Instead, falling barometric pressure explains both the stormy weather and the falling barometric readings. A surprising number of operations in cells depend on the Ca^{2+} concentration. Changing the intracellular Ca^+ concentration is likely to impact several different reaction rates, only some of which are directly relevant to neurotransmitter release. It is crucial for understanding such biochemical cascades, however, that one understand what causes what and what is merely correlated with what for some other reason (such as the existence of a common cause). Good explanations explain effects with causes.

One last feature of this example deserves attention: the relationship between action potentials and the release of neurotransmitters is stochastic. Only 10–20 percent of action potentials (and instances of Ca^{2+} influx) eventuate in release events. It is clearly not required of this explanatory relationship that all action potentials eventuate in release events. Nor is it required that no release events occur without action potentials. Nor is it required that action potentials make release events probable, for they evidently do not (see Bogen 2005). Action potentials are reminiscent of the case of Mr. Jones, whose untreated syphilis terminates in paresis despite the fact that only one in five cases of untreated syphilis do so. His bout of syphilis is relevant to his paresis despite the fact that one would not expect him to develop paresis on the basis of knowing that he has syphilis.

No other norms of explanation could be illustrated with this example. I have said nothing, for instance, about the complexities of designing and conducting these experiments. However, the main points can now be summarized as follows:

(E1) mere temporal sequences are not explanatory (temporal sequences);
(E2) causes explain effects and not vice versa (asymmetry);
(E3) causally independent effects of common causes do not explain one another (common cause);
(E4) causally irrelevant phenomena are not explanatory (relevance); and
(E5) causes need not make effects probable to explain them (improbable effects).

Salmon (1984) uses constraints (E1)–(E5) to attack the once-dominant CL model of explanation and to argue in favor of his causal-mechanical view. Salmon's most penetrating insight was to abandon the idea—explicit in the CL model and Kitcher's U–model—that explanations are arguments. Instead, he defended an *ontic* view, according to which explanations are objective features of the world. This idea can be brought out by considering an ambiguity in the term, "explanation." Sometimes explanations are texts—descriptions, models, or representations of any sort that are used to convey information from one person to another. Explanatory texts are the kinds of things that are spoken, written, and drawn. They are the kinds of things that can be more or less complete and more or less accurate. They are representations. Other times, the term explanation refers to an objective portion of the causal structure of the world, to the set of factors that bring about or sustain a phenomenon (call them objective explanations). What explains the accident? The ice on the road, the whiskey, the argument, the tears, and the severed brake cables. What explains the release of neurotransmitters? The action potential, Ca^{2+} influx, vesicular binding, and fusion. There are mechanisms (the objective explanations) and there are their descriptions (explanatory texts). Objective explanations are not texts; they are full-bodied things. They are facts, not representations. They are the kinds of things that are discovered and described. There is no question of objective explanations being "right" or "wrong," or "good" or "bad." They just are.

Objective explanations, the causes and mechanisms in the world, are the correct starting point in thinking about the criteria for evaluating explanatory texts in neuroscience. The normative criteria expressed in (E1)–(E5) are embodied in the idea that good explanatory texts reveal the causal structure of the world. Good mechanistic explanatory texts (including prototypes) are good in part because they correctly represent objective explanations. Complete explanatory texts are complete because they represent all and only the relevant portions of the causal structure of the world.[3] Explanatory texts can be accurate enough and complete enough, depending on the pragmatic context in which the explanation is requested and given. Objective explanations are not variable in this way.

[3] See Coffa (1974) and Salmon (1989) for discussion of the "ontic approach" to explanation as I intend it here. At times, I will switch back to using the word "explanation" to describe explanatory texts or explanatory models. I will sometimes talk about explanations as describing mechanisms. My limited point here is that there are objective explanations and that good explanatory texts describe those objective explanations. There are perhaps many interesting things to be said about explanatory texts, but one crucial aspect of their adequacy has to do with whether explanatory texts accurately characterize the causal structure of the world.

In order to display the virtues of this ontic and causal-mechanical view of explanation, I now consider three popular views of scientific explanation. Each has difficulty satisfying E1–E5.

3. Explanation and Representation

According to one large family of views, explanations explain by subsuming a phenomenon under a general representation, prototype, or schema (see Bechtel and Abrahamsen 2005; P. M. Churchland 1989; Machamer et al. 2000). The representations can be understood as mental representations, as diagrams or models, or as textual descriptions or equations. My concern is with the minimal suggestion that the explanatory relationship between an *explanandum* and an *explanans* should be conceived as a case of bringing an abstract representation to bear on an *explanandum phenomenon*, for example, as activating a mental representation, as applying a diagram to an example, and as using equations to derive the phenomenon to be explained. While this idea is an intriguing hypothesis about the psychology of understanding and about how scientists represent the world to themselves and to one another, it is too weak to serve as a guide to the norms that distinguish good explanations from bad and complete explanations from incomplete.

To see this, consider Paul Churchland's (1989) parallel distributed processing (PDP) account of explanation. Churchland uses a broadly connectionist framework (see Rummelhart and McClelland 1986) to construct a neurally inspired theory of understanding. He then applies that theory to traditional philosophical discussions of explanation. On his view, explanation is prototype activation in a connectionist network, or in a brain that works like one:

Explanatory understanding consists in the activation of a particular prototype vector in a well-trained network. It consists in the apprehension of the problematic case as an instance of a general type, a type for which the creature has a detailed and well-informed representation. (P. M. Churchland 1989: 210)

This pattern of activation, Churchland emphasizes, is not merely a "label":

The vector has structure, a great deal of structure, whose function is to represent an overall *syndrome* of objective features, relations, sequences and uniformities. Its activation by a given perceptual or other cognitive circumstance does not represent a loss of information. On the contrary, it represents a major and speculative *gain* in information, since the portrait it embodies typically goes far beyond the local and perspectivally limited information that may activate it on any given occasion. (P. M. Churchland 1989: 212; emphasis in original)

Explanations assimilate a phenomenon to a prototype and thereby generate novel features of the item from a few input features.

Churchland emphasizes that there are many different types of understanding that have different kinds of prototype in different domains (see P. M. Churchland 1989: 212–18). His taxonomy of explanatory prototypes includes: *property-cluster prototypes,* such as "Jadeite" or "pyramidal cell"; *etiological causal prototypes,* such as the explanation of neurotransmitter release by Ca^{2+} influx; *means–ends prototypes,* such as procedures or functional explanations; *superordinate prototypes,* such as those invoked to explain why the interior angles of a triangle sum to 180 degrees; *social interaction prototypes,* such as those involving ethical, legal, or etiquette-involving norms; and *motivation prototypes* of the sort in folk-psychological explanations. I add *constitutive causal prototypes* to this list to accommodate, for example, the explanation of the Ca^{2+} channel opening in terms of the underlying mechanism within the channel. (Perhaps this is a species of means–ends prototype, but it is different from many other kinds of functional explanation). The account of mechanistic explanation that I develop in this book shows what etiological and constitutive mechanistic prototypes would have to represent.

Churchland's general approach to scientific explanation involves two steps. The first is to construct a neural model of understanding. The second is to apply the model to scientific explanation.

As to the first, Churchland does not say how those instances of prototype-activation that constitute understanding are different from those that do not. Prototype activation vectors are widespread in the functioning of the brain. Populations of neurons also control balance, posture, and reaching; they produce and direct saccadic eye movements; and they regulate endocrine release and body fluid homeostasis. The systems responsible for such phenomena can be explained by appeal to state spaces and activation vectors in populations of neurons. However, it is a strain to see these systems as understanding (or having explained) anything at all.

To focus on cognitive systems in a more narrow sense, consider the distinction between recognizing a phenomenon and understanding it. One can recognize Ike[4] in a crowd without explaining anything about him.[5] Suppose that one wants to understand why Ike is a bookie, or why Ike has only a junior high education. One cannot answer these questions by merely recognizing Ike. This is because Ike's surface features (his gait, his hair line, his shape) are in most cases not explanatorily relevant to his professional and educational status. The distinction between recognition and understanding is supported by empirical evidence. Experimental psychologists, for example, recognize different levels of processing in memory, distinguished (in part) by different encoding procedures (see Craik and Tulving 1975). Lower levels of processing encode memories of visually presented words by, for example, representing surface features of the printed word (does it contain an "e"?), or by representing its phonological properties (does it rhyme with cat?), or by making semantic associations (what could one do with it?). Each of these is a case of prototype activation on the PDP view, but only the latter contains information that is explanatorily relevant to the phenomenon that the word describes.

In the years since Churchland first made this suggestion, cognitive scientists have learned more about causal understanding. For example, some models treat explanation as a matter of tracking the unobservable structure of the world (Povinelli 2000), or picking up on statistical dependency relationships (Cheng 1999; Glymour 2001; Rescorla and Wagner 1972), or making inferences to the best explanation (Ahn and Kalish 2000), or mentally modeling the behavior of a mechanism (Hegarty, Just, and Morrison 1988; Thagard 1999; Bechtel and Abrahamsen 2005). Perhaps Churchland can meet some of the above-mentioned challenges by building further constraints into his model.

Suppose, then, that we accept Churchland's PDP model as an adequate account of the neuropsychology of human understanding. Can this neuropsychological account do double-duty as an account of the norms of scientific explanation? Churchland is explicit that his interests are not primarily normative (P. M. Churchland 1989: 198). However, the goal of

---

[4] The example is a reference to McClelland (1981).

[5] Recognition and explanation can begin to blur if one endorses the idea that perception is a kind of inference to the best explanation. The size, shape, and pattern of movement of that person are best explained by the hypothesis that the person is Ike, and the image of a triangular cell body is best explained by positing that I am looking at a pyramidal cell. Granting that this is a form of explanation, however, what is explained in such cases is the set of stimulus features, not anything about the object itself.

thinking more clearly about what is required of an adequate neuroscientific explanation cannot be satisfied without thinking about norms for evaluating explanations. Consider Churchland's description of etiological causal prototypes:

> An etiological prototype depicts a typical temporal sequence of events, such as cooking of food upon exposure to heat, the deformation of a fragile object during impact with a tougher one, the escape of liquid from a tilted container, and so on. These sequences contain prototypical elements in a prototypical order, and they make possible our explanatory understanding of the temporally extended world. (P. M. Churchland 1989: 213)

But as the example of neurotransmitter release suggests, some temporal sequences are explanatory, and some are not. An account of explanation should help one to distinguish the two. Churchland acknowledges this limitation: "Now just what intricacies constitute a genuine etiological prototype, and how the brain distinguishes between real causal processes and mere pseudoprocesses, are secondary matters I shall leave for a future occasion" (P. M. Churchland 1989: 214).[6] Those who would develop a normative account of explanation, however, cannot avoid this question. The way to understand how brains distinguish causes from temporal sequences is to start by considering how causes differ from temporal sequences—that is, by examining the objective explanations in the world rather than the way that they are represented in the mind/brain.

A separate problem arises in accounting for explanatory relevance (E4). Grant that explanatory texts are prototypes and that explanation involves activating such prototypes. Different features of the phenomenon are relevant for different explanatory purposes. Suppose that Ike is a Shark (a member of the gang, the Sharks); he is single and thirty years old; he weighs 210 pounds; he has a junior high education; he is a bookie; he idolizes Johnny Thunders; and he plays guitar. To explain why he is a bookie, it would be relevant to note that he is a member of a gang and perhaps that he has a junior high education, but it would not be relevant to note that he weighs 210 pounds or that he plays guitar. To explain why he plays guitar, it might be relevant to note that he is a single, thirty-year-old male who idolizes Johnny Thunders, but not (I suppose) that he is a bookie or

---

[6] Churchland (1995) repeats the same account of the etiological prototype without amendment.

that he has a junior high school education. All of these features are in the Ike prototype (which, if we know him well, contains innumerable other features of varying degrees of explanatory relevance). All of these features are activated in the Ike prototype. Yet only some of these features are relevant to Ike's being a bookie, only some are relevant to his playing guitar, and possibly no feature is relevant to both.

What goes for Ike goes for the categories of neuroscience. Ca^{2+} channels can be characterized along a number of dimensions: molecular weight, primary structure, voltage sensitivity, maximum conductance values, primary structure, and so on. Different features of the Ca^{2+} channel are relevant for different explanatory purposes. An account of explanation that can be used to sort good explanations from bad should help to sort explanatorily relevant information from explanatorily irrelevant information. But the PDP account cannot be so used unless the activation–vector story is supplemented with an account of explanatory relevance. Perhaps the PDP account can be supplemented to resolve this difficulty. However, to supplement it, one will have to begin by assessing what explanatory relevance is, and this thrusts our attention away from representation and out onto the causal structures that good explanations describe.

Churchland discusses some normative conclusions that follow from the PDP account. In particular, he stresses that good explanations are rich, warranted, correct, and as unified as possible. The first three of these virtues are not particular to explanations; any representation should be at least sufficiently detailed, warranted, and accurate for the purposes at hand. So I focus on unity.

Churchland justifies his appeal to unity on instrumental grounds: unified prototypes are the best predictors. Churchland draws this conclusion from the behavior of connectionist networks. If they contain too many hidden nodes, or if they have too many connections for a given task, standard training algorithms will configure the network such that it stores each trial stimulus as its own separate representation. If so, it fails to generalize to novel cases. If, alternatively, one places computational limits on the network by reducing the number of hidden nodes and connections, the same algorithms configure the network so that it readily generalizes to novel input patterns. Churchland concludes, "Conceptual unification, evidently, is a cognitive virtue of enormous importance, at least as conceived on the present model of cognition. It is important for the very good reason that cognitive configurations having that virtue do much better at generalizing their past experience to new cases" (Churchland 1989: 221).

One might reasonably wonder at this point how the value of unity is to be weighed against the value of generating explanations that satisfy constraints such as (E1)–(E5). Grant that more unified theories afford better predictions. The question is whether prototypes that merely unify diverse phenomena will be better predictors than those that, *in addition*, satisfy (E1)–(E5). There are long-standing philosophical arguments that one good way to build theories that make accurate novel predictions is to build theories that accurately describe hidden causal mechanisms (see Psillos 1999). Prototypes of temporal sequences, correlations, and irrelevant factors are not as useful for this purpose. I return to the discussion of unification as a virtue in Section 5.

A final point serves to underscore the importance of shifting attention away from the representations used in explanations and toward the causal structure of the world. Some phenomena might be so complex that they overwhelm our limited cognitive systems. Perhaps a mechanism has so many parts with so many interactions that it is impossible to understand. Felleman and Van Essen's (1991) "subway map" of the visual cortex in the macaque monkey, for example, contains thirty-two distinct brain regions and over 300 connections among them. Biochemical cascades and gene regulation often involve a bewildering number of molecules and interactions. For very complex mechanisms, human working memory is so limited that it cannot entertain all of the explanatorily relevant information at one time (compare Rosenberg 1985, 1994). Mary Hegarty shows that even simple mechanisms overwhelm our processing capacities if they have over a handful of parts or if the interactions among them cannot be represented in two dimensions (Hegarty, Just, and Morrison 1988). For this reason, neuroscientists who revel in the complexity of the brain are increasingly using computational tools and databases (such as Van Essen's SuMS database and the Genome Database) that allow them to make explanatory connections that would escape them if they relied only on their unaided cognitive abilities.[7] It would be wrong to say that the

---

[7] One might develop an externalist view of explanation, in which this computational scaffolding, as Clark (1997) would call it, is included in the cognitive account of understanding. Perhaps Churchland's model could be combined with Clark's active externalism. I do not pursue that possibility here.

phenomena produced by such complex mechanisms have no explanation. The explanations exist even if we cannot represent them cognitively.[8]

4. The Covering-Law Model

One way to strengthen representational models would be to place restrictions on what can appear in explanatory representations and on how the representation can be applied to the *explanandum phenomenon*. According to the CL model (Hempel and Oppenheim 1948; Hempel 1965), scientific explanations are arguments from premises describing laws of nature and antecedent conditions to a conclusion describing the phenomenon to be explained.

Explanations explain, on this view, by showing that the phenomenon described in the conclusion *was to have been expected on the basis of the laws of nature* (Hempel 1965: 336). The relevant sense of "expectation" is not psychological but epistemic: the *explanandum* is the conclusion of a sound argument with premises that state laws of nature and the relevant antecedent and background conditions. For deductive explanations, expectation means that a description of the phenomenon follows with certainty from universal laws (plus the relevant antecedent and background conditions). For inductive explanations, expectation means that a description of the phenomenon follows with high probability (that is, $P > 0.5$) from statistical laws. Advocates of the CL model frequently claim that prediction and explanation are symmetrical; the only difference is that in explanations the conclusion of the argument is presumed true (or well-confirmed). The CL account of explanation is sometimes called an epistemic or inferential model (by, for example, Coffa 1974; Salmon 1989) to highlight its reliance on this sense of expectation. This is the central point of contrast with the ontic view that I recommend.

Hempel develops variants of the CL account to accommodate explanations of singular events, such as the occurrence of a particular action

---

[8] A similar point can be made by appeal to the social nature of science. Scientific explanations need not be housed in the minds of individual cognitive agents but might be distributed across many researchers or entire traditions. Many papers have multiple authors, and each author understands some aspect of the posited explanation more than the other co-authors. This is why the authors share the intellectual burden of the paper. (See Keil and Wilson 2000.)

potential, and general regularities, such as the characteristic waveform of the action potential. *Classical theory reduction* is the CL account of explanation for general regularities. A special case of such reduction is the explanation of macro-regularities in the behavior of wholes in terms of the micro-regularities in the behaviors of components. Advocates of classical theory reduction (and many of its opponents) are thus among those who at least tacitly endorse the CL account. Reduction is then understood as an explanatory relationship between a basic theory, T_B, and a reduced theory, T_R. The *explanandum*, T_B, reduces T_R if and only if: (i) the predicates in T_R are defined in terms of the predicates in T_B; (ii) T_R is derivable from T_B by use of such definitions together with sentences specifying boundary conditions and limiting assumptions; and (iii) T_B contains at least one law of nature. Requirement (i) links the vocabularies in the two theories, requirement (ii) expresses the derivability requirement, and requirement (iii) ensures that the explanation contains at least one law, as the CL account demands.

In Chapter 1, I claim that the CL account performs poorly as a description of explanations in neuroscience, which are more likely to be explanations in terms of underlying mechanisms. The primary virtue of the CL account, however, is not as a description but as a regulative ideal. According to that account, explanations are arguments. When the argument is a good argument—when the premises are true, when at least one nontrivial premise states a law of nature, and when the inference is warranted—the explanation is a good explanation. Likewise, explanations are complete when it is possible to write out the argument without suppressing premises. Here I focus on the CL model's shortcomings as a regulative ideal for explanations.

The CL model suffered sustained attack well into the 1980s (see especially Lewis 1983; Salmon 1984). It is now widely regarded among philosophers of science as a relic of logical positivism (even though this tradition traces back at least as far as Aristotle). There are many reasons for this attitude. I discuss three: (i) the problem of distinguishing laws of nature from accidents and other non-explanatory generalizations; (ii) the problem of providing an account of explanatory relevance; and (iii) the fact that one need not show that a phenomenon was to be expected in order to explain it. These objections are familiar to many, so I keep the discussion short.

(i) One central challenge for the CL model is to account for the distinction between laws of nature, which are genuinely explanatory, and accidental generalizations, which are not. (E1)–(E3) address three ways that a generalization can fail to be explanatory. It can describe mere temporal sequences (E1). It can describe mere correlations (E2). And it can describe non-explanatory effect-to-cause relations (E3). It will not do, for example, to adopt the naïve regularity view that laws are universal generalizations of unrestricted scope because relationships violating (E1)–(E3) can easily be formulated within this restriction (see Armstrong 1983; Ruben 1999; Salmon 1984). Nor will it do to add that the universal generalizations must support counterfactuals (as Weber 2005 recommends). There are true counterfactuals, for example, asserting that if the cell were to release neurotransmitters then it is likely to have generated an action potential and asserting that if the cell had not increased its intracellular Na^+ concentration, then it would not have released a neurotransmitter. For this reason, Lewis (1983) requires that explanatory generalizations support "non-backtracking" counterfactuals, that is, those that cannot be used to describe the relationship between an effect and its cause. The CL model's strength as a regulative ideal depends, in large part, on the availability of a satisfactory account of laws, and much of the normative force of the CL model is contained within the restrictions placed on the notion of a "law." For this reason, in Chapter 3, I defend one strategy for meeting this challenge (though not as a defense of the CL model, which I reject).

(ii) A second problem for the CL model is to provide an account of explanatory relevance (E4). The rise in membrane voltage rather than the rise in intracellular Na^+ concentrations explains the opening of the Ca^{2+} channels. Nonetheless, there is a generalization to the effect that if the Na^+ concentrations had been high, then the cell would be more likely to release neurotransmitters.

To use a philosopher's example, consider an experiment in which neurons are first blessed by an ordained parson (for example, by sprinkling them with isotonic holy water) and then stimulated with a 10-nanoampere (nA) current for one second. This experiment would no doubt confirm the general regularity that blessed neurons produce action potentials when stimulated with a 10 nA current. From this regularity, one could conclude that when a given cell has been blessed and stimulated with a 10 nA current, it will generate an action potential. But the blessing is not part of the explanation.[9] It is irrelevant. Note here a crucial difference between arguments and explanations (stressed by Salmon 1984). The strength of an argument is not diminished one bit by the addition of any number of irrelevant premises. The strength of an explanation, on the other hand, depends crucially upon whether the factors described in the explanatory text are relevant.

No neuroscientists believe that blessing neurons makes any difference, but all neuroscientists are confronted at some point with the task of discerning which of a number of competing possible variables explains a phenomenon. One might legitimately wonder, for example, whether an action potential was caused by the injection of current, or the injection of a volume of fluid, or the physical disruption of the membrane. Such considerations are part of the reason why neuroscientists run controlled experiments. They try to determine which factors make a difference and which do not. Mere correlations are insufficient to establish that an item is explanatorily relevant. Instead, one seeks evidence that the correlation is underwritten by a causal relationship between the explanatory factor and the event to be explained.

Although constraints (E1)–(E4) raise serious problems for the CL account, and although others argue that the problems are fatal (for example, Salmon 1989), one might preserve the CL account by rejecting these constraints. Causal skeptics treat (E1)–(E4) as folk notions that have been abandoned in the mature sciences and will (or should) be abandoned in other sciences as they mature. Bertrand Russell (1913), for example, would no doubt embrace the Hodgkin and Huxley model (discussed in Section 5) as a developmental milestone for neuroscience—a first step toward abandoning causal explanations in favor of explanations that subsume phenomena under differential equations. John Norton (2003) follows Russell in treating causation as a "folk notion" on par with caloric or phlogiston. Talk of causation, he claims, can be retained in "hospitable environments," such as certain areas of biology and physiology, because many phenomena in those domains are sufficiently regular to evoke the illusion of a causal relation. But such apparently causal relationships are ultimately nothing but regularities sustained by noncausal laws at the most fundamental level.

---

[9] This example parallels Kyburg's (1965) classic case of "hexed salt," which always dissolves in water.

I cannot rule out a priori the possibility that neuroscientists will some day follow in the path of physicists and reject (E1)–(E4) (if this is really what physicists have done). Nonetheless, two considerations argue against taking the skeptical path.

First, even if the skeptics are right, biology appears to be one of those hospitable environments in which some occurrences depend upon others and in which not every correlation is equally explanatory. Where the phenomena of fundamental physics can perhaps exhaustively be explained by differential equations, there is more to learn in neuroscience about why variables are correlated. Neuroscientists search for mechanisms because in their domain there are mechanisms to be found. In fact, physicists use mechanistic explanations when they descend levels, for example, from particle physics to strings or branes. Unlike fundamental physicists, neuroscientists *can* look to a finer grain to understand how the regularities described in such equations are sustained. Norton and Russell argue from the structure of the best physics to conclusions about causation generally. One might just as easily argue from the structure of the best neuroscience to conclusions about the importance of causation in neuroscience. There is no reason (absent separate metaphysical arguments) to take the developmental trajectory of physics as a projectable trend to be read onto the development of all sciences.[10]

Second, unlike some areas of fundamental physics, the search for neuroscientific explanations is driven by goals of treating illnesses, improving brain function, preventing cognitive decline, and developing new ways to manipulate and record from the brain in the laboratory. Explanation is a tool for determining how to intervene into the brain and manipulate it for our various purposes. Intervening to change a mere temporal predecessor, a mere correlate, or an irrelevant factor will, at least in most cases, do nothing to control and manipulate the brain. In such contexts, the notion of "cause," its asymmetry, and its difference from correlations and mere temporal sequences are simply indispensable. The fact that physicists can do without this distinction (if, in fact, they can) is not germane.

Short of endorsing causal skepticism, one could defend the CL account by fine-tuning the notion of a law of nature to accommodate (E1)–(E4).

---

[10] Pearl (2000) argues that the notion of causation cannot really get a grip in an open system, but applies only once one has drawn boundaries around a system and imagined an intervention imposed from outside the system.

Doing so would move the CL account in the direction of the causal model of explanation developed here.[11] However, it will not do to simply stipulate that laws satisfy (E1)–(E4). The ad hoc character of this stipulation would stand out all the more because, as Salmon (1984) argues, (E1)–(E5) are readily addressed if one views explanation *not* as a matter of showing *that* a phenomenon fits within the *nomic* nexus but rather as a matter of showing *how* a phenomenon fits into the *causal* nexus. Causal dependencies satisfy the restrictions that (E1)–(E4) place on a model of explanation: earlier events explain later events only when they are causally connected (E1). Later events do not cause earlier events (E2).[12] The effects of a common cause are not causally related to one another, although each is caused by a common ancestor event (E3). Explanatorily relevant features are those that are causally related to the *explanandum* effect (E4). In Chapter 3, I defend a view of causal relevance, and I show that it satisfies these basic constraints on a model of explanation.

(iii) The final problem with the CL account as a regulative ideal strikes at the heart of the *nomic expectability thesis*: that to explain an event is to show that it was to be expected on the basis of the laws of nature (and the antecedent and background conditions). As I note above in connection with E5, only 10–20 percent of action potentials eventuate in the release of neurotransmitters. Ion channels (such as $Ca2^+$ channels) can (and frequently do) open under conditions in which their opening is improbable. Mr. Jones's syphilis terminates in paresis despite the fact that only one in five cases of untreated syphilis do so. Each of these examples illustrates that explaining a phenomenon need not require showing that it was to be expected (see Salmon 1984).[13]

In response to examples of this sort, Peter Railton (1978) develops a deductive-nomological-probabilistic (DNP) model of explanation. Although Railton retains several features of the CL account (such as its

---

[11] Lewis proposes to do this by demanding that the laws underwriting causal truths be axioms in the simplest and most systematized axiomatic system. There are questions whether this requirement can in fact capture the norms expressed in (E1)–(E5). My discussion of Kitcher's view of unification casts some doubt on whether such a solution can be worked out in detail.

[12] If there were backwards causes, then later events would explain earlier events, but, at least in this world, the causal relations described in neuroscientific explanations seem to run from earlier to later.

[13] Valerie Hardcastle (personal communication) correctly points out that the probability of getting paresis is much greater if you have syphilis than if you do not. However, having syphilis does not make getting paresis probable, as required by the nomic expectability thesis. See also below the discussion of Kitcher's treatment of this problem case.

appeal to laws), he rightly rejects the nomic expectability thesis for explanations of improbable events. If the event is irreducibly improbable, meaning that there is nothing more to learn about the set-up that would raise one's expectations, then it would be wrong to insist that explanations must show the event to be expected. Explanations proceed, according to the DNP model, by describing a mechanism that gives rise to a probability distribution over possible outcomes and by showing that the *explanandum* event is an instance of one of those possible outcomes. For Railton, then, to explain unexpected phenomena one must describe the mechanisms that produce them—here the mechanisms of transmitter release, and the mechanisms by which syphilis crosses the blood–brain barrier. When it comes to providing an account of mechanisms, however, Railton says only that he will "not have much to say here by means of demystification" (Railton 1978: 208). The account of mechanisms I develop in this book makes Railton's proposal concrete. In neuroscience (and, in fact, also in physics, chemistry, and almost everywhere else) improbable things happen, and when they do, mechanisms can explain them as well (if, in fact, there are mechanisms to be found). The CL model functions as a regulative ideal for explanation because of the nomic expectability thesis. Good explanations lead one to expect the *explanandum phenomenon*. This requirement cannot be relinquished without abandoning the CL model's central motivation. Railton's suggestion is therefore more congenial to a causal-mechanical account of explanation than to Hempel's inferential account.

For these three reasons, the CL model of explanation has generally faded from philosophical currency. Also for these three reasons, the CL model is not an especially useful starting place for thinking about the norms of explanation in neuroscience.

5. The Unification Model

According to the unification model of explanation (henceforth, U-model), explanation is not a matter of deriving the *explanandum phenomenon* from laws but a matter of unifying diverse beliefs under a few simple argument patterns (compare Friedman 1974; Kitcher 1989). The appeal of the U-model derives from the fact that many of the most successful explanations in the history of science (such as Newton's laws, Maxwell's equations, and Darwin's theory of evolution by natural selection) encompass large domains of phenomena within the purview of few basic argument patterns. Philip Kitcher expresses the unificationist ideal succinctly:

Science advances our understanding of nature by showing us how to derive descriptions of many phenomena, using the same pattern of derivation again and again, and in demonstrating this, it teaches us how to reduce the number of facts that we have to accept as ultimate. (Kitcher 1989: 423).[14]

More formally: start with a set K of accepted beliefs at a time. Scientists construct *argument patterns* that allow one to derive some members of K from others. Argument patterns contain *schematic sentences* in which nonlogical terms (terms other than "and," "or," "not," "if," etc.) are replaced by variables. Some of the schematic sentences are premises, and some are conclusions. The variables in schematic sentences are filled in accordance with *filling instructions*, constraints on the values these variables can take. One systematizes K by developing one or more argument patterns that can be used to derive some members of K from others. Explanatory systematizations are those that have the smallest available set of argument patterns that is adequate for deriving the other members of K. Kitcher calls this minimal set the *explanatory store*, or E(K). Progress toward unification is made to the extent that the systematization of one's beliefs approaches E(K). Good explanations have argument patterns in the explanatory store.

One could unify K trivially with vacuous argument patterns. Wondering why any given thing happens, one might appeal to the schematic sentence, "all things happen because God wills them," and to the undemanding filling instructions for "things," to infer the conclusion that this given thing happens. To block examples of this sort, Kitcher requires that explanations be *stringent*. One argument pattern is more stringent than another if that pattern "sets conditions on instantiations that are more difficult to satisfy than those set by another pattern" (Kitcher 1989: 433).

---

[14] Kitcher builds on an earlier suggestion by Friedman (1974), who expresses the unificationist intuition as follows: "Science increases our understanding of the world by reducing the total number of independent phenomena that we have to accept as ultimate or given. A world with fewer independent phenomena is, other things equal, more comprehensible than one with more" (1974: 15). Friedman has technical difficulties defining the metric of unification. Kitcher develops his version of unification to address these difficulties.

These conditions include both the accepted rules of inference (Kitcher calls them "classifications") and the filling instructions. Stringency is a condition of adequacy on unifying explanations.

In what follows, I argue that the unificationist model cannot satisfy the explanatory ideals implicit in the practices of neuroscientists unless it is supplemented with attention to the causal structure of the world. First, I argue that the model is insufficient to distinguish explanation from other varieties of scientific achievement (such as justification and categorization). Second, I argue that Kitcher's model does not satisfy the above constraints on an account of explanation.

Nonexplanatory Unification: several kinds of scientific achievement unify without explaining (see Woodward 2003: 363–5). Taxonomies are one example. The Linnaean taxonomic system systematizes the biological world, but few believe that categorizing an organism within that taxonomy constitutes an explanation. The periodic table shows elements sorted according to atomic number, molecular weight, and the like, but it is not an explanation of the elements. The development of a taxonomy of kinds is crucial for building scientific explanations. Taxonomies are often useful because they arrange items according to explanatorily relevant features. By recognizing a molecule as dopamine, one learns its molecular weight, its mode of synthesis, the enzymes that break it down, its molecular structure, and so on. These features of dopamine can then be deployed in explanations. But merely slotting items into a category, even systematically, is not explanatory. Instead, one gives an explanation by using the relevant features in the taxonomy to explain specific properties and activities of the dopamine molecule. Sorting is preparatory for, rather than constitutive of, explanation.[15]

Justificatory argument patterns can also unify phenomena without explaining them (see Barnes 1992: 566–70). Suppose one infers the shape of a Neanderthal brain from the shape of its fossilized cranium. One might begin with a schematic sentence asserting that fossils of a given type indicate the existence of a Neanderthal with a brain shape of a certain type. One could then infer from the discovery of a given fossilized cranium that a Neanderthal with a given brain shape once existed. Call this the fossil pattern. Assume that K is relatively silent about the antecedent factors

[15] Kitcher would not accept these taxonomies as unifications in his rigorous sense. I do not see, however, how he can avoid accepting the justificatory arguments discussed in the next paragraph.

leading up to Neanderthals having this particular brain shape rather than some other. Given the current state of knowledge concerning the evolution of the brain, this assumption is plausible. It is also plausible that even as K develops, certain facts about the past (if not the fact under discussion) will remain forever outside of K, the past being somewhat opaque to access from the present. If so, there is unlikely to be a comparably precise argument pattern linking factors prior to the appearance of Neanderthals to the fact that Neanderthals have this particular brain shape rather than some other possible shape. The fossil pattern, in comparison, allows one to infer the shape of the brain with far greater (although not perfect) precision. The fossil argument pattern systematizes beliefs about the shape of the Neanderthal brain better than facts about its development and phylogeny. The point is that argument patterns for justifying beliefs about some feature of the world (exemplified here by beliefs about brain casts) sometimes unify more than do the argument patterns that explain those features.

Unification and Causation: given the similarities between Kitcher's U-model and the CL account, one might expect Kitcher's model to have analogous difficulties accommodating (E1)–(E5). Kitcher's range of options is further restricted by his earlier[16] commitment to the idea that the world does not, strictly speaking, contain causal relations.[17] Nonetheless, Kitcher accepts (E1)–(E5) as important constraints on explanation, and he acknowledges that it would be a blow to the U-model if there were maximally unifying yet non-explanatory argument patterns. Accordingly, he argues that the most unified systematization of K must include argument patterns that satisfy such constraints.

Take (E2), for example. This is the constraint that etiological explanations run from earlier to later and not vice versa. Kitcher addresses Bromberger's flagpole and shadow example explicitly (see Kitcher 1989: 484–7). Causal

---

[16] In *The Advancement of Science*, and more recently, Kitcher allows that he could either endorse antirealism about causes or an anti-Humean strand of causal realism (1993). My arguments here are intended to show that the causal structure of the world is not necessarily revealed in the search for unifying explanations.

[17] It should be noted, however, that Kitcher includes explicitly causal sentences in his argument schemata for various phenomena. For example, his argument schema for the Watson and Crick model includes reference to "Details of *transcription*, post-transcriptional *modification*, and *translation*" (1989: 441; emphasis added), and his argument schema for natural selection includes reference to the fact that a trait *enables* an organism to *obtain* complex benefits and advantages, *contributing* to *reproductive success* (1989: 444; emphasis added). Words for activities have snuck into these argument schemata. Thanks to Rob Skipper for calling my attention to this fact.

models of explanation are ready-made to deal with this sort of case: the relations of causal dependency run from the sun and its angle of elevation past the flagpole to the shadow, and not from the shadow's length past the flagpole to the sun and its elevation.

Kitcher's treatment is more creative than this but less direct. He compares two possible systematizations of K. One, call it S_C for common sense, includes an "origin-and-development" (O-and-D) pattern of explanation. The O-and-D pattern explains the dimensions of objects in terms of their origins and subsequent histories. The flagpole was created by a flagpole designer to be a certain length, it has been heated and cooled, it was set in the ground, and so on. The alternative systematization (S_0) contains an argument pattern that allows one to infer the dimensions of objects from their shadows (Kitcher calls this the shadow pattern). Either S_0 includes the O-and-D pattern or it does not. If it does, then S_0 contains an extra pattern (the shadow pattern) with no gain in the number of systematized phenomena. So S_0 would fare worse than S_C on unificationist criteria. If, on the other hand, S_0 does not contain the O-and-D pattern in addition to the shadow pattern, then S_0 allows one to derive fewer consequences than S_C. S_0, for example, would not allow one to derive conclusions about the dimensions of objects in the dark, perfectly transparent objects, objects that give off their own light, and objects that are too small to cast shadows. In either case, S_0 is worse than S_C on the criteria Kitcher sets for maximally unified explanations.

However, as Eric Barnes (1992) argues, in this response Kitcher relies crucially on contingent facts about the world. By imagining how those contingent features might change (in ways that might hold for examples in our world), one can use the U-model to give retroactive explanations. Suppose that our world were a world in which all objects had the disposition to cast shadows. In that world, there would be no difference in the unifying strength of the O-and-D pattern and the shadow pattern, and Kitcher, against his stated inclinations, would have to accept that the two patterns are equally explanatory. Alternatively, suppose that the competitor to the O-and-D pattern is a dispositional shadow pattern (DS) with which one can infer the dimensions of objects from the shapes of all of the shadows that they are disposed to produce in the right circumstances (see Kitcher 1989: 485–6). Unilluminated objects might be illuminated, translucent objects might be coated with black paint, and light sources can take on any angle.

If our world were one in which all objects cast shadows, or one in which all objects have the disposition to cast shadows if treated properly, then the shadow and dispositional shadow patterns would have unifying power equal to that of the O-and-D pattern. In those worlds, Kitcher would have no way to rule out the shadow or dispositional shadow patterns in favor of the O-and-D pattern.

In response, Kitcher claims that the predicates of DS are not projectable (see 1989: 486–7). The central predicate of DS could be analyzed as something like this: "x has the disposition to produce a shadow if illuminated, or x has the disposition to produce an absorption pattern if is covered with silver and irradiated, or x has the disposition to produce shadows if painted black and illuminated ... and so on."[18] Such mongrel predicates are the traditional target in discussions of projectability (Goodman 1955). However, Kitcher does not say what makes a predicate projectable within his unificationist framework. He cannot assume that appeals to projectability are benign additions to his unificationist world-view. One plausible way to understand projectability is in terms of natural kinds: projectable predicates are those that refer to natural kinds, where natural kinds are kinds that exhibit a stable cluster of properties and are capable of participating in regular causal interactions by virtue of a common underlying mechanism (compare Boyd 1991; Griffiths 1997; Kornblith 1993). Clearly, Kitcher's aversion to causality prevents him from endorsing this account of projectability. If Kitcher does appeal to such causal notions in his account of projectability, then he might as well have endorsed a causal solution to the asymmetry problem in the first place. One unificationist alternative to this approach is to hold that the projectable predicates with respect to K are those predicates featured in E(K).[19] However, the point of comparing DS to O-and-D is that they equally unify K. Considerations of projectability are supposed to favor O-and-D over DS despite the fact that they equally unify K.

A parallel example, in which problems concerning projectability do not arise, is that of the motions of the planets. Newton's laws are time symmetrical. They can be used both to derive future positions of the planets

---

[18] Note that the filling instructions for "objects," "origins," and "histories," are also complicated and disjunctive. It is not clear that these predicates are projectable.

[19] In *The Advancement of Science*, Kitcher writes "To say that a particular predicate picks out a natural kind is to claim that marking out the extension of that predicate would figure in the ultimate (ideal) practice" (1993: 172–3).

from the past, and past positions of the planets from the future. Either way, one can (I suppose) derive the same number of phenomena from the same number of laws. The predictive and the retrodictive argument patterns are equally stringent, and neither contains intuitively unprojectable predicates. The only difference between the two is in temporal constraints on the filling instructions. Still, one of these arguments is explanatory, and the other is not, and Kitcher's framework does not mark the difference. If this is true, then even if the contingent state of the world does allow Kitcher to dismiss some classic examples of asymmetry, it does not allow him to avoid them all.

The foregoing discussion has gotten a bit abstract and complex but the point is concrete and simple. The U-model deploys elaborate machinery to make it turn out that effects do not explain their causes. And there are real questions about whether this machinery actually succeeds. In contrast, this fact about explanation is a trivial consequence of the view that explanations show how a phenomenon is situated within the causal structure of the world.

Similar difficulties arise for the U-model's handling of the constraint that there can be explanations for low-probability effects (E5), such as the opening of an ion channel and the release of neurotransmitters. As a "deductive chauvinist," Kitcher is challenged to describe a deductive argument pattern that explains such low probability events. Here is how Kitcher responds:

We cannot explain why the mayor [Jones], rather than other syphilitics, contracted paresis ... However, the statement that the mayor had syphilis may answer a different why-question. Suppose that the why-question has an explicit presupposition: "Given that one of the townspeople contracted paresis, why was it the mayor?" Only syphilitics get paresis, and he was the only syphilitic in town. Notice that in this case, we can deduce the explanandum from the presupposition of the question and the information given in the answer.

Sometimes we show that a system is in state X by presupposing that it is in one of the states $\{X, Y_1, \ldots, Y_n\}$ and demonstrating that it cannot be in any of the Y_i. (Kitcher 1989: 457)

But, as Woodward (2003) notes, this argument schema depends on explanatorily irrelevant information. Generalize the pattern slightly by assuming that K includes beliefs that several people in town $\{X, Y_1, \ldots, Y_n\}$ have syphilis and that at least one of them has paresis. Assume further that K includes beliefs that none of the people $\{Y_1, \ldots, Y_n\}$ have paresis and that only syphilitics get paresis. From these premises, it is possible to derive that Jones, X, has paresis. Although this argument provides good reason to believe that Jones has paresis, it does not explain his paresis. Most of the crucial information in the premises is explanatorily irrelevant to Jones's health. For example, the fact that other people in the town have syphilis is explanatorily irrelevant to Jones's case. Likewise, it is irrelevant to Jones's case that other members of the town do not have syphilis. Yet all of these explanatorily irrelevant facts are included in Kitcher's argument schema.

So it is difficult to accommodate some of the basic constraints on neuroscientific explanation with the U-model. One might defend the U-model either by revising it to accommodate these constraints or by rejecting the constraints. The first response cannot be assessed in the absence of concrete proposals. However, it should be noted that there is a difference between merely accommodating criteria of adequacy once they have been found and finding those criteria of adequacy in the first place. One advantage of a causal and mechanistic approach to explanation (developed in Chapters 3 and 4) is that it focuses critical attention on the kinds of considerations that neuroscientists use to sort good explanations from bad. The alternative response is to reject the above constraints. However, to reject these constraints is to divorce the project of finding explanations from the goals of manipulation and control. Explanations that do not satisfy (E1)–(E5) would be of so little use to us that it is difficult to see why so much energy should be spent discovering them.

Assessing Explanations: the U-model offers little guidance for neuroscientists who want to build good explanations and to distinguish good (and valuable) explanations from bad. To assess explanations, one must make judgments about whether a given argument pattern will be part of E(K). But what seems now to be progress toward E(K) might appear otiose from the perspective of future science. Concerning the shadow and the flagpole, for example, perhaps E(K) could make up for the complexity involved in accepting the dispositional shadow pattern by offsetting gains in simplicity elsewhere in the system of beliefs. Kitcher provides no argument that the most unified system must satisfy these causal constraints. He argues only that on his best assessment of the available options for E(K), E(K) will accommodate these constraints. The task of envisioning E(K) is made complicated by the fact that K includes every belief; it is not restricted to a given domain of knowledge. The set of beliefs, and the adequacy of those beliefs, is sufficiently holistic that one cannot readily wall scientific beliefs off from all others (especially, for example, beliefs about mathematics, metaphysics, and epistemology). Furthermore, what one believes about neuroscience cannot be insulated from facts about, for example, physics, molecular biology, and ecology. Repeatedly in the history of science, changes in one such domain have been shown to ramify through the others. According to the U-model, assessing an explanation of the action potential requires assessing not only the best systematization of all of our beliefs about neurons, or about the brain, but all of our beliefs.

Contra Kitcher's stated view, one might adopt a more local evaluative strategy and assess individual explanations in terms of the extent to which they unify some non-global domain of phenomena. One unwelcome consequence of this local application of the U-model, however, is that explanations for uncommon phenomena are less explanatory than those for common phenomena. Compare the explanation for Parkinson's disease (involving the death of neurons in the substantia nigra) with the explanation for Kuru (involving ingestion of prion proteins from the brains of cadavers). Parkinson's disease is relatively common worldwide. Kuru was largely confined to the residents of New Guinea and has now been eradicated. Suppose complete explanations for each of these diseases are available. Given that more people get Parkinson's disease each year than have ever had Kuru, the explanation for Parkinson's disease will count as a better explanation than the explanation for Kuru. The former explains more individual phenomena than the latter.[20] Examples of this sort warn against equating the claim that a given explanation explains more with the claim that it is a better explanation. Explanations in neuroscience vary widely in their scope, but this scope variance does not correlate with explanatory strength.

To summarize, the U-model can be used to assess explanations either globally or one by one. If globally (as Kitcher prefers), then it cannot be used to assess individual explanations in the here and now without relying

---

[20] One might object that I have inappropriately saddled Kitcher with explaining individual cases of the disease rather than the disease itself. The example can be reformulated, however, so that it focuses on diseases with different numbers of symptoms, or different manifestations in different climatic environments. At any rate, there is a question about how to count *explanandum phenomena*, and this is a crucial question for the U-model, not for the mechanistic model.

on intuitive judgments concerning the best systematization of all our beliefs. The problem with this option is not merely that it rests on intuitions about unification that may turn out to be false, but that it rests on intuitions about, for example, projectability, that are most commonly guided by a prior understanding of the causal structure of the world. If, on the other hand, the U-model is used to assess explanations locally, then it leads to the counterintuitive conclusion that large-scope explanations are more explanatory than small-scope explanations. Perhaps one could find a way to avoid either conclusion, but a viable mechanistic account of explanation would allow one to sidestep the dilemma entirely. Criteria (E1)–(E5), which causal accounts readily satisfy, help to sort good explanations from bad, and the scope of causal mechanical explanations is not germane to their explanatory value in a given case.

I do not mean to suggest that unification and mechanistic explanation are exclusive. In fact, discovering mechanisms is one important way to unify beliefs. Mechanisms explain the diverse aspects of the *explanandum phenomenon*, and so unify them by relating them to an underlying causal structure (compare Salmon 1998; Glennan 2002). Mechanistic explanations also unify diverse fields of science as scientists in different fields work together to place constraints on the shape of the space of possible mechanisms for a given kind of phenomenon (see Chapter 7).

6. But What About the Hodgkin and Huxley Model?

Despite these considerations, it is hard to deny that some of the most powerful explanations in the history of neuroscience look as if they were designed to exemplify the CL model or the U-model. A classic example is Hodgkin and Huxley's model of the action potential (the HH model).[21] In this section, I argue that on closer inspection, this example shows why adequate explanation in neuroscience must show how a phenomenon is situated within the causal structure of the world.

---

[21] Weber (2005) uses the Hodgkin and Huxley model to illustrate his heteronomy thesis that explanations in systems biology (including neuroscience) are merely applications of physico-chemical theories and laws to a specific kind of system (2005: 25, 28). All of the explanatory force in such explanations is provided by physico-chemical laws (see 2005: 29–32). Here I show that derivation of laws is insufficient for explanation. I implicitly argue against this reductionist thesis and its motivation in Chapters 3 and 6.

The HH model is a model of the action potential. Action potentials consist of rapid and fleeting changes in the electrical potential difference across a neuron's membrane (shown in Figure 2.1). This potential difference, known as the membrane potential (V_m), consists of a separation of charged ions on either side of the membrane. In the neuron's resting state, positive ions line up against the extracellular surface of the membrane, and negative ions line up on the intracellular surface. In typical cells, this arrangement establishes a polarized resting potential (V_{rest}) of -60 mV to -70 mV (shown on the left side of Figure 2.1). In an action potential, the membrane becomes fleetingly permeable to sodium (Na^+) and potassium (K^+) ions. This allows the ions to diffuse rapidly across the cell membrane. This flux changes V_m. The action potential consists of (i) a rapid rise in V_m to a maximum value of roughly $+35$ mV, followed by (ii) a rapid decline in V_m to values below V_{rest}, and then (iii) an extended after-potential during which the neuron is less excitable (known as the refractory period).

Hodgkin and Huxley developed their model from the results of electrophysiological experiments in the squid giant axon. In those experiments, they used a voltage clamp to keep the membrane voltage constant as

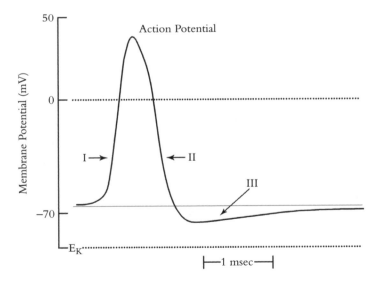

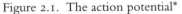

Figure 2.1. The action potential*

* Consisting of (I) a rapid rise in V_m to a maximum value of roughly $+35$ mV, followed by (II) a rapid decline in V_m to values below V_{rest}, and then (III) an extended after-potential during which the neuron is less excitable (known as the refractory period)

ion currents through the membrane varied.[22] These experiments allowed Hodgkin and Huxley to infer how membrane permeabilities for Na^+ and K^+ change at different displacements of V_m. Their crowning theoretical achievement was to represent the time-course of permeability changes as a function of V_m. They characterized the action potential in terms of the following features (modified from Hodgkin and Huxley, 1952: 542–3):

(a) the form, amplitude, and threshold of an action potential;
(b) the form, amplitude, and velocity of a propagated action potential;
(c) the form and amplitude of the resistance changes during an action potential;
(d) the total movement of ions during an action potential;
(e) the threshold and response during the refractory period (iii above);
(f) the existence and form of subthreshold responses;
(g) the production of action potentials after sustained current injection (known as "anodal break"); and
(h) the subthreshold oscillations seen in the axons of cephalopods.

Hodgkin and Huxley devised the total current equation

$$I = C_M dV/dt + G_K n^4 (V - V_K) + G_{Na} m^3 h (V - V_{Na}) + G_l (V - V_l)$$

to account for (a)–(h).[23] In this equation, I is the total current crossing the membrane. That current has four components: the capacitative current $C_M dV/dt$, the potassium current $G_K n^4 (V - V_K)$, the sodium current $G_{Na} m^3 h (V - V_{Na})$, and the "leakage current" $G_l (V - V_l)$, which is a sum of smaller currents for other ions. G_K, G_{Na} and G_l are the maximum conductance values for the different ionic currents. V is displacement of V_m from V_{rest}. And V_K, V_{Na}, and V_l are the differences between equilibrium potentials for the various ions (that is, that voltage at which diffusion and the driving force of voltage are balanced such that there is no net current flow) and V_m. The capacitance, C_M, of the membrane can be understood as the ability of the membrane to store opposite charges on the intra- and extra-cellular sides. Finally, there are three coefficients, h, m, and n, the values of which vary with voltage and time. Hodgkin and Huxley's primary

---

[22] For now, I neglect the importance of the space clamp, which was crucial for eliminating voltage gradients along the axon.
[23] This is how Hodgkin and Huxley (1952) write the equation. Contemporary textbooks use different formulations.

accomplishment (by their own lights) involved generating the equations for these variables and determining the powers that they would take in the total current equation. I discuss these further below.

Hodgkin and Huxley show that each of (a)–(h) follows from the total current equation under specifiable conditions. Figures 2.2 and 2.3 show comparisons of the predicted values of the HH equations for feature (a) to the values observed in the squid giant axon. Figure 2.2 shows the comparison between predicted (top) and observed (bottom) action potentials for initial depolarizations of 90 mV, 15 mV, 7 mV and 6 mV at 6°C. Their amplitudes, time-courses, and overall forms are roughly identical. Figure 2.3 shows the comparison between predicted (top) and observed (bottom) values for the rising phase of the action potential. Hodgkin and Huxley proceed in this manner through all of the features ((a)–(h)). In doing so, they provide a compelling example of explanation by deductive subsumption under laws of nature. The total current equation is derived from laws of nature (such as Ohm's law, the Nernst equation, and

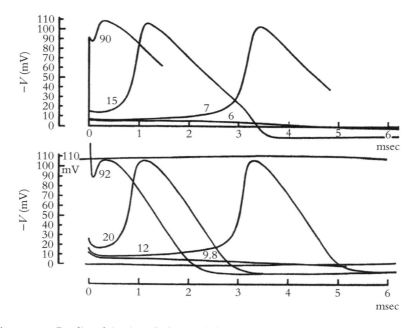

Figure 2.2. Predicted (top) and observed (bottom) action potentials*
* For initial depolarizations of 90, 15, 7 and 6 mV at 6°C
Source: Reprinted with permission from Hodgkin and Huxley (1952, 525)

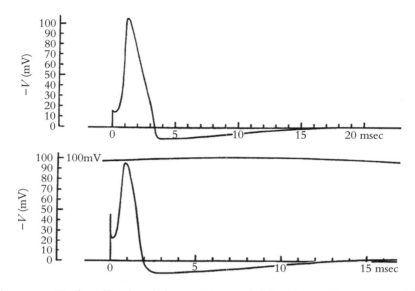

Figure 2.3. Predicted (top) and observed (bottom) rising phases of action potentials
Source: Reprinted with permission from Hodgkin and Huxley (1952: 526).

Coulomb's law), and it shows how those laws work in a given biological context to explain the action potential.

Important as these equations are, the HH equations are a mathematical description of a mechanism sketch (see Bogen 2005). They summarize decades of experiments. They embody a rich temporal constraint on any possible mechanism for the action potential. They allow neuroscientists to predict how current will change under various experimental interventions. They can be used to simulate the electrophysiological activities of nerve cells. They permit one to infer the values of unmeasured variables. And they constitute potent evidence that a mechanism involving ionic currents could possibly account for the shape of the action potential. However, Hodgkin and Huxley (1952) insist that their model of conductance changes is not explanatory:

The agreement [between the model and the voltage clamp data] must not be taken as evidence that our equations are anything more than an *empirical description of the time-course* of the changes in permeability to sodium and potassium. *An equally satisfactory description of the voltage clamp data could no doubt have been achieved with equations of very different form, which would probably have been equally successful in predicting the electrical behaviour of the membrane.* It was pointed out in Part II of this paper that certain features of our equations were capable of a physical interpretation, *but the success of the equations is no evidence in favour of the mechanism of permeability change that we tentatively had in mind when formulating them.* (1952: 541; italics added)

One could dismiss this passage as scientific modesty if it were not for the fact that Hodgkin and Huxley argue for their conclusions.

First, they insist that the equations provide nothing more than an empirical description of the time course of permeability changes. Here they are alluding to the coefficients n, m, and h. The current equation for K^+ involves the coefficient n. The current equation for Na^+ involves the coefficients m and h. Discussing the equation for the Na^+ current, Hodgkin and Huxley say that although they could have used a single variable, they found it easier to fit the curves with two. After the failure of one of their earlier hypothesized mechanisms, Hodgkin and Huxley realized that the techniques of electrophysiology would not suffice to pick out a uniquely correct characterization of the mechanism. Hodgkin writes:

We soon realized that the carrier model could not be made to fit certain results, for example the nearly linear instantaneous current voltage relationship, and that it had to be replaced by some kind of voltage-dependent gate. As soon as we began to think about molecular mechanisms it became clear that the electrical data would by themselves yield only very general information about the class of system likely to be involved. So we settled for the more pedestrian aim of finding a simple set of mathematical equations that might plausibly represent the movement of electrically charged gating particles. (Hodgkin 1992)

Their model of current changes is in this respect more analogous to Ptolemy's planetary models, which neither involve nor imply any commitment to the existence of the epicycles, deferents, and equants from which they are constructed, than it is to Newton's gravitational model of planetary motion, which Newton presents to show how and why the planets move as they do. The total current equation embodies no commitments as to the mechanisms that change the membrane conductance, that allow the ionic currents to flow, and that coordinate conductance changes so that the action potential has its characteristic shape. In the HH model, commitments about underlying mechanisms are replaced by mathematical constructs that save the phenomena (a)–(h) of the action potential much as Ptolemy's epicycles and deferents save the apparent motion of the planets through the night sky. The equations do not show *how* the membrane changes its permeability. As they said in 1952, the "Details of the mechanism will probably not be settled for some time" (1952: 504). Kenneth Cole, a collaborator of Hodgkin and Huxley, made the same point more dramatically when he said that the HH model merely "summarized in one neat tidy little package the many thousands of experiments done previous to 1952, and most subsequent ones" (1992: 151).

One might object to the judgment of these scientists on the grounds that the equations represent dependency relations among the variables in the equation. For example, the equations represent membrane conductance (permeability) as dependent upon voltage, and they describe the resulting changes in currents across the membrane. But mathematical dependencies cannot be equated with causal or explanatory dependency relations. The equations must be supplemented by a causal interpretation: one might, for example, agree by convention that the effect variable is represented on the left, and the cause variables are represented on the right, or one might add "these are not mere mathematical relationships among variables but descriptions of causal relationships in which this variable is a cause and this other is an effect, and not vice versa," but the point is that one will have to specify which variables represent causes and which represent effects, and one will have to specify which of the myriad mathematical relationships expressible within the equations are causal and which are mere correlations.[24] Of course, mere correlations and effects of common causes can be represented as mathematical dependencies of one variable upon another, and equations can always be rewritten to put any variable that one likes on the left or the right. Absent a causal interpretation in terms of the underlying causal structure, such mathematical dependencies do not specify the causal dependencies that produce the time course of the action potential.

To be sure, Hodgkin and Huxley knew a good deal more about action potentials than they included explicitly in their model. Adding this detail helps to flesh out the mathematical model into a description of a mechanism.

---

[24] I am not making the absurd claim that no explanation can be represented in mathematical form. Equations are one convention among many for specifying causal relations. My point, rather, is that the mathematical expressions, as such, are consistent with a variety of different causal interpretations, many of which embody spurious causal claims. The same equation allows one to represent the length of a pendulum as a cause or as an effect of its period, yet only the first gets the causal relationship right. The equation, absent causal interpretation, does not provide an explanation.

Hodgkin and Huxley developed their model within a long tradition of electrophysiological research that had uncovered many of the components of the electrophysiological mechanisms in neurons. They knew, for example, that the action potential is produced by changes in membrane permeability, and they knew that ions flux across the membrane toward their equilibrium potentials; they also knew that this flux of ions constitutes a transmembrane current. This background sketch of a mechanism *does* provide a partial explanation (an explanation sketch) for how neurons generate action potentials because it reveals some of the components of the mechanism, some of their properties, and some of their activities. The HH equations supplement this background knowledge with explicit temporal constraints on the mechanism. The equations include variables that represent important components in the explanation. And the equations provide powerful evidence that a mechanism built from those components could possibly explain the action potential. Supplemented with a diagram of the electrical circuit in a membrane, and supplemented with details about how membranes and ion channels work, the equations carry considerable explanatory weight. The equations without such interpretation—an interpretation that is difficult for those who know the mechanism of the action potential to imagine away—do not constitute an explanation. In order to explain, the equations of the model must be supplemented by an understanding of the mechanisms of the action potential—by an understanding of how the entities and activities in and around the membrane are organized together to produce the action potential.[25] The equations for conductance in the HH model are explanatory only to the extent that it describes aspects of that mechansm.

---

[25] Consider Hille's framing of this problem in his classic book: "The HH model certainly demonstrates the importance of Na and K permeability changes for excitability and describes their time course in detail. But does it say *how* they work? In one extreme view, the model is mere curvefitting of arbitrary equations to summarize experimental observations. Then it could say nothing about molecular mechanisms. According to a view at the opposite extreme, the model demonstrates that there are certain numbers of independent h, m, and n particles moving in the electrical field of the membrane controlling independent Na and K permeabilities. In addition, there are intermediate views. How does one decide?" (1992: 52–3). Hille's intermediate position is similar to my own. First, the model, "has important general properties with mechanistic implications that must be included in future models," such as the reversal potentials for the different currents, the fact that the ions move without metabolic input, that the channels activate and inactivate with an S-shaped time-course (1984: 55–6). Second, "fitting of models can disprove a suggested mechanism but cannot prove one. There are always other models that fit.... Therefore the

Hodgkin and Huxley insist that they have no evidence whatsoever in favor of the model that they "tentatively had in mind" when formulating their equations for conductance changes. According to that model, the membrane's permeability to Na^+ is regulated by the position of four particles in the membrane: three "activation molecules" that move from the outside of the membrane to sites on the inside, and one "inactivation molecule" that can block either the activation molecules or the flow of Na^+ through the membrane. The expression m^3h can then be interpreted as the joint probability that all three activation molecules are in their open state (with m being the probability that any one molecule has moved) and that no inactivation molecule is bound (h). When Hodgkin and Huxley say that they have no evidence for their hypothesized mechanism, they are referring to these variables in the current equations. The choice of a different strategy for building the equation (for example, using a single variable, or three rather than two) might suggest an entirely different physical interpretation (or mechanism) or none at all.

At most, this simple model of the activation and inactivation of sodium channels provides a "how possibly" sketch of the action potential. Hodgkin and Huxley take an explicitly instrumentalist stance toward their model: "It was clear that the formulation we had used was not the only one that might have fitted the voltage clamp results adequately" (Huxley 1963: 61). Indefinitely many equations could be used to predict the action potential's time-course equally well. And these different mathematical equations might be given any number of biological interpretations such as the activation model sketched above. Hodgkin and Huxley had no reason to privilege this one possible model above the others as the correct model. To explain the action potential required further details about the molecular mechanisms underlying the permeability changes. Bertil Hille describes the origins of this research program:

In the next decade, Clay and Armstrong and I began our independent research. In our first papers, we brought a clear list of "molecular" assumptions to the table.

strictly kinetic aspects of the HH model, such as control by a certain number of independent h, m, and n particles making first-order transitions between two positions, cannot be proven *by curve fitting* .... The lesson is easier to accept now that, after 50 years of work, new kinetic phenomena have been observed that disagree significantly with some specific predictions of their model" (1984: 55). One must know details about the mechanism to confirm the model.

They included the following ideas: ions are passing through aqueous pores that we called channels, ion channels are proteins, the channels for Na^+ and K^+ are different, they have swinging gates that open and close them, we can study their architecture by using electric currents to measure gating, permeation and block, and channel blockers are molecules that enter the pores and physically plug them. (Hille et al. 1999: 1106)

At the time the idea of a channel was viewed with skepticism. It was merely a filler-term for an activity or mechanism to be named later:

From 1965 to 1973, such ideas were debated annually at the meetings of the Biophysical Society. There, prominent scientists would routinely rise to request that anyone who chose to use the word "channel" avow first that it bears absolutely no mechanistic implications! It is probably fair to say that people thought the discussion about molecular mechanisms was premature. In 1969, when I had drafted a summary review of these ideas, Kenneth Cole, the dean of American biophysics, wrote to me: "I'm … worried you may be pushing some of your channel arguments pretty far." (Hille et al. 1999: 1106)

The idea of activation molecules (let alone pores or gates) was at most a useful fiction—a how-possibly model—for Hodgkin and Huxley. It helped them to model the action potential, but it could not at the time be interpreted in terms of details about the membranes of nerve cells. To leap to the end of the story, it is now well known that conductance changes across the membrane are effected by conformation changes in ion-specific channels spanning the cell membrane. Biochemists have isolated the proteins that compose these channels, they have sequenced their constituents, and they have learned a great deal about how they activate and inactivate during an action potential. It is this wealth of detail about how these channels regulate the timing of the conductance changes that accounts for the time-course of the action potential.

Only with the discovery of these molecular mechanisms will the action potential be not merely modeled but explained. As Michael Mauk notes:

There was little to be learned from the particular mathematical implementation that H[odgkin] and H[uxley] used to represent voltage-dependent conductances. Because they were intended only as mathematical tools to produce the correct input/output behavior, the ingredients of the [phenomenological] model did not need to reflect the underlying biological processes. For example, the conductances could have been described in lookup tables. Thus, like experiments with only one possible outcome, the ability to build these [phenomenological] models meant little mechanistically. (2000: 650)

The equations for the conductance changes (specifically, the equations governing the values of n, m, and h) are merely phenomenological models.[26] These equations characterize how specific ion conductances change with voltage and time, but they do not explain why they change as they do, when they do. Without an account of the underlying mechanisms of the conductance change, the buck of accounting for the temporal features of the action potential (as specified in (a)−(h)) is merely passed on to some-conductance-changing-process-we-know-not-what. This filler-process was later completed as Hille and his colleagues investigated the structure and function of ion channels and gradually weeded merely how-possibly mechanisms out of the space of plausible mechanisms.

These considerations raise serious doubts as to whether the Hodgkin and Huxley model should be seen as a triumph of the CL model or the U-model of explanation. For it is now clear that neither the ability to subsume a phenomena under laws of nature, nor the ability to unify its diverse features under a common argument schema, is alone sufficient for explanation. Appeal to such models is thus insufficient for sorting good and complete explanations of the action potential from bad and incomplete explanations.

While constraints (E1)−(E5) apply to causal explanations of particu-lar events, analogous constraints apply to constitutive explanations of the behaviors of wholes (such as the action potential) and the activities of their parts (such as the movements of ions). Because classical micro−reduction is a model of constitutive explanation, these constraints apply to that model as well: (C1) action potentials are not explained by mere temporal sequences of events in the cells that produce them, but are explained instead by the causal relationships among them; (C2) action potentials are explained by a particular ordering of conductance changes from beginning to end, and one could not reverse this ordering and still produce an action potential—in constitutive mechanisms involving feedback, explanations follow the direction of dependency among the component stages, so if an

---

[26] It turns out, in retrospect, that aspects of the equations for these conductance changes do correspond to features of the ion channels, but this, as Hodgkin and Huxley would have noted, is not a perfect fit, and it is at any rate merely fortuitous.

explanation does not characterize those dependency relations, then it is not an adequate explanation; (C3) when Na$^+$ channels open, the gating charge across the membrane and the rise in Na$^+$ conductance are correlated, but neither explains the other—rather both are explained by the voltage change that opens the channel; (C4) blessing the membrane adds nothing to the explanation of the action potential, for in describing a constitutive mechanism, one must distinguish relevant from irrelevant components and properties—one might be able to derive facts about a phenomenon from laws concerning its parts, but (C1)–(C4) (as well as the Hodgkin and Huxley example) show that mere derivation is insufficient for explanation.[27] As I suggested above, because the view of constitutive explanation expressed within the CL account is classical reduction, (C1)–(C4) provide reasons to suspect that the reduction model does not provide an adequate regulative ideal for constitutive explanations. More positively, (C1)–(C4) provide constraints on any adequate model of constitutive explanation in neuroscience.

One other constraint is sufficiently important to be given its own heading even though it is implicit in others:

(C5) Mere neural correlates are not explanatory.[28]

Neuroscientists know that merely finding that a brain region regularly lights up (that is, shows signs of increased metabolic activity or blood flow) during a cognitive task does not allow one to infer that the brain region is involved in the task. The brain region might be tonically active, or it might be a component in a different phenomenon that is experimentally inseparable from the one under study. For example, the volume of blood flowing to the visual cortex is tightly correlated with reading, but this does not mean that increasing blood flow explains my ability to read. In fact, as all MRI (magnetic resonance imaging) researchers know, the changes in blood flow measured by these devices lag well behind the performance of the task, and researchers have to adjust for this time lag to interpret

---

[27] Hempel and Oppenheim mention a similar problem in what Salmon (1989) calls the "infamous footnote 33." They admit that they cannot block trivial reductions, such as the derivation of Kepler's law from the conjunction of Kepler's laws and Boyle's law. One aspect of this "triviality" is that Boyle's law is irrelevant to Kepler's law (Hempel and Oppenheim 1948).

[28] Although (C1)–(C4) correspond to (E1)–(E4), I do not discuss whether there is a constitutive sister to (E5). There is a question about whether constitutive relations can be stochastic, but I do not discuss that here. (C5) has nothing to do with (E5).

their data. Similarly, the mere fact that performance on a task degrades with the destruction or inhibition of a brain region does not mean that the brain region's activity is part of the explanation for the performance of that task. Removing the kidneys will eventually degrade the ability to generate past-tense verbs from present-tense verbs, but that does not mean that kidney activities are part of the explanation for generating past-tense verbs. I return to this issue in Chapter 4. For now, the point is that the idea of a "neural correlate" is too weak to be taken seriously as an account of explanation, despite the fact that neural correlates can be used to derive descriptions of higher-level phenomena from descriptions of lower-level phenomena.

If deductive subsumption under laws or argument schemata is insufficient for a good explanation, might it nonetheless be necessary? In Section 4 above, I argue that improbable events can be explained despite the fact they cannot be seen as deductive consequences (or even as probable consequences) of the laws of nature in specific antecedent and background conditions. Etiological explanations, I conclude, need not show that the phenomenon to be explained *was to be expected* on the basis of the laws of nature. The nomic expectability thesis is the core idea behind the CL model of explanation; it is the reason for thinking that explanations are arguments. In showing that this thesis is questionable in cases of etiological explanation, I have raised doubts about whether rational expectability is an essential aspect of constitutive explanations as well.

7. Conclusion

In the remainder of this book, I develop a model of explanation that accommodates constraints such as (E1)–(E5) and (C1)–(C5). I thus provide an existence proof for the possibility of a normatively rich account of explanation that does not require anything like argumentative subsumption of phenomena under general representations of any sort. Good neuroscientific explanations are distinguished from bad not by the features of an inference but by the fact that good explanations accurately describe the causal structure of the world. Complete neuroscientific explanations are distinguished from incomplete explanations not by the ability to avoid enthymemes (that is, arguments with suppressed premises), but by the fact that complete explanations capture all of the relevant causal relations among the components in a mechanism. Understanding the "mechanisms of permeability change" (as Hodgkin and Huxley say), the "mechanistic implications" (as Hille says), and the "underlying biological processes" (as Mauk says) requires understanding the causal structures—the mechanisms—that explain how neurons produce action potentials.

3

Causal Relevance
and Manipulation

Summary

I provide a view of causal relevance that accommodates the mechanistic
fragility and historical contingency of neuroscientific generalizations but
that nonetheless satisfies constraints (E1)–(E5). I review the limitations
of two alternative accounts of causation—Stuart Glennan's mechanical
account, and Wesley Salmon and Philip Dowe's transmission account. I use
an example from the contemporary neuroscience of learning and memory
to defend Woodward's (2002, 2003) view that the causal relevance relations
in neural mechanisms are relationships that can potentially be used for the
purposes of manipulation and control.

1. Introduction

In Chapter 2, I discuss five constraints on explanations in neuroscience, and
I argue that any acceptable account of explanation in neuroscience should
make sense of their importance. These constraints are:

(E1) mere temporal sequences are not explanatory;

(E2) causes explain effects and not vice versa;

(E3) causally independent effects of common causes do not explain one
another;

(E4) causally irrelevant phenomena are not explanatory; and

(E5) causes need not make effects probable to explain them.

These constraints are explained by the fact that successful explanations in neuroscience describe the causal structure of the world. This claim, however, presupposes a view of the causal structure of the world, and one that accommodates (E1)–(E5). In this chapter, I argue for an account of causal relevance that satisfies these constraints. In doing so, I provide an account of causal relevance that makes sense of the norms that scientists use to search for causes and to evaluate causal claims.

My focus on the norms implicit in the practice of neuroscience contrasts with traditional metaphysical projects concerning the nature of causation. First, I do not define "causation" in terms of non-causal concepts, such as "regularity" and "temporal succession." I doubt that any such reductive definition is possible. My colleagues and I have argued elsewhere that at least many cases of causation should be understood in terms of the diverse *activities* that scientists describe in their theories (Machamer et al. 2000; Darden and Craver 2002).[1] Such activities include collision, diffusion, electrostatic attraction and repulsion, gravitation, magnetism, oxidation, and phosphorylation. Activities are no less mysterious than most entities in our best scientific theories (such as atoms, fields, molecules, nuclei, and pituitary glands), and they are no more in need of reductive analysis. From my perspective, causation requires normative regimentation, not metaphysical demystification.

Second, I do not provide an account of the secret connection that Hume sought between a cause and its effect. I will argue that the search for this connection (this cement, glue, spring, or string)—as exemplified by Salmon (1984, 1998) and Dowe's (2000) transmission account and by Glennan's (1996) mechanical account of causal relevance—is sometimes misguided and often distracts philosophers from the aspects of causation that are most important for an account of explanation. This search is sometimes misguided because many causes in neuroscientific explanations are not connected to (that is, in contact with) their effects. For example, in cases of omission and prevention (as when the absence of activity in an inhibitory interneuron allows the post-synaptic cell to fire, or when a competitive antagonist prevents a neurotransmitter from binding to a receptor) there is no hidden connection between the cause and the effect. Such causes work by absences and gaps in connections (or so I will argue). The search for a

---

[1] This view is further elaborated in Bogen 2004, 2005; Machamer 2004.

connection is distracting because even in cases where one can identify an unbroken connection between a putative cause and an effect, that alone is insufficient to establish that the putative cause is *relevant* to the effect. The search for hidden connections can thus distract one from providing an account of causal relevance, which is much more central to the practice of distinguishing good explanations from bad.

In this chapter, I consider three accounts of causal relations: Glennan's (1996) mechanical account (Section 3), Salmon (1984, 1998) and Dowe's (2000) transmission accounts (Section 4), and Woodward's (2003) manipulationist account (Section 5). The first two—the mechanical and transmission accounts—are each advanced as part of an account of mechanistic explanation, and so it is fair to ask whether they are adequate for that purpose. Each also attempts to identify a hidden connection between causes and their effects. These two views of causation, I believe, are separate paths to the idea that all bona fide causes are found only at the most fundamental ontological levels. All of the real work, one might suppose, is being done by contact action or exchanges of conserved quantities among the most fundamental things. Once one recognizes the limitations of these views of causation, it is much easier to make room for the causal relevance of nonfundamental properties. In the final section, I argue that Woodward's manipulationist view of explanation embodies the standards that neuroscientists (among others) use to discover and evaluate claims about causal relevance, and I show that it satisfies constraints (E1)–(E5). I begin my discussion with the example of Long-Term Potentiation.

2. The Mechanism of Long-Term Potentiation

It is widely believed—and there are polls (Stevens 1998)—that brains learn through changes in the strengths of synapses, that is, by changes in the efficiency with which a single action potential in the pre-synaptic cell depolarizes the post-synaptic cell. The most studied form of synaptic plasticity is known as Long-Term Potentiation (LTP). Many believe that LTP, a laboratory phenomenon in which a synapse is strengthened through exposure to a high-frequency pulse, reflects the existence in the synapse of a mechanism for encoding and storing memories. Here, I focus on a type of LTP mediated by a subtype of glutamate receptors that is highly responsive to the pharmacological agonist, N-methyl-D-aspartate (NMDA). These receptors are called NMDA receptors, and this variety of LTP is commonly called NMDA-receptor dependent LTP. My description of LTP and its mechanisms follows the classic description by Bliss and Collingridge (1993). (For more recent developments, see Squire and Kandel 2000; Lynch 2004; Malenka and Bear 2004.)

A common protocol for inducing LTP involves delivering a tetanus, a high frequency train of stimuli, to populations of pre-synaptic neurons. This stimulus results in a reliable increase in synaptic efficiency. This increase in efficiency is commonly operationalized as: (i) an increase in the slope and amplitude of the excitatory post-synaptic potential in populations of post-synaptic neurons (indicating a larger effect of individual pre-synaptic cells on the post-synaptic response); (ii) an increase in the amplitude of the "population spike" (indicating the synchronous generation of action potentials in the individual post-synaptic cells); and (iii) reduced latency in the population spike (indicating that the post-synaptic action potentials occur faster).

In saying that the tetanus potentiates the synapse, neuroscientists clearly do not mean to assert that whenever one tetanizes a pre-synaptic cell one potentiates the synapse. Nor do they mean to assert that there is a strict law of LTP, in the way that Newton's laws or Ohm's law might reasonably be said to be strict. Of course, one might use the term "law" in a more relaxed sense. It does not matter for my point here. I will show how causal generalizations in biology can function in explanations even if we grant the now well-known reasons for thinking that there are no distinctively biological laws (Beatty 1996; Bechtel and Abrahamsen 2005; Rosenberg 1985; Smart 1963; Weber 2005). Here are four such reasons.

First, LTP is *limited in scope*. It is not a feature of all cells, or of all chemical synapses, or even of all glutamatergic synapses. Its features vary from organism to organism, brain region to brain region, and synapse to synapse. It also varies with developmental stages, with different experimental manipulations, and with the cellular mechanisms used to produce it. In the first full-length report of LTP, Bliss and Lømo (1973) note that the phenomenon varies both across subjects and in the same subject over time. There are several types of LTP, and there are other forms of short- and long-term potentiation that happen at other synapses in the brain. Compared to the genetic code and the theory of evolution by natural

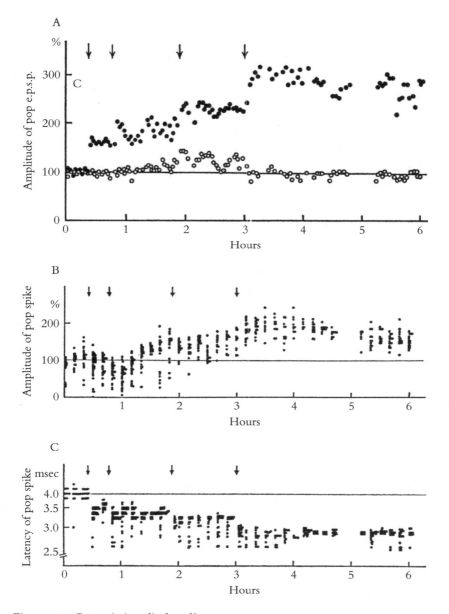

Figure 3.1. Potentiation displayed*

* As (i) increased amplitude of the population e.p.s.p. in A; (ii) the amplitude of the population spike in B; and (iii) the latency of the population spike in C

Source: Compiled and reprinted with permission from Bliss and Lømo (1973: 339–41)

selection, such generalizations as there are to describe LTP have very narrow application.

Second, these generalizations are *stochastic*. Even in those organisms and synapses in which they hold, they hold only some of the time. Bliss and Lømo found all three signs of potentiation ((i)−(iii)) in only 29 percent of their trials. Only feature (ii) appeared in more than 50 percent of the trials. And in only 26 percent of the trials did the synapses show any sign of potentiation thirty minutes after the tetanus. Today, after over thirty years of LTP research, neuroscientists can induce LTP in only roughly 50 percent of their trials.

At least part of the reason that these generalizations are stochastic is that LTP is *mechanistically fragile*.[2] Like most other biological phenomena, LTP varies with features of the stimulus, with background conditions, and with the integrity of the underlying mechanism. By lowering the frequency of the tetanus, one can weaken the synapse rather than strengthening it. By increasing the frequency, one can exhaust or simply incinerate the cell. One can also intervene in myriad ways in the machinery of the pre- and post-synaptic cells such that no potentiation ever occurs. LTP has been reported to vary with such factors as temperature, pH, and time of day (Sanes and Lichtman 1999). If one insists on saying that there are laws of LTP, such laws are at best *ceteris paribus* laws: meaning, roughly, that they hold except when something defeats them, and neuroscientists cannot (now or possibly ever) specify all of the conditions under which they are defeated.[3] Still, neuroscientists know quite a bit about LTP, about the conditions under which it can be induced and maintained, and about the

---

[2] This point is familiar to philosophers of biology. Rob Wilson, for example, characterizes biology as one of the fragile sciences. This is not the same notion of fragility that Lewis uses to discuss causation in "Causation as Influence" (which has to do with criteria of event individuation), although it is related to other themes in Lewis's paper, especially the discussion of alterations.

[3] There is considerable debate over how to understand *ceteris paribus* laws, about whether they exist, and about whether they can explain anything. As I have formulated the notion of a *ceteris paribus* law, such a law is vacuous either because it is a tautology (the law holds unless it does not) or because we have no idea what it says (the law holds unless X, where X is unspecifiable). The *ceteris paribus* law could also be understood as asserting that the law holds unless there is some factor X that can explain why it does not (Pietrosky and Rey 1995). As Earman and Roberts (1999) point out, this allows there to be a *ceteris paribus* law linking any F to any G, even where F is utterly irrelevant to G. Puffins could act as coincidence detectors in the LTP mechanism if only they were small enough, if they had binding sites for glutamate, if they could change their conformation, and so on, and the fact that they do not meet these requirements explains why the *ceteris paribus* law breaks down. The urge to ground explanatory generalizations in *ceteris paribus* laws has its roots in the idea that one can only explain with strict laws and that *ceteris paribus* laws are hedged strict laws (see Roberts 2004). I do not accept the first

conditions under which it fails, and neuroscientists count statements about LTP as explanatory.

Finally, the generalizations describing LTP are *historically contingent* (Schaffner 1993a; Beatty 1995; Rosenberg 2001).[4] They are not time-less truths about the brain and its components, but the products of machines cobbled together through evolution by natural selection and soft-constructed in development. The fact that these generalizations are true, in other words, is a contingent product of how life happens to have developed and how a given life happens to develop for each organism. Because of this historical fact, the regularities currently exhibited in biological organisms are not physically necessary, if by that one means that that they could not be different given the laws of physics. There was a time when no organisms in the world exhibited LTP, and there might well be another such time in the future.

These four features of the generalizations describing LTP are not unique to LTP. Instead, they are common to most generalizations in neuroscience and biology generally.[5] They are true, for example, of the causal generaliza-tions describing the mechanism of LTP. Three features make LTP plausible as a potential mechanism of learning: its cooperativity, its associativity, and its input-specificity.[6] Suppose that the experimental set-up involves

---

of these assumptions. I advocate a different view about how mechanistically fragile generalizations can be explanatory in Section 5.

[4] The exact sense in which these regularities are contingent is difficult to make precise. Rosenberg argues that, "every regularity in biology will be falsified (or turned into a stipulation) eventually" (2001: 141). This fact about generalizations in biology leads him to claim that there can be no distinctively biological explanations. As he puts it, "One historical fact cannot by itself explain another" (2001: 155; see also Weber 2005: 34). Explanation, on Rosenberg's view, requires the kind of physical necessity found in some of the laws of physics. This conclusion is implausible in the face of the apparent explanatory successes of contemporary neuroscience and biology. I see no reason to believe that one historical fact cannot explain another. They can and they do. Indeed, it is hard to generate examples of explanations that do not explain historical facts by historical facts. Why did the US invade Iraq? Why did the dinosaurs go extinct? Why did AIDS take root among IV drug users? I would accept Rosenberg's conclusion only after exhausting the available options for thinking about how contingent regularities might be explanatory.

[5] Consider Crick's (1988) claim: "Evolution is a tinkerer. It is the resulting complexity that makes biological organisms so hard to unscramble. Biology is thus very different from physics. The basic laws of physics can usually be expressed in exact mathematical form, and they are probably the same throughout the universe. The 'laws' of biology, by contrast, are often only broad generalizations, since they describe rather elaborate mechanisms that natural selection has evolved over billions of years" (p. 5).

[6] There is a sense in which these features of LTP are misleadingly associated with learning. The loose connection is that learning is associative (pairing two co-occurring stimuli, for example), that memories can be primed (cooperativity), and that learning must be specific to associations formed in

stimulating a population of pre-synaptic neurons that converges on a single set of post-synaptic neurons, and that many pre-synaptic neurons converge on the same post-synaptic cells. Depending on whether the pre-synaptic stimulus is weak or strong, it will produce action potentials in a few or in many pre-synaptic neurons. LTP is *cooperative* in the sense that there is a stimulus threshold below which too few pre-synaptic neurons are active to induce LTP. Using a strong stimulus to recruit more pre-synaptic neurons makes LTP more likely at each of the stimulated synapses. LTP is *associative* in the sense that a weak (or sub-threshold) stimulus can produce LTP if it is paired with a strong stimulus to a separate set of pre-synaptic neurons converging on the same post-synaptic cells. Finally, LTP is *input-specific* in the sense that only those synapses that are active during the stimulus are potentiated. These three features point to a common defining mark of LTP: it is induced only when the pre- and the post-synaptic cells are simultaneously active. The synapse thus exhibits a Hebbian form of learning (Hebb 1949).

This defining mark of LTP is explained by a coincidence detector mechanism involving the NMDA receptor (see Figure 3.2). The NMDA receptor gates the diffusion of Ca^{2+} into the post-synaptic cell. When the pre-synaptic neuron is active, it releases the neurotransmitters, glutamate and glycine, which traverse the synapse and bind to receptors on the post-synaptic cell, including NMDA receptors. The NMDA receptors change their conformation to form a Ca^{2+}-selective channel through the membrane. If the post-synaptic cell is polarized (that is, resting), the channel is blocked by large Mg^{2+} ions. When the post-synaptic cell depolarizes as a result of activity at non-NMDA receptors (specifically, α–amino-3-hydroxyl-5-methyl-4-isoxasolepropionic acid, or AMPA receptors), the Mg^{2+} ions are repelled from the channels, removing the Mg^{2+} blockage. At this point, Ca^{2+} begins to flow through the channel. The influx of Ca^{2+} and the consequent rise of intracellular Ca^{2+} concentrations then activate a number of intracellular biochemical pathways leading to the changes that constitute a potentiated synapse. In the short term, these pathways add

the environment. Few if any contemporary neuroscientists think that complex associative memories are stored in single synapses, and so it is questionable whether these features of LTP make it directly relevant to learning in the way that these words suggest. The associations relevant to complex forms of learning (for example, semantic memories) are far more likely, given our current understanding of learning, to be formed among distributed representations across populations of neurons than they are to be formed at single synapses.

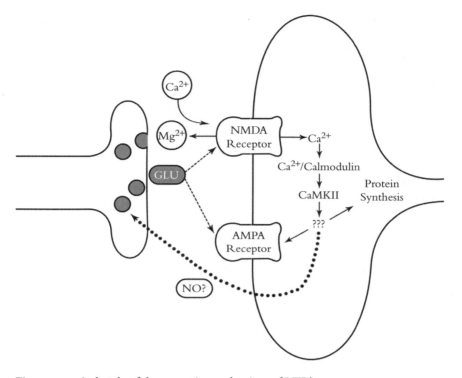

Figure 3.2. A sketch of the synaptic mechanism of LTP*

* Beginning with the release of glutamate (GLU) from the pre-synaptic neuron (left) and termi-
nating with changes to the post-synaptic neuron (right) and/or the pre-synaptic neuron (via nitric
oxide, NO)

new receptors to the membrane, or alter their sensitivity to glutamate,
or change their Ca^{2+} conductance. Such changes could account for the
rapid induction of LTP. In the long term, the biochemical pathways lead
to the production of proteins used to alter the structure of the synapse.
Some suspect that there is also a pre-synaptic component of this mechanism
whereby, for example, the pre-synaptic cell releases more glutamate with
each action potential. What matters most for present purposes, however, is
that the NMDA receptor gates the induction of LTP. LTP is cooperative
because weak inputs do not depolarize the post-synaptic cell sufficiently
to remove the Mg^{2+} block. LTP is associative for the same reason: the
independent strong input depolarizes the post-synaptic cell sufficiently to
remove the Mg^{2+} from the channel. Finally, LTP is input-specific because
glutamate opens the NMDA receptors only at the active synapses.

The generalizations describing the causal relationships in this mechanism share all of the features mentioned above for the causal generalization describing LTP. They are *narrow in scope*, holding only for pyramidal cells, or only in NMDA receptors. Many of the causal relationships in this mechanism are stochastic, such as the diffusion of ions or the opening and closing of NMDA receptors. The causal relationships in this mechanism are *mechanistically fragile*. If the concentration of glutamate is too high or too low, if the temperature and pH are not within physiological ranges, or if there is a missing amino acid in the NMDA receptor, many of these causal relationships can break down. Finally, these generalizations are *historically contingent*; before there were NMDA receptors, this mechanism could not work.

Despite the fact that these causal generalizations are limited in scope, stochastic, mechanistically fragile, and historically contingent, they nonetheless describe causal relations in mechanisms that work. They are not mere descriptions of temporal sequences. They relate causes to effects and not vice versa. They do not describe relationships among effects of common causes. And they describe relationships among relevant factors. How must we think about causal generalizations in neuroscience, and the relations that they describe, in order for them to be explanatory despite the fact that they are fragile and contingent? Before getting to my positive view, I first consider two views of causation designed to explicate mechanistic explanation.

3. Causation as Transmission

A widespread, if largely implicit, belief about causation is that it involves objects coming into contact and exchanging or transmitting something between them. When the eight ball careens off the two ball into the side pocket, the balls touch and exchange momentum; this exchange constitutes the two ball's causal influence on the eight ball. This view of causation has historical precedent in both science and philosophy, and one might reasonably believe that causal relations in neuroscience (and hence explanations in neuroscience) ultimately are grounded in fundamental causal relations of this sort.

The most influential contemporary expression of this view is found in transmission accounts of causation, especially those of Wesley Salmon

(1984, 1997, 1998) and Phil Dowe (1992, 2000). Salmon developed two transmission accounts: the Mark Transmission account (MT; Salmon 1977, 1984) and the Conserved Quantity account (CQ; suggested by Skyrms 1980; Dowe 1992; elaborated by Salmon 1994 and Dowe 2000). Salmon abandoned MT in favor of CQ, and he ultimately recognized a number of limitations to CQ (Salmon 1989). In each case, the reasons for Salmon's change of opinion show why this view of causation is ultimately unsatisfactory for understanding causal relevance in neuroscience.

The two central constructs of MT and CQ are *causal processes* and *causal interactions*. In this context, processes should *not* be understood as extended events or occurrences, such as production processes or computational processes. Rather, processes are world-lines in Minkowski space–time diagrams; they are things that exhibit consistency of characteristics over time. To introduce three examples that will recur below, a glutamate molecule crossing the synapse, a Ca^{2+} ion entering a cell, and a shadow moving along the ground as a car moves down the highway are all processes. Salmon distinguishes two kinds of process: causal processes and pseudo-processes. According to MT, these are distinguished by the fact that causal processes are capable of transmitting a mark. A mark is a change in some characteristic of a process that occurs when processes intersect. For example, glutamate can be tagged with a radioactive tracer, the NMDA receptor changes its conformation when it binds to glutamate, and a car's shadow is deformed as it passes telephone poles. What distinguishes causal processes (such as glutamate or Ca^{2+} ions) from *pseudo-processes* (such as shadows) is that the causal processes can *transmit* the mark beyond the space–time point at which the processes intersect. A process transmits a mark from space–time point A to space–time point B if and only if the mark appears at each space–time point between A and B in the absence of additional interactions. Once the tracer is attached to the glutamate molecule, additional interactions are not necessary for the glutamate molecule to continue to bear the mark. Likewise, a mark introduced into the car at a local intersection with a pebble (for example, a crack in the windshield) is borne by the car from that point on. The pebble is marked by being broken, compressed, and accelerated. This is not true of the shadow, which is deformed as it passes the telephone pole. The shadow is a pseudo-process because it cannot transmit marks beyond local points of intersection. Two processes (for example, a car's windshield and the pebble) *interact* causally when they intersect, when both processes are marked, and when the marks are transmitted beyond the point of intersection in the absence of additional interactions. This is an elegant view, indeed.

For both MT and CQ, explaining a phenomenon is a matter of situating it within the causal nexus.[7] As shown in Figure 3.3 (redrawn from Salmon 1984), etiological explanations situate the event to be explained within the causal nexus by tracing the relevant portion of the causal nexus in its past. To say that an event X is part of the explanation for an event Y is to locate X in Y's past light cone and to trace the physical connections—the processes and interactions—linking X to Y.

MT places few restrictions on what constitutes a process or a mark. At least in many cases, neural mechanisms involve parts interacting with one another through contact, and those interactions introduce changes in

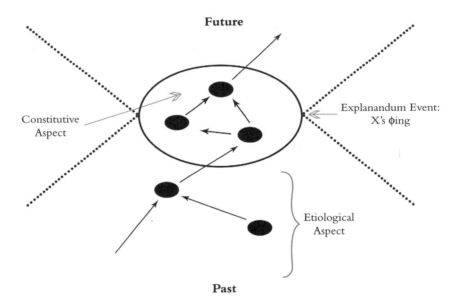

Figure 3.3. Two aspects of causal–mechanical explanation*
* The etiological aspect traces the antecedent causes of the explanandum event (X's ϕ-ing); the constitutive aspect traces the mechanisms that make up X's ϕ-ing
Source: Adapted from Salmon (1984)

---

[7] This is a view of etiological explanation. This simple and appealing story does not apply to what Salmon and I call "constitutive" explanations, in which components are not causally (but rather componentially) related to the *explanandum phenomenon*. See Chapter 4.

the properties of the interacting parts. When an enzyme phosphorylates a molecule, and when an electrode injects current, marks are transmitted through local interactions. Despite this prima facie plausibility, neither MT nor CQ can provide a general account of causation in neuroscience.

For example, MT has difficulty accommodating transitory interactions involving marks that are borne only *during* local intersections between processes. Consider the interaction between the glutamate molecule and the NMDA receptor. When glutamate binds to the NMDA receptor, the NMDA receptor changes its conformation and exposes a channel through the membrane. When glutamate detaches from the receptor, the channel returns to its original conformation. The mark is not borne beyond the locus of the interaction. Many of the enzyme-substrate interactions that appear in most molecular explanations in neuroscience have this basic scheme. MT is prevented from accommodating such interactions by its device for distinguishing causal processes from pseudo-processes.[8] Salmon is insistent on this distinction in part because it corresponds to the distinction in special relativity between processes that can be accelerated beyond the speed of light (such as shadows) and those that cannot. Those that can are pseudo-processes, and those that cannot are causal processes. An account of causation in neuroscience, however, need not be bound by a distinction peculiar to physics, especially if the effort to honor this distinction prevents one from accommodating unproblematic kinds of causal relations accepted in neuroscientific explanations.

From Salmon's perspective, however, MT suffers from a more serious limitation. Part of his motivation for developing MT is his desire to treat causation as an empirical phenomenon, open to investigation with the methods of physical science. For Salmon, this involves developing an account of causation free of appeal to counterfactuals (that is, free of statements of the form "if X were to happen, then Y would happen"). Salmon could not see a way to evaluate the truth-values of counterfactuals within his broadly empiricist (though realist) epistemological framework; more specifically, he eschewed efforts to determine their truth-values by

---

[8] Salmon might respond that the mark fails to persist because of additional interactions inside the channel. Similar counterexamples can arise for fundamental interactions of this sort that cannot be analyzed into interactions among constituent parts. Salmon recognized difficulties accounting for what he calls Y-type interactions that do not involve two processes coming together but rather one process splitting. The channel example involves a Y-type interaction.

considering what happens when counterfactual possibilities (such as X) happen in nearby possible worlds.[9] When he realized that MT makes tacit appeal to counterfactual relations, he abandoned the account (see Salmon 1994). To see how MT makes such tacit appeal, imagine that a shadow (a paradigm pseudo-process) intersects with a glutamate molecule (a causal process) at the same time that the glutamate molecule interacts with a vehicle bearing a radioactive tracer (a causal process). During the intersection with the shadow, the glutamate molecule is marked with a radioactive tracer, and that mark persists beyond the locus of the intersection. The intersection with the shadow, however, is irrelevant to the marking of the glutamate molecule. To rule out cases of this sort, Salmon recognized the need to stipulate that in causal interactions, the mark *would not have been transmitted had the interaction not occurred*. The vehicle satisfies this criterion, but the shadow does not. Salmon's empiricist convictions, however, led him to find this reliance on counterfactuals intolerable.

In "Causality without Counterfactuals" (Salmon 1994), Salmon abandoned MT, citing these concerns about counterfactuals as his primary motivation. He adopted Phil Dowe's (1992) CQ account of causal transmission. According to the CQ account, causal processes and interactions are defined as follows:

(CQ1) A *causal process* is a world-line of an object that possesses a non-zero amount of a conserved quantity (for example mass, energy, charge).

(CQ2) A *causal interaction* is an intersection of world-lines that involves exchange of a conserved quantity.[10]

---

[9] Although Salmon did not express the problem in this way, one can put the problem in terms of the thesis of Humean Supervenience: the idea that there can be no difference in causal facts without a difference in past, present, or future occurrent facts. Roughly, if two worlds are identical with respect to what in fact happens, where, and when, then they cannot differ with respect to what causes what. Failing to conform one's view of causation to this requirement threatens to make causal facts unknowable in principle. If two worlds are identical with respect to their occurrent facts but differ in their causal facts, then no amount of evidence gleaned from the world could ever settle the question of what the causal facts are. Given these epistemic consequences, it seems wise to conform one's account of causation to the principle of Humean Supervenience unless there is a good reason for not doing so. Counterfactual accounts, Salmon might have thought, force one to consider facts other than occurrent facts (for example, facts about nearby possible worlds), thus violating this empiricist loyalty test. Salmon did not develop arguments against counterfactual approaches, such as Lewis (1983), which is intended to be consistent with Humean Supervenience.

[10] It is doubtful that CQ can serve as a reductive account of causation since conservation is an implicitly causal notion. Quantities are conserved if their values remain constant in closed systems,

CQ obviates the need for counterfactuals by appeal to conserved quantities that remain constant in the absence of interactions. CQ also presents a view of causation tailor-made for physicalists/fundamentalist metaphysics. If causal interactions are exchanges of conserved quantities, and if conserved quantities are found only at the fundamental level, then all causation is located at the fundamental level.

The added ontological restrictions on processes and interactions in CQ remove the generality that MT has for describing causal interactions in neuroscience. A mark is *any* persistent alteration to a characteristic; so described, marks are ubiquitous. Conserved quantities are not so prevalent. In electrophysiology, as discussed in Chapter 2, explanations appeal to the movement of charges and matter across the membrane. The folding of proteins is similarly described in terms of transitions among stable states through energy-conserving interactions. But the claim that voltage causes NMDA receptors to open makes no explicit appeal exchanges of conserved quantities, and interactions among neurons, such as the LTP phenomenon itself, are not, and do not require for their intelligibility that they be grounded in, conservative interactions.[11] As soon as one begins to talk about causal relations that arise when parts are organized into mechanisms, the transmission view loses traction; its austere descriptive vocabulary no longer applies. When a tetanus induces LTP, there is a causal relationship between an injection of current and the strength of a synapse. Conservation laws do not describe this relationship, and nothing is passed from the tetanus to the strength of the synapse. Although I know of no explanations in neuroscience that violate conservation laws, very few explanations in neuroscience appeal directly to exchanges of conserved quantities. Such exchanges almost always occur well below the "level" of the causal interactions that neuroscientists care about. As a result, very few causal relationships described in neuroscience textbooks can usefully be regimented by assimilating them to conservation laws.

Leaving this descriptive matter aside, however, there are two reasons to doubt that CQ can provide an adequate account of causation in

and closed systems are those that have no causal transactions with their environments (see Hitchcock 1995a).

[11] I neglect here the empirical hypothesis that synaptic changes in the central nervous system are regulated to maintain a constant overall synaptic strength across all of the synapses in a region or system. This could possibly be true. I am merely insisting that its truth is not required for LTP to count as a causal phenomenon.

neuroscience. The first is that transmission theories do not provide a satisfactory account of causal relevance (as required in E4). The second is that transmission theories do not accommodate negative causal relations, such as cases of omission and prevention. MT and CQ can perhaps be supplemented with additional apparatus to remedy these shortcomings. In each case, though, the additional apparatus is an ad hoc adjustment that is untrue to the original motivations for the account and that gives up the simplicity that makes transmission accounts attractive in the first place. A univocal account of causal relations that can do all of the work of CQ and MT without the additional apparatus, such as the manipulationist account I defend in Section 5, looks more promising as an account of the causal relations in neuroscientific explanations.

3.1 Transmission and causal relevance

Causal relevance cannot be analyzed in terms of exchanges of conserved quantities alone. The causal nexus is a complex reticulum of causal processes and interactions. Only some of them are relevant to any given *explanandum phenomenon*. Providing an etiological explanation involves not merely revealing the causal nexus in the past light cone of the *explanandum phenomenon*. It involves, in addition, selecting the relevant interactions and processes and picking out the relevant features of those processes and interactions (see Hitchcock 1995).

Consider blessed neurons. Suppose our parson electrophysiologist blesses the pre-synaptic neuron with isotonic holy water while delivering a tetanus. The holy water is a causal process transmitting marks and conserved quantities from the micropipette to the neuron. Likewise, the tetanus is induced by injecting current and so involves movement of ions from an electrode into the cell. Matter and energy are conserved in each case. The isotonic holy water is as much a part of the antecedent causal nexus of LTP as is the injection of current. But the blessing is causally irrelevant to LTP.

This example represents a situation at the heart of the search for causes, not just in neuroscience, but generally. The search for causes is not merely a search for what marks what, or what engages in conservative interactions with what, but rather what factors make a difference to the effect. Follow the glutamate molecule from the pre-synaptic cell to the NMDA receptor. The molecule no doubt engages in any number of conservative interactions: it bumps the pre-synaptic membrane; it collides with other molecules; it attracts a passing ion; and it exchanges energy with synaptic enzymes. Each of these interactions involves causal processes exchanging marks or conserved quantities. But only some of these processes and interactions are causally relevant to LTP.

Similar problems arise for causal interactions in which multiple conserved quantities are exchanged. To use an example due to Christopher Hitchcock: a pool cue strikes a cue ball, imparting both momentum and a blue dot of chalk. In the first case, momentum is exchanged. In the last, matter is exchanged. Yet only the first is relevant to the trajectory of the cue ball. We could remove the dot, or change it from blue to green, or change its material constituents in many ways without affecting the trajectory of the ball. Similarly, when an electrophysiologist (ordained or not) lowers the electrode into the cell, the electrode punctures the cell membrane, adds matter to the intracellular fluid, collides with various intracellular molecules, and injects current. Each of these involves an exchange of marks and conserved quantities, but only the current is relevant to LTP. The challenge is to determine which exchanges of conserved quantities are relevant. Because an account of transmission alone does not distinguish relevant from irrelevant markings and exchanges, transmission accounts do not meet condition E4. If explanation is a matter of situating something in the causal nexus, and if the causal nexus contains myriad causally irrelevant processes, features, and interactions, then the explanation includes causally irrelevant features (in violation of E4).

Salmon (1994) acknowledges these problems with his CQ model and admits that they are serious setbacks to his vision of the causal nexus.[12] The problem of explanatory relevance requires a conditional solution. What makes the blessing irrelevant is that the tetanus would strengthen the synapse even if the neuron were not blessed. What makes the blue dot irrelevant is that the imparted momentum would send the cue ball into the eight ball even if the cue did not leave a dot. The goal of an account of causal relevance is to say what makes a difference to what. That goal requires appeal to claims about what would happen or what would be likely to happen if the circumstances were different (or, if it be preferred, to claims about what does or is likely to happen when the circumstances are different; see Bogen 2004).

---

[12] Dowe (2000) addresses this matter (see his Chapter 7). For criticism of his account, see Hausman (2002); Ehring (2003).

3.2 Omission and prevention

A second difficulty for transmission accounts concerns the prevalence of explanations that appeal to negative causal factors. This brings me back to the coincidence detector mechanism in LTP. LTP is induced only when both the pre- and the post-synaptic neurons are simultaneously active. As I note above, the crucial features of LTP are explained by the fact that unless the post-synaptic neuron is depolarized when the pre-synaptic neuron is stimulated, Mg^{2+} ions block the NMDA receptor channel and prevent Ca^{2+} from flowing into the post-synaptic neuron. To induce LTP thus requires removing the Mg^{2+} block. Depolarizing the post-synaptic neuron causes Ca^{2+} to enter through the NMDA receptor. But this causal relationship cannot be understood as an exchange of conserved quantities (or transmission of marks) between the depolarization of the pre-synaptic cell and the influx of Ca^{2+}.

To see why, focus on the stage in which Mg^{2+} is expelled from the channel in the NMDA receptor. The absence of Mg^{2+} allows Ca^{2+} to enter the cell. The depolarization removes the Mg^{2+} ion from the channel in an interaction that involves exchanging conserved quantities. But no conserved quantities are exchanged between the absence of the Mg^{2+} ion and the influx of Ca^{2+} ions. Absences do not bear or exchange conserved quantities. They are not processes; they are not "things," properly speaking, and they do not exhibit consistency of characteristics over time. Nonetheless, the absence of the Mg^{2+} block does seem to cause Ca^{2+} to enter the cell. At least this is what controlled experiments suggest: when the Mg^{2+} block is in place, the Ca^{2+} does not enter the cell. When the Mg^{2+} block is removed, the Ca^{2+} current begins to flow. In this sense (further restrictions will be added below), the absence of the Mg^{2+} ion makes a difference to intracellular Ca^{2+} concentrations. To the extent that causal relevance is a matter of making a difference, the removal of the Mg^{2+} block, and so the opening of the channel pore, is causally relevant to the induction of LTP.

The example can also be described the other way around. When the Mg^{2+} ion is in the channel, it prevents intracellular Ca^{2+} concentrations from rising despite the fact that glutamate is bound to the NMDA receptor. Does the presence of a Mg^{2+} ion in the channel cause Ca^{2+} not to enter the cell? The Mg^{2+} ion does exchange conserved quantities with Ca^{2+} ions as they enter the channel, but this is not the same as *preventing* an increase in intracellular Ca^{2+}. The failure of Ca^{2+} concentrations to rise is not the sort of thing that bears conserved quantities, and it is not the sort of thing with which Mg^{2+} ions can exchange marks. Still, there is no difficulty saying that Mg^{2+} is causally, and so explanatorily, relevant to LTP. The reason is simple: the Mg^{2+} ion *makes a difference* to the Ca^{2+} concentration of the cell, a difference that is revealed, and so can be tested, by removing the Mg^{2+} block.[13]

These examples exhibit two varieties of negative causation.[14] The first, in which the absence of the cause allows an effect (that is, not-C causes E), is commonly called *omission*. The second, in which a cause inhibits or precludes an effect (that is C causes not-E), is commonly called *prevention*. Omission and prevention are common in neuroscience and everyday life. Neurons fire because inhibitory neurons are inhibited. Cells produce proteins because molecules inhibit repressors. Aberrant movements appear in Huntington's disease because of damage to systems that would normally suppress such movements. One does not need to look hard in neuroscientific textbooks to find crucial causal roles for antagonists, blockers, gates, inhibitors, repressors, derepressors, negative feedback, and switches. These are the kinds of systems for which negative causes are crucial.

Jonathan Schaffer (2004) argues, convincingly in my view, that any view of causation that does not include negative causes is sharply at odds with common-sense talk about causes, with scientific judgments about what causes what, and with theoretical applications of the concept of the cause (for example, to understand human agency and moral responsibility). LTP is not unique or in any way exceptional in this respect. Different areas of neuroscience have learned at different rates that they had to include negative causation in their theories for different aspects of brain function. Inhibitory neurons in the brain were not discovered until the middle of the twentieth century. Physiologists and pharmacologists studying the chemical synapse quickly learned that they had to discuss the means by which neurotransmitters are enzymatically inactivated and/or removed from the synapse. The neuroscientists who developed functional brain imaging began

---

[13] Negative causation also raises problems for Glennan's (1996) mechanical view because absences are not physical parts and cannot "interact," in Glennan's sense of the word, with other parts.

[14] These two can be combined to generate a family of test-problems for views of causation, including cases of double prevention, preemptive prevention, and so on. See Collins et. al. (eds) (2004) for discussions of these and other cases.

by studying only increases in activation during the performance of a task and then realized that they should also systematically investigate reductions in activation as well. Neuroscientists have learned time and again that brain systems can make a big deal out of nothing.

I would add an epistemic point. One discovers and tests negative causal relationships with the same experimental strategies, and negative causal claims are evaluated according to the same normative standards used to evaluate positive claims. If the evidence for testing causal relations is blind to the distinction between negative and positive causes, then our epistemic access to them is no more and no less problematic than it is to positive causes. These considerations make a strong case for accepting negative causes and so place the burden of proof on those who would deny that negative causes exist.

Some philosophers, however, deny that cases of omission and prevention are true cases of causation. There are metaphysical reasons for this view, grounded in the idea that absences, as nothings, have no causal powers.[15] This is a thorny issue, and it is hard to imagine it being resolved decisively. The issue turns in part on how one construes the relata in the causal relations. (Are they events, processes, states of affairs, values of variables, properties, or objects? See Schaffer 2003.) According to the view I recommend, which follows Dretske (1977), Hitchcock (1996), Northcott (forthcoming), and Schaffer (2005), the causal relata are contrasts. For the cause variable, the contrast is between the value of the variable as fixed by the ideal intervention and the value that the variable has in the control condition (that is, without intervention). For the effect variable, the contrast is between the value of the variable in the control condition (when one does not intervene on the cause variable), and its value in the experimental condition (when one does intervene on the cause variable). Causal statements are thus most clearly articulated when they describe a relationship between contrasts: C rather than not-C causes E rather than not-E. Different choices of contrast classes yield different causal claims. To use Dretske's example, it is true that Socrates' ingesting (rather than not ingesting) the hemlock (rather than some non-poisonous beverage) caused him to die (rather than live). It is false that Socrates' ingesting (rather than injecting) the hemlock caused

---

[15] This consideration would at best preclude the possibility of omission. It raises no difficulties for prevention, so long as the preventer is a presence.

him to die (rather than live). I defend this contrastive view in Chapter 6. Note further that cases of omission and prevention are in many cases merely extremes on a continuum of positive or negative causal relevance. Raising the dose of a drug improves pain relief. Lowering the dose of the drug reduces pain relief. Removing the drug entirely reduces it to a zero-point. Cases of omission and prevention are not outliers in our scientific conception of causation.

A second problem raised against the acceptance of negative causes is that there are too many of them, and most negative causes are of no use for understanding explanation in neuroscience. As Dowe (2004) and Beebee (2004) argue, many instances of negative causation run counter to our common sense, scientific, and theoretical uses of the concept of "cause," and no available account of negative causation accepts all and only the intuitively satisfactory instances. If omissions count as causes, then it would appear that I am a cause for all of the things that I might have acted to prevent. Whenever someone spills coffee in someone's lap in a Vienna café, I could have prevented it had I been there and moved the coffee cup, or distracted the waitress, or placed a puffin on the counter, or whatever. I am also the cause of every window's not breaking, for the simple reason that I might have tossed a rock through it. I take very little pride in that fact. It would appear that, in the context of neuroscience, treating cases of omission and prevention as on par with causal processes and interactions makes the project of explaining the brain (that is, discovering its causal structure) much more complicated. The complete etiological explanation (that is, the complete cause) for a phenomenon includes not only all of the factors that actually contributed to its occurrence, but also all of the factors that might have prevented it, no matter how remote. In short, some examples of negative causation are intuitively satisfying and explanatorily salient, and some are not. Such considerations lead many to draw a clear line where they can find it: between positive causation (involving physical connections) and negative causation (not involving physical connections). Dowe (2000, 2004), in particular, argues that the common-sense notion of causation (including cases of negative causation) should be bifurcated into genuine causation, involving exchanges of conserved quantities, and causation*, a counterfactual-laden quasi-causation without connection.

Dowe offers separate accounts of omission and prevention and he shows how these accounts might be extended to cover more complex examples of negative causation. It suffices for present purposes to examine cases of prevention. On his account, to say that X prevented Y is to say that X caused* not Y. X caused* not Y if:

(P1) X occurred and Y did not, and there occurred an m such that
(P2) there is a causal relation between X and the process due to m, such that either
    (i) X is a causal interaction with the causal process m, or
    (ii) X causes n, a causal interaction with process m, and
(P3) If X (or an alternative preventer) had not occurred, m would have caused Y. (Modified from Dowe 2000, 133−4).[16]

To return to the LTP example, the Mg^{2+} ion is lodged in the channel (X) and the Ca^{2+} does not enter the post-synaptic cell (Y), in accordance with (P1). There is a causal interaction between the Mg^{2+} ion in the channel and Ca^{2+} ions entering the channel (m), in accordance with (P2). If the Mg^{2+} ion had not blocked the channel, then the ion would have moved into the cell, in accordance with (P3). In this way, the Mg^{2+} ion prevented the influx of Ca^{2+} ions, or caused* the ions not to enter the cell.

This account does not so much solve the problem of there being too many negative causes as rename it as a problem for causation*. Dowe recasts the problem in (P1) and (P2), and then appeals to counterfactuals in (P3) to show how the problem can be solved. Dowe does not claim to provide an account of counterfactuals, or a means for distinguishing those generalizations that sustain counterfactuals from those that do not, or a story about how their truth-values are determined. Nor does he provide a means to distinguish those appeals to causation* that are appropriate (the intuitive cases) from those that are not. All he really wants to show is that there are genuine cases of causation that do not require appeal to counterfactuals. The problem of providing an account of the counterfactual in (P3) can then safely be left to those interested in causation*. This strategy is legitimate for Dowe's goal of constructing an empirical account of causation. Dowe's bifurcation effectively banishes omission and prevention from the domain of phenomena over which his theory of causation is required to range. However, my objective is to develop an account of causation that satisfies the norms of explanation in neuroscience. Explanations in neuroscience

---

[16] Machamer (personal communication) has also suggested an informal version of this view.

typically involve instances of both causation and causation*, and so the task of understanding (P3) cannot be left to others. Dowe's account is thus incomplete for present purposes.

The extravagant cases of negative causation can be handled in a number of ways. Some negative causes are too improbable or abnormal to be included in explanatory texts or even counted as causes. Others are ruled out by, for example, legal, moral, and epistemic factors that determine the salience of a fact in a particular discussion (see Beebee 2004). For example, I cannot be held responsible for the coffee spillage in Vienna because I did not know about it (an epistemic claim), I could not reasonably be expected to go to Vienna today for this purpose (a moral claim), and I am under no obligation, legal or otherwise, to prevent the spillage (in the way that perhaps a personal assistant would be). Consider a neuroscientific example: is the gasoline in my car's tank a cause of the instance of LTP in the Petri dish? It is likely true that if I had doused the dish with the gasoline, then the cells would not induce LTP, but it seems odd to think of the absence of gasoline as a cause of LTP. Although I do not have a general formula for ruling out nonexplanatory causes of this sort, it is clear enough that gasoline is neither normally part of cells nor part of their extracellular environment. Gasoline is not part of the set-up or background conditions under which the cell normally operates. It is not a cellular constituent. Gasoline levels do not vary as the mechanism works. The distinction between intuitive and counterintuitive cases is a psychological distinction that is drawn on a number of different grounds in different epistemic contexts.

However, it is a psychological distinction that all parties in this dispute have to accommodate. To remove negative causation from the extension of the term "cause" is only to relocate the problem as a problem for causation*. For the question that naturally arises is: what is the difference between the intuitive and counterintuitive cases of causation*? For the goal of building an account of mechanistic explanation, one cannot simply banish negative causes from consideration. They play too central a role in biological (and neuroscientific) mechanisms. And once they are admitted (either as bona fide causes or as mere causes*), then the extravagance follows automatically.

The problem of causal relevance that I discuss in Section 3.1 and the problem of negative causation that I discuss in this section together present a significant challenge to transmission accounts. For the transmission account to provide an account of causal relevance, it needs to be supplemented with the idea that causes make a difference to their effects, a difference that can be assessed with controlled experiments. The cue ball, after all, would still have gone in the corner pocket even if it had not been marked with the blue dot. For the transmission account to provide an account of negative causation, it also needs to be supplemented with the idea that causes make a difference to their effects. If the Mg^{2+} ion does not leave the channel, the Ca^{2+} does not enter the cell. But once one has introduced this idea of difference-making (one that many believe requires counterfactuals, such as Dowe's (P3); see Hitchcock 1995; Woodward 2003; see also Bogen 2004) into the account of both positive and negative causation, it is reasonable to ask what further work is left to be done by the requirement that the entire causal chain must involve physical connections or transmission of marks. What justification is there for this further ontological restriction on the notion of "cause"? It is more appropriate to say that even though many cases of causation involve transmission of marks or conserved quantities, this is but one way for something to make a difference to something else. The manipulationist approach that I recommend in Section 5 makes this reliance on difference-making (and the experimental procedures to test it) explicit, shows how this notion should be regimented, and thereby provides a univocal account of positive and negative causal relevance.

4. Causation and Mechanical Connection

Let's turn then to Glennan's (1996) mechanical account of causation.[17] His view contains some important insights about how mechanistically fragile and historically contingent generalizations can be explanatory. However, Glennan advances his account as a response to Humean skeptical challenges to causation,[18] and his focus on this classic problem prevents him from developing a normatively adequate account of causation or, consequently, of mechanisms. Glennan has since amended his view (see Glennan 2002) in

---

[17] I call Glennan's account of causation "mechanical," which should not be associated with my *mechanistic* view of explanation. As my criticisms make clear, I do not think that causation can be explicated in terms of mechanisms, as the mechanical account claims, but I do believe that explanations often describe mechanisms.

[18] I use the term "Humean" to acknowledge debates over Hume's thoughts about causation. I am merely reporting Glennan's rendition of a set of worries traditionally attributed to Hume.

a way that can perhaps handle the objections I raise and in a way that brings his view much closer to my own.[19] Here, I focus only on the earlier view because its limitations bring out some general lessons about the notion of causal relevance in neuroscience.

Glennan (1996) describes Hume's challenge as follows: given a putative cause X and an effect Y, at best, one can observe that X and Y are contiguous, that X precedes Y, and that X-type things and Y-type things are constantly conjoined. One cannot observe the necessity or hidden power by which X causes Y. For Glennan, the challenge is to identify this hidden power connecting X to Y, because that hidden causal power distinguishes cases in which X causes Y from those in which X is merely correlated with or merely precedes Y. Glennan argues that for nonfundamental causes, the hidden causal power is a mechanism linking X to Y: "a relation between two events (other than fundamental physical events) is causal when and only when these events are connected in the appropriate way by a mechanism" (Glennan 1996: 56, 1997). For Glennan, a mechanism is a complex system that produces its behavior by the interaction of a number of parts according to direct causal laws (Glennan 1996: 52). On his account, the tetanus causes the strengthening of the synapse because there is a mechanism (involving glutamate, NMDA receptors, and Ca^{2+}) that connects them.

Glennan argues that his mechanical account of causation offers a partial solution to Hume's problem:

To what degree have we uncovered the secret connexion that binds together causally connected events? At the level of fundamental physics, Hume's problem still remains. We can observe certain regularities, but we cannot offer an explanation of why those regularities obtain. It is not good enough to say that in physics there just are regularities, for there are still questions about which regularities are lawful and causal. Despite the difficulties that remain, we have shown that Hume's problem is not a universal one. In the case of higher-level laws, we can distinguish connections and conjunctions, because we can understand the mechanisms which produce higher level regularities. Very often, the connexion is not so secret after all. (Glennan 1996: 68)

Causation is thus to be understood in two tiers. For nonfundamental causal relations, mechanisms fill the gap between cause and effect with

---

[19] Indeed, we agree on many aspects of this general framework. My view centers on the same basic ideas and builds from the same philosophical literature. I focus on our differences for purposes of explication.

intermediate causal relations. For fundamental causal relations, there are by definition no mechanisms. While Glennan acknowledges that Hume's problem still arises at the fundamental level, he claims that it is not a problem he needs to confront to understand nonfundamental causes.

Glennan's use of the words "direct causal law" to describe the interactions in a mechanism (Glennan 1996, 1997) has attracted criticism from those who believe that the mechanistic fragility and historical contingency of causation in nonfundamental sciences make talk of universal laws inappropriate (see, for example, Machamer et al. 2000; Woodward 2002; Darden 2002; Glennan 2002). While I agree with the spirit of these criticisms, I also believe that they obscure the progress Glennan makes in thinking about these matters.

Glennan explicitly addresses mechanistic fragility. On his account, nonfundamental causal regularities are sustained by a working mechanism in a range of background and stimulus conditions. Mechanisms (such as the LTP mechanism) break down in inappropriate stimulus conditions, or in abnormal background conditions, or if the components of the mechanism break. Nonfundamental causal regularities are fragile because the mechanisms that sustain them can fail to work.

Although Glennan (1996) does not discuss the historical contingency of nonfundamental causes, the same point applies. Nonfundamental regularities (and the mechanisms that sustain them) are in many cases contingent products of evolution and development. Biological mechanisms are tinkered together (Jacob 1977), and their components are adjusted as variants arise and perish in the course of evolutionary history and as organisms change and develop over their life histories. Such mechanisms have changed considerably over the history of life. They also change over the life of individual organisms. On Glennan's account, such historical contingency subtracts nothing from the ability of a mechanism to act as a hidden connection between present causes and effects. The difference between causal regularities and accidents, for Glennan, is not that causal regularities are timeless and that accidents are historically transitory, but rather that causal regularities are sustained by mechanisms and accidents are not.

To attack Glennan for his use of the term "law" also distracts attention from a serious problem with his attempt to ameliorate the force of Humean causal skepticism, a problem that ultimately ramifies through Glennan's account of causation. The problem derives from a tension between

Glennan's anti-fundamentalism and his attempt to analyze causation in terms of lower-level mechanisms. Glennan states his anti-fundamentalism as follows:

The mechanical theory of causation rejects a widespread assumption about the nature of causation. I think that it is generally assumed that whatever causal connections are, they ultimately have something to do with the most fundamental physical processes. The closer we are to fundamental physics, the more our statements are about the true causes of things; the further we stray into the higher-level sciences, the more we move away from causal statements and toward mere empirical generalizations. This assumption, however, is what makes Hume's skepticism so devastating. ... Causal statements are typically statements about events regulated by mechanisms, and mechanisms are complex higher-level entities. Only when we talk about interactions governed by fundamental laws does causal talk become problematic. (Glennan 1996: 67)

I believe that mechanists should follow Glennan in resisting causal fundamentalism, but not because such resistance addresses the Humean challenge.

Glennan's anti-fundamentalism does not solve the Humean problem. Although he rejects the view that nonfundamental causal relations are grounded in fundamental metaphysical glue (Glennan 1996: 67), he accepts the weaker intuition that they are grounded in metaphysical glue at lower, yet nonfundamental, levels. For Glennan, the causal relationship between the tetanus and LTP is grounded in causal relations among glutamate, NMDA receptors, and Ca^{2+} ions. Likewise the causal relations between glutamate and NMDA receptors, and NMDA receptors and Ca^{2+} ions, are grounded in still lower-level mechanisms. Glennan's mechanisms are *causal* mechanisms. They are *complex systems* composed of *interacting* parts that *produce* the behavior of the whole according to direct *causal* laws. The italicized words are transparently causal, and the Humean will rightly request an account of these causal terms. If Glennan grounds these causal terms in still lower-level causal mechanisms, then he only staves off ignorance of the nature of causes a little longer. He responds:

The circularity [or regress] is only apparent. In describing the mechanism that connects the two events I have explained how the events are causally connected. How the parts are connected is a different question. I can try to answer the second question by offering another account of the mechanisms which connect them, but I need not give an account to explain the connection between the events. Indeed such an account would only obscure the causally relevant features of the original explanation. ... I refer to a mechanism which in turn refers to causal relations, but these latter causal relations are different (and more basic) relations, than the one which I am seeking to explain. (Glennan 1996: 65)

This response is unassailable as a point about *explanation*, but it does not address the worry about *causation*. I agree that one makes progress in explaining LTP by appeal to activities such as binding, changing conformation, diffusing, and phosphorylating. These activities are different from and relatively more basic than LTP. I agree further that it would obscure the understanding of LTP to keep descending through levels of explanation all the way to quarks, strings, and branes. But the Humean problem as stated above is not about explanation. Hume asks, "What is the necessary connexion between cause and effect?" For that question, Glennan's answer is unsatisfying: the mysterious connections at higher levels are grounded in many more and equally mysterious connections at a lower level.

One way out of the regress is to allow it to terminate. One way to do this is to claim that those fundamental causal relations involve exchanges of conserved quantities; I discuss the limitations of that option above. Glennan takes a related approach by claiming that the regress terminates in fundamental laws. He admits that he has no account of how fundamental laws are distinguished from fundamental accidents: "Hume provides a convincing argument that we can have no knowledge of this glue [at fundamental levels], and that talk of such glue may even be unintelligible ... Only when we talk about interactions governed by fundamental laws does causal talk become problematic" (Glennan 1996: 67). Here, Glennan echoes a familiar claim of physicists and many philosophers of physics: belief in fundamental causes is no longer tenable (if it ever was). Many of these physicists and philosophers also argue on these grounds that belief in causes is untenable (or literally false) *tout court* (see, for example, Russell 1913; Norton 2003). This strategy, however, threatens the heart of Glennan's view of causation in a more direct way.

Suppose that one is trying to understand the necessary connection between X and Y (that is, $X \to Y$) at one level above the fundamental level. Glennan (1996) says that the necessity in the connection between X and Y should be understood in terms of the connections between items at the fundamental level, say, $X \to a \to b \to Y$. Glennan grants that a and b have no necessary connection between them and that talk of such a connection may be unintelligible. But how can a necessary causal connection between X and Y be built out of relations in which there is no necessary connection and for which such talk is unintelligible? The problem then scales up: if the necessary connection between X and Y is problematic, then so are any causal relationships built out of that connection. If the Humean is right about causation at fundamental levels, then when Glennan arrives at the font of causal power at the fundamental level, the well will be dry. In short: the regress terminates or it does not, and either way Glennan fails to solve Hume's problem.

Similar considerations show why Glennan's (1996) mechanical account cannot satisfy (E1)–(E5). Consider (E1), the idea that causal relations are not mere temporal sequences. To meet this constraint, Glennan appeals to the fact that causal relations (as opposed to temporal successions) are underwritten by mechanisms. However, the same worry arises for the causal relations in the mechanism. How are the causal relations in mechanisms distinguished from mere temporal sequences? Glennan answers that the causal relations in mechanisms are interactions governed by direct causal laws. And what are direct causal laws? He answers that they are not mere temporal sequences but necessary connections.[20] Glennan does not explain what it means to say that the direct causal laws are "necessary." It appears that, contrary to the spirit of his mechanical account, Glennan appeals to "direct causal laws" to distinguish causal relations from mere temporal sequences. If so, he does not (and perhaps cannot, given his remarks about fundamental causal laws) develop the resources to adequately distinguish direct causal laws from mere temporal sequences.

A like problem arises concerning the effects of a common cause (E3). Glennan says that "the stipulation that the laws [composing the mechanism] be causal is meant to exclude lawful generalizations which can be explained by common causes" (1996: 55). However, the challenge of (E3) is to find a principled means to distinguish effects of a common cause from causal relations, not merely to stipulate that there is such a difference. Note that there *is* a set of causal relations between the effects of common causes: namely, one that passes via a series of interactions from one effect, through the common cause, to the other effect. Unless Glennan stipulates that the

---

[20] This response is inconsistent with Glennan's claim, discussed above, that talk of necessity is unintelligible for fundamental causal laws.

bona fide interactions in mechanisms run from causes to effects (that is, stipulates (E2)), there is no way to rule out this set of causal relations as a mechanism linking the two effects of a common cause. Again, the buck of providing an account of causation is passed ever lower in a hierarchy of mechanisms until it is discharged by stipulation in fundamental causal relationships.

Finally, consider the problem of distinguishing relevant from irrelevant causes (E4). Here is a possible description of the LTP mechanism: A glutamate molecule with molecular weight w crosses the synaptic cleft at velocity v, collides with a passing protein, alters the position of various amino acids in the NMDA receptor, and lowers the concentration of Na^+ in the intracellular fluid. Each step in this bizarre description is true: the molecular weight, the velocity, the collision, the position of the amino acids, and the changes in Na^+ concentration each hold for the mechanism producing LTP. This description includes a set of parts and mechanistically explicable interactions. Each stage is linked via a mechanism to its predecessor. Yet no one would claim that this is a good explanation of LTP. This is because the putative explanation is composed of irrelevant features of the synapse. It is not the molecular weight of the glutamate molecule or its velocity that matter, but rather its conformation and charge configuration. It is not the position of a particular amino acid in the glutamate receptor that matters (at least in many cases), but rather the appearance of a pore through the membrane. And it is not the drop in Na^+ concentration, but rather the rise in intracellular Ca^{2+} concentration that is relevant to the occurrence of LTP. An account of causation suitable for use in an account of explanation must distinguish causally relevant from causally irrelevant factors. Glennan does not show how this can be done, and so he has not provided a normatively adequate account of the causal relations in mechanisms. As a result, he does not provide a normatively adequate account of mechanisms.

Glennan offers a useful way to explain the mechanistic fragility and historical contingency of neural mechanisms. However, his desire to solve Hume's problem for nonfundamental causes ultimately backfires, driving his account deeper and deeper into a hierarchy of mechanisms. I suspect that many are convinced of the truth of fundamentalism because they endorse a view of causation very much like Glennan's. If this is right, my objections to Glennan's account should help to weaken that motivation. For in Glennan's account, the most pressing questions for a normatively adequate account of causation are stipulated as features of "direct causal laws" at the fundamental level. As a consequence, Glennan neither ameliorates Hume's worries nor satisfies (E1)–(E5). In Section 5, I show how the manipulationist approach satisfies (E1)–(E5) without stipulation and without descending into fundamentalism.

5. Manipulation and Causation

I dwell at some length on the mechanical and transmission approaches to causation because each is associated with mechanistic explanation and because each can be used (intentionally or not) to support explanatory fundamentalism. The mechanical view grounds higher-level causal relations in lower-level mechanisms, a grounding process that ends, if ever, only in the most fundamental causal laws. The transmission account is more explicit in its association between causation and properties found only at the most fundamental levels (that is, conserved quantities). The fact that neither of these views provides an adequate account of causation—and in particular, that each struggles to provide an account of causal relevance and negative causation—weakens the attraction of fundamentalism.

To repeat a central theme: causal relevance, explanation, and control are intimately connected with one another. This is particularly true in biomedical sciences, such as neuroscience, that are driven not merely by intellectual curiosity about the structure of the world, but more fundamentally by the desire (and the funding) to cure diseases, to better the human condition, and to make marketable products. The search for causes and explanations is important in part because it provides an understanding of where, and sometimes how, to intervene and change the world for good or for ill. This connection between causation, explanation, and control is also reflected in the procedures that neuroscientists use to test explanations. These tests involve not only revealing correlations among the states of different parts of a mechanism but, further, intervening in the mechanism and showing that one has the ability to change its behavior predictably. More explicitly: to say that one stage of a mechanism is productive of another (as I suggest in Machamer et al. 2000; Craver and Darden 2001), and to say that one item (activity, entity, or property) is relevant to another, is to say, at least in part, that one has the ability to manipulate one item by intervening to change another. More concretely, to say that LTP is caused by tetanic stimulation is to say that one can potentiate a synapse by tetanizing it.

In embracing this view, I rely closely on James Woodward's account of the role of invariance in explanation (see, especially, Woodward 1997, 2000, 2002, 2003; and Woodward and Hitchcock 2003a, 2003b). Woodward is not especially concerned with neuroscience; however, he is concerned with developing an account of causation adequate for explanations that involve mechanistically fragile and historically contingent generalizations. Woodward (2002) shows how his account of causal relations might be fitted into an account of mechanisms, and Glennan (2002) has followed him in this idea. In this section, I build on that idea by showing how the manipulationist account of causal relevance can satisfy (E1)–(E5). I also show how it can accommodate negative causation.

Woodward's view is currently the most defensible and readable exposition of the manipulationist tradition in thinking about causation both in philosophy (see, for example, Collingwood 1940; von Wright 1971) and in statistics (Cook and Campbell 1979; Freedman 1997). Related ideas appear in Pearl's (2000) notion of a "do operator," the notion of an intervention by Spirtes et al. (1993), and Glymour's (2001) idea of surgically intervening into a causal graph. The central idea is that causal relationships are distinctive in that they are potentially exploitable for the purposes of manipulation and control. More specifically, variable X is causally relevant to variable Y in conditions W if some ideal intervention on X in conditions W changes the value of Y (or the probability distribution over possible values of Y). In the context of a given request for explanation, the relationship between X and Y is explanatory if it is invariant under the conditions (W) that are relevant in that explanatory context. Now I consider the different components of this basic statement.[21]

Woodward construes X and Y as variables, that is, as determinables capable of taking on determinate values. Although this is a common way of speaking in some areas of science and statistics, philosophers have generally

---

[21] Again, I do not offer this account as a reductive analysis of causation. It would clearly be circular, given that intervention is an ineliminably causal concept. Instead, my account is intended as a necessary condition to be met by relationships of causation and to be explained by any satisfactory metaphysics of causation. Lewis's view of causation, for example, ably captures many of the crucial features of this necessary condition (see Woodward and Hitchcock 2003a for a discussion).

preferred other relata in their accounts of causation. Davidson (1969) and many other philosophers, for example, describe causation as a relationship between events. Salmon (1984, 1998) and Dowe (2000) describe it as a relationship among processes. Others describe it as a relationship among objects, facts, and contrasts. Each of these ways of speaking and thinking about causation can be translated without loss into talk of variables. For example, talk of event and object causation can be translated into talk of a variable that can take on two values {E occurs/is present, E does not occur/is not present}. Talk of causation among processes can be translated by assigning variables to the features of a process or to the magnitudes of the conserved quantities.[22] Similar translations can be made for the other ways of thinking about causation. To view causal relevance as a relationship among variables allows one to consider cases in which the variable may take on any value in a continuum (for example, a dose), to make relative assessments of causal efficacy along that continuum (for example, a dose-response relation), and to consider cases in which there are sharp discontinuities in the effect between one portion of the continuum and another (threshold events, such as action potentials).[23]

The term "intervention" denotes, roughly, a manipulation that changes the value of a variable. It is helpful to think of interventions as well-designed experimental interventions. However, one must not think of manipulations as exclusively the products of human agency. When a stroke damages a brain region, this counts as an intervention on that brain region's functioning. When a meteor strikes the moon, it intervenes in the moon's environment.

The manipulationist view of causal relevance requires that the relationship between X and Y must be *potentially* exploitable for the purposes of manipulating Y in conditions W. One need not actually be able to manipulate X. One might not know how to intervene on X, one might not have the tools, or X might be too small, too big, or too far away for human intervention. Many believe, for example, that a spatial map in the

---

[22] Those who think of causation as involving activities can make use of the fact that activities have precipitating conditions or enabling properties (that are necessary for or conducive to the occurrence of the activity) and termination conditions or signatures (that is, effects). One can then apply the strategy just described for causation among events, objects, or properties. See Darden and Craver (2002).

[23] As I note above and discuss further in Chapter 6, a contrastive formulation is even more perspicuous. It is a variable X's having one value (rather than some other value) that causes the effect to occur (rather than some alternative). (See Dretske 1977; Hitchcock 1996.)

hippocampus is causally relevant to the ability of rodents to navigate their environments (as argued by O'Keefe and Dostrovsky 1971; O'Keefe and Nadel 1978; Wilson and McNaughton 1993). They believe this in spite of the fact that neuroscientists currently lack the ability to drive a rat through a novel maze by manipulating its spatial map. The ability to do so would no doubt be convincing evidence that the hippocampus is involved in navigation, but this evidence is not required to know that there is a causal relation. What matters is that there is a relationship between X and Y that can possibly be exploited to change Y by changing X, even if no human can or will ever be able to so exploit it. It is a very interesting question how (and how much) we can manage to learn about the causal structure of the world in cases where we cannot intervene in this way. This question is best answered through a detailed look at specific experimental practices in neuroscience. I do not pursue such a detailed investigation in this book (see, for example, Bogen 2001; Bechtel forthcoming). I focus instead on more abstract and general features of the evidence required to establish causal claims.

An *ideal* intervention I on X with respect to Y is a change in the value of X that changes Y, if at all, *only via* the change in X. More specifically, this requirement implies that:

(I1) I does not change Y directly;

(I2) I does not change the value of some causal intermediate S between X and Y except by changing the value of X;

(I3) I is not correlated with some other variable M that is a cause of Y; and

(I4) I acts as a "switch" that controls the value of X irrespective of X's other causes, U. (Adapted from Woodward and Hitchcock 2003a)

These restrictions on ideal interventions are represented graphically in Figure 3.4. Unidirectional arrows represent causal relations, bidirectional dotted arrows represent correlations, and bars across arrows represent a restriction against the represented relation. In this figure, an intervention changes the value of X, surgically removing other causal influences, U, on X (I4). This intervention produces a change in Y that is not mediated directly (I1), by affecting an intermediate variable, S (I2), or by being correlated with some other variable, C, that can change the value of Y

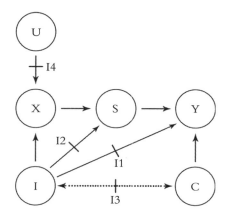

Figure 3.4. An ideal intervention on X with respect to Y*
* Solid arrows represent causal relations; dotted arrow represents correlations; hashes represent the absence of the cause or correlation

(I3). Note that conditions (I1)–(I4) represent the kinds of control that are routinely used and required to test causal and explanatory claims.

The focus on ideal interventions will give rise to objections that experimental situations are often in many ways non-ideal. This is true, and it is an important insight about our epistemic situation with respect to the causal structure of the world. More work remains to be done to say how one can learn about the causal structure of the world if criteria (I1)–(I4) are relaxed, removed, or replaced in order to more accurately describe the complex epistemic situation in which most experimentalists work. The best inroad into that discussion, it seems to me, is to work first on the clear cases and then to see how (and if) the account can be adjusted so that it can regiment non-ideal experimental situations.

Consider the LTP example again. When is it appropriate to assert that a tetanus in the pre-synaptic cell is causally relevant to LTP? One might establish this relationship experimentally by intervening into the pre-synaptic cell, delivering a tetanus, and observing subsequent changes in the strength of the synapse. An experimenter could intervene by injecting current into the cell, by creating an electrical field in a population of pre-synaptic cells, by applying neurotransmitters to the pre-synaptic cell, or by allowing a population of cells to enter its normal burst cycle. What matters is that the intervention makes the pre-synaptic cell fire rapidly and repeatedly. Suppose that one performs such an intervention and observes a subsequent increase in the strength of the synapse. Such a finding would not warrant belief in the claim that the tetanus is causally relevant to synaptic strength. It is possible that the intervention strengthened the synapse for reasons having nothing to do with the tetanus. Perhaps merely breaking the cell membrane or inserting an electrode into a population of neurons can strengthen synapses (in violation of (I1)). Or perhaps inserting the electrode changes features of neurotransmitter release (in violation of (I2)). Or perhaps one inserts electrodes only when one has the cells in a particular bath solution, and the bath solution strengthens synapses (in violation of (I3)). Or perhaps the injected current is swamped by input from other neurons into the cell (in violation of (I4)). If any of the conditions (I1)–(I4) fails in an experimental protocol, the observed changes in synaptic strength would not be good evidence of a causal relationship between the tetanus and the changes in synaptic strength. When one asserts a causal relevance relation between the firing rate of the pre-synaptic cell and the strength of a synapse, one asserts when one alters the firing rate of the cell in specified ways using an ideal intervention, then one either strengthens the synapse or changes the probability that the synapse would be strengthened.

Each of the activities in the LTP mechanism can be described in the same way. Neuroscientists believe that glutamate opens NMDA receptors because they open when glutamate is applied, but not (or not to the same extent) when isotonic saline or some other neurotransmitter is applied, and not when the binding site for glutamate has been blocked or altered. They are convinced that Mg^{2+} blocks the flow of Ca^{2+} into the post-synaptic cell because they can manipulate Ca^{2+} levels in the cell by changing the concentration of Mg^{2+} or by manipulating the electrical potential that holds Mg^{2+} ions in the NMDA receptor's pore. They are convinced that depolarizing the post-synaptic cell is relevant to the eventual occurrence of LTP because they can keep everything else the same and eliminate LTP simply by clamping the voltage of the post-synaptic neuron at rest. Experiments of this sort show neuroscientists what can manipulate what. On the further assumption that such manipulations are relevantly similar to changes occurring in the brain under the conditions in question, neuroscientists can assume that natural interventions (that is, those not wrought by human hands) produce similar changes in the brain.

5.1 Invariance, fragility, and contingency

The explanatory generalizations describing these causal relevance relations are stable, or as Woodward says invariant, though not necessarily—or even usually—universal. To say that a generalization is stable is to say that the specified relation between the cause variable and the effect variable holds under a (generally nonuniversal) range of conditions. The conditions under which a generalization might be stable include *stimulus conditions, intermediate conditions,* and *background conditions.* Stimulus conditions include conditions explicitly represented as independent variables in the description of the relationship; in the case of $X \rightarrow Y$, the stimulus condition is X. The relationship need not be stable across all stimulus conditions. Outside of a normal range of stimulus conditions, the stimulation might have no effect, might weaken the synapse, or might simply damage the cells. The generalization might also be more or less stable under a range of values for the variables intermediate between X and Y, such as Ca^{2+} concentration and Mg^{2+} concentration. Finally, the relationship holds only under a range of background conditions, such as temperature, pH, and available energy. Stable causal relations in neuroscience, in other words, do not hold under all conditions but only under a narrow range of conditions.

The idea that a relationship between variables must be stable to be explanatory is also weaker than the requirement of "contextual unanimity" found in many accounts of causation (for example, Cartwright 1983; Eells 1991; Skyrms 1980). The requirement of contextual unanimity demands, roughly, that if X causes Y, then the relationship between X and Y holds in all contexts. This requirement is too strong for the causal relations in neuroscience precisely because these causal relationships often depend crucially upon the absence of counteracting causes, on the absence of interaction effects, and on background conditions within relatively circumscribed ranges (see Glennan 1997). In contrast to the contextual unanimity requirement, the manipulationist approach allows explanatory generalizations to vary considerably in their stability or invariance and requires only that the generalization should be stable in the conditions relevant to a particular request for explanation (see below).

The fact that generalizations can be more or less stable and still be explanatory is useful for dealing with the fact that causal generalizations in neuroscience are limited in scope, mechanistically fragile, and historically contingent. Causal relations need not be universal to be explanatory, nor need they be unrestricted in scope, nor need they lack any reference to particulars. All that matters is that there is some stable set of circumstances under which the variables specified in the relation exhibit the kind of manipulable relationship sketched above. Mechanistically fragile generalizations are invariant over a range of values for the stimulus variable, the intermediate variables, and the background conditions. Furthermore, the fact that the relationship is historically contingent, and so in some sense unnecessary, makes no difference to whether the relation is explanatory here and now. Na^+ channels produce action potentials today even if no creatures produce action potentials that way 20 million years from now. What matters, again, is that there exists a range of conditions under which one can reliably manipulate the effect variable by intervening to change the cause variable.

Which are the relevant conditions for assessing the stability of a generalization? There is no general answer to that question. Woodward often confines his attention to changes in the values of the variables appearing in the statement of the causal relevance relation. However, this requires at once too much and too little. It requires too much because, as just noted, such relationships might break down under extreme values of the variables appearing in the statement of the relation. It requires too little because, although neuroscientists are often interested in physiologically relevant conditions (that is, the conditions found in intact and healthy organisms), they are just as often interested in disease states in which the stimulus, intermediate, and background conditions are abnormal or pathological. Sometimes they are interested in background conditions well outside the physiological range, as when they try to explain highly contrived experimental effects, to design drugs to interact with the CNS, or to commandeer some part of the CNS for their own purposes. The appropriate range of conditions in which a causal generalization must be stable thus depends crucially upon one's explanatory interests. This does not mean that the causal relations are interest-relative. The causal relevance relations under different ranges of conditions are objective features of the world. However, which of those objective relations is relevant depends on what you are trying to explain.

5.2 Manipulation and criteria for explanation

According to the manipulationist account, explanatory texts describe relationships between variables that can be exploited to produce, prevent, or alter the *explanandum phenomenon*. Merely being able to manipulate a phenomenon, of course, is not sufficient to explain it. People made babies long before they understood how DNA works. But the wider the range of possible manipulations, and the deeper one's knowledge of how such manipulations change the *explanandum phenomenon*, the more complete is the explanation. As Woodward puts it, a good explanation allows one to answer a range of "what-if-things-had-been-different questions" (w-questions, for short). Deep explanatory texts (or models) provide the resources to answer more questions about how the system will behave under a variety of changes than do shallow explanatory texts. The answers to such questions are evaluated experimentally according to the standards described above.

The manipulationist view readily satisfies criteria (E1)–(E5). Consider mere time-courses (E1). The ability to lay down long-term memories invariably appears after the development of the primary sexual characteristics, but (so far as I know) the latter is explanatorily irrelevant to the former. In contrast, delivery of a rapid and repeated stimulus to the pre-synaptic cell is explanatorily relevant to the entry of Ca^{2+} into the post-synaptic cell. The difference, according to the manipulationist account, is that one could not manipulate the ability to lay down long-term memories by intervening to change the development of primary sexual characteristics (so far as I know), but one can manipulate the tetanus to change the concentration of Ca^{2+} in the post-synaptic cell. This way of dealing with the difference between causation and regular succession has clear advantages over both regularity-based accounts of causation and certain counterfactual views. Both of these alternative views of causation treat at least some cases of regular temporal succession as cases of causation. This is because the values of the two variables, X and Y, are constantly conjoined (*ex hypothesi*) such that whenever the first variable occurs, the second does as well. One could then infer that if X takes a particular value, then Y will take the corresponding value. Nonetheless, it is not the case that one could change Y by intervening to change X. In cases of this sort, the relationship between X and Y supports what Lewis (1979) calls "backtracking counterfactuals," but, as Lewis notes, such counterfactuals are not explanatory. The manipulationist-based approach instead requires causal regularities to fulfill a more demanding requirement, namely that if X is set to x in accordance with (I1)–(I4), then Y will take on the value f(x). This kind of statement is tested in controlled experiments. Relations that meet this requirement allow one to answer w-questions.

The same strategy can be used to show why causal explanations tend to run from earlier to later (E2). The reason is that, at least in all known cases in neuroscience, one cannot change the past by intervening in current states of affairs. No matter what one does to the pre- or post-synaptic neuron now, one will not change the way that it behaved yesterday. There is no need to *insist* that all causes precede their effects on metaphysical grounds. There are still debates about whether backwards causation is possible in physics (see, for example, Price 1996). Were such a relationship to be demonstrated (using the sorts of ideal experimental manipulations discussed above), one would be justified in asserting that past events can be caused by future events and in asserting that at least in some cases one needs to appeal to future events to explain the past. However, there have been no such demonstrations in neuroscience, and this helps to explain the presumption that explanations in neuroscience are temporally asymmetrical.

Constraint (E3) is that two effects of a common cause do not explain one another in spite of the fact that the occurrence of one allows us to infer the occurrence of the other. Suppose that one pre-synaptic neuron (A) synapses upon two unconnected post-synaptic neurons, N_1 and N_2; that stimulating A reliably causes N_1 and N_2 to fire action potentials; and (for simplicity) that N_1 and N_2 are quiescent in the absence of activity in A. Let X be a variable representing the electrical activity of N_1 with the values {firing, not firing} , and let Y be a like-valued variable representing the electrical activity of N_2. Under these suppositions, one could reliably infer the value of X from the value of Y and vice versa because N_1 and N_2 always fire in tandem. That is, there is a robust regularity between X and Y that sustains certain backtracking counterfactuals. Were X to take the value {firing}, then Y would take the value {firing}. And if Y were to take the value {not firing}, then X would take the value {not firing} as well. However, one could not change X's activity by intervening directly to change Y. Nor could one change Y's value by intervening directly to change X. The regularities here do not satisfy requirement W. Examples such as this generalize: if the relationship between two variables is merely a correlation, then one will not be able to manipulate one variable by intervening to change the other. If the two are causally related, then one can manipulate one of them by manipulating the other.

The manipulationist approach also sorts relevant from irrelevant properties and interactions, as required by criterion (E4). (I extend this basic model considerably in Chapter 6 to address issues of nonfundamental causal relevance). To begin with the parson and his micropipette, while it may be true that all pyramidal cells blessed with holy water produce LTP when tetanized, the holy water is irrelevant. One can establish this by intervening in the above sense to remove the blessing, or to change the blessing to a curse, while leaving everything else the same. If one finds that such interventions have no effect on the occurrence (or incidence) of LTP, then one should conclude that the blessing is irrelevant to LTP. Of course, experiments are rarely so clean in the real world. In the history of LTP research, for example, it has been very difficult to determine which of the myriad interactions among intracellular molecules are relevant to the occurrence of LTP (see, for example, Sanes and Lichtman 1999). Part of the reason that these relevance relationships have been so difficult to disentangle is that the intracellular molecular cascades are so complex and causally interwoven that it is difficult to perform the sorts of ideal interventions described above. It is complex, in practice, to determine that one's intervention acts only on the target variable X, and that the intervention changes Y only via X and not through a host of myriad other connections. But these practical difficulties, which are part of what make science challenging and rewarding, do not impugn the overall idea that what one ideally wants to establish is precisely such well-controlled relationships of manipulability.

The final criterion, that the account of causation should allow for improbable effects (E5), requires only a slight modification of the basic argument scheme applied to (E1)–(E4). Many of the causal relationships posited in neuroscience are probabilistic. Tetanizing a pre-synaptic cell produces LTP only 50 percent of the time (with current techniques). If X and Y are only probabilistically related, then any particular intervention to change X might have no effects on Y. As remarked above, what the manipulationist account requires in such cases is that manipulating X changes the probability distribution over possible values for Y. For example, depolarizing the neuron should change the probability that the Na^+ channel will open or that the synapse will be potentiated. In neither case is it required that manipulating X makes Y probable (that is, $p(Y \mid X) > 0.5$). The probability of Y might be quite low even under the maximally effective manipulations of X. Indeed, this matches precisely the way that researchers assess stochastic relationships in neuroscience and elsewhere.

One last point requires emphasis. Nothing in this view of causal relevance makes reference to a privileged level at which all causes act or at which all relevant causes are located. Variables can be fundamental (spin, charm) or nonfundamental (socio-economic status, priming, inflation). All that matters is that they exhibit the patterns of manipulability discussed above.

5.3 Manipulation, omission, and prevention

A final promising feature of the manipulationist approach to causal relevance is that it accommodates causation by omission and prevention (see Woodward 2002). In cases of omission, such as when the absence of an attractive force allows the Mg^{2+} ion to float out of the NMDA receptor channel, what matters is not the transmission of marks or conserved quantities from the beginning of this mechanism to the end, but rather the fact that one can prevent the Mg^{2+} ion from floating out of the channel by polarizing the cell. Likewise in cases of prevention, such as when the Mg^{2+} ion blocks the channel and thereby prevents Ca^{2+} from entering the cell, what matters is not an exchange of conserved quantities between the Mg^{2+} ion and the non-increase in Ca^{2+} (for there can be no such exchange), but rather the fact that by manipulating the putative cause (positive or negative), one can make a difference in the putative effect (positive or negative).

The ability of the manipulationist account of causal relevance to satisfy (E1)–(E5) and to accommodate cases of negative causation is directly tied to the ability of such generalizations to answer w-questions. This ability provides the kind of rich information about the *explanandum phenomenon* that is typically required of a good explanation. When one knows the relations of manipulability, one can say which interventions make a difference to the *explanandum* and which do not (for example, mere temporal predecessors, temporal successors, irrelevant properties, and the like). In cases where interventions do make a difference, knowing these relations allows one to predict how the *explanandum phenomenon* will be different under a variety of conditions. There is a strong appeal in this connection given that one way to test one's understanding of a phenomenon (as any good test-writer knows) is to test whether someone can say how it will change in novel conditions.

6. Conclusion

This view of causal relevance adds an essential normative component to previous accounts of mechanistic explanation. For example, Bechtel and Richardson (1993), like Glennan (1996), argue that mechanistic explanations describe parts and their interactions, but they do not say how to sort interactions from correlations or relevant from irrelevant parts. My co-authors and I (Machamer et al. 2000) describe mechanisms as partly constituted by "activities productive of regular changes," but we do not say what distinguishes productive activities from mere correlations. The manipulationist account clearly makes some progress on this question: X is causally relevant to Y if one can manipulate Y (or, more generally, the probability distribution over values of Y) by intervening ideally on X. X is explanatorily relevant to Y if it is causally relevant.

It is worth noting how much progress can be made in thinking about causation and causal relevance without resolving metaphysical worries about the ultimate nature of causation. The manipulationist approach does not reduce talk of causation to some less problematic notion; the idea of manipulation is causal, and conditions (I1)–(I4) are all stated in causal terms. But it is not clear that a reductive account of causation can provide a satisfactory treatment of causal relevance (that is, one that satisfies (E1)–(E5)). An account of causal relevance should allow one to say which of a number of putative causes actually makes a difference to the effect even if it cannot alone resolve the question of what difference-making *really is*. The diverse examples discussed above (especially cases of omission and prevention) should cast some doubt on the thesis that there is one and only one thing answering to the word "causation." This is one reason why the manipulationist view also remains silent concerning the "hidden connection" between causes and effects. As I have argued, the search for such a connection has led more than one philosopher to develop an account of causation that includes no account of causal relevance. One can complain that the manipulationist account presupposes a metaphysics of causation, and refuse ascent until an account of the metaphysics is provided, or one can recognize the manipulationist account of causal relevance as a normative framework that any adequate metaphysics should satisfy, or better, explain. I do not discuss here whether such metaphysics is required or what the available metaphysical options are. Even if the manipulationist view does not identify the truth-maker for causal claims, it is nonetheless an illuminating analysis of the causal truths themselves, and it is crucial for the project of deciding which putative metaphysical explanations (that is, which truth-makers) are adequate and which are not.

Although I display some of the merits of the manipulationist approach relative to some competitors (mechanical and transmission accounts), I do not argue that one can make sense of causal relevance only by appeal to manipulability relations. I do not rule out the possibility that (E1)–(E5) might be satisfied by other accounts of causation. Nor do I rule out the possibility that there is more to learn about causation by investigating such alternatives. I believe, for example, that Hitchcock's comparative conception of the statistical dependency relations involved in causation (Hitchcock 1996) can help to remove certain ambiguities in the manipulationist approach (I build on this idea in Chapter 6). I believe further that the notion of "productive activities" developed by Machamer et al. (2000) and deployed by Craver and Darden (2001) and Darden and Craver (2003) is extremely useful for describing the history of science, for understanding aspects of scientific change, for thinking about how to build explanations, and for thinking about the metaphysics of causation (for a discussion of this issue, see Tabery 2004). Nonetheless, I now have a view of causal and explanatory relevance that can resolve some of the problems that plague the CL model, the U-model, and the PDP model. This seems to me a very friendly amendment to many current mechanistic views of etiological explanation, including my own (Machamer et al. 2000; Craver 2001). By supplementing the account of mechanisms in this way, one adds a normative dimension, showing what it means to correctly identify causally relevant factors within a mechanism. In the next chapter, I show how this view of causal relevance can be embedded within an account of mechanisms and can be extended to provide an account of *constitutive* explanatory relevance.

4

The Norms of Mechanistic Explanation

Summary

In this chapter, I develop a causal-mechanical model of constitutive explanation. The account satisfies two goals: first, to provide an alternative to classical reduction for thinking about constitutive explanation, and second, to show how the systems tradition (exemplified by Cummins's view of explanation as functional analysis) would have to be amended and revised if it is to offer a normatively adequate account of constitutive mechanistic explanation. I build my account by considering the discovery of the mechanism of the action potential and the diverse kinds of experiment required to show that a component is relevant to such a mechanism. The resulting view is a causal-mechanical competitor to reduction as a way of understanding interlevel relationships in neuroscience and beyond.

1. Introduction

Explanations in neuroscience describe mechanisms. Some mechanistic explanations are etiological; they explain an event by describing its antecedent causes. Dehydration is part of the etiological explanation of thirst. Prion proteins are part of the etiological explanation of Creutzfeldt-Jacob disease. Excessive repetition of the CAG nucleotide pattern on the fourth chromosome is part of the etiological explanation for Huntington's disease. Other mechanistic explanations are constitutive or componential;[1] they explain a phenomenon by describing its underlying mechanism. The NMDA receptor is part of the constitutive explanation of LTP. The hippocampus is part of the constitutive explanation for spatial memory. Ions are part of the constitutive explanation for the action potential. In this chapter, I develop a normatively adequate account of constitutive explanation.

There are two dominant and broad traditions of thought about constitutive explanation: the reductive tradition and the systems tradition. My view is a development and elaboration of one strand in the systems tradition.

The reductive tradition construes constitutive explanation as a species of CL explanation holding between theories at different levels. The explanation proceeds by constructing identity statements (or partial identity statements) between the kind-terms of the higher-level theory and those of the lower-level theory and then deriving the laws of the higher-level theory from the laws of the lower-level theory. The derivational requirement serves two purposes. First, it provides an epistemic account of explanation, according to which understanding is *rational expectation* of the *explanandum* on the basis of the *explanans* (in accordance with the nomic expectability thesis discussed in Chapter 2). Second, it offers a *regulative ideal* for explanation. If the explanation is ideally complete, one should literally be able to derive the *explanandum* from the *explanans*. Even if few explanations in neuroscience or elsewhere live up to this standard, the reduction model nonetheless provides a clear statement of what is required of an adequate explanation.

Although most philosophers of neuroscience (including John Bickle 1998, 2003; P. S. Churchland 1986; and Schaffner 1993a and b) fall in the reductive tradition, this classic view of reduction has few remaining advocates among philosophers of mind and philosophers of science. The most cited reason is that it is impossible to formulate the requisite identities because higher-level kinds are multiply realized by lower-level kinds to such an extent that there is no question of forming identities between the kind-terms in the higher-level theory and those in the lower-level theory. The conceptual taxonomies at different levels are askew, and therefore the one-to-one mapping that reduction requires is unlikely to fit the facts.

---

[1] I borrow the term "constitutive" from Salmon (1984). I mean by "constitutive" a relationship between the behavior of a mechanism as a whole and the organized activities of its individual components. I understand that the word "constitutive" is used for other purposes in metaphysics, but I am following Salmon's usage.

A second reason why reduction is unpopular is that real explanations in neuroscience look nothing like the explanations that the reduction model requires. Defenders of reduction have been forced to endorse the limited claim that the model serves mainly as a "regulative ideal" that is entirely "peripheral" to the practice of biology and neuroscience (see Schaffner 1974; P. M. Churchland 1989). A third, and least cited, reason why reduction has few supporters is that the deductive model of explanation on which reduction is premised has the varied shortcomings I discuss in Chapter 2. It is not sufficient to explain a theory merely to be able to derive it from another theory. The required derivation can be constructed on the basis of mere correlations, temporal sequences, effect-to-cause generalizations, and incomplete explanations.

The systems tradition, in contrast, construes explanation as a matter of decomposing systems into their parts and showing how those parts are organized together in such a way as to exhibit the *explanandum phenomenon*. In this tradition, I include philosophers of biology and psychology who discuss explanation by functional analysis (Fodor 1968; Cummins 1975, 1983, 2000), by decomposition (Simon 1969; Wimsatt 1974; Haugeland 1998), by identifying homunculi (Fodor 1968; Dennett 1978; Lycan 1987), by reverse engineering (Dennett 1994), by taking the design stance (Dennett 1987), by describing the articulation of parts (Kauffman 1971), and, finally, by discovering mechanisms (Bechtel and Richardson 1993; Glennan 2002). Lycan, following Dennett (1978), describes this form of explanation with the metaphor of little men:

We explain the successful activity of one homunculus not by idly positing a second homunculus within it that successfully performs the activity, but by positing a team consisting of several smaller, individually less talented and more specialized homunculi—and detailing the ways in which the team members cooperate in order to produce their joint or corporate output. (Lycan 1987; in Lycan 1999: 51)

Dretske mobilizes several different metaphors in his article, "If you can't make one, you don't know how it works":

All I mean to be suggesting by my provocative title is something about the spirit of philosophical naturalism. It is motivated by a constructivist's model of understanding. It embodies something like an engineer's ideal, a designer's vision, of what it takes to really know how something works. You need a blueprint, a recipe, an instruction manual, a program. (Dretske 1994: 468)

Cummins's account of explanation by functional analysis is the most rigorous formulation of the systems tradition prior to recent discussions of mechanisms and mechanistic explanation. I reference Cummins's account throughout this chapter. On his view, the *explanandum* is some capacity ψ of a system S. S's ψ-ing is explained by analyzing it into subcapacities $\{\phi_1, \phi_2, \ldots, \phi_n\}$ and showing that ψ is produced through the programmed exercise of the subcapacities. To show that ψ can be produced, in this sense, through the programmed exercise of the subcapacities, one specifies a box-and-arrow diagram showing how the subcomponents work together such that they ψ. For example, the capacity of the neuron (S) to generate action potentials (ψ) would presumably be explained by a box-and-arrow diagram that exhibits the programmed exercise of such capacities as rotating, changing conformation, and diffusing.

As Cummins's account illustrates, systems explanations involve showing how something works rather than showing that its behavior can be derived from more fundamental laws (Dretske 1994; Cummins 2000; Bechtel and Abrahamsen 2005). This view of explanation has several advantages over the model required by the reductive tradition. For example, it does not matter for the systems tradition that the *explanandum phenomena* might be multiply realized. If the multiple realizability of nonfundamental phenomena raises a problem for classical reduction (there is debate on this matter), it is because classical reduction requires the translation of kind-terms in one theory into those of another theory. Translation is not required because the systems tradition rejects the idea that explanations are arguments. All that matters is that the phenomenon is realized by some underlying mechanism. Furthermore, systems explanations are not peripheral to the practice of neuroscience; they are much more accurate descriptions of neuroscientific explanations than the reduction model supplies. Finally, systems explanations need not inherit the limitations of the CL model; they promise an altogether different vision of scientific explanation.

But what, exactly, is that alternative vision of explanation? What does it mean to "know how something works" or to "reduce a capacity to the programmed exercise of sub-capacities" if not that one can derive the behavior of a mechanism as a whole from the organized behaviors of its parts? What distinguishes good constitutive explanations from bad? What does it mean to have a complete systems explanation? How does one decide which parts should be included in a systems explanation and which parts are irrelevant? If the systems tradition is to present a complete alternative to reduction, then it must provide an alternative set of norms by which explanations should be assessed. Otherwise, it provides an adequate surface description of constitutive explanations in neuroscience without challenging the core idea of explanation underlying classical reduction.

In this chapter, I construct a normatively adequate *mechanistic* model of constitutive explanation (henceforth, mechanistic explanation). Chapter 1, Section 2 contains a sketch and overview of my basic position. Those wanting merely a summary should consult that sketch and the conclusion of this chapter. The primary purpose of this chapter is to move beyond that sketch and to show how the simple idea of explanation by decomposition can be made precise and normatively rigorous. In doing so, I present a more detailed and elaborate exposition of the systems tradition than is currently available, and I provide it with the tools to challenge reduction as a normative model of constitutive explanation in neuroscience and beyond.

I construct my model of mechanistic explanation to serve two ends: (1) to distinguish how–possibly explanations from how–actually explanations, and (2) to distinguish mechanism sketches from mechanism schemata. These distinctions are introduced in Section 2. In Section 3, I illustrate progress along these two dimensions by considering how neuroscientists moved beyond the Hodgkin and Huxley model of the action potential in order to provide a complete explanation of the conductance changes constituting the action potential. In subsequent sections, I show how Cummins's account of functional analysis (and so the systems tradition generally) can be supplemented and transformed to become an account of mechanistic explanation that rivals reduction as a regulative ideal for explanation. The regulative ideal is that constitutive explanations must describe all and only the component entities, activities, properties, and organizational features that are relevant to the multifaceted phenomenon to be explained. I build my account slowly by considering separate aspects of mechanistic explanation sequentially. These include:

(i) the nature of the *explanandum phenomenon* (Section 4);
(ii) the constitutive relationship between a phenomenon and its components (Section 5);

(iii) the difference between real components and useful fictions (Section 5);
(iv) the nature of capacities or activities (Section 6);
 (v) the nature of mechanistic organization (Section 7); and
(vi) the nature of constitutive explanatory relevance (Section 8).

This last topic—the problem of saying what it means for a component to be explanatorily relevant to a phenomenon—has thus far been entirely neglected by both the systems tradition and the reduction tradition. In Section 8, which could be considered a chapter within this chapter, I introduce this problem and offer a causal-mechanical solution.

2. Two Normative Distinctions

Throughout this chapter, I am guided by two normative distinctions that are implicit in the practices of constructing and evaluating mechanistic explanations. An adequate account of mechanistic explanation should help one to understand how these distinctions are drawn.

First, the proposed account should have resources adequate to distinguish how-possibly models from how-actually models. *How-possibly models* have explanatory purport, but they are only loosely constrained conjectures about the sort of mechanism that might suffice to produce the *explanandum phenomenon*. They describe how a set of parts and activities might be organized together such that they exhibit the *explanandum phenomenon*. One might have no idea if the conjectured parts exist or, if they do, whether they are capable of engaging in the activities attributed to them in the model. Some computer models are purely how-possibly models. For example, one might simulate aspects of the visual system in LISP without any commitment to the idea that the brain is somehow executing CARs and CDRs (the basic operations of LISP) through its neural networks. How-possibly models are often heuristically useful in constructing and exploring the space of possible mechanisms, but they are not adequate explanations. *How-actually models*, in contrast, describe real components, activities, and organizational features of the mechanism that in fact produces the phenomenon. They show how a mechanism works, not merely how it might work. Between these extremes is a range of *how-plausibly* models that are more or less consistent with the known constraints on the components, their activities, and their organization.² To continue Dennett and Lycan's metaphor for functional analysis, without some restrictions on who can be a homunculus, on which homunculi are on the team, and on how the team members work together to produce a corporate output, the account of explanation lacks the resources to distinguish how-possibly from how-actually explanations. One guiding question in this chapter is: How would one have to restrict functional analysis to distinguish how-possibly from how-actually mechanistic explanations?³

Second, the account of mechanistic explanation should distinguish mechanism sketches from complete mechanistic models. A *mechanism sketch* is an incomplete model of a mechanism. It characterizes some parts, activities, or features of the mechanism's organization, but it leaves gaps. Sometimes gaps are marked in visual diagrams by black boxes or question marks. More problematically, sometimes they are masked by *filler terms* that give the illusion that the explanation is complete when it is not. A list of common filler terms in neuroscience is shown in Table 4.1. Terms such as "activate," "inhibit," "encode," "cause," "produce," "process," and "represent" are often used to indicate a kind of activity in a mechanism without providing any detail about exactly what activity fills that role. Black boxes, question marks, and acknowledged filler terms are innocuous when they stand as place-holders for future work or when it is possible to replace the filler term with some stock-in-trade property, entity, activity, or mechanism (as is the case for "coding" in DNA).⁴ In contrast, filler terms are barriers to progress when they veil failures of understanding. If the term "encode" is used to

Table 4.1. Common filler terms in neuroscience

Activate	Generate	Process
Cause	Influence	Recognize
Control	Inform	Represent
Encode	Inhibit	Regulate
Excite	Modulate	Store
Filter		

---

² Both the distinctions among how-possibly, how-plausibly, and how-actually descriptions and between a schema and a sketch are introduced in Machamer et al. (2000). (The term "how-possibly explanation" is used in Brandon 1990).

³ I do not claim that all explanations are mechanistic explanations.

⁴ Stock-in-trade items (cf. Kauffman 1971) are those that are accepted and understood by a science at a time; they are part of its ontic store (Craver and Darden 2001).

stand for "some-process-we-know-not-what," and if the provisional status of that term is forgotten, then one has only an illusion of understanding. For this reason, neuroscientists often denigrate the authors of black-box models as "diagram makers" or "boxologists." Between sketches and complete descriptions lies a continuum of *mechanism schemata* whose working is only partially understood. A second guiding question in this chapter is: how would one have to restrict the systems tradition to distinguish sketches, schemata, and complete descriptions of mechanisms?

Progress in building mechanistic explanations involves movement along both the possibly-plausibly-actually axis and along the sketch-schema-mechanism axis. I now describe how neuroscientists made such progress in the discovery of the mechanism of the action potential.

3. Explaining the Action Potential

The history of the discovery of the mechanism of the action potential serves three purposes in this chapter. First, it provides an example of a successful mechanistic explanation. Second, it illustrates the distinctions that I have just introduced. And, finally, it illustrates many of the norms implicit in the practice of constructing constitutive mechanistic explanations.

I begin where I leave off in Chapter 2. In 1952, Hodgkin and Huxley constructed a mathematical model of the action potential, which they characterize in terms of a list of features (a)–(h) (see Chapter 2, Section 6). They began their project with a background sketch of a mechanism. They knew some of its entities and activities. They knew that action potentials are produced by the movement of ions across a lipid membrane. They knew that action potentials are produced by depolarizing the cell body (that is, by making V_m greater than V_{rest}).[5] And they knew that the shape of the action potential, as described in (a)–(h), could possibly be produced by the voltage-dependent *activation* and *inactivation* of membrane conductance for specific ions, as represented by the variables n, m, and h in their total current equation. Hodgkin and Huxley did not engage in boxology. They used the more informative representational conventions for diagramming electrical circuits shown in Figure 4.1. Left to right, in parallel, are a capacitor and

[5] Here I neglect the possibility of spontaneous action potentials, resulting from the stochastic opening of even a few Na^+ channels.

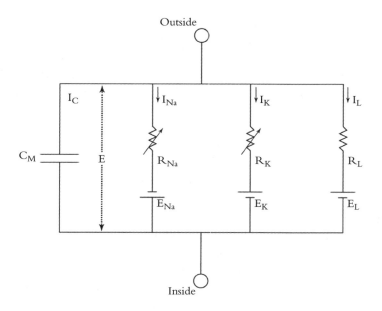

Figure 4.1. The equivalent circuit model of the neuronal membrane*

* I is current, R is resistance, E is the equilibrium potential, and C is capacitance

three pathways for the component currents in the total current equation. Each of the three pathways contains a battery (representing the equilibrium potential for the ion) and a resistor (the inverse of conductance for the ion) in series. The HH model shows that the coordinated changes in the resistances to Na^+ and K^+ currents could account for items a–h.

The primary reason for calling this background mechanistic model a *sketch* is that "activation" and "inactivation" are filler terms. Hodgkin and Huxley (1952) consider some ways to complete these filler terms. They consider the possibility that ions are conveyed across the membrane by active transport. They suggest that perhaps a number of "activation" particles could weaken the integrity of the membrane. They hint at a biological interpretation of their model according to which activation and inactivation particles move around in the membrane and somehow change the membrane's resistance. They admit, however, that they have no evidence favoring their model over other possible models. This admission spurred research on the biophysics of the membrane and the search for ion channels. Nonetheless, well into the 1970s most neuroscientists regarded talk of ion-specific channels as mere metaphor at best and boxology at worst.

C. M. Armstrong (1981) and Bertil Hille (1992) among others elevated talk of ion-specific channels above the status of filler terms. On Hille's model, which is now textbook neuroscience, the conductance changes in action potentials are explained by the temporally coordinated opening and closing of transmembrane channels. Action potentials are generated in the axon hillock, a region at the interface of the cell body and the axon, the "sending" end of a neuron. The hillock is rich in Na^+ channels, and depolarizing the cell body opens these voltage-sensitive Na^+ channels. The resulting increase in membrane conductance (as represented by the dotted line in Figure 4.2) allows Na^+ ions to diffuse from the Na^+-rich extracellular fluid into the relatively Na^+-poor intracellular fluid. This inward Na^+ current is balanced at low values by the effects of depolarization on outward K^+ and leakage currents, the latter of which I ignore for the moment. Above a threshold depolarization, the high voltage sensitivity and rapid activation of the Na^+ channel overwhelms these balancing currents. The flood of Na^+ drives the voltage of the cell towards the Na^+ equilibrium potential (E_{Na}; roughly $+55$ mV), where the forces of diffusion and voltage balance. This flood accounts for the rapid rising phase of the action potential.

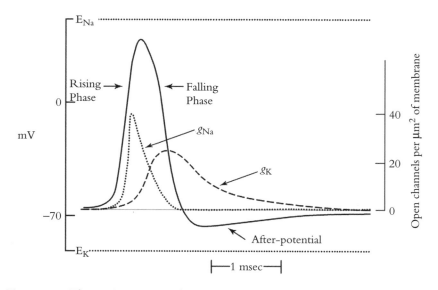

Figure 4.2. The action potential superimposed on a graph of changes in the membrane's conductance for Na^+ and K^+

Depolarizing the membrane has two consequences that account for the declining phase of the action potential. The first is inactivation of Na^+ channels, which slows and eventually stops the ascent of V_m towards E_{Na}. The second is activation of voltage-sensitive K^+ channels, which increases the K^+ conductance of the membrane (as indicated by the dashed line in Figure 4.2) and allows K^+ to diffuse from the K^+-rich intracellular fluid into the relatively K^+-poor extracellular fluid. The diffusion of K^+ out of the cell drives the membrane potential back down towards the K^+ equilibrium potential (E_K; roughly -75 mV) and even below the resting potential of the membrane.

Thus begins the after-potential phase of the action potential, characterized by both hyperpolarization of the membrane (that is, V_m is lower than V_{rest}) and reduced excitability of the neuron. The membrane hyperpolarizes after the action potential because K^+ channels are slow to return to their resting closed state (they are sometimes called "delayed rectifiers" for this reason). The K^+ current tugs V_m away from V_{rest} and towards E_K. This hyperpolarization makes the neuron less excitable, because a larger depolarization is required to move V_m to the threshold for an action potential. This refractory effect is reinforced by the residual inactivation of Na^+ channels, which temporarily prevents them from conducting Na^+ ions. The above is the intermediate elaboration of the action potential mechanism as it appeared when talk of channels gained acceptance through the 1970s and 1980s.

Still, Armstrong and Hille's intermediate elaboration remains a sketch. It fills in some of the details. For example, talk of channels replaces less precise talk about activation and inactivation of conductances, and the focus on channels eliminates speculation about active transport across the membrane. But filler terms remain. In particular, questions remain about how *channels* "activate" and "inactivate." To illustrate how these filler terms were replaced and how how-possibly models gave way to how-actually mechanisms, I focus specifically on how rising membrane voltage can activate and, at higher voltages, inactivate, the Na^+ channel. Hille started work on these mechanisms by conjecturing the set of how-possibly models shown in Figure 4.3. These models of the mechanism have different parts, with different activities, organized in different ways. There are swinging gates, sliding gates, free-floating blockers, tethered balls and chains, rotating cylinders, and assembling components. Hille intended these as merely how-possibly models because he had no idea whether channels would turn

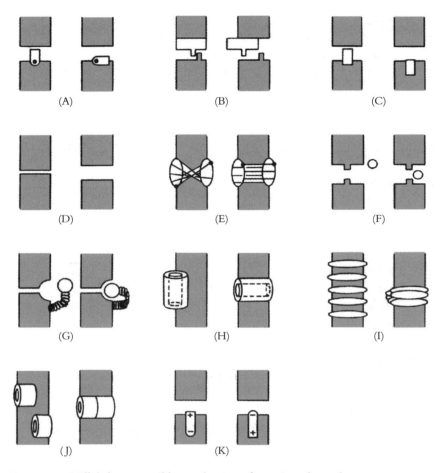

Figure 4.3. Hille's how-possibly mechanisms for gating channels
Source: Reprinted with permission from Hille (1992: 479)

out to have parts of the requisite sort, or whether the parts could act as the model requires, or whether their activities were organized in the way that the model suggests. Hille (1992) rules out many of these how-possibly mechanisms in the face of known constraints and plausibility arguments, leaving only A, B, and C as contenders to account for activation. None of these, however, anticipates the model that subsequently emerged from several independent lines of investigation.

Clues about the Na^+ channel came from sequencing the channel protein, reconstructing its three-dimensional structure, identifying its hydrophilic and hydrophobic regions (hydrophilic regions are more likely to be inside the membrane, and hydrophobic regions are more likely to be outside) and recording the behavior of individual Na^+ channels under a range of electrical, pharmacological, and genetic interventions.[6] These studies show that the Na^+ channel consists of four subunits, each of which is composed of six membrane-spanning regions (see Figure 4.4). One membrane-spanning region, known as the S4 region, is arranged such that every third amino acid residue is either arginine or lysine. This ordering produces a helical structure, known as an α-helix, with evenly spaced positive charges (see Figure 4.5). At V_{rest}, a positive extracellular potential holds the α-helix in place. Weakening that potential, which happens when the cell is depolarized, allows the helix to rotate out toward the extracellular side (carrying a "gating charge" as positively charged amino acids move outward). This rotation, which occurs in each of the Na^+ channel's subunits, destabilizes the balance of forces holding the channel in its closed state and bends the pore-lining S6 region in such a way as to open a channel through the membrane. Another consequence of these conformation changes is that the pore through the channel is lined with hairpin turn structures, the charge distribution along which accounts for the channel's selectivity to Na^+. Part of the evidence for these conclusions comes from experiments involving site-specific mutagenesis: point mutations induced in the α-helix prevent the channel from opening, and mutations to the hairpin turn regions alter the channel's ion selectivity. The α-helix and the hairpin turn are thus parts of a more complete how-actually model of the rising phase of the action potential.

How does the Na^+ channel close? The currently accepted hypothesis invokes the ball-and-chain model shown in (G) of Hille's diagram. One of the protein subunits composing the channel is thought to contain a long protein strand on the intracellular side of the membrane that terminates in a small "ball" of protein. As V_m reaches a threshold value, this proteinaceous ball and chain swings into the channel, blocking the flow of Na^+ ions. Evidence for this hypothesis includes the fact that removing the ball and chain, either with site-specific mutations or with a pharmacological agent, eliminates inactivation entirely.

---

[6] For a more detailed discussion, see Catterall (2000) and Hille (1992).

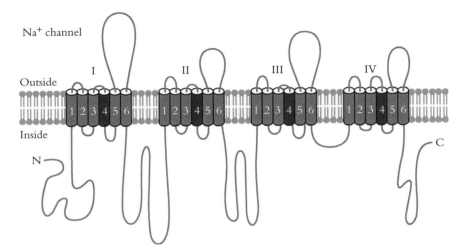

Figure 4.4. Transmembrane regions of the Na^+ channel
Source: Adapted from Hall (1992: 109)

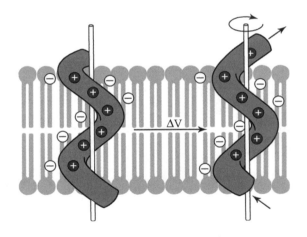

Figure 4.5. A plausible mechanism for activating Na^+ channels*
* An α-helix with regularly spaced positive charges rotates outward
Source: Redrawn from Hall (1992: 112)

There is a great deal more to be said about the mechanisms of Na^+ channel activation and inactivation. Recent studies of the Shaker K^+ using X-ray crystallography and electron microscopy provide detailed accounts of the internal structure of voltage-sensitive K^+ channels and are leading researchers both to recognize multiple voltage-sensitive regions in channels and to rethink how these voltage-sensitive components work. (For a recent review, see Swartz 2004). The above rotating-helix model of voltage-sensing in the Na^+ channel now has competitors, although it is not currently clear which, if any, is the how–actually model (see Sands, Grottesi, and Sansom 2005). On one model, the S4 region does not move substantially across the membrane but rather causes other parts of the channel to do so, thereby accounting for the gating charge. According to another model, parts of the S4 and S3 regions form paddle-like structures on the external surface of the channel that translocate en masse during voltage changes, thereby opening the channel. According to a third model, two segments within the S4 region twist relative to one another, exposing a channel through the membrane. Although these details are exciting, and although they illuminate the structure of the Na^+ channel, the above textbook sketch is sufficient to reveal the relevant features of mechanistic explanation that I focus on in the remainder of this chapter.

This textbook sketch of one component of the mechanism for the action potential calls attention to three aspects of mechanistic explanation. First, mechanistic explanations are framed by the *explanandum phenomenon* (represented at the top of Figure 4.6), in this case, the action potential as partially described by Hodgkin and Huxley's items (a)–(h). Second, the explanation is *constitutive*; the action potential is explained by reference to component parts of the action potential mechanism. There are component

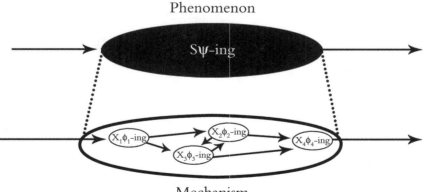

Figure 4.6. A phenomenon (top) and its mechanism (bottom)

entities (the parts), such as ions, ion channels, α-helices, and protein chains, and there are component *activities*, such as diffusion and changes in conformation. The circles and arrows at the bottom of Figure 4.6 represent the mechanism's entities and activities. Third, these entities and activities are *organized* together such that they jointly exhibit the phenomenon to be explained. It matters, for example, that the α-helix contains evenly spaced positive charges, and that the ball at the end of the chain is large enough to block the channel, and that the thresholds for activation and inactivation of the channels are such as to explain the temporal features of the conductance changes. In short, mechanistic models describe how constituent entities and activities are organized to exhibit a phenomenon (compare Bechtel and Richardson 1993; Glennan 1996; Kauffman 1971; Machamer et al. 2000).

Cummins's account of functional analysis can be grafted onto the abstract diagram in Figure 4.6. S's ψ-ing represents the *explanandum phenomenon*, and the circles and arrows represent the analyzing capacities $\{\phi_1, \phi_2, \ldots, \phi_n\}$. This is why functional analysis provides an appropriate starting place for constructing an adequate account of mechanistic explanation. However, Cummins intends his account of explanation to be more general than mechanistic explanation, including in addition what he calls "interpretive explanations," and his effort to develop such a general account prevents him from supplying the kind of detail required for an adequate account of mechanistic explanation. Cummins's commitment to functionalism also leads him to a view of explanation that is abstracted away from the details of the mechanism that realize the functions. This abstraction makes Cummins's account inappropriate as an account of specifically *mechanistic* explanation. In what follows, I show how the basic structure of Cummins's account would have to be elaborated and transformed to provide a normatively adequate account of mechanistic explanations—that is, an account that can distinguish how-possibly from how-actually models, and sketches from complete mechanistic models. Such an account rivals reduction as a normative account of constitutive explanation.

4. The *Explanandum Phenomenon*

The core normative requirement on mechanistic explanations is that they must fully account for the *explanandum phenomenon*. As Kauffman (1971) and Glennan (1996, 2002) argue, mechanisms are always mechanisms *of* a given phenomenon. The mechanism of protein synthesis synthesizes proteins. The mechanism of the action potential generates action potentials. The boundaries of mechanisms—what is in the mechanism and what is not—are fixed by reference to the phenomenon that the mechanism explains. Consider some ways that a description of the phenomenon can fail. These failures provide clues to the standards of success.

One way that the search for mechanistic explanations can fail is by trying to explain a fictional phenomenon. Prior to Galvani's eighteenth-century work on animal electricity, natural philosophers entertained a number of hypotheses about how nerves work (see Pera 1992). Descartes and Borelli believed that nerves are hollow conduits for the flow of animal spirits, and that they activate muscles by inflating them. Starting with this idea, one would be led to search for mechanisms that explain, for example, how nerves shunt the flow of animal spirits into this nerve or that, how they activate muscles, and how light or auditory stimuli impact upon this hydraulic machine. David Hartley, the self-proclaimed Newton of the Mind, believed that neurons work by vibrating. He sought to understand how such vibrations could be distinguished from one another, how they could be stored in the "medullary substance," and how the occurrence of one vibration might cause another to be produced (as demanded by his associationist view of memory). Just as the CL model requires that the *explanandum* sentence should be true, the mechanistic model requires that the *explanandum phenomenon* should exist.

Slightly less obvious are the diverse *taxonomic* errors that one might make in characterizing the phenomenon. If the goal is to provide a mechanistic explanation, the phenomena should be delimited in such a way that they correspond to underlying mechanisms.[7] One kind of taxonomic error is a *lumping error,* which involves assuming that several distinct phenomena are actually one. Cognitive neuroscientists of memory, for example, argue that they have made progress on this front. Daniel Schacter writes that: "We have now come to believe that memory is not a single or unitary faculty

---

[7] One need not enter the process of discovery with the right taxonomy of phenomena. As Churchland and Sejnowski (1992) illustrate, neuroscientists' understanding of a phenomenon often "co-evolves" with their understanding of underlying mechanisms. Bechtel and Richardson (1993) argue that this co-evolution frequently involves "reconstituting the phenomenon" in the process of searching for mechanisms.

of the mind, as was long assumed. Instead, it is composed of a variety of distinct and dissociable processes and systems. Each system depends on a particular constellation of networks in the brain that involve different neural structures, each of which plays a highly specialized role within the system"(Schacter 1996: 5).[8]

Conversely, one might commit a *splitting error*, which involves incorrectly assuming that one phenomenon is many. For example, it was once assumed that rusting, burning, and breathing are different phenomena with different mechanisms rather than different expressions of a common oxidation mechanism. Taxonomic errors are not always confined to single phenomena, but sometimes infect entire taxonomies. Franz Joseph Gall (1810–19), for example, believed that philosophers were wrong to explain the mind in terms of such mere abstractions as action, memory, perception, cogitation, and will. Gall's system, in contrast, was tailored to identify the set of talents that might vary from individual to individual. His organological map contains cranial regions dedicated to the instinct to murder, tenderness for one's offspring, mechanical skill, facility with colors and coloring, and the impulse to propagation. Contemporary cognitive scientists have a different taxonomy. They divide the mind into such phenomena as motion detection, working memory, change blindness, and pitch perception. The point of this comparison is that it is possible that an entire taxonomic system could be ill-matched to the mechanistic structures of the brain. If so, the taxonomic system is clearly not suited to the search for mechanistic explanations.[9]

One can also err by underspecifying the phenomenon. What is required to fully characterize the *explanandum phenomenon*?[10] For Cummins, the *explanandum phenomenon* is a capacity or disposition, ψ.

To attribute a disposition [ψ] to an object [S] is to assert that the behavior of [S] is subject to (exhibits or would exhibit) a certain law-like regularity: to say [S] has

---

[8] Similar arguments are given by Weiskrantz (1990), Schacter and Tulving (1994), and Squire and Knowlton (1994). Such arguments have been discussed by Churchland and Sejnowski (1989); Bechtel and Richardson (1993).

[9] Note that I have not said that this is ground for eliminating the taxonomy. Mismatch between phenomena and the mechanistic structure of the world need not carry eliminativist implications.

[10] Some workers in the systems tradition assume or stipulate that all *explanandum phenomena* have been selected by evolution by natural selection (Lycan 1987, in Lycan 1999: 52–3; Schouten and Looren de Jong 1998: 242–5) or that the phenomena are otherwise adaptive (that is, the phenomenon is how something behaves when it is behaving properly; see Bechtel 1986; Mundale and Bechtel 1996: 485). In the philosophy of biology, Cummins is best known for his attacks on Wright's (1973) adaptive view

[ψ] is to say that [S] should manifest [ψ] (shatter, dissolve) were any of a certain range of events to occur ([S] is put into water, [S] is struck sharply). (Cummins 1975, in Sober 1984: 401)[11]

Several years later, Cummins reiterates: "A capacity is specified by giving a special law linking precipitating conditions to manifestations—that is, by specifying input–output conditions" (Cummins 1983: 53). This terse characterization of the phenomenon downplays the wealth of detail that can be used to distinguish how-possibly from how-actually explanations and to distinguish sketches from complete descriptions of mechanisms.[12] Consider some dimensions along which this basic characterization might be elaborated.

Phenomena are typically *multifaceted*. Action potentials are complex phenomena, when compared to shattering and dissolving. Part of characterizing the action potential phenomenon involves noting that action potentials are produced under a given range of *precipitating conditions* (for example, a range of depolarizations in the cell body or axon hillock). But, as Hodgkin and Huxley's (a)–(h) illustrate, there is more to be said about the *manifestations* of an action potential. It is necessary to describe its rate of rise, its peak magnitude, its rate of decline, its refractory period, and so on. Consider, for example, how different values of the peak magnitude of the action potential demand (and exclude) different mechanistic explanations. In 1902, Julius Bernstein hypothesized that nerve impulses might be produced by a sudden breakdown in membrane resistance. If so, the action potential should peak at a value no higher than 0 mV. And so it was widely believed until the 1930s, when Kenneth Cole and Howard Curtis (1939) confirmed that the membrane resistance drops by roughly two orders of magnitude during

---

of functions. I side with Cummins. Neuroscientific explanations often focus on malfunctions, disease states, laboratory phenomena, pharmaceutical contrivances, and industrial and military applications (for example, how the vestibular system works in zero-gravity). There also seems no reason to presuppose that all of the functions currently operating in organisms have selective histories. Traits can become entrenched through genetic drift and exaptation. The considerations below also provide reasons for concluding that adaptive functional characterizations of the phenomenon omit much of the crucial information for distinguishing how-possibly from how-actually models. No doubt, some of the features of the brain have straightforward adaptive etiologies, but I do not want to presuppose for present purposes that all of them do. Either way, one still needs the more limited sense of role-functions, activities that make some crucial contribution to the behavior of a containing system (Cummins 1975; Craver 2001).

[11] I have changed the variables for consistency.

[12] Cummins (2000) has explicitly abandoned this connection between functional analysis and laws (more about which in Section 6).

the action potential. However, Hodgkin and Huxley (1939) demonstrated that the action potential overshoots 0 mV, peaking at +40 to +50 mV. Curtis and Cole (1940) later redid these experiments with a different kind of electrode and found much higher peak magnitudes. They published one of their most dramatic examples of the overshoot, which peaked at +110 mV. Because the Na^+ equilibrium potential is roughly +55 mV, Hodgkin and Huxley's finding was consistent with the possibility that the rising phase of the action potential is constituted by a breakdown in the resistance to Na^+. Curtis and Cole's finding, on the other hand, could not be explained by that mechanism (or at least not by that mechanism alone). Note that this is only one of multiple aspects of the manifestation of the action potential. If the peak magnitude can be characterized as an "output," then the action potential is characterized by a very large array of input–output relationships, each of which must be satisfied by any explanatory model of the mechanism. The understanding of the action potential has expanded considerably since 1952. A how-possibly model that accounts for features (a)–(h), but not the subsequent discoveries concerning action potentials, would be merely a how-possibly model. It would not explain the action potential.

Second, it is insufficient to characterize the phenomenon only under standard precipitating conditions. A complete characterization of the phenomenon requires one to know its *inhibiting conditions*—that is, the conditions under which the phenomenon fails to occur. Action potentials can be prevented, for example, by applying tetrodotoxin (TTX), which blocks the flow of Na^+ through Na^+ channels, or by removing Na^+ from the extracellular fluid. If one truly understands the mechanism of the action potential, one should be able to say why they are *not* produced under these conditions. A complete characterization of the phenomenon also requires knowing the phenomenon's *modulating conditions*—that is, knowing how variations in conditions alter the action potential. For example, one wants to know how the action potential changes if one changes the neuron's diameter, or the density of ion channels in a given stretch of membrane, or the extracellular concentration of Na^+. One has not fully characterized the action potential unless one also knows how it behaves under a variety of *non-standard conditions*. Most laboratory conditions are nonstandard. If one connects a squid giant axon (the experimental system in which most of these experiments were performed) to a space clamp or a voltage clamp (crucial experimental innovations in this historical episode), one observes the behavior of cells under conditions that would never occur in a normal organism. Although such experiments are not physiologically relevant (that is, relevant to the behavior of neurons in a normal cell under standard operating conditions),[13] they are nonetheless part of how the mechanism works if manipulated in specific ways. Two how–possibly mechanisms can account equally well for the capacity of a neuron to produce standard action potentials under physiologically normal precipitating conditions but nonetheless diverge considerably in their ability to account for features of action potentials in inhibiting, modulating, and otherwise nonstandard conditions.

A variety of *by-products* or side effects of the phenomenon can also be crucial for sorting how-possibly from how–actually models and sketches from complete mechanistic models. By-products include a range of possible features that are of no functional significance for the phenomenon (for example, they do not play any role in a higher-level mechanism) but are nonetheless crucial for distinguishing mechanisms that otherwise account equally well for the phenomenon. Cummins now recognizes that describing phenomena as capacities is an oversimplification, and that it is often "a matter of some substance" to specify what the *explanandum* is (Cummins 2000: 123–4):

Given two theories or models of the same capacity, associated incidental effects can be used to distinguish between them. ... Even when two models are not weakly equivalent, they may be on a par empirically, that is, close enough that the differences between them are plausibly attributed to such factors as experimental error, idealization, and the like. Again, incidental effects that may have no great interest as explananda in their own right may serve to distinguish such cases (2000: 124).

As noted above, the activation of Na^+ channels is accompanied by a gating charge, a very slight movement of charges across the membrane. Why

---

[13] "Normal" and "standard" conditions amount to something like "the way that the mechanism behaves under the conditions that we consider most appropriate for our current explanatory purposes." Sometimes this is assessed in terms of the healthy and fit organism, and normal means something like "behavior consistent with or conducive to overall system health and function." Sometimes it is assessed in terms of evolutionary stories, and so means something like "behavior similar to that which preserved the trait in the population of organisms." Sometimes normalcy is assessed in terms of its utility for an experiment, and so means something like "behavior consistent with or conducive to manipulation and detection with my experimental protocol." There is no need to be more restrictive about this notion. "Normal" and "standard" are defined relative to an implied investigative context.

is there a gating charge? According to the standard textbook model, the activation of Na^+ channels involves rotating an α-helix, which is composed of regularly spaced positive charges (see Figure 4.5). It turns out that the gating current is precisely equal to the amount of charge moved across the membrane as the α-helix rotates. All of the competing models of voltage sensor mentioned in Section 3 have to, and are designed to, accommodate the gating charge. Gating charge apparently plays no role in the electrical activities of nerve cells, but it is nonetheless an aspect of the voltage sensor, and it is one that any how-actually model has to account for.[14]

In summary, mechanistic explanations can fail because one has tried to explain a fictitious phenomenon, because one has mischaracterized the phenomenon, and because one has characterized the phenomenon to be explained only partially. One can conjecture a mechanism that adequately accounts for some narrow range of features of the phenomenon, but that cannot accommodate the rest. For this reason, descriptions of the multiple features of a phenomenon, of its precipitating, inhibiting, modulating, and nonstandard conditions, and of its by-products, all constrain mechanistic explanations and help to distinguish how-possibly from how-actually explanations. Similarly, mechanism sketches, with large gaps and question marks, can explain some aspects of the *explanandum phenomenon* but fail to explain others. Hodgkin and Huxley's background sketch explains the shape of the action potential in terms of changes in component currents, but the sketch does not explain the conductance changes that regulate the current flow. To characterize the phenomenon correctly and completely is a crucial step in turning a functional analysis into an acceptable mechanistic explanation.

5. Components

Mechanistic explanations are *constitutive* or componential explanations: they explain the behavior of the mechanism as a whole in terms of the organized activities and interactions of its *components*. Components are the entities in a mechanism—what are commonly called "parts." Action potentials are

---

[14] Such by-products are not functionally relevant but they nonetheless are part of the phenomenon to be explained. This is an additional reason to think that the character of the phenomenon should not be restricted to those features that contributed to survival, or that contribute to current health, etc.

explained by appeal to components such as Na^+ and K^+ channels, ions, and protein chains.

This is a crucial point of contrast between my mechanistic view of constitutive explanation and Cummins's account of functional analysis. Unlike other exponents of the systems tradition, Cummins insists that, "it is important to keep functional analysis and componential analysis conceptually distinct" (Cummins 1983: 29, 2000: 123). He insists on this point because he wants to allow for *non*constitutive analytic explanations—analytic explanations in which both the analyzed and the analyzing capacities (ψ and ϕ, respectively) are capacities of the system as a whole.[15] He gives the following example: if one wants to explain how a cook (S) bakes a cake (ψ), one will appeal to analyzing capacities (ϕ) that are also "cook-level" capacities, such as reading recipes, stirring, and salting to taste. He also discusses John B. Watson's explanation of maze-running in terms of capacities such as stimulus substitution and "the ability to respond in certain simple ways to simple stimuli," which are also properties of the rat as a whole (1975: 761).[16] Cummins makes this allowance to accommodate "interpretive explanations," which appeal to the flow of information or to the manipulation of representations in a system. Indeed, Cummins is not primarily interested in constitutive mechanistic explanations, but rather with forms of psychological explanation that are functional and largely independent of the implementing mechanisms. I agree with Cummins that these two varieties of explanation must be kept distinct, especially in discussions of explanation in neuroscience. Lumping both together under the rubric of functional analysis blurs this distinction. So let us make it explicit that functional analysis and mechanistic explanations are distinct in that in mechanistic explanations, *S's ψ-ing is not explained merely by the subcapacities of ψ, but by the capacities $\{\phi_1, \phi_2, \ldots, \phi_n\}$ of S's component parts $\{X_1, X_2, \ldots, X_m\}$.*

The distinction is crucial because how–actually explanations are often distinguished from how-possibly explanations on the grounds that the latter appeal to component parts that do not exist and because models

---

[15] Cummins often frames his account of functional analysis without any reference to component parts. For example: "Functional analysis consists in analyzing a disposition into a number of less problematic dispositions such that the programmed manifestation of these analyzing dispositions amounts to a manifestation of the analyzed disposition" (2000: 125).

[16] Thanks to Uljana Feest for calling my attention to this ambiguity.

of mechanisms are often distinguished from sketches on the grounds that the latter contains black boxes or filler terms that cannot be completed with known parts or activities. In some functional explanations (such as interpretive explanations), explanations describe a *program* that *could possibly* produce the phenomenon. Cummins repeatedly emphasizes that, "there is no unique right answer to the question 'Which program does this system execute?'" (1983: 30–43). Further:

> Any way of interpreting the transactions causally mediating the input-output connection as steps in a program for doing [ψ] will, provided it is systematic and not *ad hoc*, make the capacity to [ψ] intelligible. Alternative interpretations, provided they are possible, are not competitors; the availability of one in no way undermines the explanatory force of another. (Cummins 1983: 42; symbol substituted for consistency)

For interpretive functional explanations, then, any set of how-possibly φ-ers will suffice so long as they can be strung together in a program that accounts for S's ψ-ing. Not so for mechanistic explanations. If it did suffice, then Hodgkin and Huxley would have counted their equations for the conductance changes as explanations, but as I show in Chapter 2, they insist that their proposed sequence of biological activities, involving activation particles and their motion in the membrane, is only a convenient fiction.

In a more recent paper, Cummins acknowledges that in neuroscientific explanations in particular one cannot be so cavalier about how different psychological capacities are realized in the parts of organisms:

> Neuroscience enters the picture as a source of evidence, arbitrating among competitors, and ultimately, as the source of an account of the biological realization of psychological systems described functionally. (Cummins 2000: 135)

And furthermore:

> a complete theory for a capacity must exhibit the details of the target capacity's realization in the system (or system type) that has it. Functional analysis of a capacity must eventually terminate in dispositions whose realizations are explicable via analysis of the target system. Failing this, we have no reason to suppose we have analyzed the capacity as it is realized in that system. (Cummins 2000: 126)

No neuroscientist would claim that it makes no difference whether action potentials are produced by passive diffusion through Na^+ and K^+ channels or by active transport through some energy-intensive membrane mechanism. Mechanistic explanation is inherently componential. Box-and-arrow diagrams can depict a program that transforms relevant inputs onto relevant outputs, but if the boxes and arrows do not correspond to component entities and activities, one is providing a redescription of the phenomenon (such as the HH model of conductance changes) or a how-possibly model (such as their working model of conductance changes), not a mechanistic explanation.

Distinguishing good mechanistic explanations from bad requires that one distinguish real components from fictional posits. The most dramatic examples of fictional posits include animal spirits, entelechies, and souls, but fictitious entities can be far more mundane than these. It might have turned out that Bertil Hille's channels did not exist. The movement of charge across the membrane might well have been a matter of active transport (as Hodgkin and Huxley once thought), or degradation of the membrane (as Bernstein suggested), or it might have involved no movement of ions across the membrane at all. Many of the how–possibly mechanisms in Figure 4.3 require parts (and activities) that do not exist.

There is no clear evidential threshold for saying when one is describing real components as opposed to fictional posits, or for detecting when one is pushing one's hypothesis a bit far (as Hille's older colleagues claimed). Nonetheless, the following four criteria are satisfied by real parts and help to distinguish mere how-possibly from how-actually explanations. Real parts have a stable cluster of properties, they are robust, they can be used for intervention, and they are physiologically plausible in a given pragmatic context.

First, the parts should have a *stable cluster of properties* (compare Boyd 1991). Hille's speculative channels were gradually transformed into stock-in-trade entities as it became possible to identify them as proteins, to determine the linear order of their amino acids, to recover their secondary and tertiary structure, to describe their interactions with neurotransmitters and with chemical agonists and antagonists, to characterize their voltage-dependence and rapid inactivation, and so on. Discovering clusters of such properties also allowed researchers to distinguish multiple kinds of channel proteins, selective for different ions, sensitive to different agonists and antagonists, composed of different sequences of amino acids, and the like. As details mounted about the shapes of the channels, their components, their causal interactions, and their subtypes, it became increasingly difficult to dismiss channels as a mere hypothesis being "pushed too far."

Second, and related, the parts should be *robust* (Wimsatt 1981). They should be detectable with a variety of causally and theoretically independent devices. The convergence of multiple lines of independent evidence about Na^+ channels convinced neuroscientists of their existence. Ion channels can be isolated from the membrane, purified, and sequenced. Their behavior can be detected en masse through intra- and extracellular recording techniques, and they can be monitored individually with single-channel patch-clamp techniques. They can be manipulated with pharmacology, they can be altered with site-specific mutagenesis, they can be crystallized and X-rayed, and they can be seen through an electron microscope. Using multiple techniques and theoretical assumptions to reason for the existence of a given item decreases the probability that conclusions drawn from any single technique or mode of access are biased or otherwise faulty (Salmon 1984; Culp 1994, 1995; Psillos 1999; Achinstein 2002).

Third, it should be possible to use the part to *intervene* into other parts and activities (Hacking 1983). It should be possible, that is, to manipulate the entity in such a way as to change other entities, properties, or activities. One can manipulate Na^+ channels to alter the membrane potential, to change Na^+ conductance, to open K^+ channels, and to balance current. As I argue in Chapter 3, the ability to manipulate items in this way is crucial evidence for establishing causal and explanatory relationships among the mechanism's components. This criterion is also crucial for distinguishing real components from fictional posits.

Finally, the component should be *physiologically plausible*. It should not exist only under highly contrived laboratory conditions or in otherwise pathological states. Of course, what constitutes a contrived condition or a pathological state varies across explanatory contexts. If one is trying to explain healthy functions, then pathological conditions might be considered physiologically implausible. If, on the other hand, one is trying to explain a disease process, one's explanation might be physiologically implausible if it assumes conditions only present in healthy organisms. What matters is that the parts' existence should be demonstrable under the conditions relevant to the given request for explanation of the phenomenon

This is neither an exhaustive list of criteria nor an exhaustive discussion of the items in it. Nonetheless, in making these criteria explicit, I take steps toward spelling out when one is justified in presuming that one has moved beyond providing merely a how-possibly account or a filler term (black or grey boxes), and toward describing an actual mechanism. Hille and Armstrong's channel hypotheses moved from a how-possibly posit to a how-actually description of a mechanism as findings about membrane-spanning ion channels satisfied the above criteria. To adequately describe mechanistic explanation, functional analysis must be restricted to constitutive explanations in which some property or activity of a whole is explained in terms of the properties or activities of its parts. And it should be restricted to cases in which the components in the explanation are not mere fictions but real components in the system.

6. Activities

The systems tradition and Cummins's account usefully shift attention away from etiological explanation and toward the kinds of explanation found in neuroscience and psychology. As Cummins notes:

The concern to distinguish causal laws from noncausal correlations, to shun uncaused or idle events, and to make provision for independent access to causes and effects are, of course, not the only methodological concerns to manifest themselves in scientific practice and in writings on the scientific method, but they are, perhaps, the most fundamental and pervasive. ... It should become clear shortly, however, that these concerns are simply out of place in the context of property theories and the analytic strategy of explanation. (1983: 14)

Cummins is right to call attention to this philosophical tunnel vision. However, functional analyses are made up of capacities, and mechanisms are partly constituted by activities and interactions. An adequate account of constitutive explanation must address traditional philosophical problems about causation.

Cummins describes capacities as input–output relations that relate precipitating conditions to manifestations. He requires further that there must be "laws *in situ*" relating input to output conditions, that is, "laws that hold of a special kind of system because of its peculiar constitution and organization. The special sciences do not yield general laws of nature, but rather laws governing the special sorts of systems that are their proper objects of study" (2000: 121). Laws *in situ* are what I describe in Chapter 3 as mechanistically fragile generalizations.

Cummins's appeal to laws to analyze capacities raises two issues. The first is the matter of squaring this view with his insistence that laws are not explanatory. Cummins rejects the CL model because "No laws are explanatory in the sense required by the [CL model]. Laws simply tell us what happens; they do not tell us why or how" (2000: 119). If capacities or dispositions are analyzed in terms of special laws, and special laws are not explanatory, then it is hard to make sense of Cummins's claim that "[functional] analysis allows us to explain how the device as a whole exercises the analyzed capacity, for it allows us to see exercises of the analyzed capacity as programmed (that is, organized) exercises of the analyzing capacities" (2000: 125). Cummins needs to distinguish the laws used in CL explanations from the laws underlying the capacities in functional analyses, but he does not articulate the difference.

The second issue is that Cummins needs a way to distinguish bona fide capacities from pseudo-capacities. One can use Cummins-style input–output pairs to describe mere temporal sequences (input crowing roosters, output dawn), effect-to-cause pairs (input refractory period, output rising phase), correlations between the effects of a common cause (input falling barometer, output storm), and irrelevant pseudocause-to-effect pairings (input blessing, output action potential). It will not help to require that the input–output regularity support counterfactuals (as Weber 2005 requires), because not all counterfactual supporting generalizations are explanatory. If the rooster were to be crowing, dawn would be coming. If my barometer were falling, a storm would be on the horizon. Cummins requires an account of analyzing capacities sufficiently robust to satisfy criteria such as (E1)–(E5).

In Chapter 3, I show that the manipulability account distinguishes laws from accidents while honoring Cummins's accurate assessment that the laws of neuroscience and psychology are mechanistically fragile. The causal relationships in mechanisms are not mere capacities in Cummins's sense; they are relationships that are potentially exploitable for purposes of control.

7. Organization

Mechanistic explanatory texts can begin with a correct and complete characterization of a phenomenon, and with real parts and bona fide capacities, and still fail to understand how these components are *organized*. Cummins defines organization as something that can be described in a flow chart or a program. But almost anything can be described in a flow chart or a program. Arguments, libraries, time-lines, taxonomic systems, chains of command, legal precedent, and words in a book all can be described with boxes and arrows. Yet some forms of organization are distinctively mechanistic.

The distinctively mechanistic form of organization can be brought out by contrasting mechanisms with mere *aggregates* (Wimsatt 1985, 1997). In an aggregate, the whole is literally the sum of its parts. Suppose that a property or activity (ψ) of the whole (S) is explained (in an ontic sense) by the properties or activities $\{\phi_1, \phi_2, \ldots, \phi_n\}$ of its parts $\{X_1, X_2, \ldots, X_m\}$. The ψ-property of S is an aggregate of the ϕ-properties of X's when:

(W1) ψ is invariant under the rearrangement and intersubstitution of Xs;

(W2) ψ remains qualitatively similar (if quantitative, differing only in value) with the addition or subtraction of Xs;

(W3) ψ remains invariant under the disaggregation and reaggregation of Xs; and

(W4) There are no cooperative or inhibitory interactions between Xs that are relevant to ψ. (Modified from Wimsatt 1997)

Wimsatt's (W1)–(W4) are criteria for diagnosing the importance of organization in a system and are also a set of strategies for discovering a mechanism's organization. Compare the mechanism for generating action potentials (S_1) to a neat glass of gin (S_2) and, likewise, Na^+ channels, K^+ channels, and the membrane (the Xs in S_1) to unit volumes of gin (the Xs in S_2). The mechanism of the action potential (S_1) generates action potentials (ψ_1), and the glass of gin (S_2) has a given volume (ψ_2). The parts (Xs) of the action potential mechanism, such as the Na^+ channels and K^+ channels, cannot be intersubstituted with one another (W1). They are ion specific. Only judicious removal or multiplication of certain parts of the action potential mechanism is compatible with its continued working as a whole (W2). Changing even the spatial relations among the components of the mechanism would, at least in many cases, completely disrupt the behavior of the whole system (W3). Finally, there are cooperative and inhibitory interactions between the components of the action potential mechanism (W4). This is why alterations to the entities and activities of the action potential mechanism can destroy it. The volume of gin, in contrast, stays the same any way you shake it.

The above description of the mechanism of the action potential displays three varieties of mechanistic organization: active, spatial, and temporal. Different kinds of organization predominate in different mechanisms.

Most fundamentally, the components in the action potential mechanism are *actively organized*. In direct violation of W4 they act and interact with one another in such a way that the ψ-ing of S is more than just a sum of ϕ-properties. In fact, the ϕ-properties of a working mechanism are not just properties; they are the activities of and interactions among the entities in the working mechanism. The different components act in cooperation or competition, and they do so with some components and not with others. It matters which Xs ϕ with which others, and it matters how they interact. This is why the parts of mechanisms often cannot be reorganized randomly (W1), added or subtracted at will (W2), or taken apart and put back together again (W3) without disturbing their corporate ability to ψ.

Active organization also distinguishes mechanistic explanations from what John Haugeland calls "morphological explanations." Haugeland (1998) illustrates the contrast with the transmission of an image along a fiber optic cable. An image projected on one end of the cable is transmitted to the other by an array of bundled fibers. Each fiber is an isolated conduit of light for a given dot in the image, the brightness and color of which is transmitted along the length of the wire. So long as the relative spatial arrangement of the wires in the bundle is the same at each end, the input image is conserved in the output image. In such explanations, mere spatial organization does most of the work. The fibers do not relevantly interact with one another or work together, and they can become hopelessly tangled in the middle of the wire so long as the spatial arrangement remains the same at the end. This relationship is a matter of degree, however, because many morphological explanations also essentially involve interactions among the parts (for example, the shapes of crystals are determined by the shapes of the molecules, their spatial arrangement, and their packing). Mechanisms, in contrast, are not mere static or spatial patterns of relations, but rather patterns of allowance, generation, prevention, production, and stimulation. There are no mechanisms without active organization, and no mechanistic explanation is complete or correct if it does not capture correctly the mechanism's active organization.

Finally, active organization distinguishes mechanistic models from taxonomic schemes or temporal sequence displays. The periodic table organizes the elements in terms of their underlying atomic structures by exhibiting, for example, some as noble gases and others as radioactive isotopes. Although there are mechanistic models for explaining why certain elements are possible or impossible, and although these allow one to predict the existence of hitherto unobserved elements, mere taxonomic ordering is not a mechanism. Similarly, the Linnaean taxonomic system, which sorts organisms on the basis of their phenotypic traits, is not a mechanistic explanation: the components in this system do not *do anything* that contributes to a behavior of all of the parts taken together. The same can be said of purely sequential theories, such as those describing developmental stages of an organism or the life cycle of a cell. Purely sequential models describe time-slices of a four-dimensional object and show how its parts are arranged at different stages. However, such models do not show how one stage arises from its predecessor, or how the configuration of parts at one stage produces the configuration at the next.

Active organization in mechanisms is sustained by the *spatial* and *temporal organization* of the component parts. The same entities and activities joined in different spatial and temporal organization often yield different mechanisms. The spatial organization of a mechanism includes, for example, the sizes, shapes, structures, locations, orientations, directions, connections, and compartments of its components. Several kinds of spatial organization are crucial for understanding the mechanism of the action potential. It matters, for example, that the ion channels have appropriate *sizes* to allow the flow of ions, that they are long enough to traverse the membrane, and that they are small enough to fit in a small patch of membrane. It matters that the components have appropriate *orientations*, for example, that the ball and chain is inside the membrane and that the α-helix is roughly perpendicular to the membrane. The conformations (or *shapes*) of the ion channels under different membrane voltages allow them to act as channels and to gate the flow of ions appropriately. Furthermore, it matters that large numbers of Na^+ channels are *located* in the axon hillock, and that the α-helix is in the S4 region of the protein.[17] In many mechanisms, it

---

[17] Bechtel and Richardson (1993) emphasize the importance of localization in discovering mechanistic explanations.

matters that the different components are in *contact* with one another: it matters that the S4 region is *connected* to the rest of the channel or that the ball and chain comes into contact with the walls of the channel. This is not an exhaustive list of spatial forms of organization found in mechanisms. Furthermore, one should not expect each form to be equally represented in all mechanisms. Some mechanisms, such as biochemical cascades in the cytoplasm, depend less on the precise location of the activities than on the structures of the entities involved and the temporal arrangement of their activities. But in many cases—and the action potential is an excellent example—spatial organization provides the structure by virtue of which mechanisms work. Getting the relevant aspects of the spatial organization right is part of developing a good and complete mechanistic explanation.

The third aspect of mechanistic organization, is temporal. The order, rate, and duration of successive component activities are crucial for the action potential. There is a sequence of stages from beginning to end, and it is not possible to change their order without interfering with how the mechanism works (or making it a different mechanism entirely). The activation and inactivation of the Na^+ and K^+ channels are appropriately timed so that the action potential rises, falls, and exhibits its characteristic refractory period. The rates at which the channels open and close, and the duration over which they are open or inactivated, are similarly crucial for the overall shape of the action potential. One much-noted problem with programs in classical artificial intelligence is that they often ignore real-world temporal constraints on processing. One might be able to simulate object recognition in LISP, but such a model is unlikely to work as fast as the visual system. Good mechanistic explanations incorporate temporal constraints.

In Cummins's account, the notion of organization is underspecified, requiring only that it be possible to describe the system with a box-and-arrow diagram. He requires this abstraction in order to accommodate interpretive functional explanations (such as Watson's explanation for how a mouse runs a maze). Mechanistic explanations, however, are embodied. They are anchored in components, and those components occupy space and take time to act. A description of a mechanism is not merely a summation of parts or capacities; it is a description of how they work together. That description involves—in addition to a list of component entities $\{X_1, X_2, \dots, X_m\}$ and activities $\{\phi_1, \phi_2, \dots, \phi_n\}$—an account of how they are organized together actively, spatially, and temporally in S's ψ-ing.

As the discovery of the mechanism of the action potential illustrates, neuroscientists distinguish how-possibly from how-actually models by adding such constraints on organization (see Craver and Darden 2001). In the final chapter of this book, I show how the mosaic unity of neuroscience is achieved when different fields, with different techniques and theoretical vocabularies, place different constraints on the same mechanism.

8. Constitutive Relevance

To recap the basic features of my account thus far: The *explanandum* of a mechanistic explanation is a phenomenon, typically some behavior of a mechanism as a whole.[18] The central criterion of adequacy for a mechanistic explanation is that it should account for the multiple features of the phenomenon, including its precipitating conditions, manifestations, inhibiting conditions, modulating conditions, and nonstandard conditions. The explanans is a mechanism. The model of a mechanism does not describe capacities of the mechanism as a whole; it describes the activities of the mechanism's components. How-possibly models can be composed of fictional components, but how-actually models describe real components that have multiple properties, that are detectable with multiple techniques, that are utilizable for the purposes of intervention, and that are physiologically relevant. The model of the mechanism also describes the causal relations (activities) that compose the mechanism. These are not mere input–output relationships or *laws in situ* but relationships of manipulability as described in Chapter 3. Finally, mechanistic explanatory texts do more than exhibit box-and-arrow diagrams; they reveal the active, spatial, and temporal organization of a mechanism. These restrictions make significant progress in defining mechanistic explanation, in distinguishing it from other kinds of explanation, and in distinguishing good explanations from bad.

However, this model of mechanistic explanation is not yet complete. There are two reasons: first, I have not said what it means for a model of a mechanism to "account for" the phenomenon. According to the CL model—the model of explanation at the core of classical reduction—one accounts for the phenomenon by showing that its diverse features *are to be*

---

[18] In an explanatory text, the *explanandum* is a description of the phenomenon and the *explanans* is a description, or schema, of a mechanism.

expected on the basis of the description of the mechanism; this means that one can infer the features of the phenomenon from a complete specification of the mechanism, the initial conditions, the background conditions, and the relevant transtheoretic identities. In Chapter 2, I argue that this is an inadequate view of the nature of explanation on the grounds that it is impossible for most explanations in neuroscience and that it is too weak to distinguish explanatory derivations from, for example, mathematical models that merely save the phenomena. However, I have not yet provided an alternative vision of how a mechanism accounts for, and so explains, the phenomenon.

Second, I have not provided an account of *constitutive* explanatory relevance.[19] That is, I have not said when a part of S is a component in the mechanism of S's ψ-ing. Not all parts are components. Consider again the difference between mechanisms and machines. Machines contain many parts that are not in any mechanism. The hubcaps, mud-flaps, and the windshield are all parts of the automobile, but they are not part of the mechanism that makes it run. They are not *relevant* parts of that mechanism. Good mechanistic explanatory texts describe all of the relevant components and their interactions, and they include none of the irrelevant components and interactions. The failure to address constitutive relevance is a major lacuna not just in Cummins's model of explanation, but also in the systems tradition generally, in recent discussions of mechanistic explanation (including my own), and, in fact, in all discussions of "mircroreduction" in the philosophy of biology and the philosophy of mind. Considerable philosophical effort has been expended on the topic of etiological (that is, causal) relevance, but almost none has been dedicated to the problem of constitutive relevance.

In Section 8.1, I show that any adequate account of mechanisms must supply an account of constitutive relevance. I build my positive account by considering the experimental strategies that neuroscientists use to test whether a given entity, activity, property, or organizational feature is relevant to the behavior of the mechanism as a whole and by considering some well-known ways that these strategies can fail (8.2). The account of constitutive relevance should block these failures in much the same way that

---

[19] Again, I am using this term as Salmon uses it, that is, to refer to an underlying mechanism. The goal is to specify the sense in which a component is relevant to, and so is part of the explanation for, the phenomenon.

the manipulationist account of etiological relevance in Chapter 3 blocks the kinds of failures expressed in (E1)–(E4).[20] I then offer a sufficient condition for interlevel relevance: the *mutual manipulability* account. According to that account, a part is a component in a mechanism if one can change the behavior of the mechanism as a whole by intervening to change the component *and* one can change the behavior of the component by intervening to change the behavior of the mechanism as a whole.

8.1 Relevance and the boundaries of mechanisms

One cannot delimit the boundaries of mechanisms—that is, determine what is in the mechanism and what is not—without an account of constitutive relevance. To see that this is the case, consider the shortcomings of some efforts to delimit the boundaries of mechanisms without appealing to explanatory relevance.

One might, for example, equate the boundaries of mechanisms with compartmental boundaries. Some mechanisms are entirely contained within physical compartments, such as a nucleus, or a cell membrane, or skin. Transcription (typically) happens within the nucleus, and translation occurs in the cytoplasm. Detection of plasma ion concentrations happens within the circumventricular organs and outside of the blood–brain barrier. However, mechanisms frequently transgress compartmental boundaries. The mechanism of the action potential relies crucially on the fact that some components of the mechanism are inside the membrane and some are outside. The membrane allows the intracellular and extracellular concentrations of ions to be different, allows a diffusion gradient to be set up, and allows for a separation of charge. Likewise, many cognitive mechanisms draw upon resources outside of the brain and outside of the body to such an extent that it may not be fruitful to see the skin, or the surface of the CNS, as a useful boundary (as Haugeland 1998; Wilson 1995, 2004; Clark 1997; and Clark and Chalmers 1998 emphasize). Examples such as this are commonplace.[21]

Cartesian mechanists faced this challenge as well. If the extended world is devoid of goals and purposes, composed only of corpuscles operating

---

[20] The failure of (E5) is not germane in the case of constitutive explanations.

[21] von Eckardt and Poland (2005) criticize my view of mechanisms in Craver (2001) for my failure to accommodate outward- and upward-looking explanations. Craver (2001) is motivated in part by the desire to accommodate such explanations.

blindly by motion and contact, what principles could possibly define the unity of a machine, organ, or organism? Descartes at times favors principles of spatial organization: the parts are within a spatial boundary, they move together, and they can be transported together from one place to another while maintaining fixed relative positions with the other components (see Des Chene 2001). Others (such as Salamone De Caus) appeal to contact among the parts. Few contemporary scientists hold to the idea that all causal interactions require contact among components, but even granting this possibility, there are several counterexamples to each of these suggestions. I have already noted that mechanisms frequently defy tidy physical boundaries (although every mechanism can, trivially, be circumscribed). Parts of mechanisms often move in separate directions (as any multiple-pulley system illustrates). Some mechanisms are more ephemeral than others;[22] they work only as components happen to come into the appropriate spatial arrangement. For example, in many biochemical cascades, the relevant reactions could happen anywhere in the cytoplasm. Such mechanisms lack stable spatial relations; they cannot be picked up and carried from one place to the next.

Some members of the systems tradition define the boundaries of mechanisms by appeal to the *intensity of interaction* among its components. Herbert Simon (1969) takes this approach in his discussion of "near complete decomposability." Systems, for Simon, are sets of state variables and their interactions. A system can be decomposed into distinct (that is, bounded) subsystems by comparing the relative strengths of interactions among the variables in the system as a whole. Variables are clustered into subsystems when their interactions with one another are stronger than are their interactions with variables outside of that set. Wimsatt (1976b) adopts the same view, but notes that the threshold of strength required for inclusion in a mechanism depends upon one's pragmatic interests. If one requires exacting control or exceptionally precise predictions, then even weak interactions must be included in the model. For other purposes, one might be willing to tolerate error or imprecision and so can neglect weak interactions. John Haugeland develops a third variant. He describes systems as "relatively independent and self-contained composites of components interacting at interfaces" (1998: 215), where to be relatively independent and

---

[22] I borrow this term from Stuart Glennan (personal communication).

self-contained is to interact more often and more intimately with items inside the interfaces than with those outside (215). Intimacy, in turn, "means something like how 'tightly' things are coupled, or even how 'closely knit' they are" (215). Grush (2003) has elaborated Haugeland's position (for the purposes of criticizing it), as distinguishing mechanisms from their environment by the *bandwidth* of their interaction. By bandwidth, Grush means the number of state variables describing a component that appear in the equations describing the evolution of the other state variables. The narrower the bandwidth, the more appropriate it is to identify the inter-action as an interface. Grush's elaboration of Haugeland's view is the most sophisticated interactionist account of the boundaries of mechanisms.[23]

The bandwidth criterion, it would seem, needs to be supplemented by the kinds of pragmatic considerations that Wimsatt discusses in order to specify a threshold of bandwidth below which the components are separate and above which the components are not separate. The location of this threshold is likely to depend upon one's error-tolerance and one's purposes. Leaving this issue aside, however, neither strength nor bandwidth criteria suffice to pick out the right boundaries. First, they do not readily distinguish components from *background conditions*. The beating of my heart and my ability to read are strongly connected to one another, on any notion of causal strength. If my heart were to stop beating for any stretch of time, or if it were to speed up dramatically, my ability to read would quickly decay. The action potential shares high-bandwidth interfaces with protein synthesis mechanisms and glucose metabolism, for example, because ion channels are constantly recycled in the membrane and because the ion pump that establishes the V_{rest} is energetically demanding. Although the distinction between a mechanism and a background condition is likely to be vague, it is nonetheless a common distinction and one that a view of constitutive relevance can help to sort out.

There is also the problem of *sterile effects*. Components of mechanisms have many effects that are irrelevant to the behavior of the mechanism.

---

[23] Grush (2003) develops his own view, according to which distinct mechanisms are plug-and-play components that can readily be ejected from and plugged into a systemic context. This works well for the case that Grush considers (the importance of the skin as a boundary for cognition), but it works less well for biochemical cascades and physiological systems, which are often spatially quite distributed and so tightly interwoven into their systematic context that it is very difficult to see them as self-contained in this way. Furthermore, whether a mechanism is truly plug-and-play depends on whether it contains all of the relevant components.

Such effects might provide evidence for or against a given how-possibly mechanism, but they are not part of the mechanism itself. Action potentials affect a host of other processes in cells, such as protein synthesis, metabolism, membrane turnover, and packaging of neurotransmitters. Na^+ channels exert attractive and repulsive effects on ions and other particles in the cytoplasm and in the extracellular space, they deform the membrane, and so on. But these activities are sterile in the mechanism: they either produce no changes in the other components of the mechanism, or the changes they do produce make no difference to action potentials. In contrast, the rotation of the a-helix, the movement of the ball and chain, and the diffusion of ions are all tightly coupled in a way that does make a difference to action potentials.[24]

The boundaries of mechanisms, it appears, cannot be defined by strength of interaction or bandwidth alone. The spatial and interactive boundaries of mechanisms depend on the epistemologically prior delineation of *relevance boundaries*. Spatial boundaries are those that circumscribe all the relevant entities and activities. Temporal boundaries are those that include all the relevant activities. An account of constitutive mechanistic explanation must include an account of constitutive relevance. The causal-mechanical alternative to derivation as a regulative ideal is that the mechanism should describe all of the components, activities, and organizational features that are *relevant* to the *explanandum phenomenon*.

8.2 Interlevel experiments and constitutive relevance

The norms of constitutive relevance are implicit in the experimental strategies that neuroscientists use to test claims about componency and in the rules by which neuroscientists evaluate applications of those strategies (Bechtel forthcoming; Bechtel and Richardson 1993; Craver 2002b). Neuroscientists use these experiments to establish which parts are components in a mechanism and which are not, that is, to distinguish relevant components from mere constitutive correlates (as discussed in C5 of Chapter 2), sterile effects, and background conditions. These experimental strategies,

---

[24] I have not discussed the possibility that the boundaries of mechanisms might be defined by grouping together those items that were selected for the performance of some function. This answer, however, presupposes a solution to the problem under consideration here. To establish that a component was selected for its contribution to a function, one must first show that the part contributes to the function and so is relevant in the sense under discussion here. (As a purely epistemic point, neuroscientists often know very little about how features of the brain evolved.)

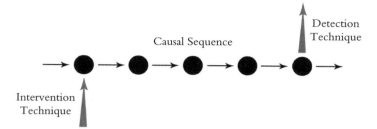

Figure 4.7a. Abstract representation of an experiment for testing etiological (causal) relevance

and their various well-known weaknesses, provide a valuable window on the norms of constitutive relevance.

To start with the more familiar case, etiological causal claims are test-ed with experiments of the sort diagrammed in Figure 4.7a. That figure represents an intervention (I) into a causal sequence to change variable (X) and a detection technique (D) that monitors the consequences (if any) of that intervention on some downstream variable (Y). In interlevel exper-iments, in contrast, the intervention and detection techniques are applied to different levels of mechanisms. (For present purposes, X's ϕ-ing is at a lower level than S's ψ-ing if X's ϕ-ing is a component of S's ψ-ing.) *Interlevel* experiments test the relationship between the components of a mechanism (the entities, activities, and organizational features at the lower level[25]) and the *explanandum phenomenon* (at the higher level). The left side of Figure 4.7b shows a bottom-up experiment, in which one intervenes to change a component in a mechanism (X's ϕ-ing) and detects changes in the behavior of the mechanism as a whole (S's ψ-ing). The right side of Figure 4.7b shows a top-down experiment, in which one intervenes to manipulate the phenomenon (S's ψ-ing) and detects changes in the activities or properties of the components in the mechanism (X's ϕ-ing).

Let me clarify the relationships involved in such experiments. X's ϕ-ing is a component in S's ψ-ing. S's ψ-ing can be understood as a complex input—output relationship. The inputs include all of the relevant conditions required for S to ψ. In the case of the action potential, this includes the

---

[25] By "level" in this context I mean the relationship between a mechanism as a whole and the entities, activities, properties, and organizational features of the mechanism taken individually. See Chapter 5.

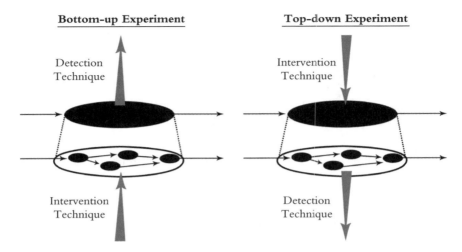

Figure 4.7b. Abstract representation of experiments for testing constitutive (or componential) relevance

stimulus delivered to the pre-synaptic cell and a host of other conditions of the sort described in the methods sections of scientific papers. The output is an action potential. Between these inputs and outputs is a mechanism, an organized collection of parts and activities. X is one of those parts, and ϕ is one of those activities. One intervenes on S's ψ-ing by intervening to provide the conditions under which S regularly ψs. Top-down experiments intervene in this way. Bottom-up experiments involve intervening into the components of the intermediate mechanism. Often they also involve putting S in the conditions for ψ-ing in order to see whether the intervention into the part changes whether S ψs or the way that S ψs. In each case, the goal is to show that X's ϕ-ing is causally between the inputs and outputs that constitute S's ψ-ing.[26]

Three varieties of interlevel experiment are common in contemporary neuroscience: interference experiments, stimulation experiments, and activation experiments.[27] They differ depending on whether the experiment

[26] I stress again that this relationship should not be understood causally. Nor should it be understood as a relationship between a supervenient event or property and its supervenience base. Rather I am talking about a relationship between a component in the mechanism and the behavior of a mechanism as a whole.

[27] There is a fourth kind of interlevel experiment, deprivation experiments, which I neglect here because they are so rare in neuroscience. In such experiments, one inhibits the behavior of a mechanism as a whole and detects changes in the behaviors of the parts. I am thinking, for example, of the

is top-down or bottom-up, and on whether the intervention is excitatory or inhibitory. To reveal the criteria for assessing constitutive relevance, I examine some inferential challenges that these different kinds of experiment face. Neuroscientists are aware of these challenges. I mention them not as objections to interlevel experiments (which I take to be indispensable), but as data points in building a descriptively and normatively adequate account of constitutive relevance. A complete discussion of these methods, their strengths and weaknesses, and their relationships to one another is much needed but beyond the scope of this book. What follows is a skeletal framework that can be used for that purpose.

8.2.1. Interference experiments   Interference experiments are bottom-up inhibitory experiments. They are represented on the left side of Figure 4.7b. In interference experiments, one intervenes to diminish, disable, or destroy some putative component in a lower-level mechanism and then detects the results of this intervention for the *explanandum phenomenon*. The assumption is that if X's ϕ-ing is a component in S's ψ-ing, then removing X or preventing it from ϕ-ing should have some effect on S's ability to ψ. In the simplest case, removing X or preventing it from ϕ-ing would eliminate or inhibit S's ψ-ing. If X is an inhibitory component, then intervening to remove X or to inhibit its ϕ-ing might produce or augment S's ψ-ing. The point of an interference experiment is to show that one can change S's ψ-ing by intervening to manipulate X's ϕ-ing.

Lesion experiments, for example, are interference experiments in which something intervenes to remove a portion of the brain and one then detects the effects of the lesion on task performance (see, for example, von Eckardt Klein 1977; Glymour 1994; Bub 1994). Clinical case studies, such as the cases of Leborgne (Broca 1861), H. M. (Scoville and Milner 1957), and Phineas Gage (Harlow 1868), are dramatic examples of interference studies. Interference experiments have also been crucial for discovering the mechanism of the action potential. When one intervenes to introduce mutations to the primary structure of the S4 region, or to cleave the ball-and-chain inactivation gate in the Na^+ channel with proteolytic enzymes, or to inhibit channels with TTX or TEA, and then detects the effects of

experiment in which David Hubel sutured the eyes of kittens and monkeys to observe how the cortex develops when deprived of visual input.

the intervention on the shape of the action potential, one is conducting an interference experiment.

It is well known among scientists that interference experiments face significant challenges. One is that the mechanism sometimes compensates for the intervention. A second is that the intervention can sometimes influence the behavior of the mechanism as a whole indirectly.

(F1) Compensation: there are circumstances under which S's ψ-ing does not change after X and its ϕ-ing are disrupted, even though X and its ϕ-ing are relevant to S's ψ-ing. X could be redundant. The work of one kidney, or of one bilateral brain region, can sometimes be assumed by its partner with no diminution of function. In other cases, the mechanism might compensate for the loss of a part by recovering (healing the part), by making new use of other parts, or by reorganizing the remaining parts. Each of these possibilities is illustrated in people who have suffered strokes. Over the weeks following their stroke, many of the affected functions often return because the affected brain regions recover or reorganize, or because the person learns new ways to perform old tasks. The failure to see effects of interference is, as all neuroscientists know, insufficient to show that the part is irrelevant to the mechanism.[28]

(F2) Indirect interference: there are also circumstances in which interfering with X's ϕ-ing can change S's ψ-ing even though X's ϕ-ing is irrelevant to S's ψ-ing. For example, a brain lesion can disrupt the blood supply to surrounding brain regions, or it can produce swelling in the surrounding tissue that disrupts normal functioning in those areas. In these cases, the lesion delivered to brain region X has indirect effects on other areas, and those indirect effects are responsible for the observed deficit in S's ψ-ing. For example Anand and Brobeck (1951) report that lesions to the lateral hypothalamus stop rats from eating. They conclude that the lateral hypothalamus is a hunger center. Subsequent research confirms that the rats stop eating. They also stop *moving*. Electrolytic lesions to the lateral hypothalamus damage not only indigenous cells, but also a pathway of

---

[28] Compensatory responses are frequently incomplete. I am assuming the worst-case epistemic scenario for the neuroscientists and, conversely, the best-case recovery scenario for the patient, in order to make the interpretive challenge as stark as possible. Thanks to John Bickle for urging me to make this point.

neurons passing through the hypothalamus (the nigrostriatal bundle) that is thought to be a component in mechanisms regulating general arousal.[29] Again, neuroscientists are aware of this problem; Anand and Brobeck's paper would not be accepted for publication in any contemporary neuroscience journal because it does not conform to the norms that have subsequently evolved for evaluating interference experiments. In cases of this sort, however, one intervenes to change X and detects a change in S's ψ-ing, although the observed relationship is not due to the fact that X is a component, but rather to the fact that the disruption of X changes A, and A is a component in the mechanism of S's ψ-ing.[30]

An adequate account of constitutive relevance should help us to understand how each of these interpretive difficulties (compensation and indirect interference) is met. I return to this in the next major section.

8.2.2. Stimulation experiments Stimulation experiments are bottom-up, excitatory experiments. They are represented along with inhibition experiments on the left side of Figure 4.7b. In stimulation experiments, one intervenes to excite or intensify some component in a mechanism and then detects the effects of that intervention on the *explanandum phenomenon*. The assumption is that if X's ϕ-ing is a component in S's ψ-ing, then one should be able to change or produce S's ψ-ing by stimulating X. In the clearest case, one could make S ψ by making X ϕ. If X and its ϕ-ing play an inhibitory role in the mechanism, then stimulating X to ϕ would diminish or eliminate S's ψ-ing. If X or its ϕ-ing has only a modulatory role in S's ψ-ing, then stimulating X would change S's ψ-ing.

The classic example of stimulation experiments is Gustav Fritsch and Eduard Hitzig's (1870) work on the motor cortex (see Bechtel forthcoming). Fritsch and Hitzig performed a series of experiments on dogs in which they delivered low-grade electrical stimuli to a cortical area now known as the motor strip (see Bechtel forthcoming). Localized stimuli along

---

[29] One can dissociate these possibilities by using techniques that kill the dopaminergic fibers passing through the hypothalamus but that leave the indigenous cells intact and vice versa.

[30] Again, I am not arguing for skepticism about the results of these experiments. There are standards for distinguishing good interference experiments from bad, and one task of the philosophy of neuroscience is to make those explicit and to justify them. Here, I am using the well-known problems of interference experiments as a basis for showing what neuroscientists mean when they say that a part is a component in a mechanism. I am merely explaining why neuroscientists often claim that mere lesion experiments are insufficient for that purpose.

this area produce regular and repeatable movements in specific muscles, including the legs, the tail, and the facial muscles. The ability to produce focal movements predictably by stimulating areas of the brain is potent evidence that the stimulated area plays a role in motor mechanisms. Many of the electrophysiological experiments leading to the discovery of the mechanism of the action potential involve stimulating cells by injecting current.

Stimulation experiments give rise to interpretative complexities similar to those generated by interference experiments, as shown below (see Bechtel and Stufflebeam 2001 for examples).

(S1) Compensation: just as a neural mechanism can sometimes recover from interference, it can also sometimes recover from stimulation. Stimulating X to ϕ thus might not lead to S's ψ-ing even though X's ϕ-ing is relevant to S's ψ-ing. For example, homeostatic mechanisms might work to "siphon off" the stimulation or to adjust activities elsewhere in the mechanism to compensate for its effects. One example of such compensatory responses is drug tolerance, in which repeated exposure to a drug might lead to the need for larger doses to achieve the required effect. Tolerance to morphine is thought to result from compensatory responses within the endogenous opioid receptors, and the diminishing returns from L-Dopa in the treatment of Parkinson's disease are thought to result, at least in part, from downregulation of dopamine receptors in the basal ganglia. In most cases of stimulation, such compensatory responses are sufficiently delayed that they pose no threat to the interpretation of controlled experiments that test for a drug's effect, but it is not always possible to rule out short-term compensatory responses that would not be so evident.

(S2) Indirect effects: another challenge facing stimulation experiments arises from the possibility of indirect effects of the stimulation. For example, the stimulation delivered to X might spread to some other component B, where B is a component of S's ψ-ing. In that case, one can manipulate S's ψ-ing by manipulating X's ϕ-ing, but X's ϕ-ing is not a component in the mechanism for S's ψ-ing. Fritsch and Hitzig worried that their stimuli spread to other portions of the cortex. Subsequent experimenters refined the intensity of the electrical stimulus to localize the effects of the stimulation to just the brain regions under study. Similar refinement has taken place in experimental protocols involving pharmacological agents

and genetic manipulations. One goal in designing a good stimulation experiment is to confine the stimulus to just the putative component or property under study.

8.2.3. Activation experiments   The last kind of interlevel experiment is activation experiments. In activation experiments, one intervenes to activate, trigger, or augment the *explanandum phenomenon* and then detects the properties or activities of one or more putative components of its mechanism. These excitatory, top-down experiments are represented on the right side of Figure 4.7b. The basic assumption behind activation experiments is that if X is a component in S's ψ-ing, then there should be some difference in X depending on whether S is ψ-ing or not. In the most intuitive case, X would become active, or would increase its activity from baseline, when S begins to ψ. In parallel with cases of omission and prevention, however, it is also possible that X's ϕ-ing inhibits S's ψ-ing, and that activating S's ψ-ing therefore attenuates or eliminates X's ϕ-ing. Regardless, the point of an activation experiment is to show that interventions that change S's ψ-ing are accompanied by changes in X's ϕ-ing.

There are several common varieties of activation experiment at all levels in neuroscience. In PET and fMRI studies, one activates a cognitive system by engaging the experimental subject in some task while monitoring the brain for markers of activity, such as blood flow or changes in oxygenation. (For philosophical discussion of these techniques, see, for example, Bechtel and Stuffelbeam 2001; Bogen 2001, 2002. For a state of the art look at the techniques and its challenges, see Raichle and Mintun 2006). In single- and mutli-unit recording experiments, one engages the subject in a task while recording the electrical activity in neurons. In other studies, researchers monitor the production of proteins, or the activation of immediate early genes such as c-fos and c-jun. The experiments leading up to Hodgkin and Huxley's model of the action potential involved generating action potentials and monitoring single ionic currents while the neuron spiked. Activation experiments also face inferential perils, as described below.

(A1) Mere correlates: one challenge for activation experiments is that the activated component might be a mere correlate of the phenomenon. For example, engaging a subject in a cognitive task increases blood flow to brain regions activated by the task. PET researchers routinely take the increase

in blood flow as a marker of activity in components, but no researcher believes that the increase in blood flow is itself part of the mechanism for such cognitive tasks. Instead, the changes in blood flow are treated as poorly understood background conditions rather than as established components in the mechanism under study.[31] More generally, intervening to make S ψ might activate some component X of S, but the activation of that component has sterile effects, relative to S, on some irrelevant part, C. C would then be strongly correlated with task activation, but it would not be part of the mechanism. The lesson is that compelling top-down results, while an important part of establishing constitutive relevance, cannot alone establish constitutive relevance.

(A2) Tonic contributions: a major assumption of activation experiments is that X and its ϕ-ing must change during S's ψ-ing. Yet it is possible that a component plays a static role in the mechanism. Consider, for example, the contribution of the non-channel regions of the membrane, or perhaps Schwann cells, to the action potential. There can be no potential difference without a membrane that is largely impermeable to ions. Although channels change the permeability of the membrane, other portions of the membrane remain crucially impermeant. The existence of insulating Schwann cells that wrap the axon of a nerve cell allow the action potential to propagate quickly along its length. Schwann cells do not change during the propagation of action potentials; their insulating effect is a static, or tonic, contribution (or at least they are often described this way).

These experimental strategies—interference, stimulation, and activation—cannot be understood fully in isolation. They are typically used in conjunction because the strengths of one strategy compensate for the weaknesses of the others.[32]

8.3 Constitutive relevance as mutual manipulability

The close analogy between causal experiments and interlevel experiments suggests that the manipulability account of etiological relevance might provide a model for thinking about constitutive mechanistic relevance. My

---

[31] If one were to cut off blood flow for very long, the brain region would no longer function, but that is not the point. I am referring to the increase in blood flow subsequent to activation.

[32] Philosophers of neuroscience have said very little about the structure and limitations of these experimental strategies; see Bogen 2002; Hardcastle 2002; Uttal 2001.

working account of constitutive relevance is as follows: a component is relevant to the behavior of a mechanism as a whole when one can wiggle the behavior of the whole by wiggling the behavior of the component *and* one can wiggle the behavior of the component by wiggling the behavior as a whole. The two are related as part to whole and they are *mutually manipulable*. More formally: (i) x is part of S; (ii) in the conditions relevant to the request for explanation there is some change to X's ϕ-ing that changes S's ψ-ing; and (iii) in the conditions relevant to the request for explanation there is some change to S's ψ-ing that changes X's ϕ-ing. This simple formulation needs considerable refinement.[33]

There are significant differences between etiological and constitutive relevance. Because X is part of S (and ϕ is part of ψ), the relationship between them is only uncomfortably viewed as causal. Constitutive relevance is symmetrical in a way that etiological (that is, causal) relevance typically is not. In constitutive mechanistic relations, one can change the *explanandum phenomenon* by intervening to change a component (as illustrated by interference and stimulation experiments), or one can manipulate the component by intervening to change the *explanandum phenomenon* (as illustrated by activation experiments). Although there are *some* cases of cause and effect variables in which the manipulability relationships are bidirectional (as in cases of feedback), many, if not most, causal relationships are unidirectional. In contrast, all constitutive dependency relationships are bidirectional. This is the core reason why constitutive relevance should be understood in terms of *mutual* manipulability rather than in terms of the unidirectional variety introduced in Chapter 3. Second, in the constitutive relation, a token instance of the property ψ is, in part, constituted by an instance of the property ϕ; as such, the tokening of ϕ is not logically independent of the tokening of ψ. At least since Hume, many philosophers have held that causes and effects must be logically independent. If one endorses this restriction on causal relations, then one should balk at positing a causal relationship between constitutively related properties. Finally, because the constitution relationship is synchronic, ϕ's taking on a particular value is not

---

[33] This should not be confused with a claim about supervenience. Supervenience, in this case, amounts roughly to the claim that there can be no difference in S's ψ-ing without a difference in the mechanism for S's ψ-ing. Supervenience so stated is a relation between a phenomenon and the corporate behavior of the organized components. The relevance relation, in contrast, holds between the phenomenon and one of the components. The supervenience claim, note, is not symmetrical. I have no reason to deny weak and global forms supervenience, but that is not what I am discussing here.

temporally prior to ψ's taking on its value.[34] If one is committed to the idea that causes must precede their effects, then constitutive relationships are not causal relationships. These differences warrant caution in thinking of constitutive (interlevel) relations as causal. It seems appropriate to acknowledge these differences by marking the linguistic distinction between causation and componency, and so between etiological relevance and constitutive relevance.

I return now to the proposed sketch of constitutive relevance. According to that sketch, X's ϕ-ing is constitutively relevant to S's ψ-ing if the two are related as part to whole and the relata are mutually manipulable. There should be some ideal intervention on ϕ under which ψ changes, and there should be some ideal intervention on ψ under which ϕ changes.

With respect to the first of these conditionals, an *ideal* intervention I on ϕ with respect to ψ is a change in the value of ϕ that changes ψ, if at all, *only via* the change in ϕ. This implies that:

(I1$_c$)   the intervention I does not change ψ directly;

(I2$_c$)   I does not change the value of some other variable ϕ^* that changes the value of ψ except via the change introduced into ϕ;

(I3$_c$)   that I is not correlated with some other variable M that is causally independent of I and also a cause of ψ; and

(I4$_c$)   that I fixes the value of ϕ in such a way as to screen off the contribution of ϕ's other causes to the value of ϕ.[35]

Consider these briefly. Requirement (I1$_c$) is intended to rule out cases in which the putative intervention on X and its ϕ-ing directly fixes the value of ψ. (Remember, ψ does not supervene on ϕ. Rather, ϕ is part of the mechanism for ψ-ing.) If one were testing whether Na^+ channels are relevant to changes in membrane voltage, and one intervened to activate Na^+ channels by raising membrane voltage, the observed change in membrane voltage might be due to the intervention rather than to the activation of Na^+ channels. Requirement (I2$_c$) excludes those cases of indirect effects mentioned in F2 and S2 above. In those cases, an intervention has indirect effects (ϕ^*) that account for the observed changes to ψ. (I3$_c$) is required to rule out cases in which the intervention is

---

[34] For a detailed discussion, see Kim (2000) and Craver and Bechtel (forthcoming).

[35] The numbering here is intended to parallel that for etiological causal claims introduced in Chapter 3.

correlated with other determinants of the value of ψ. For example, the control organisms in lesion experiments typically undergo sham surgeries to ensure that the observed effects are not due to anesthesia or other correlated aspects of the surgical procedure rather than the lesion. It is not intended to rule out cases in which, for example, M is causally intermediate between I and X, as ruled out by ($I2_c$). Finally, ($I4_c$) is required to ensure that the intervention in fact changes the value of ϕ as intended.

Consider the first of the two conditionals that constitute the mutual manipulability account, that which asserts a conditional relationship between low-level interventions and high-level consequences. Putting it roughly:

(CR1) When ϕ is set to the value ϕ_1 in an ideal intervention, then ψ takes on the value $f(\phi_1)$.

CR1 reflects the importance of bottom–up experiments, such as interference and stimulation experiments, for testing claims of constitutive relevance. Let ϕ be a variable representing the activity of a brain region, and let ϕ_1 represent the activity produced by ablating the region (that is, $\phi_1 =$ off). If X's ϕ-ing is necessary for S's ψ-ing, then S should no longer ψ (that is, $f(\phi_1) =$ off). If one removes the ball-and-chain inactivation gate from Na^+ channels, then the channel should not longer inactivate.

CR1 must be further restricted to conditions germane to a request for explanation. This is required to accommodate the fact that in neuroscience and elsewhere, one is not interested in whether just any change to ϕ could change ψ, or in whether changes to ϕ under just any conditions could change ψ, but rather in whether the changes can be observed in conditions that are explanatorily salient. What counts as an experimentally salient condition should be judged on a case-by-case basis, but the general idea is that if one is trying to understand the way a mechanism works in a healthy organism, and one is positing a constitutive explanatory relationship that holds only under extreme laboratory or pathological conditions, then one will not have identified a component of the mechanism in explanatorily relevant conditions. If one is interested in explaining the behavior of a mechanism under diseased or industrial conditions, then one will be interested in componency relations under those conditions. Although we are often interested in states of health or features that have been selected for, there is no reason to insist upon this restriction. There is no way to know what constitutes the "appropriate" conditions without specifying the pragmatic context in which one is operating.

One can exclude sterile effects and other mere correlates by requiring that the experiment satisfy CR1. Sterile effects are properties or behaviors of a component that are irrelevant to the behavior of a mechanism as a whole. Performance of cognitive tasks, for example, is routinely correlated with hemodynamic changes, but this does not mean that the hemodynamic changes are part of the mechanism involved in task performance (as all MRI researchers know). Hemodynamic changes can be ruled out as components of the mechanism on the grounds that intervening to prevent the increase in blood flow during a task will not prevent one from performing the task. Of course, preventing blood flow to a region can quickly degrade task performance, and perhaps preventing the increase in blood flow would have long-term consequences as well. However, because hemodynamic changes typically *follow* the performance of a task, it is safe to assume that preventing those changes cannot alter task performance. Most generally, CR1 excludes correlations from constitutive explanations because intervening to change a mere correlate will not alter the phenomenon. Knowing that one can manipulate S's ψ-ing by manipulating X's ϕ-ing in various ways allows one to say how S's ψ-ing is different when X is removed, or when X's ϕ-ing is altered. In other words, a relationship that satisfies CR1 allows one to answer a range of what-if-things-had-been-different questions about how the mechanism will behave under a variety of interventions into its components. Mere correlations across levels do not allow one to answer such a range of questions.

Nonetheless, satisfying CR1 is neither necessary nor sufficient for X's ϕ-ing to be relevant to S's ψ-ing. Consider these in turn.

Satisfying CR1 is unnecessary because compensatory responses (such as recovery, redundancy, and reorganization) can prevent changes to S's ψ-ing (as noted in (P1) and (S1) above). One way that scientists solve problems of this sort is to design experiments that avoid or prevent the compensatory response. They try to show that the intervention on X's ϕ-ing induces changes in S's ψ-ing if one detects S's ψ-ing before S has had time to recover, or if the other redundant components are occluded or taxed, or if one prevents the system from reorganizing. More formally, there should be an ideal intervention on X's ϕ-ing that changes the value of S's ψ-ing under the conditions (CR1a) that the intervention, I, leaves all of the other dependency relations in S's ψ-ing unchanged and (CR1b) that other interventions have removed the contributions of other redundant components. CR1a rules out cases of recovery and reorganization in the mechanism. CR1b rules out cases of redundancy. These two conditions are not merely ad hoc additions to the account. They correspond to the kinds of experiment that researchers do to overcome these inferential challenges. Although a system might reorganize in response to an intense stimulus (as in cases of drug tolerance), such effects are often delayed, allowing researchers to observe short-term changes before recovery or reorganization is complete. In some cases, researchers may be able to intervene to prevent the system from reorganizing. Problems of redundancy, likewise, can be met with experiments that inhibit the redundant mechanisms and, thereby, unmask the causal contribution of the part in question. Even if removing one kidney has little physiological effect, removing the second has dire physiological consequences. A final way that experimentalists deal with this kind of problem is by intervening in a way that does not prompt the system to compensate. As I show below, activation experiments can be used to detect correlated activity in multiple redundant parts, and they can usually be carried out in ways that do not prompt the system to reorganize. One of the virtues of such top-down experiments is that they sidestep inferential perils that bottom-up experiments cannot.

CR1 is also insufficient to establish a component's constitutive relevance because interventions into *background conditions* can change S's ψ-ing even though they are not part of the mechanism (see (F2) above). Lesioning the heart can prevent word-stem completion, but the heart is not part of the word-stem completion mechanism. In such cases, the lesioned or stimulated item *is* relevant to *explanandum phenomenon* in the sense that one can manipulate the phenomenon by intervening to change parts, but the parts are not components in the mechanism.

No doubt, the distinction between background conditions and components is often drawn on pragmatic grounds. However, such pragmatic decisions can be made on an objective base. Here are some ways of doing so. First, sometimes mere background conditions are identified by conjoining interference and stimulation strategies. Intervening to inhibit a background condition B's ϕ-ing may inhibit S's ψ-ing, but one cannot stimulate S's ψ-ing by stimulating B's ϕ-ing. For example, while interfering with the heart interferes with word-stem completion, one cannot produce word-stem completion by stimulating the heart. Second, sometimes background conditions can be ruled out on the basis of activation experiments. Although one can interfere with S's ψ-ing by interfering with background condition B's ϕ-ing, at least in many cases, one cannot alter B's ϕ-ing by manipulating S's ψ-ing. For example, lesioning the heart might produce deficits in word-stem completion, but engaging a subject in word-stem completion will not change the behavior of the heart (except under torturous word-stem completion tasks outside of the context of the request for explanation). Third, the effects of interfering with background conditions tend to be nonspecific, that is, they affect many phenomena besides the one under study. Researchers learned, for example, that the lateral hypothalamus is not a hunger center by recognizing that the hypothalamic lesions prevent the animals from doing most of the things that animals do. Lesions to the heart would impair not only word-stem completion but also everything else distinctive of a living organism. Finally, the effects of interventions that change background conditions on the behaviors of mechanisms are often unsubtle. One cannot reliably produce subtle changes in word-stem completion by even arbitrarily subtle interventions to change the heart; interventions on the heart that have any effect seem to have switch-like effects. Slowing the heart, for example, will have no effect up to a threshold beyond which word-stem completion rapidly ceases. One who truly understood word-stem completion, however, if provided with the appropriate tools (a sizeable if), would be able to intervene into the mechanism to subtly manipulate the mechanism's output.[36] Criteria of this sort might provide a means for drawing the distinction between background conditions and components in a mechanism and for showing how CR1 might be supplemented to meet this problem case.

Part of the motivation for associating constitutive relevance with *mutual* manipulability is that bottom-up and top-down experiments are mutually reinforcing in the search for components in a mechanism. The inferential complexities involved in interpreting one such experimental strategy are often resolved by applying another strategy. None of the strategies is, by itself, sufficient to establish the constitutive relevance of a putative component. The strategies cannot be assessed fully in isolation from one another.

---

[36] James Woodward mentioned the third and fourth of these criteria in personal conversation.

For this reason, the mutual manipulability account contains the second conditional:

(CR2): if ψ is set to the value ψ_1 in an ideal intervention, then ϕ takes on the value $f(\psi_1)$.

CR2 is intended to describe the effects of top-down experiments, such as the use of functional imaging or the use of other biological markers of activity. One compares, for example, brain scans taken during a task (ψ_1) to brain scans during rest (ψ_2) in order to see which areas of the brain change across these two conditions. One compares, for example, cfos and cjun expression in cells during a task and not during the task to see if the cells are producing proteins relevant to the task. As discussed in the preceding section, these experimental strategies are common and useful.

Nonetheless these strategies face the challenges of mere correlation and tonic activation. Blood flow might increase during a task even if the increase in blood flow is not part of the mechanism performing the task. The tonic activity of a part might be relevant to performance of a task even if task performance does not change its level of activity (that is, not all parts of a mechanism have to change when the mechanism is working). In practice, these problems can be overcome by bottom-up experiments. Mere correlates of task performance cannot be manipulated to change task performance, but task performance can be manipulated by manipulating tonic activities. This is why I argue that constitutive relevance should be understood as *mutual* manipulability. What the second conditional adds, as I argued above, is a tool for dealing with problems of compensatory responses and for sorting components from background conditions. For these reasons, in addition to recognizing that such experiments are crucial in contemporary neuroscience, I include CR2 in the account of constitutive relevance.

In sum, I conjecture that to establish that X's ϕ-ing is relevant to S's ψ-ing it is sufficient that one be able to manipulate S's ψ-ing by intervening to change X's ϕ-ing (by stimulating or inhibiting) and that one be able to manipulate X's ϕ-ing by manipulating S's ψ-ing. To establish that a component is irrelevant, it is sufficient to show that one cannot manipulate S's ψ-ing by intervening to change X's ϕ-ing and that one cannot manipulate X's ϕ-ing by manipulating S's ψ-ing. The complexities in the componency relationship make it difficult to say more about the intermediate cases in which only one half of the mutual manipulability account is satisfied. What to say in such cases, I suspect, depends on details peculiar to given experiments that admit of no general formulation. Nevertheless, the mutual manipulability approach is a suitable starting point for an account of constitutive relevance.

Relationships of mutual manipulability can and should replace the requirement of derivability as a regulative ideal on constitutive explanations in neuroscience. One need not be able to derive the phenomenon from a description of the mechanism. Rather, one needs to know how the phenomenon is situated within the causal structure of the world. That is, one needs to know how the phenomenon changes under a variety of interventions into the parts *and* how the parts change when one intervenes to change the phenomenon. When one possesses explanations of this sort, one is in a position to make predictions about how the system will behave under a variety of conditions. Furthermore when one possesses explanations of this sort, one knows how to intervene into the mechanism in order to produce regular changes in the phenomenon. Explanations in neuroscience are motivated fundamentally by the desire to bring the CNS under our control. The mutual manipulability account of constitutive relevance makes that connection explicit. Finally, the possibility of multiple realization does not even arise for the mechanistic account. It is not required that all instances of ψ-ing be explained by the same underlying mechanisms. What matters is that each instance of ψ-ing is explained by a set of components that are relevant to ψ in that particular mechanistic context. There are no doubt epistemic difficulties of determining when two mechanistic contexts are equal, but there is no conceptual difficulty seeing how the same type of phenomenon could be explained by different components in different contexts.

9. Conclusion

Both the systems tradition and the reduction tradition share a common goal of understanding constitutive explanation—that is, of understanding how the behavior of a whole is explained in terms of the behavior of its parts. For reasons that I discuss in the introduction to this chapter, most reductionists have now abandoned the classical model of reduction (sometimes called "strong reduction") according to which constitutive explanations involve forming transtheoretic identities and deriving one theory from another.

Those who have abandoned strong reduction commonly replace it with a weaker alternative, according to which reduction merely involves explaining higher-level phenomena in terms of underlying mechanisms (Kim 1989; Sarkar 1992; Smith 1992; Wimsatt 1976b). This move comes at a cost. When reductionists abandon strong reduction they also abandon the model of explanation that lies at its heart: namely, the CL model and the nomic expectability thesis. The problem is that there is no available account of constitutive mechanistic explanation to take its place.

My causal–mechanical account of constitutive explanation is a restricted and elaborated variant of accounts developed within the systems tradition (especially those found in the work of Bechtel, Cummins, Haugeland, Simon, and Wimsatt). The primary worry about previous such models is that they focus more on *describing* mechanistic explanations than they do on revealing the *norms* by which mechanistic explanations are and should be assessed. My friendly criticisms of Cummins's model are intended to illustrate how an accurate description of constitutive explanation can fall short of satisfying this normative objective. Because of their limitations as normative models, the models of the system tradition are not yet suitable competitors to classical reduction, the primary value of which is that it provides a regulative ideal on explanations. If the systems tradition is to challenge classical reduction as an account of constitutive explanation, it must provide an alternative regulative ideal. In this chapter, I take some steps towards rectifying that problem as well.

To see the progress that has been made, let us ask: How must Cummins-style functional analysis be restricted to provide a normatively adequate account of mechanistic explanation?

First, one needs to add the core normative requirement that mechanisms must account fully for the *explanandum phenomenon*. Ideally, it is not enough to account for just normal input–output conditions. One must also account for the multiple features of a phenomenon, including its precipitating conditions, manifestations, inhibitory conditions, modulating conditions, nonstandard conditions, and byproducts. Good explanations account for all of the features of a phenomenon rather than a subset.

Second, one needs to add that mechanistic explanations are constitutive. They explain the behavior of the mechanism as a whole in terms of the activities of its component parts. The parts should not be mere how-possibly fictions. Instead, they should exhibit clusters of properties, they should be robustly detectable, they should be able to be used for purposes of intervention, and that they should be physiologically plausible.

Third, one needs to add that the activities appealed to in a compositional analysis should satisfy the criteria discussed in Chapter 3. This addition is required to rule out mere time-courses, effect-to-cause pairs, effects of common causes, and irrelevant causes.

Fourth, one needs to add a notion of organization. Organization is not merely a matter of being describable in terms of a box-and-arrow diagram or a program. Instead, it involves the active, spatial, and temporal organization of different components. This addition is required to distinguish mechanistic explanations from aggregate explanations, morphological explanations, and taxonomies.

Finally, one needs to supplement functional analysis with an account of constitutive relevance. Without such an account, functional analysis fails to offer an alternative to reduction, and it does not have the resources to exclude irrelevant components from the mechanism. The mutual manipulability account is a plausible condition of constitutive relevance because it fits well with experimental practice and because it is an extension of the view of etiological relevance advanced in Chapter 3.

My emphasis on constitutive mechanistic explanation (and its status as a competitor to classical reduction) should not lead one to forget that I am primarily interested in defending a multilevel view of explanation. Constitutive explanation is one important kind of explanation in neuroscience. But saying so does not commit me to the view that all explanations are constitutive. Nor does it commit me to the fundamentalist view that all explanations are achieved by looking to the lowest possible levels. In the next three chapters, I develop a view of levels (Chapter 5), I argue against fundamentalist claims that causal explanations can be given only at the lowest possible levels (Chapter 6), and I argue that the unity of neuroscience is constructed in the effort to build multilevel mechanistic explanations (Chapter 7).

5

A Field-Guide to Levels

Summary

Explanations in neuroscience typically span multiple levels. The term level, however, is multiply ambiguous. I develop a taxonomy of different kinds of levels, and I show why one must be careful to keep these different kinds distinct. Using an example from contemporary neuroscience—the multilevel mechanisms of spatial memory—I argue that "levels of mechanisms" captures the central explanatory sense in which explanations in neuroscience (and elsewhere in the special sciences) span multiple levels. The multilevel structure of neuroscientific explanations is a consequence of the mechanistic structure of neuroscientific explanations. I emphasize the importance of levels of mechanisms by showing how other common notions of levels (such as levels of science, levels of theories, levels of control, levels of entities, levels of aggregativity, and mereological levels) fail to describe the explanatory levels appearing in the explanation for spatial memory.

1. Introduction

The descriptive fact that explanations in neuroscience typically span multiple levels gives rise to scientific disputes about the relative significance of different levels and to philosophical disputes about the existence and explanatory relevance of nonfundamental levels. Yet the term "level" is multiply ambiguous. Its application requires only a set of items and a way of ordering them as higher or lower. Not surprisingly, then, the term "level" has several common uses in contemporary neuroscience.[1] To

---

[1] Machamer (personal communication), Churchland and Sejnowski (1992), and Hardcastle (1998) called my attention to this fact.

name a few, there are levels of abstraction, analysis, behavior, complexity, description, explanation, function, generality, organization, science, and theory. Consequently, scientific and philosophical disputes about levels cannot be addressed, let alone resolved, without first sorting out which of the various senses of "level" is under discussion.

In this chapter, I develop a taxonomy of ways to think and talk about levels. My taxonomic approach contrasts with Wimsatt's (1976a, 1994) prototype of levels, which characterizes levels in terms of a cluster of rankable features. Wimsatt's classic treatment of levels is the appropriate starting place for any scientifically informed discussion of that topic. In his view, levels are distinguished in part by the *sizes* of objects. Objects at different levels also stand in *composition* relations. Objects at the same level are governed by the same *laws* and exhibit *forces* of similar magnitudes. Objects at the same level also have *regular* and *predictable* relations with one another and are *reliable detectors* of one another. *Theories* are found at levels because that is where the regularities are. Finally, everything at a given level is investigated with the same set of *techniques* and according to similar *disciplinary perspectives*. Wimsatt's reason for offering a prototype of levels, as opposed to a definition, is that some examples of levels lack one or more of these central features. Because the levels metaphor is ambiguous, however, the prototype account obscures the distinctions among different senses of "level." My taxonomic approach highlights the similarities and differences among different senses of level.

Because I am primarily interested in the multilevel structure of explanations in neuroscience, I begin in Section 2 with an uncontroversial example of such: the mechanisms of spatial memory. Charles Stevens praises this explanation as approaching the "dream of neurobiology ... to understand all aspects of interesting and important cognitive phenomena—like memory—from the underlying molecular mechanisms through behavior" (Stevens 1996: 1147). Squire and Kandel claim that "Memory promises to be the first mental faculty to be understandable in a language that makes a bridge from molecules to mind, that is, from molecules to cells, to brain systems, and to behavior" (2000: 3). My goal is to ask which of the different senses of level best describes the levels in this example of multilevel explanation. I develop the taxonomy of levels in Section 3. Finally, in Section 4, I introduce *levels of mechanisms* as the sense most relevant to understanding the spatial memory example and similar multilevel explanations. I show that this way of thinking about levels is consistent with many presumed features of levels (for example, that things at lower levels are smaller than things at higher levels and are studied with different techniques) but inconsistent with others (for example, that levels are monolithic strata in nature; that things at different levels interact causally; and that levels, fields, and theories correspond to one another).

I leave one significant sense of "level" out of my taxonomy for now: "levels of being," or, as I will call them, *levels of realization* (cf. the sense of "orders" in Kim 1998[2]). This is perhaps the dominant notion of "level" under discussion in metaphysics and the philosophy of mind. In levels of realization, a property or activity at a higher level is *realized by* a property or activity at a lower level of realization. The item at a lower level of realization is not part of the item at a higher level; the realized and realizing properties are properties of one and the same thing. Marr's levels of analysis (computational, algorithmic, and hardware/implementation levels) are levels of realization. Levels of mechanisms, in contrast, are a variety of part–whole relation. The property or activity at a higher level of mechanisms is the behavior of the mechanism as a whole (the *explanandum phenomenon*); the parts of the mechanism and their activities are at a lower level. I do not include levels of realization in the present discussion because any attempt to locate them within the taxonomy would be contentious. I discuss the causal relevance of realized variables in Chapter 6.

2. Levels of Spatial Memory

The explanation of spatial memory (henceforth LM), as represented schematically in Figure 5.1, is commonly said to have roughly four levels.[3] The topping-off point in this hierarchy is the spatial memory phenomenon. Call this the *level of spatial memory*.[4] This level is typically associated with scientific fields, such as experimental psychology and ethology, and with different techniques, such as mazes, for assaying different forms of spatial

---

[2] Kim (1998) describes levels of realization as "orders," and he talks about higher- and lower-order properties.

[3] I take no stand on whether this example of explanation is ultimately the right explanation. What matters is not the specific details, but rather the overall explanatory pattern of fitting items into a multilevel structure.

[4] There are many different spatial memory phenomena, but for now I gloss over that matter.

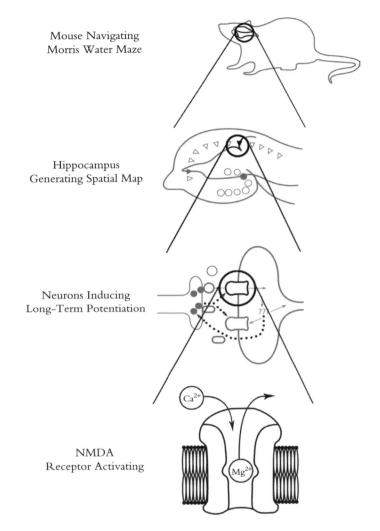

Mouse Navigating
Morris Water Maze

Hippocampus
Generating Spatial Map

Neurons Inducing
Long-Term Potentiation

NMDA
Receptor Activating

Figure 5.1. Levels of spatial memory

memory. Spatial memory is tested in radial arm mazes, sunburst mazes, three-table problems, and the Morris water maze. The last of these is a circular pool filled with an opaque liquid covering a hidden platform. Rats are trained to use various cues from the pool's environment to find the platform and escape the water. The liquid environment in the pool allows researchers to mask the olfactory cues, which is a problem with standard box mazes. In order to test different aspects of spatial memory, researchers can vary where they put the rat in the maze, features of the environment, and other cues pointing to the location of the platform. Researchers monitor the time that it takes the rat to find the platform and, in some cases, the trajectory of the rat through the pool. Experiments of this sort are used to define the phenomenon of spatial memory.

At a lower level—the level of *spatial map formation*—are the computational properties of neural systems, including brain regions such as the hippocampus and other areas in the temporal and frontal cortex. Considerable evidence suggests that the hippocampus, a structure in the medial temporal lobe, is necessary for forming spatial memories. A transverse slice of the hippocampus, with its characteristic tri-synaptic loop, is shown in Figure 5.2a. This loop runs from the perforant path fibers coming from the entorhinal cortex, through the granule cells (O) of the dentate gyrus, and from there to the pyramidal cells $\triangle$ of the cornu Ammonis region (labeled CA1 and CA3). Rats with bilateral lesions to the hippocampus exhibit profound deficits in maze learning and other tasks. Similar results can be obtained by using pharmacological agents to block the activities of crucial neurotransmitters in the hippocampus, or to prevent protein synthesis in hippocampal neurons. The results of such interference experiments have also been supported by activation experiments. If one records from single cells in the hippocampus as the rat navigates a familiar space, one will find that specific cells in the hippocampus (now known as "place cells") fire preferentially when the rat enters a given location in the maze in a particular orientation (O'Keefe and Dostrovsky 1971; Wilson and McNaughton 1993). For this reason, researchers hypothesize that the hippocampus functions as a spatial map.

How does the hippocampus generate spatial maps or contribute to the storage of spatial memories? The answer is still controversial, but answers typically appeal to phenomena at the *cellular-electrophysiological level*. The dominant hypothesis since the 1970s has been that spatial maps are formed through LTP in hippocampal synapses. This hypothesis is supported by evidence that interventions to inhibit LTP prevent spatial learning, that interventions to strengthen LTP can prime learning, and that synapses undergo LTP during learning and memory tasks.

In Figure 5.2b (top), LTP is represented as a lasting enhancement of the post-synaptic response to the same pre-synaptic electrical signal following

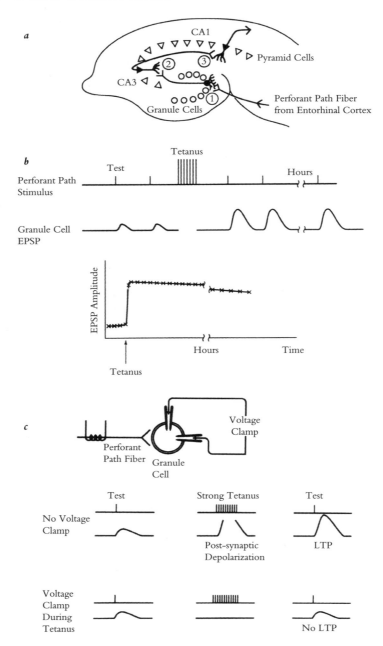

Figure 5.2. A textbook depiction of LTP

Source: Reprinted with permission from Levitan and Kaczmarek (1991)

a tetanus (rapid and repeated stimulation). The top line represents stimuli delivered to the pre-synaptic cell. The bottom line records the post-synaptic response. As shown in the first third of the diagram, a test stimulus to the pre-synaptic cell produces a regular depolarization of the post-synaptic cell (that is, an excitatory post-synaptic potential, or EPSP). The experimental intervention (in the middle third) involves applying a tetanus to the pre-synaptic cell. Following this intervention (in the last third), the same test stimulus produces a much greater EPSP than before. This facilitation lasts for hours, days, or weeks, as shown in Figure 5.2b (bottom). Figure 5.2c illustrates that LTP requires the simultaneous activation of both pre- and post-synaptic neurons. The top record is the same as in Figure 5.2b. In the bottom record, the post-synaptic cell is voltage clamped during the tetanus (in the middle), that is, an external source of current counters any voltage changes in the post-synaptic neuron. LTP is not induced in the absence of post-synaptic depolarization (in the last third). The idea is that spatial maps are created or stored by adjusting the strengths of synapses in the hippocampus.

The bottom of this hierarchy—the *molecular level*—consists of the molecular mechanisms that make the chemical and electrical activities of nerve cells possible. These molecular mechanisms are studied with molecular tools such as gene knockouts and with pharmacological agonists and antagonists that excite and inhibit different biochemical pathways. As I discuss in Chapter 3, if the post-synaptic cell remains polarized (as in Figure 5.2d), the channel through the NMDA receptor remains blocked by large, positively charged Mg^{2+} ions. But if the post-synaptic cell is depolarized, the Mg^{2+} ions are driven out of the channel, allowing Ca^{2+} ions to diffuse into the cell. The Mg^{2+} blockade is a coincidence-detection device that ensures that LTP is induced only when both the pre- and post-synaptic cells are simultaneously active. Interfering with this coincidence-detection device by, for example, removing the NMDA receptor or changing its conformation has effects that ramify throughout this hierarchy, producing deficits in LTP, spatial map formation, and performance in the Morris water maze (see Tsien et al. 1996a, 1996b; McHugh et al. 1996, which I discuss in greater detail in Chapter 7).

My decision to break this explanation into four levels is surely an oversimplification. There might be more levels. One might choose to identify networks of cells in the hippocampus, or cascades of molecules beneath a properly electrophysiological level. The hierarchy could also be expanded upward and downward. Upward, one can consider memory systems in the context of other cognitive and physiological mechanisms (such as emotion and sleep) or in the context of social groups and cultures. Downward, one can consider the protein folding mechanisms that give NMDA receptors their characteristic shapes and activities.

Even without these amendments, this explanatory sketch exhibits the kind of hierarchical structure found elsewhere in the neurosciences and beyond. The mechanisms of osmoregulation discussed in Chapter 1 span from behaviors (such as drinking and urination) to molecules (such as aquapores and oxytocin). The mechanism of the action potential discussed in Chapters 2 and 4 exhibits a similar telescoping structure from the behavior of whole cells and patches of membrane to the fine-grained conformation changes in voltage-gated ion channels. In investigating the visual system, one can focus on the visual system as a whole, on the contributions of distinct brain regions, on neural networks such as optical dominance columns, and on the chemical reactions in the retina. This kind of hierarchical structure is also used to relate Alzheimer's disease and Creutzfeldt-Jacob disease to physiological and molecular mechanisms, to link phenotypes to genotypes, and to tie polymer structure to atomic structure. LM levels are representative of multilevel explanations across the sciences, and so they are a good test case for identifying an explanatorily interesting sense of level.

3. A Field-Guide to Levels

My view is that the levels in this multilevel explanation are best understood as levels of mechanisms. Lower levels in this hierarchy are the components in mechanisms for the phenomena at higher levels. Components at lower levels are organized to make up the behaviors at higher levels, and lower- and higher-level items stand in relationships of mutual manipulability (as established with the interlevel experiments I discuss in Chapter 4). Thinking of levels in this way shows why the notion of "level" is so closely bound up with the notions of explanation and organization, and it allows one to integrate the notion of "level" with the view of explanation I have developed in the preceding chapters. In talking with other neuroscientists and philosophers, I find that most of them readily accept this view of levels.

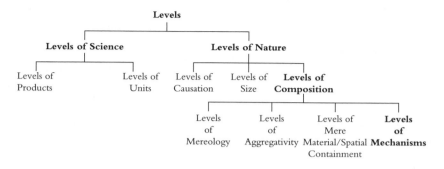

Figure 5.3. A taxonomy of levels

However, I also find that most of them confuse this view of levels with a host of unrelated and sometimes misleading associations. To guard against these misleading associations, I develop a taxonomy of levels (represented diagrammatically in Figure 5.3) to demarcate my notion of levels from its nearest neighbors. I distinguish the nodes in this taxonomy by examining three defining questions.

The first defining question is: what are the relata? That is, what kinds of things are sorted into levels? The top node of Figure 5.3, for example, marks a distinction between levels of science and levels of nature. The relata in levels of science might be either *products* of science or *units* of science (as shown one node down on the left). Products of science are epistemic constructs, such as analyses, descriptions, explanatory models, and theories. When one says that theories about molecules are at a lower level than theories about cells, or that brain regions and cells occupy different levels of description, one is talking about levels of products of science. Units of science include such groups as fields (Darden 1991), paradigms (Kuhn 1962), perspectives (Wimsatt 1994), and research programs (Lakatos 1977). When one says that nuclear physics (a field) is at a lower level than molecular biology (another field), one is talking about relationships among scientific units. One can also understand the term "levels" as describing levels of nature. These are represented on the right branch of Figure 5.3. Levels of nature relate items in the world, such as activities, entities, properties, and states. As I argue, the levels metaphor is not univocal across these different relata. Nor, I argue, do these notions of level correspond neatly to one another. To use the term level clearly, one must specify the relata (see Wimsatt 1976a: 215).

The second defining question is: what is the interlevel relation? That is, by virtue of what are two items at different levels? The three divisions under "levels of nature" in Figure 5.3 correspond to different kinds of relation: causality, size, and composition. The levels metaphor is frequently articulated as a size relationship: things at lower levels are smaller than things at higher levels (for example, Wimsatt 1976a; Kim 1998). Sometimes levels are spoken of as levels of "complexity," according to which things at higher levels are more organized than things at lower levels. Some say that things at different levels are causally related (for example, Campbell 1974). It is easy to slide from one sense of interlevel relation (for example, size) to another (for example, complexity) without noticing or acknowledging it.

The last defining question for a sense of levels is the placement question: by virtue of what are any two items at the same level? Different expositors of the levels metaphor appeal to different features in order to place items together at the same level. Some locate things at the same level if they are roughly the same size. Gould (1980) claims, in addition, that items at the same level are acted on by similar forces, are governed by the same laws, and interact (most often) with one another (see also Wimsatt 1994). I argue below that there may not be a uniquely correct answer to this question for all senses of levels. I argue, in fact, that there is no unique answer to the placement question for levels of mechanisms.

In the rest of Section 3, I move from left to right in Figure 5.3. I show that none of the notions of level, except for levels of mechanisms, adequately describes the notion of level implicit in the LM explanation. Moreover, I show that the different senses of level fail to correspond to one another, contrary to what the prototype model suggests. Once I have cleared this ground, I return to levels of mechanisms in Section 3.3.

3.1 Levels of science (units and products)

Philosophers frequently define levels by reference to divisions in science rather than by reference to divisions in the structure of the world. In this, they follow Oppenheim and Putnam's (1958) view in their "Unity of Science as a Working Hypothesis." For them, the unity of science comprises unity among either units of science (for example, fields, disciplines, and research programs) or among its products (for example, descriptions, explanations, and theories). Oppenheim and Putnam presume that units and products of science correspond to one another and that these, in turn, correspond to divisions in the structure of the world. In particular, they identify six "mereological" levels of nature: elementary particles, atoms, molecules, cells, organisms, and societies (1958: 9). Each level of nature, they suggest, also corresponds to a unique theoretical vocabulary (1958: 10) and a unique set of explanatory principles (that is, laws) that constitute a theory specific to that level (1958: 4). Each level-specific theory, in turn, corresponds to a different science, from particle physics at the bottom to the social sciences at the top. The unity of science is achieved by explaining the phenomena in the domain of one field of science with the theories of another field of science.

Oppenheim and Putnam intend this view of levels and the unity of science to be an accurate description of the science of their day. However, it is at best a caricature. The most obvious oversimplification is the six-level image of the world. Surely they did not intend these six levels to describe the world in all of its complexity, and surely they could acknowledge that science might add, delete, or modify any level in this hierarchy. Nonetheless, the descriptive shortcomings of this simplistic image help to show what would be required of a more adequate view of the multilevel structure found in many scientific explanations. First, their hierarchy has gaps. It does not include stable units formed of molecules (such as NMDA receptors), networks of cells (such as the CA1 region), organs (such as the hippocampus), or units of organization between organisms and societies (such as families or friendships). The hierarchy has no place for ecosystems, gases, planets, or solar systems. Are solar systems at a higher level than societies (because they are bigger) or are they at a lower level (because they are associated with physics)? Solar systems cannot be at a higher level than societies, because societies are not mereological parts of solar systems. Nor can they be at the same level as elementary particles, given that solar systems are composed of elementary particles. Wimsatt's branching diagram in Figure 5.4 is more accurate in these respects. There are more nodes, and the levels branch as they ascend. In this "reductive illustrative," as Wimsatt calls it, the world is structured in many different hierarchies that converge only at the lowest level. One hierarchy extends from atoms to solar objects. Another extends from atoms, through a "biopsychological thicket," to "individual thought and language." On this view, atoms are at a lower level than both plasma and organic molecules, although plasma and organic molecules are not in the same hierarchy. These changes transform

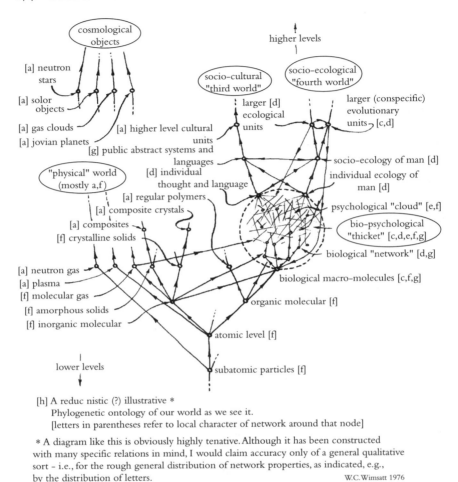

Figure 5.4. Wimsatt's branching diagram of levels

Source: Reprinted with permission from Wimsatt (1976: 253)

Oppenheim and Putnam's six levels into a much more accurate description of the hierarchies described by contemporary science.

My primary criticism, however, is not of the simplicity or descriptive inadequacy of this six-layered vision of the world. Oppenheim and Putnam could clearly grant that the world is not so tidy. Rather, I object to the supposed correspondence between levels of nature, levels of units, and levels of products of science. Oppenheim and Putnam do not seem to recognize any difficulty in moving freely between these different conceptions of levels. Consider the following passage as just one example:

It has been contended that one manifestly cannot explain human behavior by reference to the laws of atomic physics. It would indeed be fantastic to suppose that the simplest regularity in the field of psychology could be explained directly—that is, "skipping" intervening branches of science—by employing subatomic theories. But one may believe in the attainability of unitary science without thereby committing oneself to this absurdity. (1958: 7)

In this passage, Oppenheim and Putnam shift without notice from describing structures of the world (human behavior), to describing products (explanations and theories), to describing fields of science (psychology and atomic physics).

In neuroscience, this tidy correspondence breaks down. Consider the above sketch of LM levels from the perspective of Oppenheim and Putnam's view of levels. The LM explanation constitutes a theory. It is not a deductively closed and interpreted axiomatic system, as Hempel characterizes theories, but it nonetheless satisfies a view of theories as models of systems (Craver 2002a; Giere 1999; Glennan 2005; Suppe 1989). These different items are integrated in a *single* theory not because they can all be described by theoretical predicates appropriate to a level of nature, but because they can be used together to describe, predict, explain, and test aspects of spatial memory. This theory is composed of items drawn from multiple Oppenheim and Putnam-style levels. The influx of Ca^{2+} ions (atoms) through the NMDA receptor (molecules) initiates the sequence of events leading to LTP (cells), which is part of the mechanism for forming a spatial map in the CA1 region (organs). Map formation is part of the explanation for how the mouse (whole organism) navigates through familiar environments (ecosystems) and among conspecifics and predators (societies). As Schaffner (1993a, 1993b) argues, most biological and biomedical theories span levels from molecules to physiological systems. The theories of neuroscience are no exception.

There can also be multiple theories at a single level of nature on any reasonable definition of a single level. If one orders levels by size, for example, then Wimsatt's diagram picks out a single level containing neutron gases, plasma, molecular gases, amorphous solids, crystalline solids, regular polymers, and biological macromolecules. These phenomena occupy different domains of investigation, they are characterized by different theories, and different kinds of scientists study them even though all the objects under investigation are the same size. Similarly, an electrophysiologist and a cellular anatomist might be interested in the structures and activities of cells in the hippocampus, and thus focus their attention at the same level (on many standard accounts of sameness of level). Nonetheless, they approach the same level with two distinct bodies of theory. Part of what Wimsatt intends to capture in his depiction of the "biopsychological thicket," I believe, is the fact that in such domains of science, there are multiple different theories, many of which are difficult to order neatly into levels, and most of which are reticulately connected to one another. Theories in neuroscience, in short, do not correspond to tidy levels of nature.

For similar reasons, there is no tidy correspondence between the distinct fields of neuroscience (units) and Oppenheim and Putnam-style levels of nature. Single fields increasingly reach across multiple levels of nature, and different fields often approach items at the same level of nature from different perspectives. The LM theory is the combined product of anatomy, biochemistry, computational neuroscience, electrophysiology, molecular biology, neuroanatomy, pharmacology, psychiatry, and experimental psychology. Cognitive neuroscience is, by its very nature, a field that encompasses psychological, physiological, cellular, and molecular items within its domain. In the experiment mentioned above, researchers intervene to knock out the NMDA receptor and then detect the deleterious effects of that manipulation on LTP, spatial maps, and performance in the Morris water maze (McHugh et al. 1996). In a similar experiment, researchers altered the structure of the NMDA receptor and noted enhanced LTP, sharper spatial maps, and improved learning curves (Tang et al. 1999). Experiments of this sort, which are increasingly the norm in neuroscience, require contributions from several different fields. In the interdisciplinary climate of contemporary neuroscience, individual researchers often acquire competence with techniques drawn from different fields and with techniques that target various levels of nature. Contemporary neuroscience thus does not fit Oppenheim and Putnam's hierarchical structure. Fields, journals, and scientific organizations are now organized around interfield collaboration to such an extent that it is no longer possible to resolve neuroscience into well-defined strata of research.

In the case of LM levels and other hierarchically organized explanations, theories, fields, and levels of nature (in Oppenheim and Putnam's sense) dissociate from one another. Researchers in single fields do research at multiple distinct levels of nature, and sometimes multiple fields bring their resources to bear on a single level. For these reasons, I confine my attention from this point on to levels of nature rather than to levels of science.

3.2 Levels of nature

I propose then that we start by thinking of levels as primarily features of the world rather than as features of the units or products of science.[5] As possible relata in levels of nature, I include entities, activities, properties, and mechanisms. I also distinguish among three interlevel relations: causation, size, and composition. In this section, I consider each of these different relations, along with a few permutations of different relata, to illustrate how ambiguities arise from failing to keep these different relations distinct.

3.2.1. Causal levels (processing and control)   Sometimes the levels metaphor is used to describe causal relations. Two examples are levels of processing and levels of control.

In *levels of processing*, the relata are the stages of a task or an extended process. These stages are related to one another sequentially and causally (see Churchland and Sejnowski 1992: 23). Levels of processing are sometimes inscribed in the names of brain regions with such terms as "primary" and "secondary," as in "primary somatosensory cortex" and "secondary auditory cortex." For example, the flow of information through the visual system is commonly said to begin with the retina, passing through the lateral geniculate nucleus (LGN) and the primary visual cortex (V1) before being sent on to "higher-level" visual areas (such as V2, MT, or any of roughly twenty-five other major visual processing regions). The LGN is frequently said to be responsible for "lower-level" visual processing. V1 is responsible for higher-level processing, and MT (among others) processes information at a higher level still. Levels of processing are ranked relative to one another by their place in a causal (and derivatively, temporal) sequence. Processing in the retina occurs earlier than processing in the LGN, and the

---

[5] Levels of sciences and theories could then be seen as derivative upon, and at best approximations of, these ontic structures.

processing in the LGN occurs earlier than the processing in V1. Processing in the retina is causally required for, prepares the information for, or filters information into, later processing in the LGN, V1, and MT. For this reason, hydrodynamic metaphors are more appropriate for describing levels of processing than are stratigraphic metaphors: later stages are downstream in the flow of information from earlier stages.[6]

Levels of processing are relevant to understanding aspects of the LM mechanisms as well. The hippocampal trisynaptic loop shown in Figure 5.2a can be idealized into levels of processing. Perforant path fibers from the entorhinal cortex synapse on the granule cells of the dentate gyrus regions. Granule cells then project to the pyramidal cells in CA3, which, in turn, project to CA1. In this hippocampal circuit, CA1 is downstream from CA3, which is downstream from the dentate gyrus. Each region is at a higher level of processing than its predecessor.

However, the LM levels described in Section 2 are not levels of processing. The primary difference is that LM levels are relationships between a whole and its parts, while levels of processing are relationships between distinct items. LTP is part of forming spatial maps, and forming spatial maps is part of learning to navigate a novel environment. The retina is not part of the LGN. Furthermore, higher levels of processing are later in the flow of information than lower levels. They receive information that has been prepared by items at lower levels. They are "downstream" from earlier levels of processing, and items that are "upstream" causally influence them. Activities at lower LM levels, in contrast, are temporally contained within the activities at higher levels. The formation of spatial maps is not later than the induction of LTP; LTP is part of the process by which spatial maps are formed. LTP does not prepare information for consumption by the hippocampus; it is part of the consumption of information by the hippocampus. Finally, LM levels also lack the causal relations characteristic of levels of processing. This is because entities at lower levels are parts of

---

[6] The tidy division of processing units into "earlier and later" may break down in mechanisms with multiple parallel and feedback connections. Indeed, one might even suggest that it breaks down for the visual system as well, given the complex feedback from V1 to LGN to the retina. As the number of relevant causal relations in a mechanism increases, the clear temporal order among the component stages begins to break down. (See the discussion of complex mechanisms in Bechtel and Richardson 1993.) In such cases, speaking of stages as higher or lower in a hierarchy of information processing requires one to idealize away from the reticulate interconnections among components in order to see a predominant direction of causal influence.

entities at higher levels, and activities at lower levels are stages of activities at higher levels. To view LM levels as causally related, one must violate the common assumptions that causal relationships are contingent and that cause and effect must be wholly distinct. If one confuses levels of processing with LM levels, one might think of the interlevel relationship as a causal relationship despite these disanalogies.

A similar issue arises if one construes LM levels as *levels of control*. In levels of control, the relata are agents or actors (literally or metaphorically). They are related by subordination. Higher levels of control direct, dominate, or regulate activities at lower levels. Bosses and employees, generals and privates, teachers and students are all related by levels of control. The metaphor of control and subordination invites confusion when applied to nonintentional contexts, but often the metaphor is entirely appropriate. Genes are sometimes described as controlling development,[7] and the pre-frontal cortex and cingulate cortex are sometimes said to exhibit executive control over other brain regions and behavior (Fuster 1997; Smith and Jonides 1999; Posner and DiGirolamo 1998). More formally, the apparatus of control theory, with controllers, plants, and feedback connections, has been useful in many areas of biology and neuroscience (for a recent discussion, see Grush 2004). Very roughly, formal applications of this control metaphor describe controllers as receiving input from the output of the controlled system (that is, the plant), as comparing the output to a target output, and as then manipulating the plant in such a way as to bring it closer to producing the target output. Not all systems described with the language of control have these features. Sometimes the language of "control" is used merely to describe a predominant cause (as in the case of genes and the pre-frontal cortex). The important thing is that the controller and the plant are *distinct* parts of a larger system. Each part feeds input into and receives output from the other parts. Like a boss and subordinates, the pre-frontal cortex is said to monitor and regulate the behavior of *other* brain regions. This is unlike LM levels, in which objects are related as parts to wholes. The hippocampus is part of the mouse, and the synapses are parts of the hippocampus. An analogous understanding of the control system described above is to understand the whole system (including controller,

---

[7] Of course, this view is hotly debated. Genes are parts of complex mechanisms, and different perspectives lead people to privilege different components of the mechanism (or none at all) as being "in control."

plant, and feedback) as controlling the plant. This is the sort of situation envisioned by many advocates of "top-down causation." To describe LM levels in terms of levels of control is thus to import a strained understanding of the dependency relationship between levels.[8]

3.2.2. Levels of size   It is perhaps most common to describe levels of nature as levels of size. In such levels, the relata are entities (for example, mice, hippocampi, and cells), and they are ranked by relative size. Churchland and Sejnowski (2000: 16), in the classic diagram of levels shown in Figure 5.5, rank entities from molecules measured in Angstrom units to organisms measured in meters. Size is also a core feature of Wimsatt's prototype of levels (shown in Figure 5.6). Wimsatt represents levels as local maxima

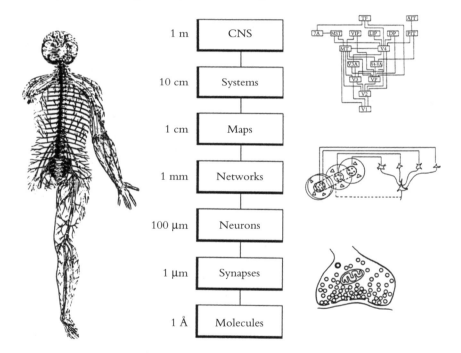

Figure 5.5. Churchland and Sejnowski's classic diagram of levels in neuroscience
Source: Reprinted with permission from Churchland and Sejnowski (1988)

---

[8] Those who suspect that the hierarchical world-view is associated with a male-centered and dominance-oriented hierarchy transparently confuse levels of the sort represented in LM levels with levels of control.

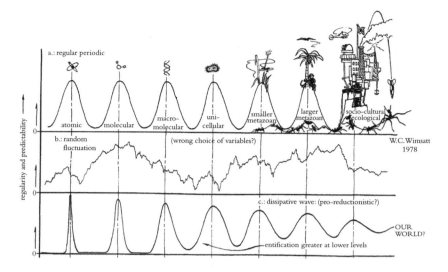

Figure 5.6. Levels as local maxima of regularity and predictability*
* Appearing over a roughly logarithmic size scale
Source: Reprinted with permission from Wimsatt (1976: 240)

of regularity and predictability in the phase space of possible ways of organizing matter. Levels appear as peaks of regularity and predictability when graphed against a "roughly logarithmic" size scale. An orderly world, with well-defined peaks of regularity and predictability at different size scales, is shown at the top. A world without levels, where regularity and predictability vary randomly with no well-defined peaks or valleys in any size range, is drawn beneath it. The bottom world (Wimsatt labels it "Our World?") shows a dissipating wave, with regularity and predictability diminishing and spreading out over broader size ranges as size increases.

Wimsatt's and Churchland's diagrams vividly illustrate the idea that levels correspond to sizes. They also illustrate an empirical hypothesis about the structure of the world, that is, that regularities tend to be found in certain size ranges and not in others. LM levels satisfy the first intuition: rats are larger than hippocampi, which are larger than cells, which are larger than molecules. The second hypothesis, concerning the clustering of regularities within size ranges, is more difficult to evaluate. One reading of this hypothesis is that those items that participate in regularities tend to be found at levels. This reading is trivial, however, because any putative between-level item for which there are robust regularities will, ipso facto, define a level. On a more substantive reading, Wimsatt's claim is that regularities hold more between items at the same level than between items at different levels. Wimsatt is led to this idea by his belief that objects tend to interact with other objects of roughly the same size (and so at the same level), and that things in the same size-range are acted on by the same forces (1976a: 237). When Wimsatt introduces Figure 5.6, he says, "Still supposing that levels are to be individuated solely on the basis of size factors, imagine a picture like that of Figure [5.6], in which regularity and predictability of *interactions* is graphed as a function of the size of the interacting entity" (1976a: 238; italics added). For Wimsatt, things at a level "interact most strongly and frequently" (1976a: 215) with things at the same level. This explains why he believes that regularities cluster within levels.

There are two problems that need to be kept separate. The first concerns causal interactions across size scales. There is a question (i) whether there can be causal interactions between things at different size scales, and a second question (ii) whether causal interactions between things at different size scales are less frequent than causal interactions between things at the same size scale. As to (i), Wimsatt and I agree that the answer is yes: large things (even arbitrarily large things) can interact with small things (even arbitrarily small things). Elephants squash fleas, planets attract molecules, and I breathe atoms. No one should disagree about any of this. However, if one recasts (i) as (i*), whether there can be causal interactions between things at different levels, the matter is more controversial. If one understands levels as involving a compositional relationship (as I am inclined to do, and as Wimsatt is sometimes inclined to do), then, as I have explained above, there is reason to be skeptical about interlevel causal claims. The skepticism arises from the fact that the ordinary concept of causation seems to carry with it a number of assumptions about the logical independence of causes and effects, the temporal precedence of causes and effects, and so on that are difficult, if not impossible, to square with the idea of interlevel (compositional) relations (see Chapter 4). The point is that the notion of levels of size carries very different implications for thinking about interlevel causes than does the notion of levels of composition. Wimsatt's prototype account makes this more confusing than it needs to be. As to (ii), I make no bets. It is an intriguing hypothesis.

The second problem to be sorted out concerns regularities. There are questions about (iii) whether there are regularities between things at different size levels, and (iv) whether regularities between things at different size scales are less common than regularities between things at the same size scale. As to (iii), the answer certainly seems to be yes again, using the same examples referenced above. As to (iv), I make no commitment. Suppose, however, that we ask the same questions about interlevel relationships and that we construe the interlevel relationship as involving a compositional relationship. Unlike the case of causation discussed in the preceding paragraph, this reconstrual makes no difference to the discussion of regularities. There are regularities between wholes and their parts. The most mundane examples are regularities of composition (for example, the fact that diamonds are composed of carbon atoms). More complex cases include the kinds of regularities revealed by interlevel experiments. The behavior of the whole is dependent on the behavior of the components in such a way that interventions to change the components can change the behavior of the whole and vice versa. While there are not interlevel causal relations in LM levels, there are many interlevel relations of dependency, and thereby interlevel relations of regularity and predictability. One can disrupt spatial memory by ablating the hippocampus or knocking out NMDA receptors. Building theories in sciences with multilevel domains involves discovering regularities that span levels and that allow prediction of how changes at one level influence changes at other levels. Regularities can be found both at and across levels.

The primary problem with understanding LM levels as levels of size is that size relations among LM levels are incidental by-products of a more fundamental *compositional* relationship among those levels. What matters is that navigating rats are partly composed of hippocampi generating spatial maps, not that navigating rats are larger than their hippocampi. These hippocampi are, in turn, composed of potentiating synapses and activating NMDA receptors. Wimsatt mentions composition as one of the features in his prototype of levels, but he is not committed to the idea that all things at different levels relative to one another also are compositionally related. This is evidenced first by his willingness to talk about the frequency of causal interaction among levels, as I discuss above. This lack of commitment to compositional relations in levels is also explicit in Figure 5.6. On the left are atoms, which are parts of molecules, which are parts of cells. On the right, however, are unicellular organisms, smaller metazoan organisms, and larger metazoan creatures. Except in very special circumstances (for example, mitochondria), these latter items are not related compositionally. The view of levels as local maxima of regularity within size ranges, while an interesting empirical hypothesis about the structure of the world, does not adequately describe the central feature of LM levels: composition.

3.2.3. Levels of composition   LM levels exhibit a special kind of composition relation. In this section, I distinguish four kinds of composition: mereological, aggregative, spatial/material, and mechanistic composition. Mechanistic composition, I claim, is the crucial feature of LM levels.

3.2.3.1. Levels of mereology   The mereological, or part–whole, relation is the most familiar variety of compositional relation appealed to in discussions of levels (see Oppenheim and Putnam 1958; Kim 1993: 337; Schaffner 1993a: 102). There are many accounts of the mereological relation, and it is not always clear which among them the authors intend to endorse. Many mereological systems contain features that are ill matched to the project of describing LM levels (Sanford 1993). Mereology, at least in many cases, ignores relations among the parts, treating every complex thing as an aggregate. This is not so much a shortcoming of mereology as a by-product of the fact that mereological systems are not designed to characterize levels in science. It might turn out that features of some formal mereological system are appropriate for describing certain aspects of levels in neuroscience. However, the best starting point for characterizing the containment relationship is to look at examples of neuroscientific explanations, and then to evaluate whether or not the formal apparatus adequately expresses that relationship. Starting with the formal apparatus of mereology requires too many assumptions, and some of these assumptions are misleading.

Consider first the *reflexivity theorem*: every object is part of itself. This theorem is in many classic formulations of mereology (including Tarski [1929] 1956; Woodger 1937), and it is a cornerstone of many proofs in formal mereology. However, the reflexivity theorem is unhelpful in describing LM levels. If the levels relationship is a part–whole relation, and every item in the LM hierarchy is a part of itself, then every item in the hierarchy is at a higher and lower level than itself. This result fits poorly with many of the functions that the levels metaphor is supposed to serve in neuroscience. First, it violates the assumption that LM levels are exclusive, that is, that each item appears at only one level in a given hierarchy. One central function of the levels metaphor is to sort items into different taxa; if the same item falls into different levels with respect to itself, that sorting function is void. Second, the levels in the LM hierarchy are closely tied to the notion of (ontic) explanation. The behavior of the hippocampus is part of the explanation for the ability of organisms to navigate their spatial environments, and LTP in hippocampal synapses is part of the explanation for how spatial maps are formed. The hippocampus, on the other hand, is not an explanation for itself. To avoid this problem, one could develop a mereology without the reflexivity axiom (as suggested by Rescher 1955). Another option is to develop an account of levels that places Y at a lower level than X only if Y is part of X according to the mereological relationship and, in addition, X is not identical with Y (that is, to specify that Y is a *proper part* of X). I have little doubt that formal mereological systems can be recast to accommodate the features of LM levels. My point, rather, is that in building an appropriate mereology for levels in neuroscience, one should begin with the sort of levels that appear in the LM hierarchy and ask what the mereology must be to adequately reflect the relevant features of those levels. One condition on an adequate mereology is that lower-level items are proper parts of higher-level items.

A second component of many formal accounts of mereology is the *extensionality theorem*: an object is completely determined by the set of its parts. A consequence of this theorem is that two objects are identical if and only if they share all their parts. This wording of the extensionality requirement rules out one of the central features of LM levels, namely, that the parts at a lower level are *organized* into the wholes that they compose (see Rescher 1955). Suppose that one took all of the cells in the hippocampus as shown in Figure 5.2a and rearranged them into an entirely different network of connections, say, a bust of Santiago Ramon y Cajal. According to the extensionality theorem, the hippocampus and the bust would be identical by virtue of the fact that they share all of their components. There is no reason to prevent people from talking this way, but it is not a useful way to talk about LM levels. LM-type levels are frequently spoken of as "levels of organization" to reflect the fact that it matters how the components are organized with respect to one another. In short: relations matter. Every complex is a mereological sum, but mechanisms are always literally more than the sum of their parts. Any account of the composition relation in LM levels must accommodate this fact.

Finally, formal accounts of mereology are sometimes formulated to apply equally to both abstract and concrete items. The NMDA receptor is, in some sense, part of the synapse. The holdings of Jones's Swiss bank account are part of his total wealth. Concepts are sometimes thought of as parts of propositions. But the part–whole relationship between Jones's holdings and his wealth is different from the part–whole relationship between the NMDA receptor and the synapse. The NMDA receptor is *materially* contained in the sense that the matter in the receptor is included in the matter that constitutes the cell, and it is *spatially* contained within the cell's boundaries. Again, there may be some common way of talking about parts and wholes that applies to both abstract and concrete objects, and this may be useful for some purposes. Starting with LM levels, however, one would not be led to this conclusion. Material and spatial containment are crucial features of LM levels.

3.2.3.2. Levels of aggregativity   There are several varieties of material/spatial containment. Some refer to LM-type levels as *levels of aggregativity*. This choice of words misleadingly suggests that properties of things at higher levels are simple sums of the properties of things at lower levels. In levels of aggregates, the relata are properties of wholes and the properties of parts, and the relation between them is that higher-level properties are sums of lower-level properties. The mass of a pile of sand is an aggregate of the masses of the individual grains. When wholes are sums of their parts, the wholes change continuously with the addition and removal of parts. Intersubstitution of parts makes no difference to the property of the whole. The parts do not interact in ways that are relevant to the aggregate property (Wimsatt 1994). The pile gets heavier continuously as one adds new grains of sand, and moving them about has no effect on the weight. Replacing individual grains with equally weighted replicas has no effect on the weight of the pile, and the grains do not interact with one another in ways that influence the weight of the pile.

Aggregative properties are rarely interesting. The total alcohol content of the gin in a glass, for example, is an aggregate of the alcohol contents of its unit subvolumes. The volume of a glass of gin, on the other hand, is technically not a mere aggregate of the volumes of the component molecules;

rather, the total volume depends on the average kinetic energy of, and electromagnetic interactions among, the component molecules. Consider synaptic transmission in hippocampal neurons. As an action potential reaches the axon terminal of the pre-synaptic neuron, Ca^{2+} channels open and Ca^{2+} rushes into the cell. As a result, a vesicle containing neurotransmitters fuses to the neuronal membrane and releases its contents into the synaptic cleft. The neurotransmitters diffuse across the cleft and act upon receptors on the post-synaptic cell. The process relies crucially on near-aggregate phenomena. Action potentials are aggregate fluxes of ions across the cell membrane, Ca^{2+} concentrations are aggregates of Ca^{2+} ions, and concentrations of neurotransmitters are aggregates of individual neurotransmitter molecules. Each of these aggregates partially depends in part on the relative spatial location of the component parts, concentration being parts per volume. As these examples illustrate, it is much more common to find levels that violate the above-mentioned conditions on aggregativity; these levels come closer to the forms of mechanistic organization that I describe in Chapter 4.

3.2.3.3. Levels of mere material/spatial containment Before I examine this mechanistic sense of levels, I examine another variety of composition relation that falls short of characterizing LM-type levels.[9] While not exactly aggregates, these levels are properly thought of as *levels of mere material/spatial containment*. In levels of mere material/spatial containment, the relata are entities. One entity is at a lower level than another entity if the lower-level entity is within the spatial boundaries of the higher-level entity and makes up part of the matter in the higher-level whole. I know of no one who advocates this view of levels, but the contrast highlights crucial features of levels of mechanisms.

Levels of mere material/spatial containment are too permissive to characterize the nature of LM levels. In particular, thinking of levels in this way does not allow one to distinguish between mere *pieces* of a system and its *components*.[10] Dividing a system or mechanism into material/spatial pieces any which way will not break it into components. One might slice

---

[9] One might argue, on the grounds presented here, that containment should not be understood as a species of composition relation.

[10] I am grateful to Tom Polger for suggesting this distinction, which is something like that originally drawn by David Sanford (1993) in his effort to develop a common-sense mereology.

it, dice it, spiral cut it, or merely hack it to bits. Each of these methods of decomposition would produce pieces, but unless one is very lucky, none of those pieces would be components. Suppose that one were to divide a rat into 1 cm cubes (cf. Haugeland 1998). Some cubes would contain no components relevant to spatial memory, most cubes would contain parts that are irrelevant to spatial memory, and no cubes (taken as a whole) would be components of the spatial memory system. The cubes would be haphazard collections of stuff that, as a whole, make no identifiable contribution to anything rats do. You could not pluck many of them out without a systematic collapse; the cubes contain crucial stuff. However, the cubes are not themselves components. Components, in contrast, are pieces that make identifiable contributions to the behavior of a mechanism. Being *a piece of* S is nothing but a compositional relation. This kind of relation holds between a glass of gin and one of its unit subvolumes. Being *a component of* S involves, in addition, being relevant to the behavior of the whole.

This example illustrates that decomposition into lower-level parts—components rather than pieces—for the purposes of mechanistic explanation is always a decomposition relative to a behavior of the system. It is framed by an *explanandum phenomenon*. As Stuart Kauffman notes:

A view of what the system is doing sets the explanandum and also supplies criteria by which to decide whether or not a proposed portion [that is, piece] of the system with some of its causal consequences is to count as a part and process of the system [that is, component]. Specifically, a proposed part will count as a part [component] of the system if it, together with some of its causal consequences, will fit together with the other proposed parts [components] and processes to cause the system to behave as described. (Kauffman 1971: 260)

The cubes fit together spatially, but unless one is very lucky, they cut across the relevant components in the mechanism. The idea of spatial decomposition is by itself too weak to rule out decomposition of a mechanism into cubes. Mechanistic decomposition cuts mechanisms at their joints.

3.3 Levels of mechanisms

The point of the foregoing considerations is that LM levels are levels of mechanisms. Levels of mechanisms are levels of composition, but the composition relation is not, at base, spatial or material. In levels of mechanisms, the relata are behaving mechanisms at higher levels and their components at lower levels. These relata are properly conceived neither as entities nor as activities; rather, they should be understood as acting entities. The interlevel relationship is as follows: X's ϕ-ing is at a lower mechanistic level than S's ψ-ing if and only if X's ϕ-ing is a component in the mechanism for S's ψ-ing. Lower-level components are *organized together* to form higher-level components. Levels of mechanisms are represented in Figure 5.7. At the top is a mechanism S engaged in behavior ψ. Below it are the ϕ-ings of Xs that are organized in S's ψ-ing. Below that are the ρ-ings (pronounced "rho-ings") of Ps (English pronunciation) that are organized in the ϕ-ing of Xs. By organization, I mean that the parts have spatial (location, size, shape, and motion), temporal (order, rate, and duration), and active (for example, feedback) relations with one another by which they work together to do something. Organization is the interlevel relation between a mechanism as a whole and its components. Lower-level components are made up into higher-level components by organizing them spatially, temporally, and actively into something greater than a mere sum of the parts.

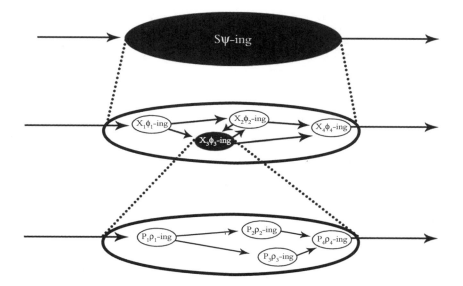

Figure 5.7. Three levels of mechanisms

Levels of mechanisms satisfy many of the central features of levels in Wimsatt's prototype. Levels of mechanisms are transparently componential, unlike mere size levels. Because components are inside the mechanism by definition, it follows that the entities in a mechanism are no larger, and are typically smaller, than the mechanism as a whole. This is consistent with the possibility that distributed components could be as large as the mechanism as a whole (for example, the circulatory system takes up most of the organism), but no component can be larger than the mechanism as a whole, in part because this would imply that the mechanism is larger than itself. Levels of mechanisms are also loci of stable generalizations, and consequently can be seen as local maxima of regularity and predictability. This is because parts of the mechanism that make an intelligible (that is, regular and predictable) contribution to the behavior of the mechanism as a whole are identified at levels. Levels of mechanisms thus satisfy many of the central features associated with levels in the first place.

However, levels of mechanisms fail to satisfy other widely held beliefs about levels. First, in contrast to the common way of speaking about levels, levels of mechanisms should not be conceived as levels of objects (for example, societies, organisms, cells, molecules, and atoms). They are levels of behaving components. In many cases, the components picked out in a mechanistic decomposition fail to correspond to paradigmatic entities with clear spatial boundaries. The synapse, for instance, is composed of part of a pre-synapatic cell (the axon terminal), part of a post-synaptic cell (the dendrite or bouton), and the gap between them. What unifies these items into a component is their organized behavior: the pre-synaptic cell releases transmitters that traverse the cleft and act on the post-synaptic cell. Synapses are not cells or parts of cells. Nor are they composed of cells alone. Rather, they are components unified by their organization in an activity.

Second, unlike Oppenheim and Putnam's six levels of nature, levels of mechanisms are not monolithic divisions in the structure of the world. The idea of monolithic levels is reinforced in Wimsatt's diagrams in Figure 5.4 and 5.6. Each size scale in Figure 5.4 contains identifiable strata across branching nodes at similar size scales. In Figure 5.6, the peaks of regularity and predictability span all atoms, all molecules, all unicellular organisms, and so on. It may turn out, as Wimsatt suggests, that the world exhibits such peaks of regularity and predictability. However, levels of mechanisms are far more local than the monolithic image suggests. They are defined only within a given compositional hierarchy. Different levels of mechanisms are found in the spatial memory system, the circulatory system, the osmoregulatory system, and the visual system. How many levels there are, and which levels are included, are questions to be answered on a case-by-case basis by discovering which components at which size scales are explanatorily relevant for a given phenomenon. They cannot be read off a menu of levels in advance.

To put the point differently, on my view of levels, it makes no sense to ask if my heart is at a different level of mechanisms than my car's water pump because there is no mechanism containing the two (except in bizarre science-fiction cases, in which case talk of levels might be appropriate). Similarly, it makes no sense to ask if ocular dominance columns are at a different level than kidneys because the two are not parts of the same mechanism. Likewise, the question of whether a given molecule and a given cell are at different mechanistic levels can be asked only in the presumed context of a given mechanism and a presumed decomposition of that mechanism. Similarities of size and functional role are not definitive of levels. My central point is that levels of mechanisms are defined componentially within a hierarchically organized mechanism, not by objective kinds identifiable independently of their organization in a mechanism.

The idea of monolithic levels of nature that I reject can be generated by abstracting from interlevel relations among particulars to interlevel relations among types. Compare the following three sentences:

(a) This pyramidal cell is at a lower level of mechanisms than this hippocampus.
(b) Pyramidal cells are at a lower level of mechanisms than hippocampi.
(c) Cells are at a lower level of mechanisms than organs.

Statement (a) has a clear mechanistic reading: a particular pyramidal cell is a component of a particular hippocampal mechanism. This statement is true if the cell is a component in a mechanism for a given task carried out by the hippocampus. For example, a given pyramidal cell can be a component in some hippocampal mechanisms but not others, and thereby be at a lower level in some hippocampal mechanisms but not others.

When Wimsatt speaks of the compositional relationship between levels, he asserts something like (b). He writes, "Intuitively, one thing is at a higher level than something else if things of the first type are composed of things of the second type" (1976a: 215). However (b) is ambiguous. It might mean:

(b1) The pyramidal cells that compose hippocampi are at lower levels than hippocampi.

Or it might mean:

(b2) All pyramidal cells are at a lower level than all hippocampi.

Clearly (b1) is a generalization of (a), in which the compositional relationship is straightforward. This reading is unproblematic and is consistent with the view of levels of mechanisms that I recommend. However (b2) has exceptions. Pyramidal cells are found in many regions of the brain, and the pyramidal cells that are not part of a hippocampal mechanism are not at a lower level of mechanisms than hippocampi. As with my heart and the water pump, it makes no sense to ask if pyramidal cells are at a lower level than hippocampi *generally*. Some pyramidal cells are at a lower mechanistic level than hippocampi, and some are not.

Precisely the same ambiguity attends (c), the monolithic view of levels that Oppenheim and Putnam (1958) propose. It may be taken as asserting that cells are at lower levels than the organs that they specifically compose, or it might mean that all cells are at lower levels than all organs. The first option follows for levels of mechanisms; the second does not. Given that not all cells are components of organs, not all cells are at lower levels of mechanisms than organs.

One consequence of my mechanistic view of levels is that there can be no unique answer to the question of when two items are at the same level. I can provide only a partial answer: X and S are at the same level of mechanisms only if X and S are components in the same mechanism, X's ϕ-ing is not a component in S's ψ-ing, and S's ψ-ing is not a component in X's ϕ-ing.[11] To say that S's ψ-ing is at a higher level than X's ϕ-ing, is to say something of local significance in contrast to the monolithic

---

[11] This has struck some readers as circular because it appears to state that X and S are at the same level if they are not at different levels. Appearances to the contrary, this is not circular. I have defined "same level" in terms of the notion of "different level," and the latter is defined in terms of componency relations. The appearance of circularity, I believe, results from the fact that most people assume that the notion of "same level" must be primitive in comparison with the notion of "different level," and I have reversed that assumed order.

relationships expressed by (b) and (c). This point is visually illustrated by comparing Figures 5.7 and 5.8. Figure 5.7 depicts three mechanistic levels: a level for S's ψ-ing (the "topping-off" point for this model), a level for the ϕ-ings of Xs, and a level for ρ-ings of Ps (the "bottom-out" point for this model). Notice that this hierarchy, like the hierarchy that I sketch for the mechanisms of spatial memory, traces a single local strand: from the mechanism as a whole, to one of its components, and on to one of its components in turn. In contrast, in Figure 5.8, S's ψ-ing is decomposed into two sequential activities ($\phi1$ and $\phi2$) of two entities (X1 and X2). Beneath each are the mechanisms for those behaviors. These mechanisms are composed of the ρ-ing of Ps and the τ-ing (tau-ings) of Ts (English pronunciation). My claim that mechanistic levels are local entails that the τ-ing of Ts is not at a lower level than the $\phi1$-ing of X1s. Mechanistic levels are levels of containment, and objects that are not related to one another as component to mechanism are not assigned to different levels.

This local view of levels provides a more solid foundation for understanding the unity of neuroscience than Oppenheim and Putnam's monolithic view of levels. Facts about cells-in-general are not explained in terms of facts about molecules-in-general. Rather, certain facts about cells are explicable in terms of some molecular items and not others. Different physiological systems have different levels of explanation and different kinds of components. Different fields of neuroscience are unified as their experimental tools, vocabularies, and conceptual structures are brought to bear upon similar problems framed by a top-most *explanandum phenomenon*. What each field contributes, and the relative importance of every contribution, however, varies from explanatory context to explanatory context. Some components appear in many different mechanistic hierarchies. Schaffner (1993a) introduces yet another sense of levels, *levels of generality*, to characterize this fact. Mechanisms of protein synthesis, for example, appear in several different neuroscientific explanations. The mechanism for the action potential also has wide application. Still, the wide scope of a privileged few components should not lead one to reintroduce the construct of monolithic levels of nature. Other parts and levels appear in only a few systems. Columnar organization, for example, appears in a few sensory systems such as the visual system and the barrel cortex, but it is not a general feature of all sensory systems, let alone all cortical systems. I develop an alternative vision of the unity of science in Chapter 7.

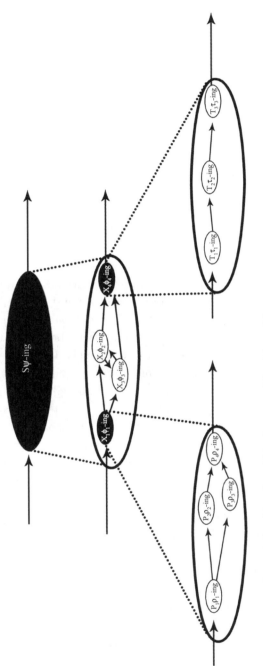

Figure 5.8. Levels are defined locally within decomposition hierarchies

The mechanistic view of levels helps to resolve some confusion about the nature of interlevel causation. First, one ought not to say that things at different levels causally interact with one another. If levels are levels of mechanisms, then there are very serious difficulties with the notion of interlevel causation. The lower-level components and their organization compose the higher level, meaning that "interlevel causation" is an interaction between the behavior of a mechanism as a whole and the parts of the mechanism. This idea is strained. On the other hand, in the case of levels of mechanisms, there is no difficulty concerning how things of one size scale can interact with things of another size scale. For example, elephants carry viruses and squash fleas. Any prejudice against these forms of causation, or prejudice in favor of rewriting them as interactions between items at similar size scales, reflects the influence of continued adherence to a monolithic view of levels (preserved as a vestige in Wimsatt's work). In the mechanistic view, what places two items at the same mechanistic level is that they are in the same mechanism, and neither is a component of the other. Two items at very different size scales can satisfy this relationship.

4. Conclusion

Talk of levels is multiply ambiguous. The levels metaphor is very flexible, and it is often used without specifying the sense of level under discussion. To prevent equivocation, I have developed a set of taxonomic principles for distinguishing different senses of levels and a taxonomy or field-guide for distinguishing different readings of the levels metaphor. This taxonomy also helps clarify a central interpretation of the levels metaphor: levels of mechanisms. The mechanistic interpretation is central because it fits core cases of neuroscientific explanation, such as LM levels. It also extends the view of mechanistic explanation I develop in the previous four chapters by showing what it means for mechanistic explanations to be multilevel. In Chapter 6, I defend the view that higher mechanistic levels are explanatorily relevant. I also show that realized phenomena (that is, phenomena at higher levels of realization) are often causally, and so explanatorily, relevant for many of the explanantia of interest to neuroscientists.

6

Nonfundamental Explanation

Summary

I argue against a possible metaphysical objection to the idea that explanations in neuroscience describe mechanisms at multiple levels. The causal exclusion argument provides reason to believe that higher-"level" phenomena have no causal powers over and above those of lowest-"level," or physical, phenomena. I show that this argument, whatever its merits, poses no threat to my view of explanation. First, the argument is targeted at levels of realization, not levels of mechanisms. It thus does not support the claim that higher levels of mechanisms have no causal powers over and above their lower-level components. Second, experimental considerations show that higher levels of realization are sometimes causally relevant in the sense that they make a difference even if, as Kim's arguments are sometimes taken to suggest, they do not make that difference through the exercise of causal powers or causal efficacy. Whether there are causal powers, and whether there are novel causal powers at higher levels of realization, are additional metaphysical questions on which the present account is officially neutral. These questions need not be answered to assess whether adequate neuroscientific explanations must span multiple levels.

1. Introduction

The fact that explanations in neuroscience span multiple levels of mechanisms raises classic metaphysical questions about whether nonfundamental (or higher-"level") properties have real causal powers over and above the powers of fundamental properties (see Heil and Mele 1993; Heil 2003;

Kim 1998). One popular argument for metaphysical physicalism is Jaegwon Kim's causal exclusion argument (1998). Given that every physical event has a complete physical cause (the doctrine of the causal completeness of the physical), there appears to be no work for nonfundamental causes to do. Suppose that an instance of a physical property P is a complete (that is, sufficient) cause of an instance of another physical property, P*. Suppose also that P is a lower-"level" supervenience base for an instance of a higher-"level" property,[1] M, that is, suppose that there can be no difference in M without a difference in P. Kim develops the argument as a challenge to specifically mental causation (hence the letter M), but the problem applies to any M that is higher-level in Kim's sense, regardless of whether it is mental or not. In any case, the question arises as to what work is left for M to do. P alone is sufficient for P*. M either makes no contribution to the occurrence of P* over and above the contribution already made by P (P being sufficient for P*), in which case it exercises no causal powers over and above those exercised by P, or M's causal contribution is entirely redundant with the contribution made by P, in which case P* has two complete causes (in fact, as many causes as there are "levels"). If one finds the idea of widespread overdetermination metaphysically unpalatable, then one seems forced to acknowledge that M does nothing beyond what P is doing—that M has no causal powers over and above the powers of fundamental properties. Either the property M is identical to the property P, or M is a dispensable ontological extravagance.

The causal exclusion argument poses no threat to the idea that explanations in neuroscience describe mechanisms that span multiple levels. There are two independent reasons, discussed in Sections 4 and 5, respectively.

First, Kim's argument, which is commonly understood as an argument against higher-"level" causal powers, is directed against levels of realization (which are related by the role/occupant relation) rather than against levels of mechanisms (which are related by a componency relation). Kim explicitly

---

[1] Here and throughout I follow Kim's formulation of the argument in terms of relations between higher- and lower-level properties. Some, such as Heil (2003), object to the very idea of higher-level properties. I do not mean to beg any questions against him. The argument, and my commentary upon it, could be formulated in terms that would be congenial to that way of thinking. When I speak of higher-level properties, such a person can replace talk of properties with talk of clusters of property instances (or tropes) related by family resemblance, falling within the extension of a given predicate, or correctly characterized in terms of a given variable. Such locution would only obscure the relatively simple points that I want to reinforce in this chapter.

accepts that wholes have causal powers that their parts individually do not have (that is, they can do things that their parts individually cannot do), and so he accepts that one can generate novel causal powers by organizing components into mechanisms. His argument simply does not apply to the central explanatory sense of levels in neuroscience. This simple point, to which all parties should agree, is sufficient to establish the importance of explanations at multiple levels of mechanisms in neuroscience.

Second, Kim's argument is designed to show that properties at higher levels of realization have no causal powers over and above those of their realizers. A multilevel mechanist need only hold that higher-level phenomena are causally relevant, not that they exercise novel causal powers. Belief in "causal powers," not only at higher levels but also at fundamental levels, is an additional metaphysical commitment beyond the manipulationist account of causal relevance advanced in Chapter 3 and extended in Sections 2 and 3 below. In this chapter, I argue that there are true generalizations describing relations of causal relevance among realized properties (that is, properties at a higher level of realization) that are not true of the causal relevance relations among their realizers. One might argue that these relations of causal relevance provide good reason to believe that there are novel causal powers among realized properties, or one might insist that these relationships can best be explained by the organized manifestation of fundamental properties and causal powers. Whatever metaphysics one chooses to endorse, however, the relations of causal relevance are robust enough to satisfy constraints (E1)–(E5), and they are useful for the purposes of manipulation and control. I begin in Sections 2 and 3 by emphasizing and elaborating certain aspects of the manipulationist view of causal relevance introduced in Chapter 3. I then return to Kim's causal exclusion argument.

2. Causal Relevance and Making a Difference

The basic idea behind the manipulationist view I defend in Chapter 3 is that a variable X is causally relevant to a variable Y if and only if there is some ideal intervention on X that changes the value of Y or the probability distribution over values of Y. Kim's talk of properties can be translated into talk of variables. In the simplest case, a variable can have two values, one for the presence of the property and one for its absence. In more complicated cases, the variable can have multiple values or a continuum of values, as when the temperature of an object can take on any value above absolute zero, or when a variable for color can take on values red, green, blue, and yellow.

An ideal intervention (I) on X with respect to Y is an intervention on X that changes the value of Y, if at all, only via a change in X. Controlled experiments are designed to rule out the possibility that the change in Y is due to the effect of variables other than I, or to the direct effect of I, or to the effect of I on some causal intermediate between X and Y, or to the fact that I is correlated with some cause of Y (expressed in (I1)–(I4) in Chapter 3). For example, to say that intracellular Ca^{2+} concentrations are relevant to neurotransmitter release implies that there are conditions under which interventions that change intracellular Ca^{2+} concentrations change the release of neurotransmitters (or the probability of neurotransmitter release) and that this change comes about via the intervention on Ca^{2+}, not via some other route. One can induce a cell to release neurotransmitters by injecting Ca^{2+}, and one can regulate the amount of neurotransmitters released by intervening to change Ca^{2+} concentrations, and one can rule out other possible explanations for these experimental findings by conducting controlled experiments. Causes make a difference to their effects, and this view of causal relevance focuses attention on those difference-making factors. Because this view of causal relevance satisfies constraints (E1)–(E5), this manipulationist view serves as the foundation of an account of explanatory relevance as well.

The manipulationist view should not be confused with the idea that causal and explanatory relevance involve subsumption under strict laws. Relationships of manipulability, it is true, can be expressed in generalizations of the form: in conditions W, if one intervenes to change X from x_1 to x_2 in accordance with (I1)–(I4), then Y will take on the value $f(x_2)$ or the probability distribution over values of Y will change as a function of x_2. However, such generalizations lack many of the features traditionally associated with strict laws. First, there is no requirement that the relationship between X and Y must be universal, that it must hold for all times and places, or that it must make no reference to particulars. Such generalizations might be true only for a limited range of values of X or only in a given species. For the relationships described by such a generalization to be explanatory, it is required only that the relationship must hold in the conditions relevant to the person requesting the explanation. Ca^{2+} makes a difference to neurotransmitter release under the conditions found in, for example, normally functioning cells of a certain type in organisms of a certain type. (Kim's argument, recall, is premised on the idea that P is causally sufficient for P*. The manipulationist view does not require that all relevant properties are sufficient for their effects.) Second, the requirement is explicitly stochastic. Interventions on X might make a difference either to the actual value of Y or to the probability distribution over values of Y. A given intervention with Ca^{2+} might produce no difference in the actual release of neurotransmitters but might nonetheless have raised the probability that neurotransmitters would be released on that occasion. Third, such generalizations are often mechanistically fragile. That is, their stability often depends upon the appropriate behavior of an underlying mechanism. If the mechanism were to break, or if one were to interfere with other components of the mechanism, the relationship would no longer hold. Finally, it does not follow from the fact that X is nomologically sufficient for Y that X is relevant to Y. X could be a mere correlate, or an effect of a common cause, or it could include irrelevant details (such as the blessing of the neurons or Jones's taking birth control pills).

To explain a phenomenon, it is neither required, nor is it enough, to show that there is a strict law of nature (one that is universal, deterministic, and insusceptible to failure) between the variable and the *explanandum phenomenon*. Such subsumption under laws would be necessary if explanations were arguments, as defenders of the epistemic accounts hold. In contrast, I advocate an ontic view of explanation according to which one explains a phenomenon by showing how it is situated in the causal structure of the world. Relationships of causal relevance (that is, manipulability) partly constitute that causal structure. One explains neurotransmitter release in part by describing the variables that can be used to make a difference to neurotransmitter release. Such explanations are useful precisely because they identify loci in a mechanism that can be commandeered for the purposes of control. Some philosophers deny that there are explanations in biology because biology lacks strict laws (for example, Rosenberg 1985), but the ability of the manipulationist account to satisfy (E1)–(E5) allows one to see that strict laws are not required for explanation.

The manipulationist view of causal relevance also contrasts with Salmon (1984, 1998) and Dowe's (1992, 2000) transmission view and from any view that construes causal relevance as a kind of physical connection: a cement, glue, spring, or string. According to such views, causal relevance is most perspicuously exemplified on a pool table, where solid objects move about when and only when they receive momentum from some other moving object. While many relationships of causal relevance are also relationships of connection in this sense, the focus on the connection misses the core idea of causal relevance: the idea that causes make a difference to their effects. Not all connections make a difference. The cue is connected to the cue ball by both an exchange of momentum and an exchange of matter (the blue chalk mark), but only the momentum sets the cue ball moving. Not all cases of difference-making involve connections. Omissions and preventions make differences through disconnections. Accounts of causation in terms of contact, or otherwise in terms of the exercise of "activities" and "causal powers," have yet to explain the sense in which activities, causal powers, and contact make a difference to their effects. Here, the manipulationist view clearly provides some insight.

Cases of omission and prevention help to underscore a difference between talk of causal relevance and talk of causal powers (as they seem to be understood in the literature surrounding the causal exclusion argument). Arguably absences are not things. They do not have properties. They do not exercise causal powers. Nonetheless, absences can make a difference. Imagine a simple network in which an excitatory and an inhibitory neuron both synapse onto a third neuron. Imagine further that both pre-synaptic cells are tonically active such that their competing efforts keep the membrane voltage of the post-synaptic cell below the threshold for generating an action potential. If one were to intervene in this system to prevent the inhibitory neuron from firing, the post-synaptic cell would fire. It is stretching a point to say that the inactivity of the inhibitory neuron has the power to cause the post-synaptic cell to fire. Nonetheless the fact that the inhibitory neuron did not fire is no doubt causally relevant to the fact that the post-synaptic cell does fire. One can make the post-synaptic cell fire by inhibiting the inhibitory interneuron or by blocking the post-synaptic effects of its activity. In this sense, the absence of activity or of an effective synaptic junction makes a difference to the post-synaptic cell's state.

I am interested in causal relevance—the idea that some properties make a difference to others—irrespective of whether the properties make their difference through the exercise of causal powers or causal efficacy, whatever these other causal notions amount to. The manipulationist approach as developed thus far provides an adequate account of what it is for one variable to be causally relevant to—that is, to make a difference to—the value of some other variable.

3. Contrasts and Switch-points

According to the manipulationist account, a variable X is relevant to a variable Y only if there is some ideal intervention on X that changes the value of Y only via the change in X. To say this is not, however, to require that all changes to X change the value of Y. For example, while the electrical state of a neuron is relevant to whether or not a neuron produces action potentials, not all changes in the membrane voltage of the neuron produce action potentials. One could, for example, hyperpolarize the cell. One could also intervene to raise the neuron's membrane voltage while keeping it well below the threshold for an action potential. The difference between the interventions that change the value of the effect variable and those that do not are explicit in the contrastive statement of the causal relation. In conditions W, interventions that change the value of X from x_1 to x_2 cause Y to change from y_1 to $f(x_2)$.

This contrastive statement enforces a more exacting specification of those properties that are relevant to the occurrence of (or to the probability of the occurrence of) the effect. A number of philosophers argue for the importance of contrast to causal and explanatory relevance (see Achinstein 1975; Dretske 1977; Woodward 1984; Hitchcock 1996; and van Fraassen 1980). The primary reason is that to assess whether a causal claim is true or false, it is often necessary to make explicit the implied contrasts in both the description of the cause and in the description of the effect. To use Dretske's example, consider whether Socrates' sipping the pint of hemlock caused his death. As stated, the question is ambiguous. This question might be asking whether Socrates' sipping the hemlock, as opposed to his guzzling or otherwise ingesting it, caused his death. In that case, Socrates' decision to sip rather than guzzle made no difference to the fact that he died. That decision perhaps made a difference to the rate at which he died (that is, to his dying at time t rather than at some time $t_1 > t$), but that is a different causal claim. Alternatively, the question might be asking whether Socrates' consuming hemlock, rather than wine or water, caused him to die. In that case, there is no doubt that Socrates' hemlock consumption is relevant. But suppose that Socrates had been given a choice of hemlock, arsenic, or cyanide. In that case, the choice of hemlock rather than arsenic or cyanide made no difference to whether he lived or died.

The contrastive formulation also spotlights ambiguities in quantitative causal claims. Hitchcock (1996) considers the question of whether smoking a pack of cigarettes per day causes lung cancer. The answer depends upon the implied contrast. If John smokes two and a half packs per day and then cuts back to one, there is little doubt that John has reduced his probability of acquiring lung cancer. One should say that John has taken steps, however feeble, to prevent his future lung cancer. On the other hand, if John increases his cigarette consumption from no packs per day to one, he has increased his probability of acquiring lung cancer, and one should say that John has put himself at risk for lung cancer. The occurrent circumstance—John's smoking a pack per day—is the same in each case, but different contrasts from that occurrent circumstance entail different truth-values for the causal claim.

The experiments used to test causal claims are contrastive. Such experiments involve comparing the value of a variable under experimental conditions with the value of that variable under control conditions. Experiments are well-designed to the extent that the experimental group and the control group differ only with respect to the value of the putative causal variable. One concludes from such experiments that the difference (if any) in the effect variable between the two groups is due to the difference in the putative causal variable. Different experiments would have to be done to test the contrasting causal claims in the two preceding paragraphs. In the smoking case, one experiment would be required to compare the incidence of cancer among one-pack smokers with the incidence among nonsmokers, and another would be required to compare the incidence of cancer among one-pack smokers with the incidence among two-pack smokers. In the case of Socrates, one experiment would be required to compare hemlock sippers to hemlock guzzlers, and another to compare hemlock drinkers to drinkers of water and wine.

Some object that this contrastive formulation of the causal relevance relation introduces pragmatic considerations that are not properly thought of as objective features of the causal structure of the world. The causal structure of the world, one might say, just is as it is; it is not a fact about the world that it is one way *rather than* another. But this is a misleading way of putting things. First, any time that one searches for a cause or attempts to formulate an explanation, one must specify the effect or the *explanandum* that one is trying to explain. Having done so, one then looks for the objective relations of causal relevance that explain the effect. The contrastive description of the *explanandum* effect is helpful merely to specify as precisely as possible what one is trying to explain—to identify precisely that feature of the world for which a cause is sought. Once the *explanandum phenomenon* has been specified (something that must be done in any search for an explanation or any search for a cause), it is then an objective matter whether or not it is possible to make a difference to that effect by manipulating certain antecedent variables and which manipulations of that variable in fact make a difference. My account is thus no more pragmatic than any view of causation or explanation would have to be. Second, changes embody contrasts. It is a perfectly objective fact about the world that things change and that some changes are correlated with others. Further, it is a perfectly objective fact, one that can be assessed experimentally, if such changes continue to be so related when one intervenes on one of the correlates and when one controls for other possible causes (in accordance with (I1)–(I4)). Pragmatic factors enter into this view of causal relevance only in the sense that relevance is always applicable to something that we want to explain. The rest can be settled experimentally.

In picking out the causally relevant changes, one is searching for a cause-contrast that is *appropriate* for a given effect-contrast.[2] This notion of appropriateness can be explicated within the manipulationist framework of causation. Consider three examples that show how the practice of designing controlled experiments helps to identify the appropriate cause-contrast for an effect-contrast.

I discuss the first example briefly in Chapter 2. An action potential reaches the nerve terminal. There is a sudden rise in Na^+ concentration in the terminal. This is followed by the opening of Ca^{2+} channels, the influx of Ca^{2+}, and then the sequence of activities that ends with the release of

---

[2] The following account is similar to Yablo's (1992) account of the "proportionality" of a cause to its effect, but I use a notion of causation that is different from his, and I make no appeal to the "naturalness" of a property.

neurotransmitters. If one uses tetrodotoxin (TTX) to block Na^+ channels, the cell will not release neurotransmitters. This finding is consistent with several possible causal relevance relations. Only experiments can sort them out. It could be, for example, that there is something specific about Na^+. Perhaps it activates or modulates some intracellular signaling cascade. It could be that the conformation changes in the Na^+ channels themselves increase Ca^{2+} conductance, irrespective of whether they allow Na^+ to flow into the cell. Finally, it could be that the influx of Na^+ raises the membrane voltage, thus opening voltage-sensitive Ca^{2+} channels. To decide among these possibilities, one must do some experiments. One could, for example, raise the intracellular concentration of Na^+ without changing the membrane voltage (perhaps using a voltage clamp) or opening Na^+ channels (perhaps by injecting Na^+). And one could change the membrane voltage without either opening channels (perhaps using TTX) or changing the Na+ concentration. The goal is to set up an experimental contrast between a case in which the putative cause is wiggled (the experimental group) and an otherwise identical case in which it is not (the control group). Such experiments (see Katz and Miledi 1967) show that neither the opening of Na^+ channels nor the rise in intracellular Na^+ concentration per se are relevant to the release of neurotransmitters. It is the rise in membrane voltage (rather than the failure of the membrane voltage to rise) that is causally relevant to opening the Ca^{2+} channels and to the subsequent release of neurotransmitters. In this case, the change in membrane voltage screens off the other causes. The changes in Na+ concentration make no difference when voltage is held constant, as is demonstrated by the appropriate experimental test.

The second example is analogous, but it is not a case of one variable screening off another. Rather the example involves deciding which partitions among the values of a single variable frame the relevant contrast for a given *explanandum* effect. The logic of the experimental situation, however, is the same. Suppose that the temperature of a room at sea level drops to $-18.6°C$ and that a bucket of water in the center of the room freezes. One can then ask, "What caused the bucket of water to freeze?" Two possible answers are: (1) the temperature's being $-18.6°C$; and (2) the temperature's being below $0°C$. How is one to decide which of these properties is the causally relevant property to the water's being frozen?

The way to decide between these competing hypotheses is to do some experiments. The obvious experiment would be to intervene to change the ambient temperature and to determine which changes in temperature change the state of the water. For example, if the water freezes when the temperature is set at −18.6°C but thaws if the temperature is −18.8°C or −18.4°C, then one would have evidence that the room's being −18.6°C is causally relevant to the freezing of the water. Of course, this is not what one would find. One could change the temperature from −18.6°C to any of a number of values (for example, −13°C, −4°C, −22°C, −29°C, and so on) without thawing the water. The only interventions that change the state of the water in the bucket raise the temperature of the room above 0°C. Clean experiments of this sort identify the relevant contrasts. An experiment that yields no difference in the effect between the experimental group and the control offers only a negative result: the difference is not causally relevant to the effect. This is the kind of result one would get if one were to intervene to change the ambient temperature from −18.6°C to −19.2°C. Such an experiment would fail to identify a causally (and so explanatorily) relevant difference.

Suppose, on the other hand, that one seeks the cause for the specific time interval, t, over which the water froze. One can ask: what caused the bucket of water to freeze in precisely t minutes (rather than faster or slower)? Again, one can do experiments by intervening to change the temperature from −18.6°C to neighboring values and measuring the time that it takes for the bucket to freeze. Changing the temperature from −18.6°C to −16.4°C or −23.2°C *does* make a difference to the rate at which the water freezes. Being below 0°C, however, is relevant only to the fact that the water freezes, not to its rate of freezing. The values of the variable are too coarse to identify the relevant differences. More precisely, the temperature's being −18.6°C, rather than any other value, made the difference between the water's freezing in precisely t minutes rather than faster or slower. In such an experiment, there would be a difference between the experimental group and the control group, and assuming that all other factors are the same (for example, same altitude and air pressure) and that the experiment is properly conducted, one identifies the precise temperature relevant to the differences in rates of freezing

The third example is due to Stephen Yablo (1992). A pigeon pecks a slip of scarlet paper. Why? Here are three competing causal hypotheses:

(1) the paper is scarlet; (2) the paper is red; (3) the paper is colored. Again, there is no way to decide among these causal hypotheses without doing experiments. To decide among these hypotheses, one should experiment by varying the color of the paper to determine whether or not the pigeon pecks. To distinguish (1) from (2), one should observe how the pigeon responds to a variety of colors in the red spectrum. One could expose the pigeon to brick, crimson, fuchsia, magenta, rose, pink, and so on. If the pigeon uniquely pecks the scarlet pieces of paper and none of the others, then one has evidence that the paper's being scarlet (rather than some other shade) is the causally relevant feature for pecking. However, if the pigeon pecks at all shades of red equally, one would have reason to favor (2).

As long as one does experiments in which the color is varied only within the red spectrum, however, one would not acquire any evidence for deciding between hypotheses (2) and (3). For that, one would have to test the pigeon on a full range of colors. If the pigeon pecks at all colors, failing to peck only white and clear pieces of paper, for example, one would conclude that the pigeon is selectively responding only to colored pieces of paper. With different experimental outcomes, one is led to suppose that different contrasts correctly identify the causally relevant variable. Suppose, however, that one were interested in some more fine-grained variable, such as patterns of activity in the dorsal-anterior region of the pigeon's nucleus rotundus (the area of the pigeon brain thought to be crucially involved in color discrimination). It might turn out that the pigeon's behavioral patterns vary with changes from red to another color, while the patterns of activation across cells in the pigeon's nucleus rotundus vary with specific shades of red.

The lesson of this example is replicated time and again in the extensive literature on pigeon object recognition (for reviews, see Huber 2001; Kirkpatrick 2001). In that literature, the question arises whether pigeons recognize objects via "particulate perception," that is, by recognizing local features of the stimulus object in isolation (see Cerella 1986), or whether pigeons recognize objects by detecting more holistic properties of the object. If pigeons are particulate perceivers, they are insensitive to global features of objects and respond regardless of how those features are arranged. If, on the other hand, pigeons are holistic perceivers, then they should respond not merely to local features but to the overall spatial arrangements among them. The pigeon should be able to distinguish a cup from a pail, for example, despite the fact that each is composed of a cylinder and an arc. Furthermore, if pigeons are particulate perceivers, their performance should degrade if the object is rotated, changing the apparent shapes of the object's component parts. If, however, pigeons were responsive to holistic properties, then one would expect their object-recognition abilities to remain more or less constant as the object is rotated. Kirkpatrick (2001) offers experimental evidence supporting the predictions of the holistic approach. What matters for present purposes, however, is not whether pigeons are particulate perceivers or holistic perceivers, but rather the simple fact that this is a legitimate experimental question of the sort that arises regularly in perceptual research and that should be settled by doing the right controlled experiments. Pigeons can discriminate cars, cartoon characters, faces, geographic scenes, leaves, letters, trees, paintings by Monet and Picasso, and different excerpts of classical music. They can learn to respond differentially depending on whether two items in a pair are the same, different, or similar. In each case, it is an experimental question which features make a difference to the pigeon's response.

These examples each illustrate that different effect contrasts (that is, the contrast between Y's having the values y_1 and y_2) lead one to identify different relevant causal contrasts (that is, the contrast between X's having the values x_1 and x_2). Each of these examples also illustrates the kinds of experiment that neuroscientists routinely do to make judgments of causal relevance. In the case of temperature, one might seek an explanation for the fact that:

(e1) the water froze rather than remaining liquid or turning to steam,

or for the fact that:

(e1′) the water froze at some particular rate t rather than at some other rate.

These effect contrasts require different cause-contrasts. The appropriate cause contrast for (e1) is:

(c1) the ambient temperature was below 0°C rather than above 0°C,

rather than the fact that:

(c1′) the ambient temperature was −18.6°C rather than some other value.

In contrast, (c1′) is the appropriate contrast for (e1′). Likewise, in the case of the pigeon, one might seek an explanation for the fact that:

(e2) the pigeon pecked, rather than ignored, the piece of paper,

or for the fact that:

(e2′) the pigeon's nucleus rotundus went into state S rather than some other state.

The appropriate cause contrast for (e2′) is that:

(c2) the paper was red rather than, for example, some other primary color,

while the appropriate cause for (e2) is that:

(c2′) the paper was some specific shade of red rather than some other shade of red.

In each of these cases, one correctly identifies the causally relevant value of the applicable variable to the extent that one formulates a cause-contrast that is *appropriate* to the given effect-contrast.

This notion of appropriateness can be explicated within the manipulationist framework. For purposes of illustration, imagine that one starts with a variable (for example, temperature) and then searches for partitions among the finest grained values of that variable that make a difference to the value of the effect variable.[3] To decide on the appropriate cause-contrast, one searches for a *switch-point* in the possible values of the cause variable that corresponds to the contrast between the different values of the effect variable.[4] In the simplest cases, there is only one switch-point. It is the rise of membrane voltage beyond a certain threshold (rather than to any subthreshold value) that causes the neuron to generate an action potential. In the case of frozen water, there is a single switch-point in the temperature variable at $0°C$. No intervention that changes the temperature from a value below this switch-point to another value below this switch-point makes a difference to whether or not the water remains

---

[3] I use a deterministic case for purposes of illustration. One can extend this to probabilistic cases, as I do in Chapter 3, by using the effect-contrast to compare different probability distributions over possible values rather than to compare particular values.

[4] Compare the discussion of testing interventions in Woodward and Hitchcock (2003a).

frozen. So long as the temperature is below $0°C$, the water remains frozen. Interventions that cross the switch-point, on the other hand, do make a difference to the value of the effect variable. Raising the temperature from below $0°C$ to above $0°C$ changes the water from frozen to liquid. The appropriate cause-contrast is the one that identifies the switch-points for the effect-contrast. In searching for the appropriate contrast, one begins with fine-grained values of a variable (temperature), one identifies the switch-point(s) in the values of those variables, and then (if necessary) one replaces the fine-grained values with coarse-grained values appropriate to the effect contrast.[5]

In the case of (e2), there are two switch-points—one at each end of the red spectrum. All values of the spectrum variable that lie between the switch-points are cases in which the pigeon pecks, and all those values of the spectrum that lie outside the switch-points correspond to the cases in which the pigeon does not peck. Interventions to change the cause-variable from one value between the switch-points to another value between the switch-points make no difference in the value of the effect variable. Those that cross switch-points, on the other hand, do make a difference in the effect variable. For (e2′), however, the switch-points are different. The pigeon's nucleus rotundus is responsive to a particular shade of red rather than to red in general. Intervening to change the shade from scarlet to pink thus makes a difference in the pattern of activation across that brain region. In this case again, one can begin by describing fine-grained values of a variable (for example, spectral reflectances), identify switch-points in the values of those variables, and then replace the fine-grained values with coarse-grained values corresponding to the effect-contrast. Again the appropriate cause-contrast is the one that identifies the switch-point for the effect-contrast.

I have perhaps said enough to clarify the manipulationist account of causal relevance. I now return to Kim's causal exclusion argument with these considerations in hand. There are two independent reasons why Kim's argument should not prevent one from endorsing a multilevel mechanistic view of explanation in neuroscience. The first is that Kim's argument attacks levels of realization, not levels of mechanisms. The second is that

---

[5] Causal inference need not proceed in this temporal sequence. One might begin with a coarse partition of the values for a variable and then make the partition more and more fine-grained in light of experimental findings.

Kim's argument is best understood as an attack on the idea of causal powers at higher levels of realization rather than on the idea that phenomena at higher levels of realization are causally relevant.

4. Causal Powers at Higher Levels of Mechanisms

In the causal exclusion argument, P usurps M's power in producing P*. Because P is sufficient for P*, there is else nothing left for M to contribute to P*'s occurrence. Either M does nothing, in which case it is an ontological extravagance, or its contribution is entirely redundant with that of P, a possibility that many philosophers find unsatisfying.[6] So, it would seem, M has no causal powers of its own.[7]

Kim points out that his causal exclusion argument does not apply to what he calls micro/macro levels: "the [causal exclusion] argument, which exploits the supervenience relation, does not have the effect of emptying macro levels of causal powers and rendering familiar macro-objects and their properties causally impotent." (1998: 86) This is because, "the exclusion-based worries about mental causation do not generalize across micro-macro levels" (1998: 84) Micro-macro levels, for Kim, are levels that stand in part–whole relations: "entities belonging to a given level, except those at the very bottom, have an exhaustive decomposition, without remainder, into entities belonging to the lower levels."[8] The exclusion argument, in contrast, applies to levels related by the supervenience relation. Sometimes he says that properties at one level are "realized" by properties at lower levels. Sometimes he says that they are different orders of properties. We

---

[6] Another possibility is that M just is P. If so, the causal exclusion argument no longer applies. M's causal powers just are the causal powers of P. See Kim (1998) and Polger (2004). In that case, higher-level properties are shown to be causally powerful because they are identical to causally powerful physical properties, and there is therefore very strong justification for pursuing multilevel explanations in neuroscience and beyond.

[7] I am adopting here the notion of a "causal power" because it is part of Kim's argument. Causal powers are sometimes described as if they need to be added into the world in addition to the entities if change is to be possible (as Machamer et al. 2000 describe activities). They are understood as forces that push and pull, attract and repel, bond and break bonds, restore equilibrium, and so on. Sometimes they are described merely as sufficient causes (as Kim seems to think of them). I assume merely that different causal powers allow the properties or objects that have them to be effected and affected by different features of the causal environment and to affect and effect different features of the world. I assume that if two causal powers differ in these respects, they are not the same causal powers.

[8] Similarly, when Heil (2003) objects to "levels of reality" or "levels of being," he is not objecting to levels of mechanisms. He is objecting to levels of realization.

can see his point in terms of the contrast between levels of mechanisms and what I call levels of realization.

Levels of mechanisms are a species of Kim's micro-macro levels. They are related by a kind of part–whole relation. Higher levels are decomposed into components at lower levels. Take some mechanism S and its behavior ψ. At a lower level are S's component entities $(X_1, X_2, \ldots, X_m)$ and their activities $(\phi_1, \phi_2, \ldots, \phi_n)$. Thus, one says that X_1 and ϕ_1 are at a lower level of mechanisms than S's ψ-ing. The relata in levels of mechanisms are a behaving mechanism and its components. The individual components are at a lower level than the behavior of the mechanism as a whole.

Levels of realization[9] are not related by the part–whole relation. Instead, they are levels of properties related by the realization relation. Kim's idea of realization (or, in his words, higher-order causes) can be summarized in four points: (i) Realization is a relationship between two properties, a realized property, ψ, and a realizing property, $\phi\#$ (pronounced phi-pound). In the special case of mechanisms, ψ is the property of exhibiting the behavior of a mechanism as a whole, and $\phi\#$ is the property (or family of properties) of having the various components (the Xs), the various activities (the ϕs), and the various organizational features in the mechanism. $\phi\#$ is thus the property (or family of properties) of being a given components-plus-organization. (ii) Both ψ and $\phi\#$ are properties of the same object, S. S has the property ψ, and S has the property $\phi\#$, that is, of being the organized collection of Xs ϕ-ing. (On this point, Gillett (2002) distinguishes between "flat" and "dimensioned" views of realization. The flat view is what Kim has in mind. On the dimensioned view, the properties of wholes (such as S's ψ-ing) are realized by the properties of their parts. The dimensioned view corresponds to my levels of mechanisms. Here, however, I am concerned with the flat view, and it is crucial to my argument that these two distinct relations are not confused with one another by sharing the common name "realization." This is why I distinguish levels of mechanisms from levels of realization.)

[9] I do not endorse this as a view of realization. (For a detailed discussion of my own views, see Wilson and Craver forthcoming). Instead, I am using it to characterize Kim's idea of "orders" (see Kim 1998: 80–7). The idea of "realization" has been part of the philosophical lexicon at least since the 1960s (Putnam 1960). It has only recently been subjected to extensive philosophical scrutiny (Gillett 2002; LePore and Loewer 1989; Kim 1998; Poland 1994; Polger 2004; Shoemaker 2001; Wilson 2001; Wilson and Craver forthcoming). I doubt that any single account of realization can accommodate the diverse ontic categories into which realizers and realized items fall, such as properties, entities, events, and processes (see Poland 1994; Craver 2004). Again, I do not mean to presuppose the existence of realized or determinable properties. Call them realized "categories" if that is preferred.

(iii) S has ψ *in virtue* of having $\phi\#$. This "in virtue of" relation can be understood in many ways. Here, I describe it as a supervenience relation: necessarily,[10] there can be no difference in ψ properties without a difference in $\phi\#$ properties.[11] Finally, (iv) it is physically possible for S to have ψ without having $\phi\#$. That is, S has ψ in virtue of having $\phi\#$, but S does not have $\phi\#$ in virtue of having ψ. This requirement distinguishes realization from type identity, which is symmetrical. Some use the term "realization" to include both type identity and weaker forms of realization (for example, Polger 2004). However, the notion of realization was originally introduced to articulate a weaker relation than identity. Different instances of ψ-ing can be realized by different properties ($\phi\#_1$, $\phi\#_2$ ...) on different occasions. That is, ψ is multiply realizable.

Levels of realization are not levels of mechanisms (as I describe them in Chapter 5). Levels of mechanisms stand in part–whole relations. The neuron (S's) ability to generate action potentials (ψ) is realized by the fact that the neuron (S) has the property ($\phi\#$) of being an organized collection of Na^+ channels, K^+ channels, a membrane, and so on. The ability to generate action potentials is at a higher level of mechanisms than the Na^+ channels, K^+ channels, and the membrane because the Na^+ channels, K^+ channels, and membrane are components of the mechanism for generating action potentials. However, the ability to generate action potentials is not at a higher level of mechanisms than the property of being a particular organized collection of acting Na^+ channels, K^+ channels, and a membrane. Rather, the parts-plus-organization realize the generation of action potentials. Having the ability to generate action potentials and having an organized collection of acting cellular components are properties of the same thing (the neuron or, more specifically, the mechanism), and the neuron generates action potentials by virtue of being an appropriately organized collection of

---

[10] This is consistent with several metaphysical explanations for why the realization relation holds between any two properties, assuming that such explanation is necessary. It might be that the two properties are identical. It might be that the individual properties in the realizer make up the realized property or otherwise constitute (in some thick metaphysical sense) that property. It might be that the causal powers of the realized property are a subset of the casual powers of the realizing property. Different understandings of this requirement might be appropriate in different cases. My argument in Section 5 is not consistent with an interpretation of (iii) in terms of type identity because my argument relies on the thesis of multiple realizability. I take no stand on what, if anything, makes realization relations true. For present purposes, I care only that some of them are, in fact, true.

[11] This requirement, coupled with item (ii) raises problems for thinking about cases of realization in which the mechanism's environment plays a crucial role in the realization (Wilson 2001), but this is not an issue that needs to be resolved for the present dispute.

parts (and not vice versa). Having the ability to generate action potentials is thus realized by an organized collection channels and membrane structures ($\phi\#$), and not by the parts ($X_1, X_2, \ldots, X_m$) and activities ($\phi_1, \phi_2, \ldots, \phi_n$) taken singularly.

The distinction between levels of mechanisms and levels of realization is crucial because there is no difficulty seeing how mechanisms can do things that their components taken individually cannot. Kim says that this point is "obvious but important":

This table has a mass of ten kilograms, and this property, that of having a mass of ten kilograms, represents a well-defined set of causal powers. But no micro-constituent of this table, none of its proper parts, has this property or the causal powers it represents. H_2O molecules have causal powers that no oxygen and hydrogen atoms have. A neural assembly consisting of many thousands of neurons will have properties whose causal powers go beyond the causal powers of the properties of its constituent neurons, or subassemblies, and human beings have causal powers that none of our individual organs have. Clearly then macroproperties can, and in general do, have their own causal powers, powers that go beyond the causal powers of their micro-constituents. (1998: 85)

Through aggregation or organization, wholes have causal powers that their parts individually do not have; they can do things that their parts individually cannot do.

Suppose, for simplicity, that the behavior of a mechanism can be characterized in terms of an input–output relation. Focusing first on the input side to the mechanism, the organization of components in a mechanism allows the mechanism to be affected by aspects of its environment that cannot so impact on the parts individually. The primate visual system, for example, is differentially responsive to motions, shapes, and objects. Take as the input the presentation of a visual stimulus, such as a vertical bar moving left to right, and take as the output a distributed activation pattern in visual cortex that encodes those features of the stimulus. None of the cells in the visual system, taken individually, can detect the shape, orientation, or motion of the bar. That task requires the organized effort of myriad neurons across several functionally distinct brain regions. When the neurons are organized in the right way, they can generate patterns of activity that correlate tightly with those features of a visual stimulus. Even if there are "grandmother cells" (that is, single cells that respond if and only if your grandmother is present), these cells gain their status as such only because they are organized within a mechanism that allows them to play this functional role. No neuron, removed from its context in the body, fires when and only when grandmothers are present. Individual neurons do not have the organization required to register these complex features of the stimulus. When neurons first came to be organized in this way, new kinds of causal relationships came into being that allowed organisms a profound flexibility in dealing with their environments. The organism could make use of this information in its behavior, and so new manipulable relationships arose between abstract features of a light stimulus (the input) and the activities of organisms in their environments (the output). New relations of causal relevance, such as that between features of ambient light and an organism's behavior, came into being.

Does this amount to a causal power for the visual system that "goes beyond" the causal powers of its individual components? However one understands causal powers, it should turn out that two causal powers differ if they have different precipitating conditions (inputs) and manifestations (outputs). If so, it seems clear that the set of input–output relations that holds for the visual system is different from the set of input–output relations that holds for any of its components. In that sense, then, this is a novel causal power. And when such input–output relationships are useful for biological organisms, they tend to be preserved in subsequent generations and to become conserved across large populations of organisms.

One might object that causal powers are always specified in combination with the various precipitating conditions required for their manifestation. To specify the power to detect moving bars, one will have to make reference to an environment in which one or more bars is moving. Those are the conditions in which the ability to detect bars is manifested. If one includes enough of the environment in one's specification of the precipitating conditions for the exercise of a power, however, one can come to see individual neurons as having the power to detect bars and grandmothers. For if they were surrounded by millions of other neurons organized just so, and if they were presented with a moving bar stimulus, then they would detect the motion of the bar. Spark plugs have the power to mow grass that is manifest when they are organized together with other components in the lawn-mower. Note, however, that in each case the generalizations that describe the input–output relations for the whole are different from those that describe the input–output relations for the parts.

The precipitating conditions for the part are much more extensive than are the precipitating conditions for the whole, given that the precipitating conditions for the exercise of the part's powers include all of the details about the organization of the surrounding components and organizational features in the mechanism.

It is now clear why the causal exclusion argument does not apply to levels of mechanisms. If one understands P in Kim's argument merely as an individual component in the mechanism for M, then it is false to say that M's causal contribution is exhausted by the causal contribution of P. P and M do not compete as complete (that is, sufficient) causes and explanations. P is just a part of M. In the notation of earlier chapters, the behavior (ψ) of the mechanism as a whole (S) does not compete with the behavior (ϕ) of its individual components (X) as a sufficient cause of any downstream effect. ϕ is a component activity in the mechanism for ψ-ing, and the causal relevance relations in which ϕ figures are not the same as those in which ψ figures. The behavior of the component is not sufficient for the occurrence of the effect, as is assumed in Kim's argument; the component must also be organized together with the other components. In Kim's argument, it is ψ and $\phi\#$ (that is the organized collection of parts-plus-organization) that compete as causes. Consequently, the causal exclusion argument does not prevent one from accepting that mechanisms can do things that individual parts cannot, that mechanisms explain things that individual parts cannot, and so that higher levels of mechanisms are legitimately included in the explanations of contemporary neuroscience.

Lest there be some confusion, I do not advocate a spooky form of emergence. It is important to keep several different senses of the term "emergence" distinct. Some philosophers and scientists use the term "emergence" to describe properties of wholes that are not simple sums of the properties of components. Mechanisms are nonaggregates, and so they are emergent in this weak sense. Mechanisms require the organization of components in cooperative and inhibitory interactions that allow mechanisms to do things that the parts themselves cannot do. Other philosophers and scientists use the term "emergence" to mean that it is not possible to predict the behavior of a mechanism as a whole from what is known about the organization of its components. This is sometimes called "epistemic emergence." Some mechanisms have so many parts and such reticulate organization that our limited cognitive and computational powers prevent us from making such predictions. Some mechanisms are so sensitive to undetectable variations in input or background conditions that their behavior is unpredictable in practice. Behaviors of mechanisms are sometimes emergent in this epistemic sense. However, one who insists that there is no explanation for a nonrelational property of the whole in terms of the properties of its component parts-plus-organization advocates a spooky form of emergence. Indeed, levels of mechanisms are levels of ontic mechanistic explanation. Advocates of the spooky emergence of higher-level properties must have in mind a different sense of "level" altogether. Advocates of spooky emergence cannot therefore appeal to levels of mechanisms to make their view seem familiar and unmysterious. When one says that atoms compose molecules, which are organized into cells, which are linked into networks from which mental properties spookily emerge, the first three steps are upward steps in a hierarchy of levels of mechanisms, but the last is not. The ability of organization to elicit novel causal powers (that is, nonaggregative behaviors and properties) is unmysterious both in scientific common sense and common sense proper (Craver 2001; Van Gulick 1993; Wimsatt 1985, 1997). Appeal to strong or spooky emergence, on the other hand, justifiably arouses suspicion.

To conclude, if one agrees that levels of mechanisms are the central sense of level in the multilevel explanations in neuroscience, and one agrees with Kim that his metaphysical worries about nonfundamental causation are irrelevant to levels of mechanisms, then one should conclude that Kim's metaphysical worries are not relevant to the sense of levels central to many explanations in neuroscience. The metaphysical arguments provide no ground for believing that things at higher levels of mechanisms lack novel causal powers. Neither do they provide ground for the weaker claims that they are explanatorily superfluous or useless for the purposes of intervention and control. The multilevel view of explanation presented in this book is neither a target of, nor is it threatened by, Kim's causal exclusion argument.

5. Causal Relevance at Higher Levels of Realization

It would be hasty, however, to conclude that neuroscientists and neurophilosophers can ignore the upshot of Kim's argument. Kim's target is levels of realization, and levels of realization have played an important, if controversial, role in the history of neuroscience. Although my view of explanation is committed only to the existence of higher levels of mechanisms, as discussed above, the manipulationist view of causal relevance can be used to argue that realized phenomena are sometimes causally and therefore explanatorily relevant. This conclusion is independent of the implications of the causal exclusion argument, whatever they should be.

Levels of realization have been discussed widely in relation to computational explanations in cognitive neuroscience. David Marr's (1982) "levels of analysis"—the computational level (the level of what is computed and why), the algorithmic level (the level of input–output transformations), and the level of hardware implementation (the level of physical parts and their organization)—are perhaps the best-known example of levels of realization. Computational processes, such as addition, are realized by algorithmic transformations, and these, in turn, are realized by an organized collection of hardware components. These are three different properties of one and the same system. The system as a whole is at once an adder, a manipulator of symbols, and an organized set of electrical circuits. The algorithmic manipulator of symbols is not a component of the computing mechanism, and the hardware implementation is not a component of the algorithmic manipulator. Rather, these are all properties of the same thing. The system is an adder by virtue of its being a manipulator of symbols, and it is a manipulator of symbols by virtue of its being, for example, an organized set of electrical circuits. Furthermore, as Marr argues, the computational and algorithmic levels are multiply realizable. The same computation can be carried out with different algorithms, and the same algorithms can be carried out by many different hardware implementations. Similar views can be found in Lycan (1987), Putnam (1960), and Lepore and Loewer (1989). The simple examples that open this chapter exemplify the realization relation as well. One and the same thing (the ambient temperature) has the property of being below 0°C and the property of being −18.6°C. The temperature is below 0°C in virtue of the fact that it is −18.6°C. Being −18.6°C realizes being below 0°C. Likewise, one and the same thing (the piece of paper) has the property of being red and the property of being scarlet. The piece of paper is red in virtue of being scarlet. Being scarlet realizes being red.

One can confuse levels of mechanisms with levels of realization in the special case in which the realized property is some behavior (ψ) of a mechanism as a whole (S), and the realizing property is S's being a particular parts-plus-organization ($\phi\#$). Kim calls properties such as $\phi\#$ "micro-based" or "micro structural" properties (1998: 82). It is true that the relationship between ψ and $\phi\#$ is in some ways different from the relationship between variables (determinables) and their values (determinates) discussed in the last paragraph. $\phi\#$ is a composite property of (or, if it be preferred, a family of properties involving) S's having its particular parts-plus-organization. Being scarlet is not a case of being an organized set of components by virtue of which something is red, and being $-18.6°C$ is not a case of being a set of components organized such that the temperature is less than $0°C$. However, the fact that $\phi\#$ is micro-based and complex is not germane. In each case, the realized and realizing properties are properties of the same object—S, the ambient temperature, and the slip of paper. In each case, the object has the realized property by virtue of having the realizing property. The room is below $0°C$ by virtue of being $-18.6°C$, and S is ψ by virtue of its being $\phi\#$. In each case, the relationship is asymmetrical. Just as the paper is not scarlet by virtue of being red, S is not $\phi\#$ by virtue of ψ-ing. The paper might be red by virtue of being brick rather than scarlet, and S might be ψ by virtue of being $\phi\#'$ rather than $\phi\#$. S's being $\phi\#$ is a realizer of S's being ψ. In each case, the realizer is a particular way of having the realized property.

To consider a concrete example of realization by a micro-based property, suppose that a neuron (S) depolarizes (ψ) to a given membrane potential. S also has a particular arrangement of ions around its membrane ($\phi\#$). It is in virtue of the fact that the ions are distributed and arranged that the neuron is depolarized. If one were to fix the spatial arrangement of the ions around the membrane and the other factors relevant to membrane potential ($\phi\#$), one would thereby fix the membrane potential (ψ). However, there are many different configurations of ions that would realize precisely the same depolarization. Think, for example, of switching the positions of like-charged ions on opposite sides of the membrane. The particular arrangement of ions is just one way of depolarizing the cell. In this respect, it is closely analogous to examples of computational explanation.

Kim's argument attacks this sense of levels. His claim is that realized properties have no causal powers over and above those of the realizing properties. What, one might ask, could the property of being below $0°C$ allow an object to do that the property of being $-18.6°C$ would not allow it to do? What causal powers could the property of being red give an object that the property of being scarlet could not? And what causal work could depolarization of the cell body do over and above what is already being done by the particular arrangement of ions in the cell body? If the answer to these questions is "nothing," then talk of causal powers at higher levels of realization will appear suspect. To borrow Heil's colorful intuition-pump, imagine that a god sets out to make the world. The god begins by creating the fundamental particles and endowing them with all of their causal powers. Then the god organizes them spatially and temporally into complex objects and interactions (such as buckets of water and neurons). Must the god add in a new set of causal powers for buckets of water, and neurons? Or are the causal powers of these things already in the organizing relations among the fundamental components? This is where Kim's metaphysical arguments potentially raise a serious challenge.

However, it is crucial to keep this metaphysical question of whether there are real properties with causal powers at higher levels of realization, whatever is required for them to be "real" in this sense, separate from the *experimental* question of whether realized properties figure in unique causal relevance relations. In asking whether realized properties figure in causal relevance relations, I am asking whether there are generalizations of the form, "In conditions W, intervening to change the value of X from x_1 to x_2 changes the value of Y to $f(x_2)$" that quantify over variables describing realized properties. I am also asking whether one can identify switch-points among realized values of variables that are appropriate to a given effect-contrast. In asking whether these causal relevance relations are unique, I am asking whether there are explanatory generalizations (i.e., those that satisfy the criteria of manipulability laid out above) that are true of realized properties and are not true of their realizers. If these questions are answered affirmatively, then one has an argument that realized properties make a difference in a sense robust enough to satisfy constraints $((E1)-(E5))$ on acceptable explanation. One can hold this much even if one endorses the metaphysical view that there are no unique causal powers among realized properties.

I have already made the experimental case for the causal relevance of three realized properties: the property of being below $0°$, the property of being red, and the property of depolarization. This discussion does not require simplified philosophical examples. Rather, the questions discussed here are just like the questions addressed all the time in neuroscience laboratories. When Miledi showed that action potentials trigger the release of neurotransmitters through depolarization rather than through the influx of Na^+ in particular, a crucial finding in the discovery of the mechanisms of neurotransmitter release, he showed that a realizing property, the rising Na^+ concentration perse, is not relevant to transmitter release. It is relevant only in virtue of the fact that rising intracellular Na^+ concentrations realize depolarization under typical cellular conditions. His experiment follows precisely the logic that I have described here. Irrespective of metaphysical worries about causal powers, it seems clear that Miledi elegantly identified and settled a causal question that is crucial for understanding how this system works. It is also crucial for understanding how to manipulate the system. Interventions that alter Na^+ concentration without changing the membrane voltage will be ineffective in triggering the release of neurotransmitters (or changing the probability of such release). Interventions that increase membrane voltage without changing Na^+ concentrations will trigger the release of neurotransmitters (or change the probability of such release). In this sense, depolarization makes a difference to the release of neurotransmitters.

Consider another example from recent experimental and theoretical work in neuroscience. Astrid Prinz and colleagues (2004) argue that realized features of even relatively simple and evolutionarily ancient neural systems are surprisingly independent of the details of the underlying micro-based properties that realize them in any given case. To put it another way, there are true stable generalizations about the behavior of these systems that are not true of the parts–plus–organization that realize them on any given occasion. The system in question is the stomatogastric ganglion in the lobster. This simple structure has roughly thirty neurons, but it is capable of generating several distinctive kinds of rhythmic electrical activity that regulate many aspects of the lobster's digestive processes, including what is known as the pyloric rhythm. By building computer simulation models of the stomatograstric ganglion, Prinz shows that the characteristic bursting pattern of the pyloric rhythm can be produced by wildly different microstructural properties. Prinz constructed over 20,000,000 models of this simple system, varying the conductance properties of individual cells and the strengths of the synapses between them. They found that roughly

20 percent of these models produce patterns of activation that have the same overall temporal patterns as those observed in lobster ganglia. Among these 20 percent, 11 percent (roughly 452,500) of the networks, with widely ranging cellular and synaptic properties, produced burst-patterns within experimentally observed ranges determined by fifteen established criteria for assessing this pattern. What the stomatogastric ganglion does—its ability to regulate the pyloric rhythm—is in large part independent of the particular cellular and synaptic connections that realize it. One could intervene to change the organization in 452,499 separate ways without changing the relevant features regulating the pyloric rhythm. Prinz concludes that similar results are likely to be found in other systems throughout the central nervous system and beyond:

> Although the pyloric rhythm of the crustacean stomatogastric nervous system was the specific example used here, we draw a general conclusion: that even tightly regulated network behavior can result from widely disparate sets of parameters in the processes that give rise to this behavior. This conclusion is relevant not only to the nervous system, but also to biochemical and signaling networks, as parallel and interacting pathways also occur in these networks. It may be possible for any given network parameter to be highly variable in different cells or in different individuals, as long as an appropriate set of compensating changes has occurred. (2004: 1349)

These stable patterns are causally integrated within the lobster's digestive system such that changes in the rhythm (irrespective of the particular organization of components) produce changes in behavior of the digestive system. There must be stable developmental mechanisms in lobsters that construct—not a particular set of connections and strengths among particular neurons in the ganglion—but rather any organization of neurons that adequately produces the functional pyloric rhythm. There are likely homeostatic mechanisms in place to maintain that rhythm in spite of perturbations that, if uncorrected, would disrupt the rhythm. If one were an adaptationist, one might argue that nature has not selected for a particular organization of cells, but rather for a behavioral profile that can be cobbled together in many ways in the process of development. If Prinz is right, neuroscientists would misunderstand the behavior of the lobster digestive system if they were to suppose that it is regulated in the stomatogastric ganglion by a particular configuration in a network of cells. If one were to focus on a particular organizational structure, one would miss a pattern in the causal structure of the digestive system that is independent of those patterns among the network realizers, just as to focus on the influx of Na^+ into the axon terminal is to miss a pattern in the causal structure of the neuron (involving changes in membrane voltage) that is independent of the particular ion flux by which the membrane voltage changes.

The key point here, however, is that there are generalizations expressing contrastive relations of causal relevance that are true of realized properties and that are not true of their realizers. Building an adequate explanation requires identifying the appropriate causally relevant property for a given effect. If the pigeon pecks because the paper is red, then changing the paper from scarlet to pink makes no difference to the pigeon's behavior, although it does change the activation vector in its nucleus rotundus. This intervention merely provides a new realizer for the value of the color variable that is causally relevant to the pecking. Because water freezes when the temperature drops below $0°C$, changing the temperature from $-18.6°$ to $-19.2°$ makes no difference to whether the water freezes, although such an intervention will change the rate at which the water freezes. Given this intervention, the water will still freeze, but the freezing will have a different realizer. Finally, as long as one depolarizes the cell body, intervening to change the particular locations of the Na^+ and K^+ ions makes no difference to whether the neuron generates an action potential so long as the membrane voltage is not changed. The neuron will still generate an action potential, but the action potential will be realized by a different configuration of ions. In each of these cases, the generalization expressed in terms of realized properties identifies a switch-point that is not represented in the generalizations describing the behavior of the particular realizers. Note further that this conclusion is independent of the question of whether the realized causal relevance relations are derivable from generalizations describing fundamental causal powers. Whether or not one can carry out such a derivation, it is still the realized contrast that is relevant. It is the paper's being red (rather than not red) that caused the pigeon to peck, not its being scarlet rather than non-scarlet. Derivable or not, the appropriate switch-point is framed among realized properties.

Eric Marcus (forthcoming) puts this point in terms of Kim's causal exclusion argument, sketched in Section 1. Suppose that if M were to occur (rather than not-M), then M* would occur (rather than not-M*), and that if M failed to occur, then M* would fail to occur. Suppose further that if P were to occur (rather than not-P), then P* would occur (rather than not-P*). And suppose that P realizes M, and that P* realizes M*. Note that in this situation, if M had occurred, and P had not, then M* would still have occurred. The reason is that, in this last case, some other M-realizer (say P′) would have occurred, and it would have caused some other M*-realizer to occur. More concretely, if the room had been below 0°C, but had not been −18.6°C, then the water would still have frozen because in that case the room would have had some other value below 0°C, and that value would have caused the water to freeze (albeit at a different rate). The true generalization describing the relationship among realized properties identifies a pattern of causal relevance that is much more encompassing than are the patterns of causal relevance identified among the realizers.

I emphasize again that these are points about causal relevance and causal explanation, not about causal powers. It is open to the metaphysician to grant these points and to insist nonetheless that the causally efficacious relations (those involving causal powers) are found only among the ultimate realizers. There is a generalization describing the behavior of the pigeon in relation to red things, but in every instance it is a particular shade of red that exerts powers in affecting the pigeon's visual system in a particular way. There is a true generalization that water freezes at temperatures below 0°C, but each instance of freezing is in fact brought about by some determinate ambient temperature. The true generalizations among realized values of variables must have truth-makers, one might think, and the obvious candidates for those truth-makers are the relations of causal efficacy or power that hold among the individual realizers (see Heil 2003). For such a metaphysician, causation is fundamentally about efficacy, activity, and production. Relations of causal relevance are second-class causal relations, derivative for their existence upon more fundamental expressions of causal power. Higher-level predicates do not refer to genuine higher-level properties but refer instead to individuals grouped by family resemblance.

The view that causal relevance relations are ultimately grounded in the exercise of causal powers is no doubt attractive. I have endorsed a similar view in other contexts (Machamer et al. 2000). Three challenges face such a view. The first is to supply an illuminating account of causal powers. To be illuminating, the metaphysical posit has to explain why causal relevance relations hold and why they satisfy constraints such as (E1)–(E5). It will not do to simply introduce a filler term, such as "power" or "activity," as a primitive causal relation and to assume that thereby a metaphysical explanation has been achieved. (E1)–(E5), in other words, characterize the phenomenon to be explained by appeal to causal powers. The challenge is to provide an account of what activities, causal powers, and causal efficacy are, that explains (not merely presupposes) why generalizations in our world satisfy (E1)–(E5). In Chapter 3, I consider two attempts at such an account: the transmission account, according to which causal processes are physically connected through the transfer of conserved quantities, and the mechanical view, according to which cause and effect are connected by a mechanism. Neither of these views satisfies (E1)–(E5). Perhaps there is some other satisfactory view of the fundamental causal relation, but this notion has been recalcitrant to philosophical analysis at least since Hume. The second challenge is to provide a compelling account of causation by omission and prevention. Causes sometimes make a difference through the dormancy of causal powers, gaps in transmission, breaks in mechanisms, and inactivity among their components. The metaphysician must then supply a separate explanation for why stable generalizations about causal relevance hold in such cases. Finally, the metaphysician should provide an account of causal powers that makes sense of the experimental and observational practices that scientists use to discover causal relations. It would, for example, be an epistemic limitation if one's account of causation made causal relationships unknowable on the basis of all possible evidence. These challenges are pressing given that the manipulationist view automatically accommodates (E1)–(E5) and provides a univocal account of both positive and negative causes while making straightforward sense of the experimental practices used by scientists in their search for causes.

Given such considerations, one might be tempted to jettison talk of causal powers as unnecessary metaphysics and to hold that to cause just is to be causally relevant in the sense specified in this book. On such a view, causation is fundamentally about making a difference, regardless of whether that difference is made through the exercise of activities or powers. There need not be a cement, glue, spring, string, or power that connects causes to their effects. What matters is that changes in the cause are accompanied by changes in the effect that occur only via the change to the cause and not via some other route. Sometimes causes act through the exercise of causal powers, and sometimes they act via absences and gaps. Any putative property that can be detected by multiple independent techniques, that is described in our best scientific theories and explanations, and that figures in patterns of causal relevance is, if not real in the full-blown metaphysical sense, at least as real as anything else known to science. For many, that is real enough (cf. Dennett 1991).

This alternative view faces two significant challenges. First, the manipulationist view of causal relevance explicitly presupposes, and so is not a reductive analysis of, the notion of causation. The idea of an intervention and the constraints (I1)–(I4) are explicitly causal. One might therefore think that the manipulationist criterion itself requires grounding in a more fundamental causal notion, and perhaps the idea of a "causal power" can play that role. This possibility will have to be assessed as more detailed accounts of causal powers and activities are forthcoming. Second, one might think that all general truths about the world have truth-makers, that is, facts in virtue of which the general truths hold. The manipulationist view might provide a revealing account of the generalizations that express causal relevance relations, but it does not provide an account of the ultimate causal facts in virtue of which these generalizations hold. The manipulationist view, to put the same point differently, lacks a semantics for the central claim that if X is changed from x_1 to x_2 then Y changes from y_1 to y_2. Solutions to this problem will likewise have to be evaluated as they are forthcoming.

These are merely two metaphysical views among many, and it is possible that the virtues of each could be combined into a more powerful view of the causal structure of the world than either can supply independently. My point is that one's convictions about realized properties, be they metaphysically fundamentalist or antifundamentalist, should not prevent one from endorsing the idea that realized properties are sometimes causally, and so explanatorily, relevant. These two metaphysical views each agree that there are nonfundamental relations of causal relevance. They disagree only about the ultimate structure of reality in virtue of which those relations hold. Questions about the metaphysics of properties and causation are therefore not relevant to what experimental scientists ought to do or to what explanations they ought to seek. Nor are they relevant to which explanations a neurophilosopher ought to endorse. Indeed, most metaphysical fundamentalists take it as a burden of their view to explain why robust and explanatory generalizations hold among realized (even multiply realized) properties if all the causal powers are located at the fundamental level. It would thus be incorrect to conclude, as some do, that causal exclusion arguments justify focusing research at the most fundamental levels of neuroscience (see Bickle 2003). If neuroscientists were to ignore generalizations among realized properties on the basis of these metaphysical challenges, they would be misled by philosophers into ignoring crucial switch-points in the causal structure of the world.

6. Conclusion

In this chapter, I show that well-known arguments against higher-level causes should not prevent one from adopting a multilevel mechanistic view of explanation. I argue that mechanisms, by virtue of their organization, are able to do things that their parts cannot do individually. They can respond to inputs that the parts alone cannot detect. They can produce behaviors that their parts alone cannot produce. There are generalizations about causal relevance that are true of mechanisms and false of their parts. Kim does not intend to deny any of this. He says it is obvious, and indeed it is.

Concerning levels of realization, I claim that there are truths about causal relevance captured in generalizations describing realized values of variables and that these generalizations cannot be expressed in generalizations describing relations among realizers. My argument for the relevance of realized properties (and my account of how to tell which level of realization is relevant in a given case) rely on the common practice of using controlled experiments to test claims about causal and explanatory relevance. Mine is an experimentalist's defense of the causal relevance of realized properties. The metaphysician wants to look deeper to the ultimate ontological structures that explain these facts. Whatever they find, however, it will not tarnish the fact that nonfundamental features are causally relevant, explanatorily relevant, and useful for the purposes of manipulation and control. We can make significant progress in the philosophy of neuroscience without settling these perennial metaphysical disputes.

7

The Mosaic Unity
of Neuroscience

Summary

In this chapter, I show how multilevel mechanistic explanations scaffold the unity of neuroscience. Philosophers of neuroscience traditionally envision the unity of neuroscience as being achieved through the stepwise reduction of higher-level theories to successively lower level, and ultimately fundamental, theories. I argue, in contrast, that the unity of neuroscience is achieved as different fields integrate their research by adding constraints on multilevel mechanistic explanations. The goal of finding multilevel explanations provides an abstract sketch or scaffold for integrating fields. The findings in different fields of neuroscience are used, like the tiles of a mosaic, to elaborate this abstract mechanism and to shape the space of possible mechanisms. The mosaic unity of neuroscience is achieved both through interfield integration at a given level and through integration across levels in a hierarchy of mechanisms. I develop this model using a putative exemplar of reduction in contemporary neuroscience: the relationship between the psychological phenomena of learning and memory and the electrophysiological phenomenon, Long–Term Potentiation (LTP). I thereby demonstrate that the mosaic view is superior to reduction as a model of the unity of neuroscience.

1. Introduction

Neuroscience is a multifield research program.[1] Its departments, journals, societies, and textbooks include perspectives from anatomy, biochemistry,

---

[1] In the spirit of Darden and Maull (1977), I understand fields as groups of researchers related by common problems, techniques, and vocabularies. The boundaries between fields are fuzzy and change with time, but there is no pressing need to tidy them up for present purposes.

computer science, radiology, developmental, evolutionary, and molecular biology, electrophysiology, experimental psychology, ethology, pharmacology, and psychiatry, to name just a few. The Society for Neuroscience (SfN) was founded in 1969 to "advance the understanding of the brain and the nervous system by bringing together scientists of diverse backgrounds, by facilitating the integration of research directed at all levels of biological organization, and by encouraging translational research and the application of new scientific knowledge to develop improved disease treatments and cures."[2] This goal of integrating and unifying neuroscience, however, is underspecified until one can say how scientists are brought together, what it means to integrate research, and in what sense work in one field can be "translated" for use in others.

Most philosophers who discuss the unity of neuroscience (for example, Bickle 1998, 2003; P. S. Churchland 1986; Schaffner 1993a, 1993b) describe it using models of intertheoretic reduction. According to the "classical" model of reduction (Nagel 1949, 1961), from which each of these authors' models descends, reduction is a species of covering law (CL) explanation: one theory is reduced to another when it is possible to define the theoretical terms of the first with those of the second and to derive the first theory from the second. None of the above philosophers of neuroscience endorses the classical view of reduction in all its rigor, but each endorses a close descendant. For example, Schaffner's model of reduction (which Churchland adopts) requires that a corrected version of the reduced theory be derivable from a restricted version of the reducing theory with the aid of transtheoretic identities.[3] These elaborations maintain the basic derivational framework of reduction, but allow the fit between reduced and reducing theory to be less than exact. Bickle's model of reduction (1998) requires that one be able to construct an "equipotent image" of the reduced theory within the structure of the reducing theory as well as "ontological reductive links" between the two. The idea of an equipotent image is a technical notion that plays the role of the derivation requirement in the strongest formulation of the classical model, but that allows degrees of homomorphism between the two theories. Ontological reductive links play the role of identity statements in the classical model. In each of these

---

[2] Society for Neuroscience web page(2003):<http://web.sfn.org/content/AboutSfN1/Mission/mission.htm>.

[3] This view of reduction has also been elaborated and defended by Hooker (1981).

models, reduction is conceived as a relationship between theories. Theories descriptive of a given level are reduced to theories descriptive of the next lowest level. Because different theories of neuroscience are associated with different fields, such reductions effect the unity of neuroscience. In still weaker models of reduction, reduction merely requires that all higher-level phenomena be explained in terms of fundamental mechanisms or laws (for example, Sarkar 1992; Smith 1992; Weber 2005). All that remains of reduction in these cases is a commitment to the primacy of downward and fundamental explanation.

There are many reasons why philosophers of neuroscience find reduction attractive for thinking about the unity of science. First, reduction can be defined precisely with formal logic (for example, Schaffner 1993a, 1993b) and set theory (for example, Bickle 2003). So the thesis that different fields of neuroscience are integrated through reduction can be formulated precisely and evaluated. This advantage is sacrificed by advocates of weaker reduction models who appeal to, for example, "explanation by mechanism" (Weber 2005) or "explanatory interfacing" (Smith 1992) without explicating precisely what counts as an explanation or what distinguishes good explanations from bad.[4] Second, because there is a long tradition of using reduction models in the philosophy of physics, chemistry, and biology, one might expect (or hope) that reduction models can be extended to the neurosciences. Finally, at least since Oppenheim and Putnam's manifesto (1958), reduction has been nearly synonymous with the explanatory unity of science: the unity of science is achieved by reducing the theories of all fields to the theories of the field that describes fundamental ontology. Thus, whoever questions the reductive unity of science might appear to be questioning the unity of science simpliciter (see Fodor 1974; Dupre 1993).

In the preceding chapters, I raise a number of problems for the above views of explanatory reduction. First, I object to the image of explanation that lies at their heart, arguing that the CL account cannot distinguish mere models from explanations, how-possibly from how-actually explana- tions, and mechanism sketches from complete descriptions of mechanisms. Precisely the same objections apply to Bickle's image-based view because

---

[4] Weber (2005), for example, explicitly declines to specify a view of explanation, appealing to the CL model, Kitcher's U-model, and Salmon's causal-mechanical account. I discuss the shortcomings of each of these possibilities in Chapters 2 and 3.

equipotent images can be how-possibly images, incomplete images, and explanatorily irrelevant images. Furthermore, Bickle does not show when the ontologically reductive links are precise enough to rule out pseudo-explanations. In Chapter 4, I provide a model of mechanistic explanation that is superior to reductive models as a regulative ideal for constitutive explanation in neuroscience. I argue in Chapter 5 that levels of science, levels of theory, and levels of nature do not coincide with one another in contemporary neuroscience. Thus, the notion that levels of nature correspond to levels of theory developed within levels of fields oversimplifies the structure within which the unity of neuroscience is achieved. Finally, in Chapter 6, I show that adequate explanations in neuroscience typically include higher-level causes. The reduction model is focused exclusively on explanations that appeal to lower-level mechanisms, and so does not accommodate these aspects of the explanatory unity of neuroscience. Reduction models thus provide an inadequate account of the explanatory unity of neuroscience. Reduction survives as a model of the unity of neuroscience largely because there is no alternative of comparable scope and clarity.

In this chapter, I use the view of multilevel mechanistic explanation developed in the preceding chapters to construct a model of the *mosaic unity of neuroscience*. The central idea is that neuroscience is unified not by the reduction of all phenomena to a fundamental level, but rather by using results from different fields to constrain a multilevel mechanistic explanation. The goal of building a mechanistic explanation, rather than an explanation *simpliciter*, provides an abstract framework or scaffold that is elaborated as different fields add constraints on the explanation. The search for mechanisms guides researchers to look for specific kinds of evidence (in the form of different constraints) and provides the scaffold by which these constraints are integrated piecemeal as research progresses. The different fields that contribute to the mosaic unity of neuroscience are autonomous in that they have different central problems, use different techniques, have different theoretical vocabularies, and make different background assumptions; they are unified because each provides constraints on a mechanistic explanation. Individual fields do not surrender their autonomy through this form of unification; in fact, their ability to contribute novel constraints on a mechanism *requires* that they maintain their autonomy (cf. Wylie 2002). Because different fields approach problems from different perspectives, using different assumptions and techniques, the evidence they provide makes mechanistic explanations robust.

To develop the mosaic model, I consider an historical example of progress toward the unity of neuroscience: the LM research program (discussed in Chapters 3 and 5). Several philosophers of neuroscience (including Bickle 1998, 2003; Schaffner 1967, 1993a; and Churchland and Sejnowski 1992) describe the LM research program as an exemplar of reduction. In Section 2, I argue that rather than being exemplary of reduction, the historical development of the LM research program more accurately exhibits the mosaic unity of neuroscience. In considering the case, I note three descriptive limitations of reduction models: first, they cannot accommodate the upward-looking aspects of the unity of neuroscience; second, they ignore *intra*level forms of interfield integration; and third, they gloss over the fact that progress in the LM research program has been achieved by abandoning reduction as an explanatory goal. This history shows how scientists integrate fields by adding constraints on mechanisms (see also Bechtel 1984). In the next portion of the chapter, I construct a model of the mosaic unity of neuroscience. Specifically, in Section 3, I show how the goal of building mechanistic explanations provides a scaffold for integrating results from different fields *at a given level*.[5] In Section 4, I show how the pursuit of mechanisms provides a scaffold for integrating results from different fields across levels. The historical considerations of Section 2 show that the mosaic model of interfield integration is more historically accurate than reduction. The constructive project of Sections 3 and 4 encompasses forms of interfield integration that the reduction model neglects, and it provides a more detailed view than does the reduction model of the kinds of constraints needed to build bridges from molecules to behavior.

I conclude by showing how the mosaic unity of neuroscience, in which autonomous fields provide independent constraints on a common multilevel mechanism, serves the epistemic function of making mechanistic explanations robust, that is, of constructing explanations that are able to withstand scrutiny from multiple independent lines of evidence and multiple independent disciplinary perspectives (compare Hacking 1983; Salmon 1984;

---

[5] Throughout this chapter, when I say that integration occurs at a level, I mean that the integration does not cross levels. My view of levels (Chapter 5) purposely leaves the idea of sameness of level undefined.

Wimsatt 1981; Wylie 2002). The mosaic unity of neuroscience is a valuable goal, not because it distinguishes science from nonscience, nor because it shows everything to be tethered to fundamental things, but because such unity is a sign of epistemic success. In sum, I argue that the mosaic model of the unity of neuroscience, based on the search for mechanistic explanations, is better suited than reduction to the descriptive, explanatory, and epistemic projects for which these classic models were designed.

2. Reduction and the History of Neuroscience

There is little agreement among advocates of reduction as a model of the unity of neuroscience as to whether or not it should be taken to be an empirical fact that neuroscience exhibits a reductive trend from early work at higher levels to more mature work at lower levels.

Many advocates of reduction admit that the reduction model poorly describes the history and practice of science. Schaffner (1993a), for example, argues that reduction is "peripheral" to scientific practice and that it should be regarded merely as a "regulative ideal," that is, the goal of an ideally complete explanation. P. S. Churchland, following Francis Crick, admits that reductions are rare and that they typically occur only after the interesting "co-evolutionary" work has been done (see 1986: 285). Such admissions insulate reduction models against evidence from the history of neuroscience. Reductionists can grant that neuroscientists have yet to achieve any (or many) complete reductions and claim, nonetheless, that neuroscientists ought to aim for the goal of reduction. They justify this normative claim by appeal to success stories in the history of other branches of science, such as the reduction of the laws of thermodynamics to the laws of statistical mechanics (Bickle 1998; and Nagel 1961), or the reduction of the laws of optics to the laws of electromagnetism (P. S. Churchland 1986).

On the other hand, it is reasonable to be suspicious of theories about neuroscience that are peripheral to what neuroscientists actually do. Why, after all, should neuroscience have the explanatory goals of physics? One difference between neuroscience and physics is that there are no laws of neuroscience comparable in scope and stability to the laws of optics and statistical mechanics. Generalizations in neuroscience are fragile, variable, and historically contingent to a far greater extent than are the gas laws or the laws of optics. A second difference is that objects in the domain of neuroscience are multiply realizable; that is, different materials, parts, or mechanisms can (and do) give rise to the same nonfundamental regularities. Even though these two differences between neuroscience and more fundamental sciences do not provide challenges to reduction in principle, they nevertheless show why the goal of achieving a classical reduction is not a priority in neuroscience. To derive higher-level regularities from lower-level regularities would require such a vast number of restrictions on background and internal conditions (even compared to the vast number required for such reductions in physics and chemistry) that actual reductions would invariably appear contrived. Furthermore, because higher-level generalizations are multiply realizable, such reductions (if possible) would likely be of only narrow significance and hold, for example, only for normal members of a subset of a species during a particular time of development. Explanatory successes in physics and chemistry are irrelevant if the domain of neuroscience (among other special sciences) requires a different kind of explanation. The peripherality of reduction, in other words, is a warning sign that it is premised on an explanatory ideal that is inappropriate for the neurosciences.

Some advocates of reduction champion reduction as an accurate description of scientific practice. Oppenheim and Putnam (1958) argue that the sciences of their day exhibit a trend toward reducing social facts to facts about psychology, then reducing facts about psychology to facts about cells, and so on down to elementary particles. They argue for a "working hypothesis" that the unity of science will ultimately be achieved through the stepwise reduction of higher-level sciences to lower-level sciences. Bickle (1998, 2003) similarly argues that contemporary neuroscience exhibits a reductive trend (2003: 280). He cites recent conference programs and journals to show that the bulk of the most exciting contemporary neuroscience is dedicated to manipulating and understanding the behaviors of cells and molecules. Furthermore, he argues that it is now possible to construct explanations for many high-level phenomena in terms of molecular mechanisms. He concludes that the best explanations in neuroscience are currently at the molecular level, and that higher-level neuroscience is at best heuristically important for directing attention to the right molecular mechanisms.[6]

---

[6] Bickle sometimes stresses that his reductionism is merely internal—a report of the explanatory ideals and practices of cellular and molecular neuroscience. Thus restricted, Bickle's advocacy of ruthless

I do not dispute that molecular biologists are making very exciting contributions to contemporary neuroscience. Nor do I dispute that the proportion of neuroscience dedicated to molecular pursuits has expanded dramatically in recent years. Even if one grants that there is an historical trend toward the molecular, there is a further question of what hypothesis best explains that trend. Bickle's hypothesis is that only molecular explanations are truly explanatory, and that neuroscientists are "going molecular" because that is where the true explanations are. However, an alternative hypotheses is at least equally plausible. Researchers have recently developed a host of new techniques for sequencing, copying, and manipulating genes, and for designing pharmaceuticals that control molecular mechanisms. These techniques allow molecular biologists to answer myriad questions about the molecular constituents of nerve cells that could not have been posed even a few years ago. As a result, the field of molecular biology has expanded greatly. In Lakatos's terms, there is now a progressive research program in molecular biology that currently generates more questions than can be answered. There have not been such exciting developments in technology in other areas of neuroscience (except perhaps neuroimaging), and so these other areas have not grown at a comparable rate. Add to this the fact that funding for genetic and other molecular research has increased dramatically, and that university research priorities are designed around funding opportunities, and one has a plausible explanation for recent trends toward molecular neuroscience. If comparable techniques for experimenting on social phenomena are developed, that field of research will boom as well.

The fact that neuroscientists are increasingly pursuing molecular research does not establish that the best neuroscientific explanations are at the molecular level. Nonetheless, knowledge of the history of a field can help philosophers keep their theories about the unity of science true to what scientists actually do. If one hopes to understand the norms implicit in the practice of science—here Bickle is exactly right—one must begin by looking at real science. My claim is that the norms implicit in the history

---

reductionism is much less controversial than it appears, amounting only to the claim that some scientists think that explanations ought to be given in terms of cells and molecules. This is a far cry from the claim that all neuroscientists endorse ruthless reductionism, and further still from the claim that all neuroscientists ought to.

of the LM research program are closer to those expressed in my mosaic model than those expressed by reduction models.

With these objectives in mind, I now examine an episode in the recent history of neuroscience—one that has become the standard exemplar of reduction in the philosophy of neuroscience: the discovery of LTP and its association across multiple levels with learning and memory (discussed in Chapters 3 and 5). In the standard scientific history of LTP, the discovery of LTP is described as the product of an intentional downward-looking search for a memory mechanism in the hippocampus. Thus understood, this discovery supports the view that there was a reductive trend from higher to lower levels. Eric Kandel (who won the Nobel Prize for his foundational work on the neuroscience of memory) and Larry Squire (an eminent memory researcher and historian of neuroscience) provide such a reductionist account of LTP's history.

> In 1973 Tim Bliss and Terje Lømo working in Per Andersen's laboratory in Oslo, Norway, made a remarkable discovery. Aware of Brenda Milner's insight about the role of the hippocampus and the medial temporal lobe in memory storage, they attempted to see whether the synapses between neurons in the hippocampus had the capability of storing information. To examine this possibility, they purposely carried out a quite artificial experiment. They stimulated a specific nerve pathway in the hippocampus of the rat and asked: Can neural activity affect synaptic strength in the hippocampus? They found that a brief high-frequency period of electrical activity (called a tetanus) applied artificially to a hippocampal pathway produced an increase in synaptic strength that lasted for hours in an anaesthetized animal and would, if repeated, last for days and even weeks in an alert freely moving animal. This type of facilitation is now called long-term facilitation, or more commonly, *long-term potentiation* (2000: 210–11).

In this passage, some of the central figures in the history are introduced. These include Per Andersen (in whose Oslo laboratory much of the story is set), Terje Lømo (Andersen's first graduate student), Tim Bliss (Andersen's post-doctoral fellow), and Brenda Milner (who performed psychological evaluations on patients with lesioned hippocampi). Yet this passage is a scientific argument for the importance of LTP rhetorically packaged as history—it is more compelling than it is historically accurate.

In a detailed examination of this history (Craver 2003), I show how misleading this history, and the reductive image that it supports, is. First, contrary to Oppenheim and Putnam's (and Bickle's) empirical thesis, the development of the LM research program extends upward and downward depending upon the problem to be solved, not just downward as the reduction model requires. This oscillation among levels is also evident in contemporary LM research. Second, the instances of interfield integration composing the history of the LM research program are, in many cases, intralevel and intratheoretic, and so are not even candidates for analysis in terms of reduction. Finally, although reduction was once an explanatory goal of the LM research program, that goal was replaced by the goal of building multilevel mechanisms. In short, reduction is not only peripheral to the recent history of LTP, but it is also incomplete and misleading as a model of the unity of neuroscience.

2.1 LTP's origins: not a top-down search but intralevel integration

Like Squire and Kandel, most neuroscientists date the discovery of LTP to a series of 1973 papers by Tim Bliss, Terje Lømo, and Tony Gardner-Medwin. Although these papers constitute a watershed in the LTP research program, the story of LTP begins much earlier than 1973 and involves an episode of intralevel (and thus nonreductive) interfield integration.

Electrophysiologists first produced and reported synaptic plasticity in the hippocampus in the 1950s. At the time, researchers worked *in vivo* by inserting electrodes through the skulls of anaesthetized rabbits. (It is now common to work on *in vitro* hippocampal slice preparations, but these techniques did not exist until the 1970s.) These researchers were under time pressure to produce as much data as they could before the anesthesia, blood loss, and repeated stimulation degraded the electrophysiological responses. As a trick of the trade, researchers knew that when the electrophysiological signals began to degrade, they could reawaken the cells by jolting them with a high-frequency stimulus for a few seconds (see Andersen 1991, 2003). While extremely important as a laboratory tool, this trick was not considered theoretically significant at the time. There are scattered references to the phenomenon in the late 1950s and early 1960s (see, for example, Green and Adey 1956: 250; Andersen 1960a: 191, 1960b: 216; Andersen, Bruland, and Kaada 1961; Gloor et al. 1964), but none of them describes it as more than an experimental curiosity. They mention it as one electrophysiological effect among many, and they accord it no special significance. It is not surprising, then, that none of these early reports connect this form of potentiation with learning or memory.

It is reasonable to assume, as the above quotation suggests, that researchers were drawn to the hippocampus because of its link with learning and memory. Wilder Penfield had published preliminary reports on hippocampal lesions in 1952, and Brenda Milner and William Scoville published their classic paper on the effects of hippocampal lesions on human memory in 1957. If electrophysiologists were studying the hippocampus because of its link with learning and memory, these reports would be evidence of a downward trend in this early phase of the LM research program.

In addition to the fact that none of the early reports of synaptic plasticity in the hippocampus contain mention of learning and memory, there are a number of reasons to reject this hypothesis. To begin with, the idea of localizing memory anywhere in the brain was generally not accepted at the time. In the 1940s, Karl Lashley's systematic lesion experiments on pigeons convinced many neuroscientists that the severity of the resulting learning and memory deficits depends not on the lesion's location, but rather on the volume of brain tissue excised:

This series of experiments has yielded a good bit of information about what and where the memory trace is not. It has discovered nothing directly of the real nature of the engram. I sometimes feel, in reviewing the evidence on the localization of the memory trace, that the necessary conclusion is that learning just is not possible. It is difficult to conceive of a mechanism that can satisfy the conditions set for it. Nevertheless, in spite of such evidence against it, learning sometimes does occur (Lashley 1950; reprinted in Cummins and Cummins 1999: 347).

Furthermore, in the 1950s, neuroscientists commonly associated the hippocampus with functions other than memory. Writers of most neuroscience texts of the day associate the hippocampus with olfaction; others hypothesize that it might be involved in behavioral inhibition, emotion, fear, ingestive behavior, sexual activity, sleep, and respiration. Given such a wide range of phenomena, it is little wonder that the early reports of hippocampal synaptic plasticity fail to include mention of learning or memory. In one of these early papers, the authors explicitly decline to speculate about the "true role" of the hippocampus. They say that "many more physiological and behavioral studies will be needed before any systematic correlation with the anatomical structure can be attempted" (Cragg and Hamlyn 1957: 483).

If these electrophysiologists were not looking for a neural correlate of memory, as reductionists claim, then why were they looking in the hippocampus? There are two primary reasons. First, the hippocampus is implicated in epilepsy. In fact, Scoville and Milner removed the hippocampus in at least one of their patients (H.M.) in a desperate attempt to cure his life-threatening seizures. Most of the electrophysiologists studying the hippocampus (including Andersen) were MDs working at medical schools, and they were no doubt aware of, if not explicitly interested in, its pathology. Second, and most importantly in the present context, the hippocampus was (and is) a valuable experimental model for studying the electrophysiology of neural circuits. It has a relatively simple organization, with three major excitatory synapses, and the same pattern is repeated, layer after layer. The anatomy of the system was well understood at the time. It is primitive and highly conserved across species. Finally, the rodent hippocampus is large and readily accessible through the skull, making it attractive for *in vivo* studies. Electrophysiologists worked on the hippocampus for the same reasons that researchers are generally attracted to any simple and well-characterized experimental model.

In Oslo, where the first long-lasting form of hippocampal plasticity was produced, researchers viewed the hippocampus as an especially useful experimental model for integrating results from anatomy and electrophysiology. This integration of fields did not occur across levels, as the reductive story suggests, but occurred at a single level as different fields added different constraints on a neural mechanism. There were several anatomists working on the hippocampus in Oslo. Chief among them was Alf Brodal, who argued influentially that to understand the brain, one must first understand its basic anatomical wiring patterns. Some of the anatomists used Golgi stains, which stain one in ten neurons and thereby show patterns of connectivity in a brain region. Others used terminal degeneration studies, in which one kills the cell body and then applies stains that show the withering axons. In each case, the goal was to identify neuronal locations, structures, and connections. This anatomical wiring diagram could then be used as a foundation for electrophysiological investigation. Using the anatomical map of the hippocampus, one could intervene to change the electrophysiological properties of specific cells or populations of cells (for example, by delivering current) and could record the effects of those interventions on other cells or populations of cells. In this way, electrophysiologists could study the propagation of neural excitation through the circuitry of the hippocampus. The findings of the anatomists and electrophysiologists were not related to one another by reduction. They did not bridge levels, create equipotent images, form bridge laws, or establish ontological reductive links relating the items of two domains. Instead, they combined different techniques to investigate different aspects of a mechanism at the same level. Their goal was to understand how neural wiring diagrams and electrical activities are related in a well-defined neural circuit. In the context of this interfield project, Lømo, and later Bliss, encountered the phenomenon now known as LTP.

To summarize the story thus far, hippocampal synaptic plasticity was not discovered in a top-down, reductive search for the neural correlate of memory; rather, it was noticed during an intralevel research project in which anatomical and electrophysiological perspectives were integrated. Such intralevel varieties of interfield integration are not candidates for description with the formalism of reduction models, but they do constitute significant progress toward the goal of a unified neuroscience. These findings from different fields provide different constraints on the same mechanism and yield a more complete image of the mechanism's organization than the fields can provide individually. In some cases, different techniques are used to provide independent evidence about a single phenomenon (as when researchers study neural connections with different staining techniques, such as Golgi stains and terminal degeneration). In other cases, different techniques expose different aspects of a single mechanism (as when researchers in one field study anatomy and those in another study electrophysiology). If the fields and techniques were *not* largely autonomous, if the results of one *could* be translated into the results of the other, then they would not provide *independent* evidence about a mechanism (cf. Wylie 2002).

2.2 *The mechanistic shift*

If LTP was not discovered in the search for a memory mechanism, then how *did* LTP come to be associated with learning and memory? This upward-looking phase of the research program, in which the lower-level phenomenon is related to a higher-level mechanism, continues to the present. This phase developed only after the discovery of potentiation in the hippocampus that lasts longer than ten minutes. Some neuroscientists in the 1950s and 1960s had a downward reductive view of the connection between synaptic changes and learning. However, after the 1973 LTP watershed, these reductive aspirations were replaced by mechanistic explanatory goals.

Warren McCulloch and Walter Pitts, for example, had clear reductive aspirations:

The "all-or-none" law of nervous activity is sufficient to insure that the activity of any neuron may be represented as a proposition. Physiological relations existing among nervous activities correspond, of course, to relations among the propositions; and the utility of the representation depends upon the identity of these relations to relations among the propositions. To each reaction of any neuron there is a corresponding assertion of a simple proposition. This, in turn, implies either some other simple proposition or the disjunction or the conjunction, with or without negation, of similar propositions according to the configuration of the synapses upon and the threshold of the neuron in question. (McCulloch and Pitts 1943: 352)

In this explanatory schema, propositions are identified with all-or-nothing activity in neurons, and the interrelationships among action potentials in a network are identified with complex propositions (for example, conjunctions, disjunctions, and negations) and with inferences among propositions (for example, from the activation of two propositions separately to the activation of their conjunction). Changes in beliefs or inference patterns, McCulloch and Pitts suggest, might be represented as changes in connection strengths among neurons. It would be difficult to find a clearer statement of reductive goals anywhere in science.

Oppenheim and Putnam (1958) cite McCulloch and Pitts and other mathematical biophysicists as having shown that phenomena at the level of the whole organism (psychology) are reducible to phenomena at the level of cells. Oppenheim and Putnam use this purported achievement as evidence for their historical thesis:

In terms of such nerve nets it is possible to give hypothetical micro-reductions for *memory, exact thinking, distinguishing similarity or dissimilarity of stimulus patterns, abstracting of "essential" components of a stimulus pattern, recognition of shape regardless of form and of chord regardless of pitch* (phenomena of great importance to Gestalt psychology), *purposeful behavior* as controlled by negative feedback, *adaptive behavior,* and *mental disorders.* (Oppenheim and Putnam 1958: 20; italics in original)

Something like the goal of reducing learning to synaptic changes is implicit in the early reports of synaptic plasticity from Oslo. The claim was not that learning in organisms is identical to synaptic changes, but rather that synaptic changes are a simple and primitive *type of* learning. Andersen and

Lømo, who in 1967 were the first to associate this form of plasticity with learning, write that the phenomenon is "of some interest in connection with," "an indication of," and "an example of" a synaptic learning process. Sir J. C. Eccles, with whom Andersen worked from 1961 to 1963, uses similar language. Unlike the Oslo community, Eccles *was* specifically interested in neural correlates of learning, and he was looking for evidence of plasticity in spinal reflex circuits. Eccles was able to produce short-term changes in synaptic strength. He thought of this potentiation in the spinal cord as a *kind of* memory. He claimed, for example, that "disused synapses are capable of 'learning' to operate more effectively" (Eccles 1953) in the sense that repeated stimulation (experience) strengthens the synapse (long-lasting change). Andersen and Lømo explicitly note that the phenomenon reported in their 1967 paper does not last long enough to be plausibly identified with learning in organisms (1967: 410). This is why they describe their phenomenon as merely a simplified model or example of memory—not as a potential memory mechanism.

In 1966, Lømo published an abstract in which he described a form of tetanus-induced plasticity in the hippocampus that lasts for hours. In 1968, when Bliss arrived for his post-doctoral fellowship, he teamed up with Lømo to characterize LTP. This work culminated in the 1973 LTP watershed (Bliss and Lømo 1973; Bliss and Gardner-Medwin 1973; Bliss, Gardner-Medwin, and Lømo 1973). These papers are the first to characterize the LTP phenomenon in detail. The authors are also the first to suggest clearly, albeit timidly, that LTP might be associated with learning. Finally, these researchers subtly reconceptualize the link between LTP and memory. They describe LTP, not as identical to memory, or as a kind of memory, but rather as a component in a multilevel memory mechanism.

This implicit shift from reductive to mechanistic explanatory objectives guided subsequent research by clarifying two basic goals. The first goal is downward-looking: to discover "the mechanisms which might be responsible for long-lasting Potentiation" (Bliss and Lømo 1973: 350). This topic is the near exclusive focus of the discussion section of this first paper. Bliss and Lømo mention learning only in passing, noting in the final paragraph that the results are interesting partly because the effect lasts so long and partly because it occurs in a cortical pathway associated with learning and memory. The second goal is upward-looking: to evaluate the role of LTP in higher-level memory mechanisms. Bliss and Gardner-Medwin

(1973) address this topic by attempting to produce LTP in awake and behaving rabbits:

Since an increase in the effectiveness of synapses may be a process underlying some forms of memory, it was considered important to establish whether long-lasting synaptic changes could be produced in animals in an approximately normal physiological condition. (1973: 358)

Sleeping rabbits do not learn. If LTP is a learning mechanism, it should be possible to produce it without anesthesia. Again, however, this paper leaves the association with learning and memory largely for the reader to infer. The primary arguments in support of the upward-looking goal are in Bliss, Gardner-Medwin, and Lømo (1973). Their introduction is an extended argument for the relevance of LTP to learning and memory. Their argument, not coincidentally, appeals to results from multiple fields. They appeal to experimental psychologists' ablation studies (Douglas 1967), biochemists' assays of the molecular constituents of the hippocampus (Hyden 1973), physiologists' EEG recordings during memory tasks (Elazar and Adey 1967), psychiatrists' evaluations of patients with brain damage (Milner 1970), electrophysiologists' theoretical considerations (Eccles 1953; Hebb 1949), and computer scientists' models (Marr 1970). Results from these different fields constrain the possibilities for situating LTP within a multilevel mechanism.

As of 1973, LTP was no longer proposed as identical to or as an example of memory, but rather as a component in a multilevel memory mechanism. This shift in explanatory perspective clearly defined the goals of the LTP research program and, at the same time, situated the LTP phenomenon in a theoretical framework for integrating fields in the young neurosciences of memory. Anatomists, biochemists, electrophysiologists, psychologists, and psychiatrists could contribute to understanding either the mechanism of LTP or the memory mechanisms that contain it.

2.3 Mechanism as a working hypothesis

This revised history helps to dislodge three reductionist assumptions about the LM research program. First, the LTP research program is a clear historical counterexample to those (such as Oppenheim and Putnam 1958; Bickle 2003) who present reduction as a general empirical hypothesis about trends in science. In the 1970s, one crucial development in the LM research program was an upward connection of LTP to learning and memory. This goal explains why it was so important for Bliss and Lømo to extend the duration of the potentiation beyond minutes to hours and days. This goal also explains why it was so important for Bliss and Gardner-Medwin to show that they could produce the phenomenon in awake and behaving rabbits. And, finally, this goal explains why Bliss, Gardner-Medwin, and Lømo (1973) open with an extended argument that LTP is relevant to memory. LTP became more than an experimental curiosity because it came to be plausibly associated with learning and memory.

The LM research program continues to involve both upward and downward connections in a hierarchy of mechanisms. Bickle (2003) is right to note that many researchers use techniques from molecular biology and electrophysiology to understand the molecular and synaptic mechanisms implicated in the phenomenon of learning and memory. Some focus on the molecular mechanisms involved in the induction and maintenance of LTP, some on the anatomy of changes in dendritic spines, and some on the structural basis for conformation changes in the NMDA receptor. Others evaluate the relevance of LTP to higher-level phenomena. Different aspects of learning and memory are found to be localized in different areas of the brain (see Buckner and Wheeler 2001). Many continue to test the link between LTP and different varieties of memory, but others also explore the role of LTP in addiction (Thomas and Malenka 2003), fear conditioning (Schafe and LeDoux 2000; Schafe et al. 2000), and pathologies of the nervous system such as Alzheimer's disease (see, for example, Rowan et al. 2003). My point is that the history of neuroscientific research on learning and memory does not show merely a trend toward downward reduction. Instead, research is focused up and down in a hierarchy as new problems are recognized and as new techniques become available. Only if one has a downward reductive bias in mind can one see the history of the LM research program, or the contemporary LTP research program, as evidence for a downward reductive trend toward a fundamental explanatory level. The mosaic model, in comparison, emphasizes the interdisciplinary richness of this historical episode.

Second, the focus of reduction models on interlevel relationships distracts attention from interfield integration at a single level. The research program at Oslo was built around the idea that anatomical and electrophysiological studies could be used in tandem to study the structure and the function of brain regions such as the hippocampus. Anatomists and electrophysiologists were not working at different levels of mechanisms. Workers in each field were concerned with neurons and hippocampal wiring diagrams. Similarly, workers who argue for the relevance of LTP to learning and memory appeal to results from different fields to show that the hippocampus is relevant to memory and that synaptic plasticity is theoretically plausible as a mechanism of learning. Again, workers in these fields do not operate at different levels; rather, they provide different perspectives on the same level. At least since Oppenheim and Putnam, reductionists have assumed that there is roughly a one-to-one mapping among fields of science, scientific theories, and levels of organization. The multifield nature of mid-twentieth-century neuroscience, as exemplified in the LM research program, shows how restrictive this assumption is. The different perspectives and techniques of different fields allow them to study different aspects of the same mechanism at a single level. Because reduction models are necessarily designed to represent relations among theories at different levels (or between a theory and its successor), they are not suited to represent the kind of interfield unity achieved at a given level.

The final lesson from this revised history is that the workers in the LM research program implicitly abandoned reduction as an explanatory goal in favor of the search for multilevel mechanisms. When they take reduction as a goal or method, researchers are driven to look for one lower-level vocabulary in terms of which the *explanandum phenomenon* can be described, or with which an equipotent image of the *explanandum phenomenon* can be constructed. This is precisely what McCulloch and Pitts tried to do by relating propositional structures to neural structures. Although the LM research program of the 1950s does exhibit a broadly reductive style of explanation, that approach was gradually replaced through the 1970s by a more ecumenical and multilevel mechanistic style of explanation. This shift in explanatory ideals allowed researchers from multiple fields to contribute to the development of neuroscientific explanations.[7]

---

[7] Kenneth Schaffner (forthcoming) describes a recent example from behavioral and psychiatric genetics. In the early 1990s, researchers hoped to find crude linkages between behavioral and psychiatric traits (for example, aggression and schizophrenia) and genes. This project largely failed to produce replicable results (see Hamer 2002). In response, researchers began to appeal to higher-level

The mid-twentieth century was a formative period in the history of neuroscience as a discipline—a period during which researchers self-consciously worked to create a multifield research program. This period witnessed F. O. Schmitt's neuroscience study program, the origins of the SfN, and the scattered appearance worldwide of departments with names like "Neurophysiology" and "Psychobiology." It would be surprising if one did not find evidence during this time of shifting standards and explanatory objectives. The origins of the LM research program span this coalescence of the neural sciences into Neuroscience. In this milieu, the goal of describing multilevel mechanisms dislodged classical reduction as the field's explanatory ideal.

Oppenheim and Putnam recommend reduction as a working hypothesis for building the unity of science. To support this thesis, they appeal to historical evidence of reductive trends in science. But their argument is flawed because they overlook evidence of upward-looking trends. It is also flawed because even if there were a downward trend before 1950, neuroscience after the 1950s became increasingly multilevel and increasingly integrative. I propose a new working hypothesis on the basis of this revised history: The unity of neuroscience is achieved as different fields contribute constraints on multilevel mechanistic explanations. Rather than reductive unity, contemporary neuroscience exhibits mosaic unity.

3. Intralevel Integration and the Mosaic Unity of Neuroscience

I now turn from historical considerations to the task of constructing a positive model of the unity of neuroscience. In this section, I focus on *intralevel* cases of interfield integration. The reduction model is not equipped to handle such cases of interfield integration because the phenomena are not at different levels, the terms used to describe them are not translated into one another, and the descriptions are not homomorphic with one another. The reductive goal of globally relating two fields through derivation of laws should be replaced by a mosaic image of multiple fields making punctate

intermediates (such as activation in brain regions) and environmental factors (such as being raised in an abusive household). Thus far, results in this multilevel tradition seem to be more promising and replicable than their predecessors.

contributions to an abstract sketch of a mechanism. This view of the unity of neuroscience derives from Darden and Maull's (1977) idea that the unity of science is often achieved by constructing interfield theories. What is missing from Darden and Maull's account, and what is provided by my account of mechanistic explanation, is an explanatory structure of interfield theories that can accommodate contributions from multiple fields. In what follows, I provide a detailed account of how progress toward the mosaic unity of neuroscience proceeds.

3.1. The space of possible mechanisms

Mechanistic theory building typically proceeds through the piecemeal accumulation of constraints on the space of possible mechanisms for a phenomenon. Different fields are integrated when their findings provide constraints on the space of possible mechanisms. The abstract goal of constructing multilevel mechanistic explanations serves as a skeletal frame-work—a most abstract mechanism schema—on which neuroscientists construct the mosaic unity of neuroscience.

The *space of possible mechanisms*, conceived most inclusively, contains all the mechanisms that could possibly explain a phenomenon. The dimensions of this space are defined by the entities, properties, and activities that compose the how-possibly mechanism at all relevant levels, and by the varieties of organization among its components. Points in this space are single how-possibly explanations. Distances between these points indicate the degree of similarity between any two possible mechanisms, and regions of this space represent classes of similar mechanisms. Scientists never consider the entire space of possible mechanisms. They typically start with a restricted space shaped by prior assumptions about what kinds of components are likely to be included, what kinds of organization are likely to be relevant, and what sorts of basic constraints are assumed to be in play (for example, gravitation, the light postulate, and energetic constraints). They thus typically work within a roughly defined space of *plausible* mechanisms, that is, the space of possible mechanisms consistent with known or assumed constraints. Hille's diagram of possible gating mechanisms (Chapter 4, Figure 4.2), for example, marks out several distinct regions in a space of possible mechanisms for Na^+ channel gating.

A constraint is a finding that either shapes the boundaries of the space of plausible mechanisms or changes the probability distribution over that space (that is, the probability that some point or region of the space accurately describes the actual mechanism). Some constraints exclude regions of the space; they show that some set of possible mechanisms is impossible given what is known about the components and their organization. On the other hand, the discovery of a new component, a new property of a component, or a new feature of the organization of a mechanism can open previously closed regions of the space of plausible mechanisms. Watson and Crick's (1953) discovery of the double helix structure of DNA immediately suggested to them a mechanism for copying the genetic material, and the gating charge suggested to Hille and Armstrong that the activation of Na^+ channels might involve the outward rotation of an α-helix. Other constraints direct attention to a given region of the space of possible mechanisms. A particular arrangement of components, a particular by-product, and the susceptibility of a mechanism to specific forms of regulation and control indicate that a specific kind of mechanism is involved, even if one is not yet in a position to describe all its components or all aspects of its organization. Constraints on the space of possible mechanisms, in short, constitute the *relevant evidence* for evaluating how-possibly descriptions of mechanisms. Progress from how-possibly to how-actually descriptions of a mechanism can thus be conceived as a process of shaping and constricting the space of plausible mechanisms.

Different fields of neuroscience are characterized by different central problems, different techniques, and different theoretical vocabularies (Darden and Maul 1977). Individually, these fields often direct their attention only to a narrow range of constraints required for constructing and evaluating a given mechanistic explanation. Researchers in a field might, for example, attend exclusively to mechanisms involved in gene regulation and protein synthesis, to biochemical cascades in the cytoplasm, or to the behavior of ion channels or receptors. Some researchers characterize the anatomical structures in neural pathways, monitor the gross activation patterns of brain regions and systems, or observe the behaviors of whole organisms. The mosaic unity of neuroscience results from the integration of constraints from multiple fields on a common mechanism.

3.2 Specific constraints on the space of possible mechanisms

One cannot know in advance how many kinds of constraint there are or which constraints are relevant to understanding a given mechanism. But a

Table 7.1. Intralevel and interlevel
constraints on multilevel mechanisms

Intralevel constraints
   Componency constraints
   Spatial constraints
     Size
     Shape
     Location
     Connection
     Compartmentalization
   Temporal constraints
     Order
     Rate
     Duration
   Active constraints
Interlevel constraints
   Accommodative constraints
     Top-down accommodation
     Bottom-up accommodation
   Spatial and temporal constraints
   Mutual manipulability constraints

number of general constraints follow from the characteristic organization of mechanisms discussed in Chapter 4. A preliminary list of intralevel constraints on the space of possible mechanisms is shown in Table 7.1. In this section, I describe these different constraints, show how they are used in the process of building theories, and I discuss cases in which they have served as loci for interfield integration.

3.2.1. Componency constraints At different times in history, neuroscientists have used different kinds of components to construct models of neural mechanisms. Renaissance anatomists described animal spirits that moved through the brain's ventricles, and they took the surrounding cerebrum to be just so much padding. For Descartes, the brain is an organ where memories are stored, and it has the power to move the body by controlling the flow of physical animal spirits through hollow nerves. Hartley described the brain as a medullary substance, in which vibrating fibers transmit sensory input and form associations. Prior to the neuron doctrine, many believed that the brain is a holistic reticulum, with all of its parts contributing to its activity. Only faint echoes of these ideas remain in contemporary neuroscience. The brain is composed of neurons. Neurons transmit signals in the form of action potentials. They communicate across electrical and chemical synapses. They are composed of a complicated array of cytoplasmic molecules. They have characteristic ways of generating electricity, of repairing themselves, and of eliminating waste products. They are organized into networks of cells that make up systems, many of which have widely conserved patterns of organization. These diverse items constitute the ontic store of contemporary neuroscience: the set of stock-in-trade items out of which models of mechanisms can be built. Introductory neuroscience textbooks acquaint students with this store.

The store of entities and activities expands and contracts with the addition and removal of established entities and activities over time. In early theoretical discussions of synaptic plasticity, for example, researchers conjectured that synapses could be strengthened as axons and dendrites swell and move closer to one another, as neurons grow and shrink, as new neurons are born and die, and as glial cells enter and recede from synapses. Current models of LTP describe a mechanism that adds new receptors to dendrites, changes the shape of dendritic spines, and activates silent synapses. These mechanisms contain such components as NMDA receptors, AMPA receptors, adenylyl cyclase, protein kinase A, MAP kinase, CREB, and nitric oxide. One prima facie constraint on any mechanism is that it should not add new items to the ontic store without justification. For example, the LTP researcher Robert Malinow gave faint praise to one recent mechanism for the maintenance of LTP by saying, "If nothing else, this model is attractive because it requires only established intracellular signaling mechanisms" (Malinow 1998: 1226). Conversely, by expanding the store of components, one can open up previously unrecognized regions of the space of possible mechanisms. Prior to the 1980s it was widely assumed that transmission at chemical synapses is unidirectional from axon to dendrite. Then researchers noted that nitric oxide, which can flow freely in either direction, acts as a neurotransmitter. This opened the possibility that events in the post-synaptic cell might exert influence on the activities of mechanisms in pre-synaptic cells.

Researchers in the different fields that contribute to LTP research are primarily concerned with different kinds of entities and activities. Biochemists, for example, focus on chains of reactions in the cytoplasm. Molecular biologists study the machinery of protein production. Electron microscopists investigate the structure of post-synaptic dendrites. Electrophysiologists investigate whether individual synapses are "silent" or "active." Channel physiologists study the flow of current through individual channels. Protein chemists study the structure of receptors and channels. Thus to construct the explanation of LTP, one must integrate data from several different fields. Componency constraints are one important locus of interfield integration.

3.2.2. Spatial constraints   Spatial organization is often crucial for the working of a mechanism. The components of mechanisms often must be compartmentalized, localized, connected, structured, and oriented with respect to one another (see Chapter 4, Section 7). Researchers in different fields often investigate different forms of spatial organization and are uniquely suited to provide certain spatial constraints.

Consider compartmentalization. Different components or stages of mechanisms are confined within reasonably well-defined physical boundaries, such as a nuclear membrane, a cell membrane, or skin. In their discussion section, Bliss and Lømo (1973) generate a set of how-possibly mechanisms that might account for LTP. Some of these mechanisms involve pre-synaptic elements, such as the pre-synaptic cell's becoming more excitable by the test stimulus or an increase in the amount of neurotransmitter released per synapse (1973: 252). They also consider post-synaptic mechanisms, including an "increase in the sensitivity of the post-synaptic junctional membrane" (252) and "a reduction in the resistance of the narrow stem by which [dendritic] spines are attached to the parent dendrite" (252). Debates raged through the 1990s—and continue to some extent to this day—about whether the mechanism of LTP is located in the pre-synaptic or the post-synaptic cell, or (as a few participants in the debate argue) perhaps both. At stake in these debates, besides the truth of the matter, is the question of which fields and techniques investigate the most important aspects of LTP's mechanism. For example, if pre-synaptic mechanisms are responsible for LTP, then fields of neuroscience that focus on the mechanisms of neurotransmitter synthesis and release are the most important for elaborating the molecular aspects of this multilevel hierarchy. One can use quantal analysis (that is, analysis of the number and frequency of vesicular release events from the pre-synaptic neuron) to determine how many vesicles fuse to the membrane and dump their contents into the synapse with each action potential, and how the frequency of release changes with potentiation. One can try to assess the number of neurotransmitter molecules contained per vesicle to determine whether or not it changes with stimulation. One can experiment to determine whether or not modifications in the mechanisms of neurotransmitter release (such as changes in Ca^{2+} regulation in the axon terminal) account for any observed changes. If post-synaptic mechanisms are involved, then the molecular mechanisms of LTP would be the province of a different set of fields: those investigating the properties of receptors and ion channels, the structures of dendrites, and the synthesis and trafficking of proteins in the post-synaptic cell. The question of whether or not LTP is pre-synaptic or post-synaptic has played such a central role in contemporary discussions of LTP because compartmentalizing the phenomenon is a crucial step in determining which components are relevant to explaining the phenomenon, and also, derivatively, which techniques and theoretical perspectives are most useful for investigating the phenomenon. Compartmentalization is thus an important constraint in the integration of fields in neuroscience.

To understand a mechanism, one must often *localize* different component entities and activities. For example, Bliss, Gardner-Medwin, and Lømo (1973) argue for the importance of LTP in memory on the grounds that it can be induced in the hippocampus and that the hippocampus is a crucial brain region for various sorts of memory tasks. Bechtel and Richardson (1993) and Bechtel (1988) discuss this aspect of the search for mechanistic explanations in great detail. What I stress here is that different fields in neuroscience are uniquely capable of providing different kinds of evidence for localization. Researchers using PET, MRI, and TMS (transcranial magnetic stimulation) are well suited for discoveries concerning the localization of different kinds of brain systems in different brain regions. Electron microscopists are uniquely capable of determining whether or not new synapses (if such there be) are located in the right places to receive input from a pre-synaptic cell. As with compartmentalization, localization at several grains of size directs researchers to look within those locations for component entities in still lower-level mechanisms.

Knowing that the hippocampus is an important locus for the LM explanation, one can then begin to describe the *connections* of these hippocampal components. As discussed above, researchers at Oslo used several different techniques to trace these connections. Some used Golgi stains. Others used terminal degeneration techniques. Others used electrophysiological methods to stimulate one population of cells and to determine which other areas respond to the stimulus. Researchers using these three perspectives on synaptic connectivity address spatial organization with different sets of assumptions and techniques.

Finally, *structure* and *orientation* are often crucial aspects of a mechanism's organization. The stages of mechanisms often depend crucially upon entities with appropriate structures having appropriate orientations with respect to one another. Thus, structural aspects of the LTP mechanism are a major focus of recent research on LTP. Engert and Bonhoeffer (1999) and Maletic-Savatic, Malinow, and Svoboda (1999) present evidence that new dendritic spines are added to recently potentiated synapses. While far from conclusive, such evidence suggests a structural basis for one plausible mechanism sketch for LTP. The idea, yet to be confirmed, is that the addition of new dendritic spines makes the post-synaptic cell more responsive to glutamate. The mechanism by which such dendritic spines appear has also been subject to structural constraints investigated by constructing three-dimensional images of dendrites and surrounding cells (see Harris et al. 2003). Whether the structures involved are cells, neurotransmitters, receptors, intracellular signaling molecules, or dendritic spines, one must know which structures are involved to determine whether the parts can do what a how-possibly description demands of them. Researchers in different fields assess structural features of different kinds of entities, and their results often must be combined to assess whether a given how-possibly mechanism could work.

In sum, researchers in different fields are uniquely equipped to study different aspects of a mechanism's spatial organization. The mosaic unity of neuroscience is built, in part, through the effort to combine spatial constraints at and across levels into an adequate description of a mechanism.

3.2.3. Temporal constraints   The mosaic unity of neuroscience is also constructed through the search for temporal constraints. Findings from different fields concerning the order, rate, duration, and frequency of activities in a mechanism constrain the space of possible mechanisms.

Consider the *order* of the activities of the entities composing a mechanism—that is, their relative position in the series, forks, and cycles that make up the mechanism. Spatial organization alone does not indicate the direction of productivity in a mechanism—one must observe that electrical activity flows clockwise through the circuit of hippocampal neurons, and that NMDA receptors allow Ca^{2+} influx into the post-synaptic cell, thereby initiating protein production. Knowledge of temporal sequence alone is not sufficient to establish these productive relationships, but temporal relations place constraints on which entities and activities can be productive of which others.

Temporal constraints on the space of possible mechanisms also include findings concerning the *rates* and *durations* of different stages in the mechanism. Researchers who believe that enduring LTP might be sustained by the addition of receptors to the post-synaptic cell, for example, cannot use this mechanism to explain the initial induction of LTP because it takes around thirty minutes to produce the required proteins, distribute them, and insert them into the membrane. Short-term induction of LTP requires some faster mechanism, such as the phosphorylation of AMPA receptors. Possible mechanisms are pruned from the hypothesis space on the grounds that the stages or steps take too long or happen too slowly to produce a phenomenon with a given rate or duration.

Researchers in different fields investigate different temporal constraints on mechanisms. Electrophysiologists investigate the time-course of electrical activities in nerve cells, biochemists study enzyme kinetics and reaction rates, and psychologists study rates of learning and forgetting. Different constraints apply to different parts of a hierarchically organized mechanism. These findings, like the tiles of a mosaic, fill in the details of how-possibly sketches to bring a complete and detailed image of the mechanism into view.

3.2.4. Active constraints   To understand a mechanism, one needs to know how activities at one stage of the mechanism produce, alter, allow, or prevent activities at other stages. I offer a manipulationist account of such relations in Chapter 3.

The search for active constraints (relationships among variables under ideal interventions and the conditions under which those relationships obtain) is a frequent locus of interfield integration. Results from different fields are often required to assess which entities act and interact with one another. In many cases, the techniques of different fields will be required to intervene into one variable and to detect the other. Thus, one might intervene to prevent protein synthesis in the post-synaptic cell (pharmacology or molecular biology) and detect the effects on the ability of the synapse to induce LTP (electrophysiology); or intervene to induce LTP (electrophysiology) and detect changes in the dendrites of the post-synaptic cell (electron microscopy and cytological anatomy); or intervene to run a rat in a maze (experimental psychology) and detect spatial maps in its hippocampus (population electrophysiology). The techniques of different fields are often combined to test the active aspects of the organization of a mechanism. This constitutes progress in establishing the mosaic unity of neuroscience.

3.3 Reduction and the intralevel integration of fields

Above, I identify four main varieties of constraint on mechanistic explanations. Each of these constraints is exclusively intralevel. The unity of science thus achieved is a form of scientific integration that reduction is not equipped to handle. For intralevel interfield integration, the phenomena are not at different levels; rather, the fields investigate different components or stages of the same mechanism. The terms describing the different constraints are not translated into one another. Nor are the different constraints identified with one another. Finally, the different constraints are usually not homomorphic with one another; they may be as different as the entities and processes studied by anatomy and electrophysiology. Reduction models are focused on only a special case in the unity of neuroscience—interlevel integration—to the neglect of common forms of intralevel integration.

Darden and Maull argued in 1977 that reduction is ill-equipped to handle interfield relations. They stress that interfield integration is often achieved by constructing interfield theories rather than by reducing one theory to another. Darden and Maull do not describe the structure of interfield theories, relying instead on traditional formal models of theories as partially interpreted axiomatic systems (see Maull 1977). The account of multilevel mechanistic explanation that I develop supplements Darden and Maull's account of the unity of science with a detailed view of the structure of interfield theories. When researchers explain a phenomenon, their goal is not merely to build a "theory"; they set out to discover a mechanism, to identify its components, and to find the crucial features of its spatial, temporal, and active organization. The goal of discovering a mechanism acts as an abstract framework that guides researchers' attention to specific kinds of evidence (that is, the constraints) that are relevant to evaluating potential explanations. The mosaic unity of neuroscience is achieved as researchers in different fields integrate their results as constraints on multilevel mechanistic explanations.

4. Interlevel Integration and the Mosaic Unity of Neuroscience

The mosaic model also has many advantages over reduction for understanding *inter*level forms of interfield integration. According to classical reduction models, levels are integrated by identifying the kind-terms describing phenomena at one level with the kind-terms describing the phenomena of another. Less formally precise models of reduction involve the formulation of "ontological reductive links" and the construction of a homomorphic model of the higher-level theory within the lower-level theory. The mechanistic approach I develop in the preceding chapters provides an alternative, causal-mechanical, approach to interlevel integration. It has four main advantages over reduction for thinking about interlevel integration. First, it provides a straightforward way to interpret "levels" and, accordingly, the idea of interlevel integration. Second, whereas reduction models involve global relationships between theories at different levels, the mosaic model accommodates the fact that interlevel relations are often formulated piecemeal, within local mechanisms, by adding constraints on interlevel relations. Third, the mechanistic account accommodates both upward- and downward-looking interlevel integration. Finally, the mosaic view details the varied forces driving the co-evolution of work at different levels.

4.1 *What is interlevel integration?*

At least since the 1973 watershed, the theory incorporating LTP has spanned multiple levels. As I discuss in Chapter 5, there are at least four prominent levels. At the top is learning and memory (for example, the performance of some learning and memory task, such as learning to run a maze). Below that is the hippocampus generating spatial maps, consolidating information, or tutoring the cortex (there is still debate about the function of the hippocampus). Beneath the hippocampus are the chemical and electrical activities of synapses and cells. And at the lowest level are the activities of the molecules that make up the synapse, such as the NMDA receptor activating and inactivating. These are levels of mechanisms—levels that are related as parts to a whole with the additional restriction that the parts are components. According to this dominant story, the NMDA receptor is a component in the mechanism of LTP, LTP is a component in the mechanism of spatial map formation, and spatial map formation is a component in the mechanisms of spatial navigation.

What does it mean to integrate levels of mechanisms? The three papers constituting the LTP watershed, recall, define two integrative goals for the research program—one upward-looking, and the other downward-looking. Upward-looking interlevel integration involves showing that an item is a component in a higher-level mechanism. The downward-looking aspect of interlevel integration involves describing lower-level mechanisms for a higher-level phenomenon. This requires one to identify the component entities and activities, the relevant properties, and their organization.

These forms of interlevel integration are represented in Figure 7.1. Begin with X's ϕ-ing at the 0-level. X's ϕ-ing is integrated into a higher

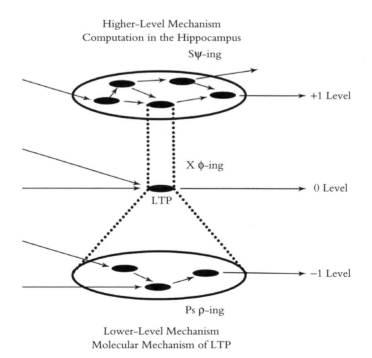

Figure 7.1. Integrating levels of mechanisms

(+1) level by showing how X's ϕ-ing is organized together with other components in the mechanism of S's ψ-ing at the +1 level. Integrating the 0-level with the lower (−1) level is a matter of describing the mechanism for X's ϕ-ing. This constitutive explanation describes the activities $\{\rho_1, \rho_2, \ldots, \rho_k\}$ and entities $\{P_1, P_2, \ldots, P_j\}$ in the mechanism along with their organization such that X ϕs. A phenomenon is integrated with adjacent levels to the extent that it is known: (i) what the relevant aspects of the phenomenon at the 0 level are; (ii) how those aspects of that phenomenon are organized within a higher +1 level mechanism; and (iii) how those aspects of the phenomenon are constitutively explained by a lower (−1) level mechanism.

This view of interlevel integration provides a much more precise and scientifically informed account of what is required to link levels in a hierarchy of mechanisms than that provided by reduction models. Integrating mechanistic levels is not a matter of establishing identities across levels but of establishing relationships of componency and explanatory relevance (see Chapter 4, Section 8). For example, it is not enough to integrate an item into a contextual mechanism that one shows merely that X's ϕ-ing is perfectly correlated with S's ψ-ing at the +1 level. Such correlation would provide limited evidence that the levels are integrated, but correlation is not integration. What is required in addition is that one should be able to manipulate S's ψ-ing by manipulating X's ϕ-ing, and one should be able to manipulate X's ϕ-ing by manipulating S's ψ-ing. In addition to satisfying the mutual manipulability requirement, integrating a component into a higher-level mechanism requires showing *how* X and its ϕ-ing are organized—spatially, temporally, and actively—with the other components such that S ψs. To situate LTP within LM mechanisms, one must provide a contextual description of how, at a given population of synapses, LTP is organized spatially, temporally, and actively with the other components in the system such that it is capable of, for example, encoding memories.

4.2 Constraints on interlevel integration

Like intralevel interfield integration, interlevel interfield integration is constructed piecemeal as constraints on a multilevel mechanism are discovered. Consider some interlevel constraints that shape the space of plausible multilevel mechanisms.

4.2.1. Accommodative constraints In sciences driven by the search for mechanisms, one goal is to accommodate the taxonomy of *explanandum phenomena* to the taxonomy of mechanistic explanations. Patricia Churchland (1986; Churchland and Sejnowski 1992) argues that levels often "co-evolve" during reduction in the sense that what is known at the different levels must be revised in order to bring them into sufficient alignment for reduction to succeed. As I argue in Section 4 of Chapter 4, there are a number of errors of fit between a mechanism and a phenomenon, including splitting errors, lumping errors, and errors of mischaracterization. These errors derive from a mismatch between the *explanandum phenomena* and the mechanisms that explain them. The attempt to accommodate these taxonomies to one another often forces researchers in different fields to change the way that they think about their domain. Researchers in different fields thus experience epistemic pressure to change their characterization of phenomena in their domain in the process of building bridges with other fields across levels. Accommodation across levels proceeds either from the top-down or from the bottom-up.

Top-down accommodation: the description of mechanisms is ineliminably perspectival (see Chapter 4). Mechanisms include all and only the entities, activities and organizational features *relevant to* the phenomenon. Researchers in fields characterizing higher-level phenomena influence those investigating lower-level phenomena by setting (if only tentatively) the boundaries of the mechanism. A world viewed only at the fundamental level would be a world of gory details unfiltered by a higher-level perspective (to borrow Kitcher's apt phrase).

Consider one example of top-down influence in the history of the LM research program. In his work on maze learning, Tolman (1948) led a generation of researchers to believe that animals navigate their environments in part by forming spatial maps. Tolman trained rats to navigate a circuitous route through a maze to reach a food reward. He then placed them in a maze containing a more direct path to the reward in addition to the original circuitous route. If spatial memory were a simple association between a stimulus (being placed in the start box) and a pattern of motor responses, as behaviorists suggest, one would expect the rat to take the circuitous route through the new maze. That is the behavior that was reinforced. In fact, however, rats prefer the direct path. Given the opportunity, rats construct efficient detours, shortcuts, and novel routes on their own (see, for example,

Chapui et al. 1987; Olton and Samuelson 1976). Experiments such as these suggest that rats learn to run mazes not by learning stimulus-response pairs but by forming internal representations—cognitive maps—which encode different locations and directions in their environment. Experimental psychologists have subsequently used a variety of techniques (for example, radial arm mazes, three-table problems, and the Morris water maze) to study different aspects of spatial memory and to identify the kinds of information that would have to be stored in a cognitive map to produce the observed behavioral profiles. The Morris water maze, one of the most popular spatial memory tests used by neuroscientists, tests the ability of rats and mice to find a platform beneath the surface of an opaque fluid in a circular pool. These protocols in experimental psychology are designed to exhibit and test different aspects of a rat's ability to navigate space, and each protocol contributes constraints on any mechanism that might explain that ability.

In the early stages of this research program, Tolman's results led behavioral neuroscientists to search for regions of the brain that could play the role of a spatial map. Because lesioning the hippocampus impairs performance in mazes such as the Morris water maze, many neuroscientists came to believe that a spatial map is located in the hippocampus. To test this hypothesis, electrophysiologists used a variety of activation experiments in which they engage a rat in various spatial tasks while recording the activity of individual cells in the rat's hippocampus. O'Keefe and Dostrovsky (1971), for example, report that individual pyramidal cells in the hippocampus fire preferentially when a rat enters a particular portion of a maze in a particular orientation. These findings led to the idea that these pyramidal cells function as "place cells" in the spatial map. Could activities in a population of such cells represent the spatial layout of a maze? Much later, Wilson and McNaughton (1993) used a cluster of electrodes to record from over 150 pyramidal cells at once while a rat explored the inside of a box. The surprising results of these experiments are that by observing the patterns of activation in the hippocampus, these systems-level physiologists were able to predict the trajectory of the rat through the box. (For more recent developments, see Hafting et al. 2005.)

The spatial map hypothesis has subsequently come under attack from those who claim that the hippocampus has a more general function (Eichenbaum et al. 1999). These challenges are based on refined behavioral experiments by experimental psychologists, and their results are leading neuroscientists to revise their understanding of the mechanism. In each case, however, the overall picture of scientific integration is the same. The effort of researchers in one field to characterize the phenomenon places accommodative constraints on the mechanism that must be honored by researchers in fields whose primary domain includes the mechanism's components.

Bottom-up accommodation: just as the description of a mechanism is constrained by discoveries concerning higher-level phenomena, so the character of the higher-level phenomenon often must accommodate findings about lower-level mechanisms. Again, this can be a locus of interfield contact. One well-known example from the history of the LM research program is the case of H.M., as reported by Scoville and Milner (1957). Scoville was a brain surgeon who worked in a psychiatric hospital, and Milner was a graduate student in psychology. As part of a search for a more benign form of psychosurgery than the lobotomy or leucotomy, Scoville decided to perform a set of experimental surgeries to remove the hippocampus bilaterally. Milner performed the psychiatric evaluations on these patients before and after the surgery. The two were in an excellent position to integrate psychological research on learning and memory with anatomical research on the functional organization of the brain. They provided compelling evidence that a crucial piece of the memory system is located in the hippocampus and, further, that declarative and procedural memory have distinct mechanisms. One conclusion drawn from this finding (and findings from subsequent animal studies) is that memory is not a single kind of thing, but a collection of loosely related phenomena. Scoville and Milner's research is but one example of how details of the underlying mechanism can lead one to revise one's assessment about higher-level phenomena. When different fields investigate the phenomenon and the mechanism, this accommodation constitutes another form of progress toward the mosaic unity of neuroscience.

4.2.2. Spatial and temporal interlevel constraints Interlevel relationships are also constrained by the spatial and temporal features of a phenomenon and its mechanism. When researchers in different fields characterize different aspects of the spatial and temporal organization of a mechanism at different levels, a second kind of interlevel interfield integration is achieved.

Localization is one of the most fundamental spatial constraints on interlevel integration (Bechtel and Richardson 1993). Not all mechanisms have easily localized components, but when they do, the location of different processes can be crucial to understanding a mechanism that incorporates them. In their effort to bridge the gap between LTP and memory, Bliss, Gardner-Medwin, and Lømo (1973) appeal to findings from anatomy, biochemistry, electrophysiology, and clinical psychology to argue that the hippocampus is an especially important location in the brain for memory. They argue that if the hippocampus is functionally implicated in learning and memory, then one would expect the cells of the hippocampus to exhibit changes (such as synaptic plasticity) that could possibly explain its ability to play that role. The fact that LTP occurs within the hippocampus, a region known for its contribution to memory, coupled with the fact that synaptic plasticity is theoretically plausible as a memory mechanism, provides suggestive evidence that LTP might be relevant to learning and memory. In contrast, Eccles's and Lloyd's (1949) discovery that synapses in the spinal cord are plastic is not taken to be evidence that such plasticity might play a role in memory, in part because the spinal cord is not a region of the CNS thought to be involved in memory encoding, storage, or retrieval (although changes in the spinal cord might account for the modification of reflexes with experience).

Temporal constraints are also crucial for the integration of levels of mechanisms. Learning and memory are inherently temporal phenomena. Despite their significant differences from one another, all forms of learning and memory involve imposing some mark or trace of past experience on a system and maintaining that trace for some time. Memory researchers study, for example, how long it takes to learn a task or to memorize a list. They ask how different practice schedules and reinforcement schedules alter the rate at which something is learned and which items in a list are more or less frequently forgotten (for example, primacy and recency effects). They investigate how quickly memories begin to fade. Answers to these questions can differ depending on, for example, the environmental conditions during the learning or training, the kind of material that is learned, the task used to evaluate the existence of the trace, the encoding strategies used by the subject, and the kind of memory system called on in the performance of the task. An adequate mechanistic explanation for memory must account for these differences and these temporal features. It should account for learning curves, forgetting curves, effects of different reinforcement schedules, and the relationship between repetition and learning, just to name a few. To my knowledge, contemporary LM researchers have explained none of these elementary temporal features of learning and memory (contra Bickle's 1998 suggestion that this represents an "accomplished psychoneural reduction"). Nevertheless, temporal arguments are relevant to interfield integration in the history of the LM research program.

Temporal constraints can be more sophisticated than these examples suggest. One can generate a number of experiments involving temporal constraints that should be done to assess hypothesized mechanisms for different kinds of memory.[8] Here is one example. Different forms of memory often have different temporal features; that is, the memories of one kind take longer to acquire than those of another kind, and the two decay at different rates. Consider, for example, the difference between semantic memory (such as a memory that Fred MacMurray stars in *Pardon My Past*) and habit formation (such as acquiring a nicotine addiction). There are important temporal differences between these kinds of memory. For example, semantic memories are quickly acquired and rapidly lost. Mere mention of the fact that Fred MacMurray stars in *Pardon My Past* can suffice for one to remember it for a while, but such memories are also often fleeting. Few will remember this fact hours, days, or weeks after reading it for the first time. Habits, in contrast, take much longer to form, but they sometimes last forever. Smoking one cigarette, or even one pack, does not doom one to a life of smoking in the way that months or years of continued smoking can. Once the habit has been acquired, however, it is very difficult to lose. Semantic memories and habit memories thus differ both in the temporal properties of their acquisition and their duration. These different types of memory are also explained by mechanisms in different brain structures. Many neuroscientists think that semantic memory is explained by mechanisms in the hippocampus and perhaps in the parahippocampal gyrus, and that habit learning is explained by mechanisms in structures such as the caudate nucleus (also the ventral tegmental area and the nucleus accumbens). These different brain regions are known to exhibit different varieties of synaptic plasticity.

If synaptic changes underlie these different forms of memory, then one would expect differences in the temporal properties of the varieties of synaptic plasticity observed in these brain regions to correspond to

---

[8] Thanks to Mortimer Mishkin for leading me to think about this sort of experiment.

differences in the temporal properties of the different kinds of memory. To assess this matter, one would need expertise both in evaluating the different kinds of memory and in evaluating the relevant temporal features of LTP. These two types of questions are in the traditional domains of different fields of neuroscience (psychology and electrophysiology). Answers to these questions would thus help integrate the findings of different fields and would constitute progress toward the mosaic unity of the LM research program.

4.2.3. Interlevel manipulability constraints   The most conspicuous varieties of interfield integration in contemporary neuroscience arise in the effort to show that phenomena at different levels are mutually manipulable. This form of interfield integration is achieved by use of interlevel experiments (activation, stimulation, and inhibition, discussed in Chapter 4, Section 9.2). If researchers in different fields study phenomena at different levels then fields must collaborate to run such experiments. This unifying function of interlevel experiments is exemplified most strikingly by experiments that span multiple levels. Consider a gene knockout experiment that provides evidence for the multilevel explanation of spatial memory (different aspects of which are reported in: Tsien et al. 1996a, 1996b; McHugh et al. 1996; and Rotenberg et al. 1996). The researchers use a technique for triggering the deletion of the NMDAR1 gene in mice that encodes an essential subunit of the NMDA receptor. They couple the deletion to a promoter of a gene that is expressed selectively in CA1 pyramidal cells and only in the later stages of the hippocampal development. As a result, this technique functionally deletes the NMDA receptor only in the CA1 region and only after the hippocampus is fully developed. Once the deletion is triggered, the researchers confirm the absence of the NMDA receptors, test for the ability of synapses in CA1 to induce LTP, monitor the formation of spatial maps across populations of hippocampal cells, and then test the mice in the Morris water maze. Knockout mice, those without functional NMDA receptors, perform far worse in the Morris water maze than do controls. When placed in a water maze *without* a platform, control mice concentrate their swimming in the platform's previous location. Knockout mice swim about randomly (Tsien et al. 1996b). The knockout mice also exhibit profound deficits in spatial map formation, as shown by multi-unit recordings from the CA1 region. Finally, knocking out the NMDA receptor eliminates

LTP induction in synapses of the CA1 region, and not in any other region of the brain (Tsien et al. 1996b).

This experiment is a bottom-up inhibitory experiment monitored at multiple levels. The intervention technique removes the NMDA receptor by deleting the NMDAR1 gene. The detection techniques register the effects of this intervention on LTP, spatial map formation, and spatial memory. I have not described all of the nuances of this experiment, and I acknowledge that these experiments are subject to various criticisms of the sort I discuss in Chapter 4. My goal is not to argue for this particular multilevel explanation of spatial memory. Instead, I use it to show how neuroscientists construct experiments that bridge multiple levels and that require the disciplinary expertise of multiple fields. This experiment has been praised as the first in which the mechanisms of spatial memory are investigated, "at all levels in a single set of experiments, from molecular changes through altered patterns of neuronal firing to impaired learning" (Roush 1997), and for taking an important first step towards the "dream of neurobiology ... to understand all aspects of interesting and important cognitive phenomena—like memory—from the underlying molecular mechanisms through behavior" (Stevens 1996). It is a mark of progress toward the mosaic unity of neuroscience that the researchers participating in this experiment are so interdisciplinary that it is difficult to pigeonhole them into tidy fields.

Nevertheless, as these quotations suggest, the techniques that these researchers use, the theoretical constructs that they apply, and the problems that they solve can be categorized roughly into different fields, including molecular biology, biochemistry, electrophysiology, systems physiology, and experimental psychology. Molecular biologists have the tools to design the knockouts. Biochemists and histologists have the tools to confirm the deletion. Electrophysiologists can determine whether or not the knockout synapses can induce LTP. Systems-level electrophysiologists can monitor hundreds of cells at once to evaluate spatial map formation. Finally, experimental psychologists are uniquely skilled at evaluating the spatial memory performance of the knockout mice. This experiment provides powerful (but inconclusive) evidence that the phenomena at each of these levels—NMDA receptor function, LTP, spatial map formation, and spatial memory—is constitutively relevant to the next. In turn, the experiment places a set of constraints on the space of possible mechanisms by identifying components at each level and by showing that each is relevant, not just to higher-level activities, but to the top-most *explanandum phenomenon*. This experiment provides compelling evidence that the mechanism of spatial memory is in the region of the space of possible mechanisms containing those mechanisms that include NMDA receptors as components in LTP mechanisms, LTP as a component in a hippocampal spatial map mechanism, and spatial map formation as a component in a spatial memory mechanism.

4.3 Mosaic interlevel integration

Fields of neuroscience are often integrated when researchers in different fields identify constraints on different levels in a multilevel mechanism or collaborate to link levels in a mechanism. Common examples of integration include the accommodation (top-down or bottom-up) of commitments about the character of the phenomenon to findings about the components of the mechanism, the identification of spatial and temporal constraints, and the use of interlevel experiments to establish interlevel relevance relations. An item is linked into higher levels when it is shown that it is a component in a higher-level mechanism and when it is shown to be organized within the higher-level mechanism. The item is integrated with lower-level components when one can describe the mechanism that explains its behavior.

The mosaic unity of neuroscience in no way resembles the effort to translate the theory of one field into the theory of another. The fields of neuroscience make only local contributions to these elaborate explanations. Nor do researchers in one field create a homomorphic image of a phenomenon studied by those in another field. Instead, researchers begin with a rather nonspecific goal, such the goal of discovering a mechanism for spatial memory. This goal provides a scaffold for their constraints. They consider how-possibly models and attempt to show that one such model (or one family of such models) is or is not consistent with the known constraints established by observation and experiment. These observations and experiments are performed by researchers in different fields who often investigate different aspects of different components at different levels in the mechanism. These different constraints are used, like the tiles in a mosaic, to elaborate the mechanism sketch, showing piecemeal which components and properties are relevant to the mechanism and how those components are organized spatially, temporally, and actively within the mechanism.

Reduction models are differentiated in part by different characterizations of the interlevel relationship, for example, as type identity, token identity, realization, and supervenience. I suggest that the relationship between levels should be understood as an explanation in terms of underlying (rather than antecedent) mechanisms. One does not establish interlevel explanatory linkages by showing that everything true of the higher level is true of the lower level, that all the regularities governing the higher can be derived from the lower, that every instance of the higher-level property is identical to some instance of the lower, or that there can be no difference in the higher level without a difference in the lower level. These claims imply additional metaphysical commitments beyond those required for a mechanistic model of explanation. One establishes interlevel explanatory linkages by describing mechanisms, by identifying the appropriate entities and activities, by showing how they are organized together, and by showing, most importantly, that each of these features of the mechanism is relevant to the *explanandum phenomenon*. The view of mechanistic explanation that I develop in the preceding chapters thus describes more concretely than reduction what is required to integrate levels in a hierarchy of mechanisms. The account is not peripheral to scientific practice but details precisely the kinds of evidence that scientists think are relevant in evaluating interlevel relations.

5. Conclusion: The Epistemic Function of the Mosaic Unity of Neuroscience

The phrase "Unity of Science" means many things to many people. For some (for example, Popper 1959) it means that all of science shares a common method, such as making risky predictions and testing them. Call this *methodological unity*. The search for a unifying methodological principle governing all of science is inextricably tied to the project of demarcating science from pseudoscience. The guiding idea is that science proceeds by a privileged set of principles for formulating and evaluating beliefs, and that forms of pseudoscience (for example, astrology, witchcraft, scientology, and philosophy) do not satisfy these principles. The search for such a set of principles, however, is widely regarded to have failed. Oppenheim and Putnam (1958) clearly distinguish their view of the unity of science from the notion of methodological unity on these grounds. Others (for example, Dupre 1993; Wylie 2002) claim that different sciences exhibit such divergent practices and criteria for success that any effort to state abstract principles that apply to all of science is likely either to be trivial or to exclude paradigm cases of scientific practice. The mosaic unity of science is not a form of methodological unity.

Dupre (1993: 226–7) criticizes nonreductive approaches to the unity of science, such as Darden and Maul's (1977), because they fail to solve the problem of demarcation. It is a mistake, however, to judge views of the unity of science exclusively by whether or not they can provide a criterion of demarcation. I believe that the unity of science serves an epistemic function, one that captures at least much of the distinction between good (neuro)science and bad. It is embodied in the normative view of explanation that I develop in the preceding chapters and in the constraints discussed above. My view is consistent with, although it is a much more precise specification of, Dupre's pluralistic epistemology (see 1993: 242–3). More on this below.

Oppenheim and Putnam (1958) characterize the unity of science reductively in terms of the ability to explain the phenomena of higher-level sciences in terms of the laws of some fundamental science. Call this *explanatory unity of science*. Their view of the explanatory unity of science has two components: a unity of scientific vocabulary, and a unity of scientific laws. The unity of scientific vocabulary is achieved by replacing the terms in a reduced theory with the terms of the reducing theory (1958: 6). Likewise, the unity of laws is achieved by making it possible to dispense with reduced laws in favor of fundamental laws. What seems right about this view of the unity of science is that higher-level (and higher-order) phenomena can often be explained in terms of lower-order phenomena. But this is not an argument for the thesis that the unity of science is achieved by reduction to a common lowest level.

The mosaic unity of science is valuable not because it serves as a criterion for distinguishing science from nonscience (it does not), nor because it relates all phenomena to a single fundamental level (it does not), but because it has the epistemic virtue of producing robust explanations—that is, explanations that can withstand scrutiny from independent perspectives and with independent techniques. Fields are individuated by different guiding questions, different theoretical vocabularies, different techniques, and different domains of phenomena (see Darden and Maull 1977). Precisely because they are independent along these multiple dimensions, different fields provide relatively independent means of access to different aspects of a mechanism. An adequate description of a mechanism must be able to withstand scrutiny from each of the different perspectives. The goal is to use these constraints from different fields to shrink the space of plausible mechanisms to a point or, short of that, to a region of the space of possible mechanisms, variation within which makes no difference for a given pragmatic aim.[9] Given that different fields have independent means of access to the mechanism, one becomes increasingly confident that the hypothesized mechanism consistent with all of the known constraints is, in fact, the actual mechanism (see, for example, Culp 1994; Wimsatt 1981). The relative autonomy of different fields affords each of them the theoretical and technical independence to provide a check on the findings in other fields and so heighten one's confidence that the explanation is correct (see Wylie 2002).

The fact that explanations in neuroscience are multilevel adds another dimension to this mosaic unity of neuroscience. For example, the different kinds of interlevel experiment provide independent paths of access to phenomena that are part of the same multilevel theory. In the first place, the intervention techniques involved in these different kinds of experiment are likely to be independent of one another. Top-down experiments manipulate a phenomenon using different interventions from those used by bottom-up experiments. Excitatory and inhibitory versions of these experiments use different forms of intervention as well. To the extent that they are distinct, they provide independent means of experimental access to the same phenomenon. If lesioning a component inhibits a phenomenon, exciting a component excites the phenomenon, engaging the phenomenon activates the component, and suppressing a phenomenon inhibits the component, one has four independent lines of evidence that the component is relevant to the phenomenon.

---

[9] Lindley Darden and I have shown how the effort to shape the space of possible mechanisms by adding constraints constitutes a methodology of discovery for mechanistic sciences, such as neuroscience (Craver and Darden 2001).

Second, the act of integrating an item into a multilevel mechanism situates it within a body of theory that both explains the item and shows that the item has an explanatory role to play. Integrating LTP into both lower and higher levels of mechanisms is one way that neuroscientists argue that LTP is both real and of significance for understanding the brain. Failure to find a lower-level mechanism can often (though not always) be decisive in the fate of such a putative component. Likewise, failure to find a role for LTP by situating it within a higher-level mechanism would leave LTP as no more than a curious laboratory phenomenon with no significance for the theories of neuroscience. Multilevel integration through interlevel experiments is thus a way of establishing the robustness of a phenomenon and of securing its place in the ontology of neuroscience.

Dupre argues that science should be understood as a "family resemblance concept." Nonetheless, he admits that good science might be distinguished from bad using a kind of "virtue epistemology":

There are many possible and actual such virtues: sensitivity to empirical fact, plausible background assumptions, coherence with other things we know, exposure to criticism from the widest variety of sources, and no doubt others. (1993: 243)

The mosaic model of the unity of neuroscience encompasses these virtues, but it adds precision in characterizing what one demands of explanations in sciences that seek mechanistic explanations. Once one recognizes the diversity of methodologies across different areas of science, it seems more fruitful to characterize explanatory and investigative virtues within subdomains of science than to formulate such abstract virtues as "make your explanation sensitive to empirical fact," or "make no implausible background assumptions." In the sciences that seek mechanistic explanations, there is a great deal more to be said about which empirical facts are most likely to be evidentially relevant, which background assumptions are likely to be plausible and implausible, and which kinds of criticism are likely to be valuable. My claim is substantiated in this and previous chapters by providing a normative account of explanation in neuroscience, by revealing the diverse kinds of constraint used to construct mechanistic explanations, by detailing the different varieties of interlevel experiments (as well as their strengths and weaknesses), and by articulating the difference between mere models, sketches, and complete mechanistic explanations. The diversity of scientific methodologies should lead one to more local epistemologies that are premised on the explanatory and investigative ideals of individual problem areas in sciences.

This mosaic view of the unity of neuroscience is broader in scope than reduction because it covers both the integration of fields in research at a given level and in research that crosses levels. This mosaic view also provides a more accurate and elaborate view of interlevel interfield integration. Where reductionists understand the unity of science in terms of stepwise reduction to lowest levels, the mosaic view treats the unity of science as the collaborative accumulation of constraints at multiple levels. Whereas reduction focuses on relations of identity, supervenience, and ontological reductive links, the mechanistic mosaic view emphasizes the importance of explanatory relevance as the bridge between levels. Finally, whereas reduction models emphasize the importance of explanatory reduction to fundamental levels, the mosaic view can be pluralistic about levels, recognizing the genuine importance of higher-level causes and explanations. The mosaic unity of science is constructed during the process of collaboration by different fields in the search for multilevel mechanisms. One task for the philosophy of neuroscience is to show how that research ought to proceed.

Bibliography

Achinstein, P. (1975). "Causation, Transparency, and Emphasis," *Canadian Journal of Philosophy*, 5: 1–23.

—— (2002). "Is There a Valid Experimental Argument for Scientific Realism?," *Journal of Philosophy*, 99: 470–95.

Ahn, W., and Kalish, C. W. (2000). "The Role of Mechanism Beliefs in Causal Reasoning," in F. Keil and R. A. Wilson (eds.), *Explanation and Cognition*. Cambridge, MA: MIT Press, 199–226.

Allen, G. (2005). "Mechanism, Vitalism, and Organicism in Late Nineteenth and Twentieth-Century Biology: The Importance of Historical Context," *Studies in the History and Philosophy of Biological and Biomedical Sciences*, 36: 261–84.

Anand, B. K., and Brobeck, J. R. (1951). "Hypothalamic Control of Food Intake in Rats and Cats," *Yale Journal of Biology and Medicine*, 24: 123–40.

Andersen, P. O. (1960a). "Interhippocampal Impulses II. Apical Dendritic Activation of CA1 Neurons," *Acta Physiologica Scandinavica*, 48: 178–208.

—— (1960b). "Interhippocampal Impulses III. Basal Dendritic Activation of CA3 Neurons," *Acta Physiologica Scandinavica*, 48: 209–30.

—— (1991). "LTP—An Exciting and Continuing Saga," in M. Baudry and J. Davis (eds.), *Long Term Potentiation*. Cambridge, MA: MIT Press, xiii–xvii.

—— (2003). "A Prelude to Long-term Potentiation," *Philosophical Transactions of the Royal Society*, 358: 613–16.

——, and Lømo, T. (1967). "Control of Hippocampal Output by Afferent Volley Frequency," *Progress in Brain Research*, 27: 400–12.

——, Bruland, H., and Kaada, B. R. (1961). "Activation of the Dentate Area by Septal Stimulation," *Acta Physiologica Scandinavica*, 51: 17–28.

Armstrong, C. M. (1981). "Sodium Channels and Gating Currents," *Physiological reviews*, 61(3): 644–83.

Armstrong, D. (1983). *What is a Law of Nature?* Cambridge: Cambridge University Press.

Ashley C. C., and Ridgway E. B. (1968). "Simultaneous Recording of Membrane Potential, Calcium Transient and Tension in Single Muscle Fibers," *Nature*, 219: 1168–9.

Barlow H. B. (1972). "Single Units and Sensation: A Neuron Doctrine for Perceptual Psychology?," *Perception*, 1: 371–94.

Barnes, E. (1992). "Explanatory Unification and the Problem of Asymmetry," *Philosophy of Science*, 59: 558–71.

Barondes, S. (1999). *Molecules and Mental Illness* (paperback edn). New York: Scientific American Press.

Beatty, J. (1995). "The Evolutionary Contingency Thesis," in G. Wolters and J. G. Lennox (eds.), *Concepts, Theories, and Rationality in the Biological Sciences*, The Second Pittsburgh-Konstanz Colloquium in the Philosophy of Science. Pittsburgh: University of Pittsburgh Press, 45–81.

Bechtel, W. (1984). "Reconceptualizations and Interfield Connections: The Discovery of the Link Between Vitamins and Coenzymes," *Philosophy of Science*, 51: 265–92.

——— (1986). "Teleological Functional Analyses and the Hierarchical Organization of Nature," in N. Rescher (ed.), *Teleology and Natural Science*. Landham, MD: University Press of America, 26–48.

——— (1988). *Philosophy of Science: An Overview for Cognitive Science*. Hillsdale, NJ: Lawrence Erlbaum.

——— (2006). *Discovering Cell Mechanisms: The Creation of Modern Cell Biology*. Cambridge: Cambridge University Press.

——— (forthcoming). "The Epistemology of Evidence in Cognitive Neuroscience," in R. Skipper, C. Allen, R. A. Ankeny, C. F. Craver, L. Darden, G. Mikkelson, and R. Richardson (eds.), *Philosophy and the Life Sciences: A Reader*. Cambridge, MA: MIT Press.

———, and Abrahamsen, A. (2005). "Explanation: A Mechanistic Alternative," *Studies in the History and Philosophy of the Biological and Biomedical Sciences*, 36: 421–41.

———, and Mundale, J. (1999). "Multiple Realizability Revisited: Linking Cognitive and Neural States," *Philosophy of Science*, 66: 175–207.

———, and Richardson, R. C. (1993). *Discovering Complexity: Decomposition and Localization as Strategies in Scientific Research*. Princeton: Princeton University Press.

———, and Stufflebeam, R. (2001). "Epistemic Issues in Procuring Evidence About the Brain: The Importance of Research Instruments and Techniques," in W. Bechtel et al. (eds.), *Philosophy and the Neurosciences: A Reader*. Oxford: Blackwell, 55–81.

Beebee, H. (2004). "Causing and Nothingness," in L. A. Paul, E. J. Hall and J. Collins (eds.), *Causation and Counterfactuals*. Cambridge, MA: MIT Press, 291–308.

Bennett, M. R. (2001). *History of the Synapse*. CRC, Overseas Publishers Association, Amsterdam.

———, and Hacker, P. M. S. (2003). *Philosophical Foundations of Neuroscience*. Oxford: Blackwell.

Best, A. R., and Wilson, D. A. (2004). "Coordinate Synaptic Mechanisms Contributing to Olfactory Cortical Adaptation," *Journal of Neuroscience*, 24: 652–60.

Bickle, J. (1998). *Psychoneural Reduction: The New Wave.* Cambridge, MA: MIT Press.

———(2003). *Philosophy of Neuroscience: A Ruthlessly Reductive Approach.* Dordrecht, Holland: Kluwer Academic Publishers.

Bliss, T. V. P., and Collingridge, G. L. (1993). "A Synaptic Model of Memory: Long-Term Potentiation in the Hippocampus," *Nature*, 361/6407: 31–9.

———, and Gardner-Medwin, A. R. (1973). "Long-Lasting Potentiation of Synaptic Transmission in the Dentate Area of the Unanaesthetized Rabbit Following Stimulation of the Perforant Path," *Journal of Physiology*, 232: 357–74.

———, Gardner-Medwin, A. R., and Lømo, T. (1973). "Synaptic Plasticity in the Hippocampal Formation," in G. B. Ansell and P. B. Bradley (eds.), *Macromolecules and Behavior.* London: Macmillan, 193–203.

———, and Lømo, T. (1973). "Long-Lasting Potentiation of Synaptic Transmission in the Dentate Area of the Anaesthetized Rabbit Following Stimulation of the Perforant Path," *Journal of Physiology*, 232: 331–56.

Bogen, J. (2001). "Functional Image Evidence: Some Epistemic Hot Spots," in P. Machamer, R. Grush, and P. McLaughlin (eds.), *Theory and Method in Neuroscience.* Pittsburgh, PA: University of Pittsburgh Press, 173–99.

———(2002). "Epistemological Custard Pies from Functional Brain Imaging," *Philosophy of Science*, 69: S59–71.

———(2004). "Analyzing Causality: The Opposite of Counterfactual is Factual," *International Studies in the Philosophy of Science,* 18: 3–26.

———(2005). "Regularities and Causality; Generalizations and Causal Explanations," in C. F. Craver and L. Darden (eds.), "Mechanisms in Biology," *Studies in History and Philosophy of Biological and Biomedical Sciences*, 36: 397–420.

Boyd, R. (1991). "Realism, Anti-Foundationalism, and the Enthusiasm for Natural Kinds," *Philosophical Studies*, 61: 127–48.

Brandon, R. (1985). "Greene on Mechanism and Reductionism: More Than Just a Side Issue," in Peter Asquith and Philip Kitcher (eds.), *PSA 1984*, vol. 2. East Lansing, MI: Philosophy of Science Association, 345–53.

———(1990). *Adaptation and Environment.* Princeton: Princeton University Press, 159–61

Broca, P. (1861). "Remarques sur le Siège de la Faculté du Langage Articulé, Suivies d'une Observation d'Aphémie," *Bulletin de la Société Anatomique*, tome XXXVI: 330–57.

Bromberger, S. (1966). "Why Questions," in R. G. Colodny (ed.), *Mind and Cosmos.* Pittsburgh: University of Pittsburgh Press, 86–111.

Bub, J. (1994). "Testing Models of Cognition Through the Analysis of Brain-Damaged Performance," *British Journal for the Philosophy of Science*, 45: 837–55.

Buckner, R. L., and Wheeler, M. A. (2001). "The Cognitive Neuroscience of Remembering," *Nature Reviews Neuroscience*, 2: 624–34.

Burdo, J. D., Antonetti, D. A., Wolpert, E. B., and Connor J. R. (2003). "Mechanisms and Regulation of Transferrin and Iron Transport in a Model Blood–Brain Barrier System," *Neuroscience*, 122: 883–90.

Burian, R. M. (1996). "Underappreciated Pathways Toward Molecular Genetics as Illustrated by Jean Brachet's Cytochemical Embryology," in S. Sarkar (ed.), *The Philosophy and History of Molecular Biology: New Perspectives*. Dordrecht: Kluwer, 67–85.

Campbell, D. (1974). "Downward Causation in Hierarchically Organized Biological Systems," in F. J. Ayala and T. Dobzhansky (eds.), *Studies in the Philosophy of Biology: Reductionism and Related Problems*. New York: Macmillan.

Cartwright, N. (1983). *How the Laws of Physics Lie*. Oxford: Oxford University Press.

Catterall, W. (2000). "Structure and Regulation of Voltage-Gated Ca2+ Channels," *Annual Review of Cell and Developmental Biology*, 16: 521–5.

Cerella, J. (1986). "Pigeons and Perceptrons," *Pattern Recognition*, 19: 431–8.

Chapui, N., Durop, M., and Thinus-Blanc, C. (1987). "The Role of Exploratory Experience in a Shortcut in Golden Hamsters (Mesocricetus auratus)," *Animal Learning and Behavior*, 15: 174–8.

Cheng, P. (1999). "Causality in the Mind: Estimating Contextual and Conjunctive Power," in F. Keil and R. A. Wilson (eds.), *Explanation and Cognition*. Cambridge, MA: MIT Press.

Churchland, P. M. (1989). *A Neurocomputational Perspective: The Nature of Mind and the Structure of Science*. Cambridge, MA: MIT Press.

—— (1995). *The Engine of Reason, the Seat of the Soul*. Cambridge, MA: MIT Press.

Churchland, P. S. (1986). *Neurophilosophy: Toward a Unified Science of the Mind/Brain*. Cambridge, MA: MIT Press.

——, and Sejnowski, T. J. (1992). *The Computational Brain*. Cambridge, MA: MIT Press.

——, and Sejnowski, T. J. (2000). "Perspectives on Neuroscience," in M. S. Gazzaniga (ed.), *Cognitive Neuroscience*. Oxford: Blackwell, 14–24.

Clark, A. (1997). *BeingThere: Putting Mind, Body, and World Back Together Again*. Cambridge, MA: MIT Press.

——, and Chalmers, D. (1998). "The Extended Mind," *Analysis*, 58: 7–19.

Coffa, J. A. (1974). "Hempel's Ambiguity," *Synthese*, 28: 141–63.

Cole, K. (1992). "Neuromembranes: Paths of Ions," in F. G. Worden, J. P. Swazey, and G. Adelman (eds.), *Neurosciences, Paths of Discovery*, vol. I. Cambridge, MA: MIT Press.

——, and Curtis, H. G. (1939). "Electric Impedance of the Squid Giant Axon during Activity," *Journal of General Physiology*, 22: 649–70.

Collingwood, R. (1940). *An Essay on Metaphysics*. Oxford: Clarendon Press.

Collins, J., Hall, N., and Paul, L. (2004). *Causation and Counterfactuals*. Cambridge, MA: MIT Press.

Cook, T. and Campbell, D. (1979). *Quasi-Experimentation: Design and Analysis Issues for Field Settings*. Boston: Houghton Mifflin.

Craik, F. I. M., and Tulving, E. (1975). "Depth of Processing and the Retention of Words in Episodic Memory," *Journal of Experimental Psychology: General*, 104: 268–94.

Cragg, B. G., and Hamlyn, L. H. (1957). "Some Commissural and Septal Connexions of the Hippocampus in the Rabbit. A Combined Histological and Electrical Study," *Journal of Physiology*, 135: 460–85.

Crane, T. (1995). *The Mechanical Mind: A Philosophical Introduction to Minds, Machines and Mental Representation*. Harmondsworth: Penguin.

Craver, C. F. (2001). "Role Functions, Mechanisms and Hierarchy," *Philosophy of Science*, 68: 31–55.

———(2002a). "Structures of Scientific Theories," in P. K. Machamer and M. Silberstein (eds.), *The Blackwell Guide to the Philosophy of Science*. Malden, MA: Blackwell.

———(2002b). "Interlevel Experiments and Multilevel Mechanisms in the Neuroscience of Memory," *Philosophy of Science* (Suppl.), 69: S83–97.

———(2003). "The Making of a Memory Mechanism," *Journal of the History of Biology*, 36: 153–95.

———(2004). "Dissociable Realization and Kind Splitting," *Philosophy of Science*, 71: 960–71.

———, and Bechtel, W. (forthcoming). "Top-down Causation without Top-down Causes," *Biology and Philosophy*.

———, and Darden, L. (2001). "Discovering Mechanisms in Neurobiology: The Case of Spatial Memory," in P. K. Machamer, R. Grush, and P. McLaughlin (eds.), *Theory and Method in the Neurosciences*. Pittsburgh, PA: University of Pittsburgh Press, 112–37.

———, and Darden, L. (2005), "Introduction: Mechanisms Then and Now," in Special Issue, "Mechanisms in Biology," *Studies in History and Philosophy of Biological and Biomedical Sciences* 36: 233–44.

———, and Darden, L. (2006). "Introduction," *Studies in History and Philosophy of Biology*, 36: 233–44.

Crick, F. H. C. (1988). *What Mad Pursuit*. New York: Basic Books.

———(1994). *The Astonishing Hypothesis: The Scientific Search for the Soul*. New York: Charles Scribner's Sons.

Culp, S. (1994). "Defending Robustness: The Bacterial Mesosome as a Test Case," in D. Hull, M. Forbes, and R. M. Burian (eds.), PSA-1994, *Proceedings of the*

Biennial Meetings of the Philosophy of Science Association. East Lansing: Philosophy of Science Association, 46–57.

——(1995). "Objectivity in Experimental Inquiry: Breaking Data-Technique Circles," *Philosophy of Science,* 62: 438–58.

Cummins, R. (1975). "Functional Analysis," *Journal of Philosophy,* 72: 741–64.

——(1983). *The Nature of Psychological Explanation.* Cambridge, MA: Bradford/MIT Press.

——(2000). "How Does It Work? Vs. What Are The Laws? Two Conceptions of Psychological Explanation," in F. Keil and R. Wilson (eds.), *Explanation and Cognition.* Cambridge, MA: MIT Press, 117–45.

—— and Cummins, D. (eds.) (1999). *Minds, Brains and Computers: a collection of essays in the foundation of cognitive science.* Oxford: Blackwell.

Curtis, H. G., and Cole, K. (1940). "Membrane Action Potentials from The Squid Giant Axon," *Journal of Cellular and Comparative Physiology,* 15: 147–57.

Darden, L. (1987). "Viewing the History of Science as Compiled Hindsight," *AI Magazine,* 8/2: 33–41.

——(1991). *Theory Change in Science: Strategies from Mendelian Genetics.* New York: Oxford University Press.

——(2002). "Strategies for Discovering Mechanisms: Schema Instantiation, Modular Subassembly, Forward/Backward Chaining," *Philosophy of Science* (Suppl.), 69: S354–65.

——(2006) *Reasoning in Biological Discoveries.* Cambridge: Cambridge University Press.

——, and Craver, C. F. (2002). "Strategies in the Interfield Discovery of the Mechanism of Protein Synthesis," *Studies in History and Philosophy of Biological and Biomedical Sciences,* 33: 1–28.

——, and Maull, N. (1977). "Interfield Theories," *Philosophy of Science,* 44: 43–64.

Davidson, D. (1970). "Mental Events," in L. Foster and J. Swanson (eds.), *Experience and Theory.* Amherst: The University of Massachusetts Press.

——[1969]. "The Individuation of Events," in D. Davidson (2001), *Essays on Actions and Events.* Oxford: Oxford University Press.

——(2001). *Essays on Actions and Events.* Oxford: Oxford University Press.

Delmas, P., and Coste, B. (2003). "Na^+ Channel $Na_v1.9$: in Search of a Gating Mechanism," *Trends in Neurosciences,* 26: 55–7.

Dennett, D. (1978). *Brainstorms: Philosophical Essays on Mind and Psychology.* Montgomery, VT: Bradford Books.

——(1987). *The Intentional Stance.* Cambridge, MA: Bradford Books/MIT Press.

——(1991). "Real Patterns," *Journal of Philosophy,* 88: 27–51.

——(1994). "Cognitive Science as Reverse Engineering: Several Meanings of 'Top Down' and 'Bottom Up'," in D. Prawitz and D. Westerstahl (eds.),

International Congress of Logic, Methodology and Philosophy of Science. Dordrecht: Kluwer International Congress of Logic, Methodology, and Philosophy of Science (9th: 1991).

Des Chene, D. (2001). *Spirits & Clocks: Machine & Organism in Descartes.* Ithaca, NY: Cornell University Press.

———(2005). "Mechanisms of Life in the Seventeenth Century: Borelli, Perrault, Régis," *Studies in the History and Philosophy of Biology and Biomedical Sciences,* 31: 245–60.

Douglas, R. J. (1967). "The Hippocampus and Behavior," *Psychological Bulletin,* 67: 416–42.

Dowe, P. (1992). "Wesley Salmon's Process Theory of Causality and the Conserved Quantity Theory," *Philosophy of Science,* 59: 195–216.

———(2000). *Physical Causation.* New York: Cambridge University Press.

———(2004). "Causes are Physically Connected to their Effects: Why Preventers and Omissions are Not Causes," in C. Hitchcock (ed.), *Contemporary Debates in Philosophy of Science.* Oxford: Blackwell, 189–96.

Dretske, F. (1977). "Referring to Events," in P. French, T. Uehling, Jr., and H. Wettstein (eds.), *Midwest Studies in Philosophy II.* Minneapolis: University of Minnesota Press, 90–9.

———(1994). "If You Can't Make One, You Don't Know How it Works," in P. French, T. Uehling, and H. Wettstein (eds.), *Midwest Studies in Philosophy, 19, Philosophical Naturalism.* Notre Dame, IN: University of Notre Dame Press.

Dupre, J. (1993). *The Disorder of Things: Metaphysical Foundations of the Disunity of Science.* Cambridge, MA: Harvard University Press.

Earman, J. and Roberts, J. (1999). "Ceteris Paribus: There is no Problem of Provisos," *Synthese,* 118: 439–78.

Eccles, J. C. (1953). *The Neurophysiological Basis of Mind.* Oxford: Clarendon Press.

Edelman, G. (1989). *The Remembered Present.* New York: Basic Books.

Eells, E. (1991). *Probabilistic Causality.* Cambridge: Cambridge University Press.

Ehring, P. (2003). "Part–whole Physicalism and Mental Causation," *Synthese,* 136: 359–88.

Eichenbaum, H., Dudchenko, P., Wood, E., Shapiro, M., and Tanila, H. (1999). "The Hippocampus, Memory, and Place Cells: Is it Spatial Memory or Memory Space," *Neuron,* 23: 209–26.

Elazar, Z., and Adey, W. R. (1967). "Electroencephalographic Correlates of Learning in Subcortical Structures," *Electroencephalography and Clinical Neurophysiology,* 23: 306–19.

Elster, J. (1983). *Explaining Technical Change*. Cambridge: Cambridge University Press.

—— (1989). *Nuts and Bolts for the Social Sciences*. Cambridge: Cambridge University Press.

Engert, F., and Bonhoeffer, T. (1999). "Dendritic Spine Changes Associated with Hippocampal Long-Term Synaptic Plasticity," *Nature*, 399: 66–70.

Felleman, D. J., and Van Essen, D. C. (1991). "Distributed Hierarchical Processing in the Primate Cerebral Cortex," *Cerebral Cortex*, 1/1: 1–47.

Fodor, J. A. (1968). *Psychological Explanation*. New York: Random House.

—— (1974). "Special Sciences (or: The Disunity of Science as a Working Hypothesis)," *Synthese*, 28: 97–115.

Freedman, D. (1997). "From Association to Causation via Regression," in V. McKim and S. Turner (eds.), *Causality in Crisis? Statistical Methods and the Search for Causal Knowledge in the Social Sciences*. Notre Dame, IN: University of Notre Dame Press.

Friedman, M. (1974). "Explanation and Scientific Understanding," *Journal of Philosophy*, 71: 5–19.

Fritsch, G., and Hitzig, E. ([1870] 1960). "On the Electrical Excitability of the Cerebrum" (G. von Bonin trans.), in *Some Papers on the Cerebral Cortex*. Springfield, IL: Thomas Springfield, 73–96.

Fuster, J. (1997). *The Prefrontal Cortex* (3rd edn). Philadelphia, PA: Lippincott-Raven.

Giere, R. (1999). *Science without Laws*. Chicago, IL: University of Chicago Press.

Gillett, C. (2002). "The Dimensions of Realization: A Critique of the Standard View," *Analysis*, 62: 316–23.

Glennan, S. S. (1996). "Mechanisms and the Nature of Causation," *Erkenntnis*, 44: 49–71.

—— (1997). "Capacities, Universality and Singularity," *Philosophy of Science*, 64: 605–26.

—— (2002). "Rethinking Mechanistic Explanation," *Philosophy of Science* (Suppl.), 69: S342–53.

—— (2005). "Modeling Mechanisms," *Studies in History and Philosophy of Biological and Biomedical Science*, 36: 443–64.

Gloor, P., Vera, C. L., and Sperti, L. (1964). "Neurophysiological Studies of Hippocampal Neurons III. Responses of Hippocampal Neurons to Repetitive Perforant Path Volleys," *Electroencephalography and Clinical Neurophysiology*, 17: 353–70.

Glymour, C. (1994). "On the Methods of Cognitive Neursopsychology," *British Journal for the Philosophy of Science*, 45: 815–45.

Glymour, C. (2001). *Mind's Arrows: Bayes Nets and Graphical Causal Models in Psychology*. Cambridge, MA: MIT Press.

Gold, I., and Stoljar, D. (1999). "A Neuron Doctrine in the Philosophy of Neuroscience," *Behavioral and Brain Sciences*, 5: 585–642.

Goodman, N. (1955). *Fact, Fiction, and Forecast*. Cambridge, MA: Harvard University Press.

Gould, S. J. (1980). *The Panda's Thumb: More Reflections in Natural History*. New York: W. W. Norton.

Green, J. D., and Adey, W. R. (1956). "Neurophysiological Studies of Hippocampal Connections and Excitability," *Electroencephalography and Clinical Neurophysiology*, 8: 245–62.

Griffiths, P. (1997). *What Emotions Really Are: The Problem of Psychological Categories*. Chicago, IL: University of Chicago Press.

Grush, R. (2003). "In Defense of Some 'Cartesian' Assumptions Concerning the Brain and its Operation," *Biology and Philosophy*, 18: 53–93.

——— (2004). "The Emulation Theory of Representation: Motor Control, Imagery, and Perception," *Behavioral and Brain Sciences*, 27: 377–96.

Hacking, I. (1983). *Representing and Intervening*. Cambridge, UK: Cambridge University Press.

Hafting, T., Fyhn, M., Molden, S., Moser, M., and Moser, E. I. (2005). "Microstructure of a Spatial Map in the Entorhinal Cortex," *Nature*, 436: 801–6.

Hall, Z. W. (1992). "An Introduction to Molecular Neurobiology". Sinaur Associates.

Hamer, D. (2002). "Genetics. Rethinking Behavior Genetics," *Science*, 298: 71–2.

Hardcastle, V. G. (1998). *How to Build a Theory in Cognitive Science*. Albany, NY: SUNY Press.

——— (2002). "What Do Brain Data Really Show?," *Philosophy of Science* (Suppl.), 69: S72–82.

Harlow, J. M. (1868). "Recovery from the Passage of an Iron Bar through the Head," *Publications of the Massachusetts Medical Society*, 2: 327–47.

Harris, K., Fiala, J. C., and Ostrof, L. (2003). "Structural Changes at Dendritic Spine Synapses During Long-Term Potentiation," *Philosophical Transactions of the Royal Society*, 358: 745–8.

Haugeland, J. (1998). *Having Thought*. Cambridge, MA: Harvard University Press.

Hausman, D. M. (2002). "Physical Causation," *Studies in History and Philosophy of Modern Physics*, 33: 717–24.

Hebb, D. O. (1949). *The Organization of Behavior*. New York: Wiley.

Hegarty, M., Just, M. A., and Morrison, I. R. (1988). "Mental Models of Mechanical Systems: Individual Differences in Qualitative and Quantitative Reasoning," *Cognitive Psychology*, 20: 191–236.

Heil, J. (2003). *From an Ontological Point of View*. Oxford: Oxford University Press.

———, and Mele, A. (eds.) (1993). *Mental Causation*. Oxford: Clarendon Press.

Hempel, C. G. (1962). "Explanation in Science and History," in R. G. Colodny (ed.), *Frontiers of Science and Philosophy*. London: Allen & Unwin, 7–33.

——— (1965). *Aspects of Scientific Explanation and Other Essays in the Philosophy of Science*. New York: Free Press.

———, and Oppenheim, P. (1948). "Studies in the Logic of Explanation," *Philosophy of Science*, 15: 135–75.

Hille, B. (1984). *Ion Channels of Excitable Membranes*. Sunderland, MA: Sinauer.

——— (1992). *Ion Channels of Excitable Membranes* (2nd edn). Sunderland, MA: Sinauer Associates.

———, and Armstrong, D., and MacKinnon, R. (1999). "Ion Channels: From Idea to Reality," *Nature Medicine*, 5: 1105–9.

Hitchcock, C. R. (1995). "Discussion: Salmon on Explanatory Relevance," *Philosophy of Science*, 62: 304–20.

——— (1996). "The Role of Contrast in Causal and Explanatory Claims," *Synthese*, 107: 395–419.

Hodgkin, A. L. (1992). *Chance & Design: Reminiscences of Science in Peace and War*. Cambridge: Cambridge University Press.

———, and Huxley, A. F. (1939). "Action Potentials Recorded from Inside a Nerve Fibre," *Nature*, 144: 710–11.

———, ———, (1952). "A Quantitative Description of Membrane Current and its Application to Conduction and Excitation in Nerve," *Journal of Physiology*, 117: 500–44.

Hooker, C. A. (1981). "Towards a General Theory of Reduction. Part I: Historical and Scientific Setting. Part II: Identity in Reduction. Part III: Cross-Categorical Reduction," *Dialogue*, 20: 38–59; 201–36; 496–529.

Huber, L. (2001). "Visual Categorization in Pigeons," in R. G. Cook (ed.), *Avian Visual Cognition* (online). Available at <http://www.pigeon.psy.tufts.edu/avc-/huber>.

Huxley, A. F. (1963). "The Quantitative Analysis of Excitation and Conduction in Nerve," Nobel lecture: <http://nobelprize.org/medicine/laureates/1963-/huxley-lecture.html>.

Hyden, H. (1973). "RNA Changes in Brain Cells During Changes in Behavior and Function," in G. B. Ansell and P. B. Bradley (eds.), *Macromolecules and Behaviour*. London: Macmillan, 51–75.

Jacob, F. (1977). "Evolution and Tinkering," *Science*, 196: 1161–6.

Ji, R. R., Kohno, T., Moore, K. A., and Woolf, C. J. (2003). "Central Sensitization and LTP: Do Pain and Memory Share Similar Mechanisms?," *Trends in Neurosciences*, 26: 696–705.

Katz, B., and Miledi R. (1967). "The Timing of Calcium Action during Neuro-muscular Transmission," *Journal of Physiology*, 189: 535–44.

Kauffman, S. A. (1971). "Articulation of Parts Explanation in Biology and the Rational Search for Them," in R. C. Buck and R. S. Cohen (eds.), *PSA 1970*. Dordrecht: Reidel.

Keil, F., and Wilson, R. A. (2000). "The Shadows and Shallows of Explanation," in F. C. Keil and R. A. Wilson (eds.), *Explanation and Cognition*. Cambridge, MA: MIT Press.

Kim, J. (1989). "Mechanism, Purpose, and Explanatory Exclusion," *Philosophical Perspectives*, 3: 77–108.

——(1993). *Supervenience and Mind*. Cambridge: Cambridge University Press.

——(1998). *Mind in a Physical World*. Cambridge, MA: MIT Press.

——(2000). "Making Sense of Downward Causation," in Peter Bogh Andersen et al. (eds.), *Downward Causation*. Aarhus: Aarhus University Press, 305–21.

Kirkpatrick, K. (2001). "Object Recognition," in R. G. Cook (ed.), *Avian Visual Cognition*. Comparative Cognition Press. Published online.

Kitcher, P. (1989). "Explanatory Unification and the Causal Structure Of The World," in P. Kitcher and W. Salmon (eds.), *Scientific Explanation. Minnesota Studies in the Philosophy of Science, Volume XIII*, 410–505.

——(1993). *The Advancement of Science*. New York: Oxford University Press.

Kornblith, H. (1993). *Inductive Inference and its Natural Ground*. Cambridge, MA: MIT Press.

Kuhn, T. (1962). *Structure of Scientific Revolutions*. Chicago, IL: University of Chicago Press.

Kyberg, H. E. (1965). "Comment," *Philosophy of Science*, 32: 147–51.

Lakatos, I. (1977). *The Methodology of Scientific Research Programmes: Philosophical Papers Volume 1*. Cambridge: Cambridge University Press.

Lashley, K. S. ([1950] 2000). "In search of the Engram," reprinted in R. Cummins and D. D. Cummins (eds.), *Minds, Brains and Computers*. Malden, MA: Blackwell, 333–50.

Lepore, E. and Loewer, B. (1989). "More on Making Mind Matter," *Philosophical Topics*, 17: 175–91.

Levitan, I. B., and Kaczmarek, L. K. (1991). *The Neuron: Cell and Molecular Biology*. Oxford: Oxford University Press.

Lewis, D. (1973). "Causation," *The Journal of Philosophy, 70*: 556–567.

——(1979). "Counterfactual Dependence and Time's Arrow," *Nous*, 13: 455–76.

——(1983). "New Work for a Theory of Universals," *Australasian Journal of Philosophy*, 61: 343–77.

_____ (2000). "Causation as Influence," *Journal of Philosophy,* 97: 182–198; reprinted in J. Collins, N. Hall, and L. A. Paul (eds.), *Causation and Counterfactuals.* Bradford: MIT Press.

Lloyd, D. P. C. (1949). "Post-Tetanic Potentiation of Response in Monosynaptic Reflex Pathways of the Spinal Cord," *Journal of General Physiology,* 33: 147–70.

Lømo, T. (1966). "Frequency Potentiation of Excitatory Synaptic Activity in the Dentate Area of the Hippocampal Formation," *Acta Physiologica Scandinavica* (Suppl.), 277: 128.

Lycan, W. (1987). *Consciousness.* Cambridge, MA: Bradford Books/MIT Press.

_____ (1999). "The Continuity of Levels of Nature," in. W. Lycan (ed.), *Mind and Cognition: A Reader* (2nd edn). Malden, MA: Blackwell.

Lynch, M. A. (2004). "Long-term Potentiation and Memory," *Physiological Review,* 84: 87–136.

McClelland, J. (1981). "Retrieving General and Specific Knowledge from Stored Knowledge of Specifics," *Proceedings of the Third Annual Conference of the Cognitive Science Society.* Berkeley, CA.

McCulloch, W., and Pitts, W. H. (1943). "A Logical Calculus of The Ideas Immanent in Nervous Activity," *Bulletin of Mathematical Biophysics,* 7: 115–33. Reprinted in R. Cummins and D. D. Cummins (eds.) (2000), *Minds, Brains and Computers: The Foundations of Cognitive Science.* Oxford: Blackwell: 351–60.

Machamer, P. (2004). "Activities and Causation: The Metaphysics and Epistemology of Mechanisms," *International Studies in the Philosophy of Science,* 18: 27–39.

Machamer, P. K., Darden, L., and Craver, C. F. (2000). "Thinking about Mechanisms," *Philosophy of Science,* 57: 1–25.

McHugh, T. J., Blum, K., Tsien, J. Z., Tonegawa, S., and Wilson, M. (1996). "Impaired Hippocampal Representation of Space in CA1-Specific NMDAR1 Knockout Mice," *Cell,* 87: 1339–49.

Malenka, R. C., and Bear, M. F. (2004). "LTP and LTD: An Embarrassment of Riches," *Neuron,* 44: 5–21.

Maletic-Savatic, M., Malinow, R., and Svoboda, K. (1999). "Rapid Dendritic Morphogenesis in CA1 Hippocampal Dendrites Induced by Synaptic Activity," *Science,* 283: 1923–7.

Malinow, R. (1998). "Silencing the Controversy in LTP?," *Neuron,* 21: 1226–7.

Marr, D. (1969). "A Theory of Cerebellar Cortex," *Journal of Physiology,* 202: 437–70.

_____ (1970). "A Theory for Cerebral Neocortex," *Proceedings of the Royal Society,* B. 176: 161–234.

_____ (1982). *Vision.* San Francisco, CA: Freeman Press.

Mauk, M. (2000). "The Potential Effectiveness of Simulations Versus Phenomeno-logical Models," *Nature Neuroscience*, 3: 649–51.

Maull, N. (1977). "Unifying Science without Reduction," *Studies in the History and Philosophy of Science*, 8: 143–62.

Miledi, R. (1973). "Transmitter Release Induced by Injection of Calcium Ions into Nerve Terminals," *Proceedings of the Royal Society London B Biological Sciences*, 183: 421–5.

Milner, B. (1970). "Memory and the Medial Temporal Lobe Regions of the Brain," in K. H. Pribram and D. E. Broadbent (eds.), *Biology of Memory*. New York: Academic Press, 29–50.

Morairty, S., Rainnie, D. McCarley, R., and Greene, R. (2004). "Disinhibition of Ventrolateral Preoptic Area Sleep-Active Neurons by Adenosine: A New Mechanism for Sleep Promotion," *Neuroscience*, 123: 451–7.

Morgan, C., and Stellar, E. (1950). *Physiological Psychology*. New York: McGraw-Hill.

Mundale, J., and Bechtel, W. (1996). "Integrating Neuroscience, Psychology, and Evolutionary Biology Through a Teleological Conception of Function," *Minds and Machines*, 6: 481–505.

Nadel, L., and O'Keefe, J. (1974). "The Hippocampus in Pieces and Patches: An Essay on Modes of Explanation in Physiological Psychology," in R. Bellairs and E. G. Gray (eds.), *Essays on the Nervous System: A Festschrift for Prof J. Z. Young*. Oxford: Clarendon Press. 367–90.

Nagel, E. (1949). "The Meaning of Reduction in the Natural Sciences," in R. Stauffer (ed.), *Science and Civilization*. Madison, WI: University of Wisconsin Press, 97–135.

—— (1961). *The Structure of Science: Problems in the Logic of Scientific Explanation*. New York: Harcourt, Brace and World, Inc.

Northcott, R. (under review). Causation and Contrast Classes.

Norton, J. (2003). "Causation as Folk Science," *Philosopher's Imprint*, 3/4.

O'Keefe, J., and Dostrovsky, J. (1971). "The Hippocampus as a Spatial Map. Preliminary Evidence from Unit Activity in the Freely Moving Rat," *Brain Research*, 34: 171–5.

——, and Nadel. L. (1978). *The Hippocampus as a Cognitive Map*. Oxford: Oxford University Press.

Olton, D. S., and Samuelson, R. J. (1976). "Remembrances of Places Past: Spatial Memory in Rats," *Journal of Experimental Psychology: Animal Behavior Processes*, 2: 97–116.

Oppenheim, P. and Putnam, H. (1958). "Unity of Science as a Working Hypoth-esis," in H. Feigl, M. Scriven, and G. Maxwell (eds.), *Concepts, Theories, and the Mind–Body Problem, Minnesota Studies in the Philosophy of Science II*. Minneapolis: University of Minnesota Press, 3–36.

Pearl, J. (2000). *Causality: Models, Reasoning, and Inference*. Cambridge: Cambridge University Press.

Penfield, W. (1952). "Memory Mechanisms," *Archives of Neurology and Psychiatry*, 67: 178–91.

Pera, M. (1992). *The Ambiguous Frog: The Galvani-Volta Controversy on Animal Electricity* (Jonathan Mandelbaum trans.). Princeton, NJ: Princeton University Press.

Perkel, D. H. (1990). "Computational Neuroscience: Scope and Structure," in E. L. Schwartz (ed.), *Computational Neuroscience*. Cambridge, MA: MIT Press, 38–45.

Pietrosky, P., and Rey, G. (1995). "When Other Things Aren't Equal: Saving Ceteris Paribus Laws from Vacuity," *The British Journal for the Philosophy of Science*, 46: 81–110.

Poland, J. (1994). *Physicalism*. Oxford: Oxford University Press.

Polger, T. (2004). *Natural Minds*. Cambridge, MA: MIT Press.

Popper, K. (1959). *The Logic of Scientific Discovery*. London: Hutchinson and Co.

Posner M. I., and DiGirolamo G. (1998). "Executive Attention: Conflict, Target Detection and Cognitive Control," in R. Parasuraman (ed.), *The Attentive Brain*. Cambridge, MA: MIT Press, 401–23.

Povinelli, D. (2000). *Folk Physics for Apes: The Chimpanzee's Theory of How the World Works*. Oxford: Oxford University Press.

Price, H. (1996). *Time's Arrow and Archimedes' Point*. Oxford: Oxford University Press.

Prinz, A., Bucher, D., and Marder, E. (2004). "Similar Network Activity from Disparate Circuit Parameters," *Nature Neuroscience*, 7: 1345–52.

Psillos, S. (1999). *Scientific Realism: How Science Tracks Truth*. New York: Routledge.

Putnam, H. (1960). "Minds and Machines," in *Mind, Language, and Reality: Philosophical Papers Volume 2*. New York: Cambridge University Press.

Raichle, M. E.. and Mintun, M. A. (2006). "Brain Work and Brain Imaging," *Annual Reviews of Neuroscience*, 29: 449–76.

Railton, P. (1978). "A Deductive-Nomological Model of Probabilistic Explanation," *Philosophy of Science*, 45: 206–26.

Reichenbach, H. (1956). *The Direction of Time*. Chicago, IL: University of Chicago Press.

Rescher, N. (1955). "Axioms for the Part Relation," *Philosophical Studies*, 6: 8–11.

Rescorla, R. A., and Wagner, A. R. (1972). "A Theory of Pavlovian Conditioning: Variations in the Effectiveness of Reinforcement and Nonreinforcement," in A. H. Black and W. F. Prokasy (eds.), *Classical Conditioning II: Current Theory and Research*. New York: Appleton-Century-Crofts, 64–99.

Roberts, J. (2004). "There Are No Laws of the Social Sciences," in C. Hitchcock (ed.), *Contemporary Debates in Philosophy of Science*. Oxford: Blackwell, 151–67.

Rosenberg, A. (1985). *The Structure of Biological Science*. Cambridge: Cambridge University Press.

—— (1994). *Instrumental Biology or the Unity of Science*. Chicago, IL: University of Chicago Press.

—— (2001). "How is Biological Explanation Possible?," *British Journal for the Philosophy of Science*, 52: 735–60.

Rotenberg, A., Mayford, M., Hawkins, R. D., Kandel, E. R., and Muller, R. U. (1996). "Mice Expressing Activated CaMKII Low Frequency LTP and Do Not Form Stable Place Cells in The CA1 Region of the Hippocampus," *Cell*, 87: 1351–61.

Roush, W. (1997). "New Knockout Mice Point to Molecular Basis of Memory," *Science*, 275: 32–3.

Rowan, M. J., Klyubin, I., Cullen, W. K., and Anwyl, R. (2003). "Synaptic Plasticity in Animal Models of Early Alzheimer's Disease," *Philosophical Transactions of the Royal Society*, 358: 821–8.

Ruben D. (1999). "Arguments, Laws, and Explanation," in M. Curd and J. A. Cover (eds.), *Introduction to Philosophy of Science*. New York and London: W. W. Norton and Company, 720–45.

Rumelhart, D. E., and McClelland, J. L. (eds.) (1986). *Parallel Distributed Processing*, vol. 1. Cambridge, MA: MIT Press.

Russell, B. (1913). "On the Notion of Cause," *Proceedings of the Aristotelian Society*. 13: 1–26.

Salmon, W. C. (1977). "An 'At-At' Theory of Causal Influence," *Philosophy of Science*. 44: 215–25.

—— (1984). *Scientific Explanation and the Causal Structure of the World*. Princeton: Princeton University Press.

—— (1989). "Four Decades of Scientific Explanation," in P. Kitcher and W. Salmon (eds.), *Scientific Explanation, Minnesota Studies in the Philosophy of Science XVIII*. Minneapolis: University of Minnesota Press, 3–219.

—— (1994). "Causality Without Counterfactuals," *Philosophy of Science*, 61: 297–312.

—— (1997). "Causality and Explanation: A Reply to Two Critiques," *Philosophy of Science*, 64: 461–77.

—— (1998). *Causality and Explanation*. New York: Oxford University Press.

Sands, Z., Grottesi, A., and Sansom, M. S. (2005). "Voltage-Gated Ion Channels," *Current Biology*, 15: R44–7.

Sanes, J. R., and Lichtman, J. W. (1999). "Can Molecules Explain Long-Term Potentiation?," *Nature Neuroscience*, 2: 597–604.

Sanford, D. H. (1993). "The Problem of the Many, Many Composition Questions, and Naïve Mereology," *Nous*, 27: 219–28.

Sarkar, S. (1992). "Models of Reduction and Categories of Reductionism," *Synthese*, 91: 167–94.

Schacter, D. L. (1996). *Searching for Memory: The Brain, the Mind, and the Past*. New York: Basic Books.

——, and Tulving, E. (1994). "What are the Memory Systems of 1994?," in D. L. Schacter and E. Tulving (eds.), *Memory Systems*. Cambridge, MA: MIT Press, 1–38.

——, Wagner, A. D., and Buckner, R. L. (2000). "Memory Systems of 1999," in E. Tulving and F. I. M. Craik (eds.), *Oxford Handbook of Memory*. Oxford: Oxford University Press, 627–43

Schafe, G. E., Atkins, C. M., Swank, M. W., Bauer, E. P., Sweatt, J. D., and LeDoux, J. E. (2000). "Activation of ERK/MAP Kinase in the Amygdale is Required for Memory Consolidation of Pavlovian Fear Conditioning," *Journal of Neuroscience*, 20: 8177–87.

——, and LeDoux J. E. (2000). "Memory Consolidation of Auditory Pavlovian Fear Conditioning Requires Protein Synthesis and Protein Kinase A in the Amygdala," *Journal of Neuroscience*, 20: RC96.

Schaffer, J. (2003). "Metaphysics of Causation," *Stanford Encyclopedia of Philosophy*.

——, (2004). "Causes Need Not be Physically Connected to their Effects: The Case for Negative Causation," in C. Hitchcock (ed.), *Contemporary Debates in Philosophy of Science*. Oxford: Blackwell, 197–216.

—— (2005). "Contrastive Causation," *Philosophical Review*, 114: 297–328.

Schaffner, K. F. (1967). "Approaches to Reduction", *Philosophy of Science*, 34: 137–47.

—— (1974). "The Peripherality of Reductionism in the Development of Molecular Biology," *Journal of the History of Biology*, 7: 111–39

—— (1993a). *Discovery and Explanation in Biology and Medicine*. Chicago, IL: University of Chicago Press.

—— (1993b). "Theory Structure, Reduction, and Disciplinary Integration in Biology", *Biology and Philosophy*, 8: 319–47.

—— (forthcoming). *Behaving: What's Genetic and What's Not, and Why Should We Care?* Oxford: Oxford University Press.

Schouten, M. K. D., and Looren de Jong, H. (1998). "Defusing Eliminative Materialism: Reference and Revision," *Philosophical Psychology*, 11: 489–509.

——, —— (1999). "Reduction, Elimination, and Levels: The Case of the LTP-Learning Link," *Philosophical Psychology*, 12: 237–62.

Scoville, W. B., and Milner, B. (1957). "Loss of Recent Memory After Bilateral Hippocampal Lesions," *Journal of Neurology, Neurosurgery, and Psychiatry*, 20: 11–20.

Shah, B. H., and K. J. Catt. (2004). "GPCR-Mediated Transactivation of RTKs in the CNS: Mechanisms and Consequences," *Trends in Neurosciences*, 27: 48–53.

Shepherd, G. M. (1983). *Neurobiology* (2nd edn). New York: Oxford University Press.

—— (1994). *Neurobiology* (3rd edn.). New York: Oxford University Press.

Shoemaker, S. (2001). "Realization and Mental Causation," in C. Gillett and B. Loewer (eds.), *Physicalism and Its Discontents*. New York: Cambridge University Press, 74–98.

Simon, H. (1969). *The Sciences of the Artificial*. Cambridge, MA: MIT Press.

Skipper, R. (1999). "Selection and the Extent of Explanatory Unification," *Philosophy of Science* (Suppl.), 66: S196–209.

Skyrms, B. (1980). *Causal Necessity*. New Haven, CN: Yale University Press.

Smart, J. J. C. (1963). *Philosophy and Scientific Realism*. London: Routledge & Kegan Paul.

Smith E. E., and Jonides, J. (1999). "Storage and Executive Processes in the Frontal Lobes," *Science*, 283: 1657–61.

Smith, P. (1992). "Modest Reductions and the Unity of Science," in D. Charles and K. Lennon (eds.), *Reduction, Explanation and Realism*. Oxford: Clarendon Press, 19–43.

Sober, E., (ed.) (1984). *Conceptual Issues in Evolutionary Biology*. Cambridge, MA: Bradford/MIT Press.

Society for Neuroscience Web Pageb <*www.sfn.org*>.

Spirtes, P., Glymour, C., and Scheines, R. (1990). *Causation, Prediction, and Search. Springer Lecture Notes in Statistics*, 2nd edn. Cambridge, MA: MIT Press.

——, ——, —— (2000). *Causation, Prediction, and Search. Springer Lecture Notes in Statistics*, 2nd revised edn. Cambridge, MA: MIT Press.

Squire, L. R., and Kandel, E. R. (2000). *Memory: From Mind to Molecules*. New York: Scientific American Library.

—— Knowlton, B. J. (1994). "Memory, Hippocampus and Brain Systems," in M. Gazzaniga (ed.), *The Cognitive Neurosciences*. Cambridge, MA: MIT Press, 825–37.

Stevens, C. F. (1996). "Spatial Memory: The Beginning of a Dream," *Cell*, 87: 1147–8.

—— (1998). "A Million Dollar Question: Does LTP = Memory?," *Neuron*, 20: 1–2.

Stricker, E., and Verbalis, J. (1988). "Hormones and Behavior: The Biology of Thirst and Sodium Appetite," *American Scientist*, 76: 261–76.

Südhof, T. C. (2000). "The Synaptic Vesicle Cycle Revisited," *Neuron*, 28: 317–20.

—— (2004). "The Synaptic Vesicle Cycle," *Annual Reviews of Neuroscience*, 27: 509–47.

Sulloway, F. (1979). *Freud: Biologist of the Mind*. London: Burnett Books.

Suppe, F. (1989). *The Semantic Conception of Theories and Scientific Realism*. Urbana, IL: University of Illinois Press.

Swartz, K. J. (2004). "Towards a Structural View of Gating in Potassium Channels," *Nature Reviews Neuroscience*, 5: 905–16.

Tabery, J. (2004). "Synthesizing Activities and Interactions in the Concept of a Mechanism," *Philosophy of Science*, 71: 1–15.

Tang, Y., Shimizu, E., Dube, G. R., Rampon, C., Kerchner, G. A., Zhuo, M. Liu, G., and Tsien, J. Z. (1999). "Genetic Enhancement of Learning and Memory in Mice," *Nature*, 401: 63–9.

Tarski, A., (1929). "Les Fondements de la Géométrie des Corps," Ksiega Pamiatkowa Pierwszkego Polskiego Zjazdu Matematycznego (suppl. to *Annales de la Société Polonaise de Mathématique*), 7: 29–33; Eng. trans. by J. H. Woodger (1956): "Foundations of the Geometry of Solids," in A. Tarski (ed.), *Logics, Semantics, Metamathematics. Papers from 1923 to 1938*. Oxford: Clarendon Press, 24–9.

Thagard, P. (1998). "Explaining Disease: Correlations, Causes, and Mechanisms," *Minds and Machines,* 8: 61–78.

——— (1999). *How Scientists Explain Disease*. Princeton: Princeton University Press.

——— (2003). "Pathways to Biomedical Discovery," *Philosophy of Science*, 70: 235–54.

Thielscher, A., and Neumann, H. (2003). "Neural Mechanisms of Cortico–Cortical Interaction in Texture Boundary Detection: A Modeling Approach," *Neuroscience*, 122: 921–39.

Thomas, M. J., and Malenka, R. C. (2003). "Synaptic Plasticity in the Mesolimbic Dopamine System," *Philosophical Transactions of the Royal Society*, 358: 815–20.

Tolman, E. C. (1948). "Cognitive Maps in Rats and Man," *Psychological Review*, 55: 189–208.

Trout, J. D. (2002). "Scientific Explanation and the Sense of Understanding," *Philosophy of Science*, 69/2: 212–33.

Tsien, J. Z., Chen, D. F., Gerber, D., Tom, C., Mercer, E. H., Anderson, D. J., Mayford, M., Kandel, E. R., and Tonegawa, S. (1996a). "Subregion- and Cell Type-Restricted Gene Knockout in Mouse Brain," *Cell*, 87: 1317–26.

———, Huerta, P. T., and Tonegawa, S. (1996b). "The Essential Role of Hippocampal CA1 NMDA Receptor-Dependent Synaptic Plasticity in Spatial Memory," *Cell*, 87: 1327–38.

Uttal, W. R. (2001). *The New Phrenology*. Cambridge, MA: MIT Press.

Van Fraassen, B. (1980). *The Scientific Image*. Oxford: Oxford University Press.

Van Gulick, R. (1993). "Who's in Charge Here? And Who's Doing All the Work?," in J. Heil and A. Mele (eds.), *Mental Causation*. Oxford: Clarendon Press, 233–56.

Von Eckardt Klein, B. (1978). "Inferring Functional Localization From Neurological Evidence," in E. Walker (ed.), *Explorations in the Biology of Language*. Cambridge, MA: MIT Press.

_____ Poland, J. S. (2005). "Mechanism and Explanation in Cognitive Neuroscience," *Philosophy of Science* (Suppl.), 71: 972–84

Von Wright, G. (1971). *Explanation and Understanding*. Ithaca, NY: Cornell University Press.

Watson, J. D., and Crick, F. H. C. (1953). "A Structure for Deoxyribose Nucleic Acid," *Nature*, 171: 737–8.

Weber, M. (2005). *Philosophy of Experimental Biology*. Cambridge: Cambridge University Press.

Weiskrantz, L. (1990). "Problems of Learning and Memory: One or Multiple Memory Systems?," *Philosophical Transactions of the Royal Society London (Biology)*, 329: 99–108.

Wilson, M. A., and McNaughton, B. (1993). "Dynamics of the Hippocampal Ensemble Code for Space," *Science*, 261: 1055–8.

Wilson, R. A. (2001). "Two Views of Realization," *Philosophical Studies*, 104: 1–30.

_____ (2004). *Boundaries of the Mind: The Individual in the Fragile Sciences: Cognition*. Cambridge: Cambridge University Press.

_____ Craver, C. F. (forthcoming). "Realization," in P. Thagard (ed.), *Handbook of Philosophy of Psychology and Cognitive Science*. North Holland.

Wimsatt, W. (1974). "Complexity and Organization," in K. F. Schaffner and R. S. Cohen (eds.), *PSA 1972, (Boston Studies in the Philosophy of Science,* vol. 2). Dordrecht, Holland: Reidel, 67–86.

_____ (1976a). "Reductionism, Levels of Organization, and the Mind–Body Problem," in G. Globus, I. Savodnik, and G. Maxwell (eds.), *Consciousness and the Brain*. New York: Plenum Press, 199–267.

_____ (1976b). "Reductive Explanation: A Functional Account," in E. Sober (ed.), *Conceptual Issues in Evolutionary Biology*. Cambridge, MA: MIT Press, 369–85.

_____ (1981). "Robustness, Reliabilty and Overdetermination," in M. Brewer and B. Collins (eds.), *Scientific Inquiry and the Social Sciences*. San Francisco, CA: Jossey-Bass Publishers, 124–63.

_____ (1985). "Forms of Aggregativity," in A. Donagan, A. Perovich, and M. Wedin (eds.), *Human Nature and Natural Knowledge*. Dordrecht, Holland: Reidel, 259–93.

_____ (1994). "The Ontology of Complex Systems: Levels, Perspectives, and Causal Thickets," *Canadian Journal of Philosophy* (Suppl.), 20: 207–74.

_____ (1997). "Aggregativity: Reductive Heuristics for Finding Emergence," in L. Darden (ed.), *PSA-1996, vol. 2. Philosophy of Science* (Suppl.), S372–84.

Woodger, J. H. (1937). *The Axiomatic Method in Biology.* Cambridge: Cambridge University Press.

Woodward, J. (1984) "A Theory of Singular Causal Explanation," *Erkenntnis,* 21: 231–62.

—— (1997). "Explanation, Invariance, and Intervention," *PSA-1996 vol. 2. Philosophy of Science,* 66: S26–41.

—— (2000). "Explanation and Invariance in the Special Sciences," *British Journal for the Philosophy of Science,* 52: 197–254.

—— (2002). "What is a Mechanism? A Counterfactual Account," *Philosophy of Science* (Suppl.), 69: S366–77.

—— (2003). *Making Things Happen.* New York: Oxford University Press.

——, and Hitchcock, C. (2003a). "Explanatory Generalizations, Part I: A Counterfactual Account," *Nous,* 37: 1–24.

——, and Hitchcock, C. (2003b). "Explanatory Generalizations, Part II: Plumbing Explanatory Depth," *Nous,* 37: 181–99.

Wright, L. (1973). "Functions," *Philosophical Review,* 82: 139–68.

Wright, W. (forthcoming). "Explanation and the Hard Problem," *Philosophical Studies.*

Wylie, A. (2002). *Thinking with Things.* San Francisco: University of California Press.

Yablo, S. (1992). "Mental Causation," *Philosophical Review,* 101: 245–80.

Index